THE
TAO OF
MUSIC

Sound Psychology

*Using Music
to Change Your Life*

JOHN M. ORTIZ, Ph.D

Newleaf

Newleaf
an imprint of
Gill & Macmillan Ltd
Goldenbridge
Dublin 8
with associated companies throughout the world

© 1997 John M. Ortiz

0 7171 2726 5

Printed by ColourBooks Ltd, Dublin

A catalogue record is available for this book
from the British Library.

3 5 4 2

To the men in my life, Manolo and Paco, for their courage, strength, and sense of humor.

To the women in my life, Gladys—who taught me reading, writing, and creativity,—and Roz, my life partner, for their support, encouragement, unconditional love, and unwavering belief in me.

Table of Contents

Acknowledgments xiii

Introduction. xv

PART ONE: CLINICAL ISSUES

1. Depressed Moods. 3
2. Pain 29
3. Self-Esteem 37
4. Stress 51
5. Anger 61
6. Sleeplessness 77
7. Control 87
8. Relaxation. 93

PART TWO: PERSONAL ISSUES

9. Memory Recall 105
10. Time Management. 111
11. Grief and Loss 119
12. Growth/Change. 125
13. Procrastination 133
14. Aging. 141
15. Physical Exercise and Music. 151

PART THREE: SOCIAL ISSUES

16. Improving Communication 165
17. Companionship 173
18. Relationship Issues 177
19. Romantic Intimacy 183
20. Motivating the Mind 201
21. How to Listen: Educating the Ear.................. 213

PART FOUR: SPECIAL ISSUES

22. Centering (Silence)............................... 223
23. Creativity 233
24. HeAr and Now 243
25. Letting Go 249
26. Being Versus Trying to Be 261
27. Clearing the Mind............................... 267

APPENDICES:

Appendix A: Explanations of Concepts and Terms
    Rhythmic Synchronicity........................... 275
    Psychological Noise and Masking.................. 281
    Contextual Cuing 287
    Acoustic Memory................................ 291
    Expectations 293
    Whys 303
    Shoulds and Musts.............................. 311

Appendix B: Techniques
    Entrainment 317
    Affirmations 325
    Thought Stopping............................... 329
    Breathing 333
    Mantric Sounds 339

Chanting. 345
Toning 349

Appendix C: Special Topics
Choosing One's Music 355
The Spiral Sojourn. 361
Your Special Place 367
Inner Guide. 371

Bibliography 375
Index. 386
About the Author 392

Exercises

Exercise 1. Lifting a Depressed Mood 8

Exercise 2. Moving Out of the Blues. 13

Exercise 3. Pain Elimination/Reduction 32

Exercise 4. Self-Enhancing: Changing Noise to Harmony. 42

Exercise 5. Letting Go of Chronic Anger. 67

Exercise 6. Diverting Another Person's Anger 69

Exercise 7. The Angry Troll:

 Dispelling Anger through Silent Humor 71

Exercise 8. Sound Sleeping 82

Exercise 9. Giving Up Control: Letting Go 90

Exercise 10. Reducing Stress. 97

Exercise 11. Spiral Sojourn through Musical Memories. 108

Exercise 12. Time Management through Music 115

Exercise 13. Using Music to Speed Your Pace 116

Exercise 14. Using Music to Slow Your Pace 117

Exercise 15. Using Music to Trigger Emotional Responses 121

Exercise 16. Creating New Memories 130

Exercise 17. Beating Procrastination 138

Exercise 18. Rejuvenation through Music 142

Exercise 19. Training through Entrainment. 157

Exercise 20. Listening and Communication Enhancement 169

Exercise 21. Enhancing Listening Sensitivity. 180

Exercise 22. The Magic Nightclub 192

Exercise 23. Using Music to Memorize Word Lists 203

Exercise 24. Improving Learning Skills 207

Exercise 25. Listening 216

Exercise 26. Sound Convergence 224

Exercise 27. Finding Your Center 227

Exercise 28. Centering through Music. 229

Exercise 29. Enhancing Creativity. 238

Exercise 30. Letting Go 254

Exercise 31. Selecting Your Soundtracks 257

Exercise 32. Clearing the Mind. 269

Exercise 33. Unexpecting 300

Exercise 34. Discovering Your Magical Breath 334

Exercise 35. Finding Your Mantric Sound 340

Exercise 36. Discovering Your Personal Chant 346

Exercise 37. Toning through Natural Release 350

Exercise 38. Toning While Making Love. 351

Exercise 39. Toning During a Stroll 351

Exercise 40. The Spiral Sojourn 362

Exercise 41. Accessing Your Inner Guide. 373

Musical Menus

Musical Menu 1. Anti-Depressed Mood Entrainment Sequence 16

Musical Menu 2. Bonding and Moving Away from a
Depressed Mood 19

Musical Menu 3. Stimulating Music. 20

Musical Menu 4. Inspirational Music 48

Musical Menu 5. Soothing Music (Rhythmic Synchronicity) 55

Musical Menu 6. Music for Dealing with Anger 73

Musical Menu 7. Top Songs of the '30s. 145

Musical Menu 8. Top Songs of the '40s. 146

Musical Menu 9. Top Songs of the '50s. 146

Musical Menu 10.Top Songs of the '60s 147

Musical Menu 11. Top Songs of the '70s. 148

Musical Menu 12. Entrainment Sequence: Big Band 160

Musical Menu 13. Entrainment Sequence: '60s Pop. 160

Musical Menu 14. Entrainment Sequence for Limited Budgets 161

Musical Menu 15. Romantic Magic Nightclub 194

Musical Menu 16. Music Box Tunes. 210

Musical Menu 17. Centering Music 228

Musical Menu 18. Meditation Music 230

Musical Menu 19. Music for Altered States. 241

Musical Menu 20. Music for Letting Go. 259

Musical Menu 21. Sixty-five Years of Song-Title Affirmations 327

Musical Menu 22. Mantric Music 342

Musical Menu 23. Chanting Music. 347

Acknowledgments

I would like to thank the following people in my life. Nancy for pointing the way and Josefina for the lifelong reminders; Bibi, Carida, and Marie—and brother Frank—for forever believing without expectations; Dr. Ed Herr, my mentor, and Betty, for opening the doors and giving me the opportunity to become; and John, Paul, George and Ringo for the soundtrack of my life.

MUSIC IS THE SOUND OF LIFE,
CELEBRATING ITSELF.

THE MUSIC OF THE TAO
IS THE BACKGROUND OF THE MOMENT,
THE ESSENCE OF THE PROCESS.
LIKE A CURIOUS DREAM
IT LIES HIDDEN BY AWARENESS
YET ACCESSIBLE TO INTUITION.
LIKE A FEELING OF DÉJÀ VU

HEARD, IT CANNOT BE RECALLED.
DANCED TO, IT CANNOT BE PLAYED.
IMITATED, IT CANNOT BE REPRODUCED.
VOICELESS, IT SINGS.
TONELESS, IT PLAYS.
THE MUSIC OF THE TAO
IS THE TAO OF MUSIC.

THE MUSIC OF THE TAO
IS THE SOUND OF ONE HAND CLAPPING.

Introduction

*The dance of life goes on
within and around us.*[1]

In 1964, the Beatles invaded my world and, for the first time in my life, I heard my inner music. From that moment on, music always provided a place where I could go; it was a friend to whom I could turn, a magical haven. When I felt sad, I knew what music would make me feel happy. When stressed, I knew which tunes would help me relax. When feeling inhibited I knew the songs that would help me to let go, that would allow me to be myself. When lonely, I knew I could "spin" a few records (black vinyl 45s), or plug in my guitar, and soon, my loneliness would disappear. If, for some reason, the loneliness refused to go away, the music somehow made it okay to be alone. Maybe it was a sense that the person who wrote or recorded those tunes had similar feelings or shared similar concerns. That commonality made my concerns a bit more universal and, somehow, less overwhelming. Through their music, those people—those famous strangers—communicated a sense of harmony and purpose that other adults could never quite get across through their lectures, rituals, or seemingly irrelevant traditions. Music, it seemed, had awoken my awareness.

1. Diane Dreher, *The Tao of Inner Peace* (New York: HarperCollins, 1991), p. 34.

The music seemed never to push from behind, but rather to pull forward. It challenged without threatening. Melodies seemed to add color to
my world, while beats and rhythms provided movement. Rather than
"This is the way it *is*," the music seemed to say, "This is one of the ways it
can be." The music never told us what we "should" do, or "why" we should
do it. It was never about "shoulds," or "whys." It was about change, energy, and vibrations.

> [M]usic represents a sort of rhythmic consensus, a consensus of
> the core culture.[2]

Well-meaning parents may tell us to "think for ourselves," but often have
little or no idea how to help our minds from recycling constant concerns,
unnecessary worries, destructive ideas, and negative images. Teachers may
be excellent at teaching us how to solve algebra problems and conjugate
Latin verbs, but there doesn't seem to be any room in the curriculum to
teach us how to handle depression, let go of anger, or simply communicate
with others effectively. Some role models are quick at telling us how we
"should" behave, what we "ought" to think, and which attitudes we
"must" have, as if there were no choices. Emphasis is typically on reliving
or avoiding the past, or planning for the future, but rarely on living here
and now, today—at this moment. Our society values "hanging on," and
frowns on "letting go." It reinforces "trying," and "doing," and totally
ignores "flowing," and simply "being." We learn to complicate simplicity
and fear silence. We take breathing for granted and often believe that
"reality" is something that just "happens." And, perhaps worst of all, we
forget to listen, both to ourselves and to others.

During the past twenty years I have been combining my professional training as a psychologist and natural abilities as a musician to help people "tune in" to their inner resources and achieve harmony in their lives.
Over the years, I have also witnessed how complementing my clinical
work and personal life-style with principles learned from years of martial
arts (Karate, Kung-fu, Tai-Chi) studies and teachings from Taoist masters
has effected significant positive differences in my life and my work with
others.

As part of my professional work, I regularly recommend relevant
books to clients who seem to benefit from our work with the aforemen-
tioned principles. However, in spite of all the excellent books available

---

2. Edward T. Hall, *The Dance of Life* (New York: Anchor Press/Doubleday, 1983), pp. 169–170.

today, I have not been able to find a book that effectively combines the techniques, ideas, and approaches that have yielded such positive results in my professional practice. The book I wanted would be based on solid scientific research, draw from years of professional training and experience, allow flexibility for personal exploration and expression, offer fresh, creative alternatives to what's already available, and address a number of common concerns experienced by most people at different points throughout their lives. It would also be based on natural, positive, and pro-active principles, and be presented in a straightforward and simple manner. Finally, I realized that I needed to write the book I was looking for.

BEFORE THERE CAN BE SOUND THERE MUST BE VIBRATION.
VIBRATIONS IMPLY MOVEMENT.
WITHOUT MOVEMENT THEN, THERE IS SILENCE.
SILENCE IMPLIES STILLNESS.
TO ACHIEVE MOVEMENT WE MUST DISRUPT THE STILLNESS.
TO ACHIEVE STILLNESS WE MUST INTERRUPT MOVEMENT.
TO ACHIEVE HARMONY IN OUR LIVES
WE MUST ACHIEVE A BALANCE BETWEEN THE TWO.

This book is about movement. In other words, it's about growth, change, and making creative choices to better our lives and the lives of those around us. It is also about stillness. It is about self-empowerment. It is about knowing when to let go, learning how to breathe and relax, and recognizing—as well as accepting—our limitations. Here psychological principles and Taoist ideas are woven together into musical packages that allow us the freedom to compose our own treatments. To help guide readers, clear and explicit guidelines are provided for conducting exercises, creating personal tapes, and choosing among musical selections. However, these guidelines have been carefully created to allow flexibility for personal expression and freedom in choosing our own path along "the way." In musical terms, the book allows us to improvise.

In short, we can blend psychological, Taoist, and musical principles to provide concise and simple guidelines to help us deal with daily concerns, while raising conscious awareness and exercising creativity. We can also learn about recognizing freedom and exercising control.

The Tao of music is experienced through the freedom that comes from flowing with our internal, natural rhythms. Although indefinable, the Tao is most often referred to as "The Way." Its essence lies in the natural forces of nature. Its teachings do not involve moral, social, or political standards, but simply call for a return to natural simplicity. Flowing with nature. "Being," rather than "trying."

While many authors have attempted to define or describe the Tao for Western readers, the primary consensus appears to be that it cannot be aptly described or defined. Regardless, attempts at interpreting its essence have been put forth. J. C. Cooper, in his book *Taoism: The Way of the Mystic,* suggests that Taoism is "an attempt to express the inexpressible." Further, regarding attempts to properly define this word/concept, Cooper adds, "The word 'Tao' is always left untranslated as it is regarded as indefinable. Its import is too great to be contained in any one word. It is best understood by inference. If it is translated, it is usually called the Way."[3] Ray Grigg, in *The Tao of Being,* similarly proposes that Tao is "the freedom that comes with not understanding," or simply—and more commonly—a "way."[4] Adding further support to the difficulties encountered by proposing Western type definitions to this Eastern concept, the authors of the book *Zen Buddhism & Psychoanalysis* suggest, "...Zen declares that the Tao is 'one's everyday mind.' By Tao, Zen of course means the unconscious, which works all the time in our consciousness." Citing a more practical example, they write, "When a monk asked a master what was meant by 'one's everyday mind,' he answered, 'When hungry, I eat; when tired, I sleep.'"[5]

> If a man hears the Tao in the morning
> and dies in the evening,
> his life has not been wasted.[6]

In effect, in musical terms, the Tao could be described as *the sound of the lost chord.*

> It is necessary for us to understand that "rhythm is nature's way," and it is up to our species to learn as much as possible about how these remarkable processes affect our lives.[7]

The Tao of Music: Sound Psychology is designed to fulfill a number of purposes. Its primary purpose, however, is to help improve our daily lives,

3. J. C. Cooper, *Taoism: The Way of the Mystic* (London: Mandala, 1991), pp. 11, 12.
4. Ray Grigg, *The Tao of Being* (Atlanta: Humanics New Age, 1989), p. xii.
5. Erich Fromm, D. T. Suzuki, and Richard de Martino, *Zen Buddhism and Psychoanalysis* (New York: Harper Colophon Books, 1970), p. 18.
6. Thomas Merton, *The Way of Chuang Tzu* (New York: New Directions, 1969), p. 20.
7. Hall, *The Dance of Life,* p. 179.

both internally and externally. We will explore the following exciting possibilities:

• Basic psychomusicology techniques—entrainment, rhythmic synchronicity, and contextual cuing;

• Creative ways to use proven psychological (behavioral, cognitive, and affective) techniques in combination with music or sound, to help improve our lives;

• Using well-known approaches, such as toning, chanting, and affirmations in psychomusical formats;

• Raising moment to moment awareness to common sounds to make these work for and with us;

• Staying in tune with our personal pace, harmonizing with our own melodies, and maintaining our own rhythms;

• Letting go of unnecessary constrictions (obsessively asking "why?," holding disruptive expectations) while staying in the present;

• Using creative "hooks," or cues (as in the phrase "heAr and now") to remind us to remain in the present;

• Implementing original terms or phrases, such as "psychological noise," or "acoustic memory," to stay in touch with the ever-important aspects of sounds in general, and listening in particular;

• Learning to "think musically" and focus on sound (*listening* for the *melody* in someone's *voice*, sorting through options as we would switch channels on a *radio* dial, *tuning* into the *rhythm* of our surroundings) and to make "sound associations" by using creative "psychomusicology" phrasings (being out of sync versus in harmony). These musical/sound connotations aim to instill new "sound ideas" and awaken a new alertness, or a tuning in, to common everyday statements;

• Presenting case histories to help personalize various approaches while illustrating the applicability of techniques;

• Providing musical suggestions for the exercises as appropriate to each section.

The normal mind is musical, and the normal body is the instrument for adequate expression of music.[8]

The Exercises

Music not only brings order to muscular movement, but also promotes order within the mind.[9]

The exercises are grounded on solid clinical research and complemented by successful results I have encountered in over twenty years of clinical practice in very diverse settings. Drawing from a number of psychomusicological concepts and techniques, the exercises and ideas combine the benefits of music—or sound—with psychological principles to assist in creating healthy, positive, and fully functioning internal (within our own bodies and minds) and external (those outside our own bodies) environments. They are designed to help deal with conditions of dis-harmony (day-to-day issues, emotional states, problematic thoughts) through creative and simple, but practical approaches.

The Koans

Koans are sayings or instructions to disciples which appear on the surface to be illogical or impossible, but which have a deeper meaning underneath. To understand a koan it is necessary to understand the context.[10]

To complement the exercises, a number of maxims or koans (short, catchy, and sometimes paradoxical phrases, grounded in Zen or Taoist philosophy, such as, "If you must expect, expect nothing.") draw on Taoist principles and ideas. The intention of "sprinkling" timely doses of these original koans throughout this book is to encourage us to examine perceptions of the world within and without while contemplating moment to moment conditions. These short teachings are also meant to function as catalysts to help further integrate the various aspects of the accompanying ideas and techniques.

8. Carl E. Seashore, *Psychology of Music* (New York: Dover Publications, 1967), p. 333.
9. Anthony Storr, *Music and the Mind* (New York: The Free Press, 1992), p. 106.
10. Hall, *The Dance of Life*, p. 92.

MUSIC IS THE BEAST
THAT CAN EXCITE THE SAVAGE BREAST.

The Music

Among the various consumption experiences that range from
simple enjoyment to ecstatic rapture, few can match listening
to music in sheer evocative power.[11]

Regardless of our budget, most of us have access to some form of music
(disc or cassette player, radio, stereo system, musical instruments) in our
homes. In effect, music—and sound in general—is so prevalent in our
lives that we often tend to take both music and sound, and their powerful
properties, for granted.

Some people think of music and sound as background embellish-
ment, something that just takes place while we go on with other, more
important day-to-day responsibilities. We do not realize the powerful
effects that music and sound constantly exert on our thoughts, moods, and
even behaviors. How many of us are aware, for instance, of the background
music playing as we meander along the corridors of our local grocery store?
Beyond that, how many of us realize that, in general, the faster the tempo
of the music which is playing, the faster we tend to walk through the store,
choose our groceries and head for the check-out counter? Few people are
aware of the fact that music that "just happens" to be playing in the background is carefully and meticulously selected by experts, who specialize in
regulating these environments for the purpose of influencing our moods.[12]

[M]usic has the potential to evoke feelings of happiness, sadness and euphoria.[13]

Background music played in grocery stores, for example, should ideally be
soothing, uplifting, lively, yet steady and in moderate tempo. The purposes

---

11. Morris Holbrook and Punam Anand, "Effects of Tempo and Situational Arousal on the Listener's
Perceptual and Affective Responses to Music," in *Psychology of Music*, 1990, 18, 2, pp. 150–162 (p.
150).
12. John M. Ortiz, "Music as Sound Campus Ecology," in *The Campus Ecologist*, 1990, 8, 4.
13. Hamid Hekmat and James Hertel, "Pain Attenuating Effects of Preferred Versus Non-preferred
Music Interventions," in *Psychology of Music*, 1993, 21, pp. 163–173 (p. 164).

behind programming background music in this manner include instilling us with a sense of comfort and relaxation while in the store, providing the store with a positive ambiance, and setting a tempo conducive to slowing us down, inducing us to take our time and perhaps purchase more than we may have initially considered, while keeping us alert and moving along. The above phenomenon, known as "entrainment," is one of many techniques we can all use in programming our own lives, controlling our environments, or regulating our actions, thoughts, and emotions.

MUSIC IS INVISIBLE, BUT WE KNOW IT'S THERE.
WE CANNOT TOUCH IT, BUT IT CAN BE PLAYED.
WE CANNOT TASTE IT, BUT IT CAN BE SAVORED.
WE CANNOT SMELL IT, YET IT FILLS THE AIR WITH FRAGRANCE.
ONCE THE TAO OF MUSIC IS FELT, IT IS NEVER FORGOTTEN.

Musical Menus

Musical preferences are relative, the creations of the musician are analogous to the creations of the painter and the sculptor; they are purely objective.[14]

Using music that we have chosen personally is strongly recommended for all exercises. The menus included here list songs intended to serve two purposes. They provide suggestions for situations when we may not be able to think of any complementary tunes to use along with a particular exercise. They are also meant to be examples that may help illustrate the type of music that *could* be used to achieve the desired result. The list presents only a microscopic piece of the collective "musical iceberg."

The various titles mentioned in the menus are a combination of songs that stimulate, calm, or balance. Many have been used by my patients, in my own research, and throughout literature in general. Please remember that *reactions to music are highly relative to each individual* and that these reactions can vary greatly. Variables include previous exposure to the music, personal preference, present mood or attitude, and so forth. None of the suggested songs, tunes, or music are guaranteed to evoke or elicit

14. Seashore, *Psychology of Music*, p. 14.

the purported reactions for all listeners or in all situations. For example, what may seem stimulating one day may feel irritating the next. What may seem soothing to one person, or in some situations, may sound depressing to another person, or in a different situation.

Sound Ideas

Life is the way it is.[15]

Included in the text are short snippets called "Sound Ideas." These are mini sound-exercises that can help us take further advantage of the basic ideas presented in those sections.

The Case Stories

[W]e are responsible for the world we create.[16]

The case stories presented here are combinations of fragments gathered from among the thousands of cases I have treated over the past twenty-two years. While the situations, examples and results are factual, they are aggregates of many distinct cases. In every case, fictitious names have been chosen at random to further discourage identifying with any particular case or event. Any similarities to actual persons, or individual cases, would be coincidental and unintended.

[M]usic is a highly specialized releaser of rhythms already in the individual.[17]

A Word of Warning

This book is not intended as a "cure all," a solution, or a panacea for severe medical problems, or emotional disturbances. It is also not intended to serve as replacement for either medical attention or mental health treatments by licensed or certified professionals. Rather, it is intended as an

---

15. Charlotte Joko Beck, *Everyday Zen* (San Francisco: HarperSanFrancisco, 1989), p. 13.
16. Diane Dreher, *The Tao of Inner Peace*, p. 53.
17. Hall, *The Dance of Life*, p. 178.

adjunct to help clear the mind so that we may better examine our alternatives. Hopefully it will help us to better realize the freedom and access some of the options we have available.

People who suffer from chronic depression, anxiety attacks, severe phobias, substance abuse, medical problems, eating disorders, or any other condition which interferes with the ability to function comfortably and effectively, should consult a medical physician, or a mental health professional, prior to pursuing the exercises in this book.

I sat and listened, fascinated. For far more than an hour I listened to the concert, to this natural melody. It was soft music, containing, as well, all the discords of nature. And that was right, for nature is not only harmonious; she is also dreadfully contradictory and chaotic. The music was that way, too: an outpouring of sounds, having the quality of water and of wind—so strange that it is simply impossible to describe it.[18]

18. C. G. Jung, *Memories, Dreams, Reflections*, Aniela Jaffé, ed. (New York: Vintage Books, 1965), p. 229.

PART ONE

CLINICAL ISSUES

*Music is God's way of
coloring sound.*

1

Depressed Moods

*If we are unable to resonate or merge with a part of ourselves, or
our environment, we become dissonant or dis-eased.*[1]

To many of us, some of the following comments may sound familiar:
"Don't worry, I'm sure things are going to work out!" "Just think
positive!" "Why don't you just snap out of it!?" "What's wrong with
you!?" "You know, you better get it together!" Over the past year, these
were some of the "pearls of wisdom" which Donna received from well-
meaning, caring friends and family members who were concerned about
her pervasive, depressive mood.

A 57-year-old, happily married mother of two daughters, Donna
presented a number of depressive symptoms that had persisted for "well
over a year." Resistant to pharmacological intervention, Donna was almost
more involved in wanting to know "why" she was so depressed than in getting over her depressed state. Although the cause of her depressed mood
became apparent quite early during our sessions, Donna's resistant and
defensive personality made it clear that she was going to have to "stumble" upon the "why" of this situation herself.

---

1. John Beaulieu, *Music and Sound in the Healing Arts* (Barrytown, NY: Station Hill Press, 1987), p. 44.

On the surface, Donna's life appeared gratifying and fulfilling. Running her own business for over thirty years, she reported an almost idyllic relationship with her husband, and the joys of having raised two talented, and beautiful daughters, now 20 and 24. Her husband was involved in his own thriving business, and both daughters were now in college, living away from home. She described her life as "full and busy," and her career as "fun and rewarding." Nonetheless, the once "fun-loving, life of the party" Donna just seemed completely missing from this new incarnation. *This* Donna was uncharacteristically tired, starting to overeat, neglecting her traditional exercise regimen, feeling "worthless," and losing sleep.

In an attempt to have Donna get in touch with her depressive mood, we discussed the idea of her making an entrainment tape. At first, Donna was very resistant. "It'll take too long . . ." was her initial reply, followed by, "This sounds silly," and "Why would that work?" Since other attempts at lifting her depression had proven unhelpful, she decided to give the entrainment tape a try, in spite of her reservations.

Instructions on creating an entrainment tape are basically the same as the ones described later in the *Entrainment* section (see Techniques, Appendix B). Back home, Donna looked over her music collection and, as suggested, chose several songs which seemed to "match her depressed mood" (always tired, sad, and pretty miserable). Having recorded the melancholy, slower tunes onto a cassette tape, she then added several increasingly more "mid-tempo" tunes which generally "moved in the direction she wanted to feel" (happier, more energized). She completed the tape with a number of tunes which closely reflected the "feel" she wanted to recapture. These songs were positive, up-beat, energizing, and full of vigor. Interestingly, Donna chose a very eclectic mix of tunes to fill her tape, including '40s big-band, '50s and '60s rock-and-roll, jazz, and a '90s country tune. As always, it was interesting to hear how these songs— always resonating somewhere in the back of her mind—were tunes that played significant roles in Donna's "life's soundtrack" over the years.

During later sessions, Donna revealed that just taking the time to select these songs had somehow helped to affect her mood. The personal meaning these tunes held for her resonated deep within her unconscious. Further, the time she took—to decide on the order, and to record the songs—provided a wonderful opportunity to do something different for herself and to reminisce over "old, friendly voices" still echoing in her life. Having completed her personalized entrainment tape, Donna found herself playing it at different times, and in different settings—in her car, while relaxing in the tub, even in her office while doing paperwork.

The songs chosen played a significant part in helping Donna get in touch with the core of her depressive mood. The self-designed entrainment sequence made her feel as if she had taken control of her own situation and devised her own "cure." After a few weeks, Donna looked forward to the bittersweet feelings and memories the introductory songs evoked, and smiled with a sense of geniality in anticipation as the more lively "in between" songs came on. The progression, she felt, served to remind her that things change—life wanes and waxes—and that taking responsibility and initiating movement in one's own situation can "feel pretty good." The concluding bouncy, energetic songs progressed from providing a sense of much needed energy to becoming "theme songs" to her newfound animated self. In a sense, the tape became a sort of compact "auditory metaphor" for her own life.

After a short time, Donna looked back and realized that her previously obsessive need to know the "why" that may have been behind her depression had somehow resolved itself.

> [W]e cannot change the cycles around us until we change those within us. . .[2]

> THE TAO OF MUSIC LIES AT THAT SPACE
> BETWEEN HARMONY AND DISSONANCE.

Clinically, depression is a mood disorder. For the purposes of this book, however, the following suggested exercises are designed to assist with lifting a *depressed mood*, rather than a clinical depression. This type of depressive mood state, or sadness, is a feeling that oppresses the mind, weighs down the body, and darkens the spirit. Like all other emotions, depressive moods have a sound all their own—"the blues." In music, these feelings are typically portrayed by the sound of a minor key on the low end of the register. We feel dejected, discouraged, unhappy. Whatever the "lyrics" to our sadness, the sound is "gloomy . . . dejected . . . melancholy . . . discouraged . . . distressed . . . desolate . . ." we sound like we are ". . . down."

> Many people are afraid of Emptiness, however, because it reminds them of Loneliness. Everything has to be filled in, it

2. Diane Dreher, *The Tao of Inner Peace* (New York: HarperCollins, 1991), pp. 112, 115.

seems—appointment books, hillsides, vacant lots—but when
all the spaces are filled, the Loneliness really begins.[3]

Contrary to some people's denial, *anyone* can become depressed. A depressive mood is not a sign of weakness, of "copping out." Depressed moods can be brought about by many things, including a major loss (loss of a loved one, fire or theft in one's home), personal crisis (accident, illness) or a significant life change whether "positive" (marriage, new birth) or "negative" (divorce, child going off to college). In effect, these moods are normal reactions to any number of life events and are experienced by all of us at one time or another, regardless of gender, age, race, ethnicity, diet, geographic locale, or chosen profession.

Chinese art teaches the importance of empty space, openness, the wisdom of Tao.[4]

Feeling empty, we may stray into compulsive eating. Weighed down, we may experience a loss of appetite. Debasing our normal state, a depressive mood can rob us of pleasure, energy, and satisfaction with life in general. Disheartened, we may struggle with insomnia, early-awakenings, or hypersomnia.

[M]usic can provide a temporary retreat from the pains of existence.[5]

Although not necessarily disabling, depressive moods are typically associated with a sense of fatigue. They can affect our bodies—making it difficult to work, and taking the fun out of play. They can be chronic in nature, and keep us from functioning effectively for sustained periods of time, disrupting daily functioning and emotionally disabling us for weeks, months, or even years.

[T]here is no doubt that music can alleviate loneliness.[6]

At one time or another, we all experience low moods which disturb our daily thinking processes, interfere with concentration, or make it difficult to deal with daily decisions. Fostering pessimism, these "blue" moods may

3. Benjamin Hoff, *The Tao of Pooh* (New York: Penguin Books, 1982), p. 147.
4. Dreher, *The Tao of Inner Peace,* p. 77.
5. Anthony Storr, *Music and the Mind* (New York: Free Press, 1992), p. 98.
6. Storr, *Music and the Mind*, p. 111.

leave us despondent, questioning our sense of identity. Depressive mood states may also impair self-esteem, leading to irrational feelings of guilt or self-blame.

Although any, or several, of the feelings mentioned above may accompany a depressed mood, the most prevalent effects usually involve low energy and lack of motivation. Somehow, it may seem more difficult to get up in the morning, or get to sleep at night. Preparing dinner may feel like a major task. Running out to the grocery store or cleaning the house may seem as demanding as climbing a mountain. Sitting in moderate traffic may be perceived as overwhelming. The joy of watching a favorite team win a major victory may be short-lived, or go unappreciated. When depressed, even if the energy is somehow mustered to accomplish a major personal or professional task, we may underestimate the significance of the event, causing us to miss out on the joy of achievement. On the other hand, hearing criticism for a minor, insignificant transgression may be misinterpreted as major rejection, leaving us feeling helpless, hopeless, or worthless. While in this state, "happy" songs tend to sound somehow irritating, while "sad" music tends to feel just about right, somewhat like a long lost friend.

> Patients with neurotic depression often associated music with Beauty/Harmony/ Tenderness, Energy/Life, and Relaxation.[7]

Depressive moods are typically felt as constrictive, or often described as somewhat paralyzing. An effective way of lifting these moods involves using music to activate or mobilize our resources. Since feeling depressed can interfere with various modes of functioning (behaviors, thoughts, moods) the following exercise is designed to attack feelings of melancholia from a number of different modalities (behavior, feelings, sensations, images, thoughts, and social-interpersonal). In effect, the following exercise combines psycho-musicology techniques and various standard psychological models.

> Music has the unique power to bring us to an awareness of our feelings in an unfettered way. Somehow it is acceptable to shed tears while listening to a Mahler symphony, the same tears we suppress when confronted with our own or another's pain.

---

7. Henk Smeijsters, Gaby Wijzenbeek, and Niek van Nieuwenhuijzen, "The Effect of Musical Excerpts on the Evocation of Values for Depressed Patients," in *Journal of Music Therapy*, 1995, 32: 3, pp. 167–188 (p. 184).

Music informs us that we are creatures of feeling, that our feelings are valid, that there is nothing wrong about experiencing them.[8]

In a sense, music can serve as a stimulus to assist us in our descent into the darkness to explore our fear. To look into its eyes, and hear its sound. Engaging us in activity music can assist us in ascending out of the darkness, brightening the path through our internal labyrinths.

EXERCISE 1:

Lifting a Depressed Mood

{D}epression, which is so common in today's world, may have its roots in the person who is out-of-sync in deep and basic ways.[9]

Take a few minutes to identify the areas (behaviors, feelings, thoughts, sensations, etc.) being affected by your depressive mood. Once identified, apply the "psycho-music" suggestions discussed below according to each modality.

EFFECTING BEHAVIOR. Use music to help you "do."

Some songs are like an old, dependable friend.

Choose several musical selections that you feel will energize you. Pick ones that will promote your desire to be active, or will help motivate you to engage in a pleasurable *physical* activity. While for some a pleasurable activity may involve something practical, such as clearing out the attic, cleaning the house, or working out in the yard, for others it may be something more fun or recreational, such as running, aerobics, lifting weights, or simply going out for a walk. For ideas on stimulating music, see the "Stimulating Musical Menu" at the end of this section.

8. Joanne Crandall, *Self-Transformation Through Music* (Wheaton, IL: Theosophical Publishing House, 1986), p. 73.
9. Edward T. Hall, *The Dance of Life* (New York: Doubleday, 1983), p. 168.

MODIFYING AFFECT. Use music to help you express feelings.

If you can't sing—whistle; if you can't whistle—hum.

If you are having difficulty expressing feelings which may be underlying— or causing—your depression, select music that will function as a
catalyst to assist you in releasing these feelings. For example, if your feelings of depression are tied to feelings of anger, animosity, or annoyance at
someone, but you feel it would be unwise, inappropriate or "politically
incorrect" to demonstrate these feelings directly (to your boss) you may
want to select some very upbeat, loud, fast, and "frenzied, turbulent, or
energetic" sounding music from your favorite genre, such as rock (classic
rock, heavy metal, punk, hard rock, alternative), classical (a vigorous piece
with explosive crescendos), new age (up-tempo, highly rhythmic), or big
band (highly charged, energized). Specific musical (album) examples may
include: for rock, "Shake Your Money Maker" (The Black Crowes) or
"Ragged Glory" (Neil Young); classical, "Symphony # 5 in C minor" (First
movement, Beethoven), or "The Messiah: Hallelujah Chorus" (Handel);
new age, "Dance the Devil Away" (Outback), or "Borrasca" (Ottmar
Liebert and Luna Negra); or big band, "In the Mood" (Glen Miller) or
"Well, Git it" (Sy Oliver). For other suggestions see the Letting Go
Musical Menu (page 259) or the Music for Dealing with Anger (page 73).

Play this music at a loud, but not uncomfortable, volume. As it
plays, either "sing" or emote along with it (act it out!). Allow yourself to
dance, exercise, or simply "respond" to the beat. If you choose, allow the
music to "give you permission" to release your feelings and express them
by—while in the privacy and comfort of your safe haven—(virtually) "hollering at your boss (neighbor, partner, child)," effectively airing any pent-
up feelings you may have of wrath or indignation. Allow yourself to let go
as you "become one," revitalized through the energy generated by the rage
and fury contained within the music.

TRANSFORMING SENSATIONS. Use music to positively alter your perceptions and sensibilities.

Music can certainly alter a person's mood, as many sufferers
from recurrent depression have realized.[10]

---

10. Storr, *Music and the Mind*, p. 122.

In this modality a person experiencing a sense of sadness may benefit from exposure to a number of cheerful, joyous, or highly animated pieces of music. Again, by use of an entrainment[11] procedure, gently modify your mood so that you may feel yourself moving upward from the depths of your depression (Beethoven's "Moonlight Sonata," or Harry Nilsson's/Mariah Carey's version of "Without You") toward a happy, uplifting, and empowering musical mode (Beethoven's "Für Elise," Ray Steven's "Everything is Beautiful," R.E.M.'s "Shiny Happy People"). For an example, please refer to the Sample Anti-Depressed Mood Entrainment Sequence, under Musical Menu 1 on page 16.

CREATING HEALING IMAGERY. Use music to help give birth to rejuvenative visualization.

Listening to music by oneself restores, refreshes, and heals.[12]

Here, you may choose to find a quiet, comfortable place where you can lie down and close your eyes without being disturbed. With soothing, but moderately upbeat, brisk, lively music in the background, visualize yourself at two progressive stages. First, following the music's cadence, imagine yourself slowly emerging from your depression. Feel yourself synchronizing with the music's dynamic rhythms, or stirring tempo. See yourself *actively* becoming more fresh and alert. Second, visualize yourself sometime in the future, being very alive and enlivened, smiling and spirited, bustling with energy and purpose.

ALTERING COGNITIONS. Use music to help convert depressive thoughts.

Depression resulting from our mental processes may very well be linked to negative, pessimistic, or irrational beliefs and self-statements. By turning to a musical background similar to the one described above (Creating Healing Imagery), use the music to mentally challenge, dispute, and reject any such mental messages, replacing them with more positive, rational, and optimistic alternatives.[13]

---

11. See Entrainment, page 317.
12. Storr, *Music and the Mind*, p. 122.
13. See Thought Stopping, page 329, and Affirmations, page 325.

Ask yourself, "How valid are these negative beliefs?" Are you dredging up past issues which do not rationally apply to the heAr[14] and now? Do these thoughts relate to pessimistic future probabilities which may, indeed, never come to pass? Are these thoughts self-destructive, or self-defeating? Are you overwhelming yourself with unrealistic and demanding "shoulds, oughts, and musts," particularly in areas of life where you have little or no control ("I *should* be taller," "I *ought* to be a better athlete," "I *must* win that award")? Is your mind consumed by useless, distressful and discouraging thoughts, images, and ideas?

With the aid of the music, replace the negative ("I'm a *loser,* a *victim,* a *failure*") and unrealistic ("*Nothing* ever goes my way!"), with positive ("I have a number of *good* qualities," "I have achieved *success* many times," "I have accomplished a lot of good things in life"), and more reality based ("*Sometimes* things go my way, *other times* they don't!") statements. Displace the pessimistic ("I'll *never* get that promotion!") and make room for encouraging, confident and comforting reflections ("I've done *my best* and I have a good shot at the promotion, if not now, I'll get it *next time!*"). Supplant irrational ("People *must* be the way I think they *should* be, if not I'll *never* be able to deal with it!") with more realistic ("Everyone is *different and entitled* to his or her own belief system," or "Diversity makes the world a *more challenging and exciting* place!") self-statements.[15]

EVOLVING INTERPERSONALLY. Use music to encourage healthy social interactions.

> (Music) gives you a sense of aloofness and inner detachment. You are helped to rise above what seemed to engulf and submerge you with the help of music. The world no longer remains so difficult and so challenging as it first appeared.[16]

Although your depression may have you feeling isolated, alienated, or simply not in the mood to be around anyone, try and get yourself out to a positive and congenial social, interpersonal environment. In accord with the Tao of music, you may choose to seek company in a variety of places—the local nightclub, lounge, pub, or your church, or other religious establish-

---

14. See HeAr and Now, page 243, and Shoulds, page 311.

15. For further reading in this area, including "shoulds," see Albert Ellis and Windy Dryden, *The Practice of Rational Emotive Therapy* (New York: Springer Publishing, 1987).

16. Joan Allekote and Marsha Maslan, "Sri Karunamayee: An In-Depth Interview," *Open Ear*, 1996, 1, p. 6. Here Sri Karunamayee is responding to a question from Marsha Maslan.

ment, anyplace where lively music and spirited socializing is the norm. On the other hand, you may choose to invite a friend, or group of friends, over to your own place for a gathering so you can socialize while listening to pleasant, lighthearted music.

ADORNING THE SEARCH MUSIC REACHES OUR
DARKEST RESOURCES. PROVIDING MOVEMENT, IT
BALANCES OUR STILLNESS. CLEARING THE CLAMOR,
IT HELPS US TO GET IN TOUCH WITH OUR
EMPTINESS. GUIDING OUR PATH THROUGH THE
MYSTERIES WITHOUT EVER DISTURBING THE
DARKNESS THAT SURROUNDS THEM.

The following exercise incorporates an entrainment technique (described in detail in Appendix B, page 317). This exercise is different from the approaches described earlier in that it provides a more structured technique to assist with lifting a depressed mood state.

> Music is effective as a therapeutic agent because, under the right circumstances, it can realign patterns of emotion, structures of consciousness or psychic energy. In very simple terms, when we feel sad or confused, a harmonious, positive piece of music will attract our negative patterns (emotions and thought forms) and carry them along into new locations or shapes.[17]

Music can help because it:

- Initiates movement (moving us from feeling sad to being cheerful, from being discouraged to hopeful, from gloomy to sunny, from negative to positive, tormented to peaceful);
- Functions as a catalyst;
- Deepens the affective experience (assisting us in effectively exploring our underlying sadness);
- Modifies our mental state by cuing us to positive affirmations.
- Helps us establish a sense of commonality, or shared experience, with others;

17. R. J. Stewart, *Music, Power & Harmony: A Workbook of Music & Inner Forces* (New York: Sterling, 1990), p. 62.

- Stimulates our physiological state from apathetic to active;
- Eliminates uncomfortable periods of silence;
- Triggers positive images;
- Induces a state of relaxation;
- Alters body chemistry;
- Provides an outlet for emotional and artistic expression;
- Serves as respite from anxiety, or stressful conditions;
- Diverts attention from fears, tensions, and other concerns.

You can not have any mood say even sorrow coming back to you unless it is felt in terms of Music. It is Music that highlights it and by highlighting even negative feelings of sorrow or sadness it provides catharsis also.[18]

◯

EXERCISE 2:
Moving Out of the Blues

1. Following the entrainment guidelines select approximately ten to fifteen minutes (two or three selections) of music, "sad" tunes which in your opinion reflect or resemble your *present* "blue" mood. Then select ten to fifteen minutes of music that "feels" moderately more positive, happy, or energizing than your present mood, music reflective of the state, or mood, that you *would like to move toward.* Finally, select ten to fifteen minutes of music that reflects the mood (positive, content, confident, energized) you *would like to be in* by the end of this session.

In other words, arrange the music so that it *begins* by reflecting how you feel *right now*, then arrange your selections in a progressive sequence culminating in a mood that reflects how you *would like* to feel by the end of the exercise.

2. Select, or compose, a number of positive affirmations relevant to combat your present emotional state (see Affirmations, page 325).

3. Find a comfortable and quiet place where you may devote approximately thirty to forty-five minutes to simply *listen* to the music comfort-

---

18. Allekote and Maslan, "Sri Karunamayee: An In-Depth Interview," in *Open Ear*, 1966, I, p. 6. Here Sri Karunamayee is responding to a question from Marsha Maslan.

ably, without interruption (disconnect phones, place a "do not disturb" sign on the door, inform others in the house that you need "a few minutes to yourself," etc.).

4. As you listen to each selection, allow the music to envelop you with its mood and vibrations. Feel each progressive mood—from sad, to content, to cheerful—wrap around you, engulfing you like a blanket. Feel the warmth of the music enveloping you snugly, like a warm, velvety glove.

5. As the music plays, do not try to focus on hearing any particular aspect of the composition. Rather, allow your heart, body and mind to passively *listen* to your thoughts and emotions as the melodies slowly mold and massage your emotional state (see Being versus Trying to Be, page 261).

6. As you feel the vibrations showering and massaging your emotions, allow yourself to join, or bond, with the music. Initially, as you play the first few, sad selections, permit your emotions to flow with the feel of the music. Allow yourself to experience an emotional release through crying or verbalizing ("I miss you," "I'm so lonely," "I feel so miserable!") your feelings of sadness. Feel the music as it comforts and consoles you, as it supports you during this time of personal expression.

7. By hearing this music, sad and blue, your heart can connect with a larger consciousness. Through its feel, the music acts as a window to your affective experience. It reminds you that someone else, somewhere, has felt similarly to the way you do at this very moment. The sheer availability of this music in the market clearly indicates that there are many kindred spirits out there, perhaps at this very moment, who can relate to how you feel *right now.* Because of the mere existence of this music, you know that—no matter how you feel—you are not alone.

8. As the musical selections move upward, in a more positively emotional direction, continue to join with the changing musical feel and begin to allow your body to relax through deep breathing (see Breathing, page 333). As you listen to your inner messages, continue to consciously bond with the changing music, allowing your mental self-statements to subtly shift from sad and hopeless, to more positive and hopeful. Feel the beat stimulating your pulse, let the musical rhythms stroke and caress you.

9. As you feel this emotional shift occurring, use your positive affirmations to counter or modify your negative thoughts, move toward your desired

mood, and accomplish a sense of control, positivity, and comfort. Allow the musical resonance to alleviate and encourage you. Let it move you forward in a positive direction.

10. As you continue to bathe in the music, feel your mental and emotional states moving slowly but steadily *upward,* continuously joining and melding with the progressively positive, up-beat melodies.

11. As the music lifts you, allow your moods to flow with the feel of the music. Feel the relief that comes from the emotional bonding, the support stemming from the common sharing of emotions with other kindred spirits. With each pulsing beat and each change in tempo, allow yourself to let go of unwanted, unnecessary, negative thoughts and emotions. Feel yourself becoming positive, relieved, and alert.

12. As the music concludes, choose one or two positive affirmations that you can return to throughout the day. These will help you consciously and emotionally "cue" back to your desired, positive emotional state. (See Contextual Cuing, page 287.)

LEAVING YOU EMPTY, MUSIC MAKES YOU FULL.
DEEP, IT FILLS WITHOUT FILLING,
YIELDING AN UNDERSTANDING THAT REQUIRES
NO COMPREHENSION.

THE TAO OF ROOTS IS DARKNESS.
THE TAO OF FLOWERS IS LIGHT.

Musical Menus

Although the same piece of music may elicit different emotions in the same individual at various times, there are many situations which tend to capture the essence of particular emotions. The following selections are provided as a general guide to assist us in joining our "blue moods," confronting them, and then moving on. The reader is encouraged to personalize his or her musical selections as often as possible.

♪

Musical Menu 1

Anti-Depressed Mood Entrainment Sequence

It is better to feel that life is tragic than to be indifferent to it.[19]

Pop-Rock Music Examples

• Selections you can choose from to start your tape (*joining with your depression*):

     Pink Floyd: "Comfortably Numb"
     Beatles: "She's Leaving Home"
     Temptations: "I Wish It Would Rain"
     Harry Nilsson/Mariah Carey: "Without You"
     Bonnie Raitt: "Louise"
     B.J. Thomas: "I'm So Lonesome I Could Cry"

• Possible selections to begin your "out of the blues" ascension (*moving up or out of your depressive state*):

     Bread: "It Don't Matter to Me"
     Tom Petty: "I Won't Back Down"
     The Carpenters: "We've Only Just Begun"
     ——— ."It's Going to Take Some Time This Time"
     Roy Orbison: "Only the Lonely"
     Bonnie Raitt: "Runaway"
     Led Zeppelin: "Stairway to Heaven"

• Potential selections to begin your entry into a happier state (*entering a brighter, more "up-beat" mood state*):

     Rascals: "I've Been Lonely Too Long"
     Beach Boys: "Good Vibrations"
     Tom Petty/The Byrds: "I Feel a Whole Lot Better"
     Bread: "Let Your Love Go"

19. Storr, *Music and the Mind,* pp. 68–69.

Buddy Holly: "It Doesn't Matter Anymore"
Elton John: "I Guess That's Why They Call It the Blues"
Led Zeppelin: "Rock & Roll"

• Selections to consider in concluding your tape (*turning the transition into positive energy*):
    Cyndi Lauper: "Girls Just Wanna Have Fun"
    Beach Boys: "Fun, Fun, Fun"
    Steve Miller Band: "The Joker"
    Beatles: "All You Need is Love"
    Three Dog Night: "Joy to the World"
    Paul McCartney (Wings): "Silly Love Songs"
    Bruce Springsteen: "Born in the U.S.A."

Classical Music Examples

• Selections you can choose from to start your tape (*joining with your depression*):
    Beethoven: First movement from Sonata No. 14 in C-sharp
        minor, "Moonlight"
    ————. Second movement, Sonata, opus 10, No. 3
    Chopin: Sonata opus 35, "Funeral March"
    Tchaikovsky: "Andante Cantabile," from Symphony No. 5 in
        E minor
        ————. Overture, "Romeo and Juliet"
        ————. Fourth movement, Symphony No. 6, "Pathetique"
    Schubert: "March Militaire"
        ————. "Serenade"
    Mendelssohn: "May Breezes"
    Wagner: Tristan and Isolde, "Liebestod"

• Possible transition selections to begin your "out of the blues" ascension (*moving up, or out of your depressive state*), and begin your entry into a happier state (*entering a brighter, or more joyful mood state*):
    Beethoven: First movement from Symphony No. 5 in C
        minor, opus 67
        ————. "Minuet in G"
    Bach: "Air, on the G-string"
        ————. "Sleepers Awake"
        ————. "Toccata & Fugue in D minor"

Debussy: "Clair de Lune"
———. "Reverie"
———. "Golliwog's Cakewalk" from *Children's Corner Suite*
———. "Afternoon of a Faun"
Mozart: Theme from *Elvira Madigan*, Concerto No. 21 in C
  major
———. "Eine Kleine Nachtmuzik" ("A Little Nightmusic")
  K. 525
Schubert: "Ave Maria"
Mendelssohn: "On Wings of Song"
Brahms: "Lullaby"
———. Third movement from Symphony No. 3 in F major

• Selections to consider when concluding your tape (*turning the transition
into positive energy*):
Bach: Preludium in E major
Rossini: "Largo al Factotum" from *The Barber of Seville*
———. Finale to the "William Tell Overture"
Beethoven: "Für Elise"
———. Third movement from Symphony No. 7 in A major
———. Turkish March from "Ruins of Athens"
Mozart: First movement from Sonata No. 15 in C major`
———. Fourth movement from Symphony No. 35 in D
  major, "Haffner"
Chopin: "Polonaise" in A-flat major
Schubert: Ballet Music No. 2 from "Rosamunde"
Mendelssohn: "Spring Song"
Sousa: "Stars and Stripes Forever" March
Handel: *Messiah*: "Hallelujah Chorus"

♪

MUSICAL MENU 2
Bonding and Moving Away from a Depressed Mood

(CD, TAPE, AND ALBUM TITLES)

Popular Music Suggestions

Jackson Browne: *The Pretender*
Tracy Chapman: *Tracy Chapman*
Pink Floyd: *The Wall*
Fiona Apple: *Tidal*
Kristin Hersh: *Hips & Makers*
Billy Holiday: *Billie's Blues*
John Lennon: *Menlove Ave.*
Cowboy Junkies: *The Trinity Session*
Joni Mitchell: *Blue*
Roy Orbison: *For the Lonely: 18 Greatest Hits*
Bruce Springsteen: *Nebraska*
Mazzy Star: *She Hangs Brightly*
Jules Shear: *The Great Puzzle; Healing Bones*

Classical Music Suggestions

Ludwig Van Beethoven: *Sonata No. 14 in C-sharp minor, opus 27, No. 2, First movement ("Moonlight")*
Frédéric François Chopin: *Sonata opus 35 ("Funeral March")*
Claude Debussy: *Sirènes (Nocturnes)*
George Gershwin: *Rhapsody in Blue (Theme)*
Franz Liszt: *Liebestraum No. 3*
Franz Schubert: *Serenade*
————. *Unfinished Symphony (Symphony No. 8), First movement*
Jean Sibelius: *The Swan of Tuonela*
Peter Ilyich Tchaikovsky: *Symphony #6 (Pathetique), Fourth movement*
Peter Ilyich Tchaikovsky: *Overture to Romeo and Juliet*

Richard Wagner: *Tristan and Isolde: Liebestod*
Various Performers: *Classic Weepies*

New Age Music Suggestions

Clannad: *Anam*
Mychael Danna: *Sirens*
Dik Darnell: *Voice of the Four Winds*
P. C. Davidoff: *Santosh*
Peter Gabriel: *The Last Temptation of Christ* (*Passion* soundtrack)
James N. Howard: *Dying Young*
Michael Jones: *After the Rain*
Daniel Kobialka: *Going Home Again*
Jon Mark: *The Standing Stones of Callanish*
Steve Roach: *Dreamtime Return*
Coyote Oldman: *In Medicine River*
Dr. Jeffrey Thompson: *Child of a Dream*

♪

MUSICAL MENU 3
Stimulating Music

New Age Music Suggestions (CD, tape, or album)

Tom Barabas: *Mosaic*
Eko: *Future Primitive* (Guitar with mandolin, keyboards, percussion, electronic sounds, and harmonica)
Strunz & Farah: *Primal Magic* (Flamenco guitars backed by Latin percussion, violin, bass, and vocals)
———. *Amèricas* (Spanish guitars backed by Latin percussion, violin, keyboards, and bass)
Deep Forest: *Deep Forest*
Kenny G.: Any selection
Trio Globo: *Carnival of Souls*

Mickey Hart: *Planet Drum* (Drums and percussion with back-up vocalists)

————. *Mystery Box*

Zakir Hussain: *Zakir Hussain and the Rhythm Experience* (Middle-Eastern, Indian, Cuban, and Brazilian drum rhythms)

Stanley Jordan: *Bolero* (Jazz)

Brent Lewis: *Earth Tribe Rhythms* (African and Caribbean rhythms on Ikauma drums)

————. *The Primitive Truth* (Ikauma drums accompanied by tabla, gourd, dumbec, and conga).

Ottmar Liebert & Luna Negra: *Borrasca* (Flamenco guitars with bass, keyboards, horns and percussion)

Hugh Masekela: *Hope*

Pat Metheny: *The Road to You* (Jazz)

————. *Secret Story* (Jazz)

The Power of Movement: *Dynamic Dancing*

Nightingale: *Light Dance* (Synthesized sounds with world-beat rhythms)

Outback: *Dance the Devil Away* (Didgeridoo and guitars with multi-cultural percussion)

City Raga: *Popol Vuh*

Steve Reid: *Bamboo Forest* (Contemporary jazz—guitar/percussion)

Gabrielle Roth and the Mirrors: *Waves* (Drums, world rhythms)

————. *Tongues*

Sacred Spirits: *Sacred Spirits*

Paul Speer and Leroy Quintana: *Shades of Shadow* (Synthesizers, piano and synthesized percussion, with some saxophone)

Omar Faruk Tekbilek: *Whirling*

Classical Music Suggestions

Johann Strauss: "Blue Danube Waltz"

Bernward Koch: "Laguna de la Vera"

W. A. Mozart: Symphony No. 35 in D (Haffner)

————. Symphony No. 41 in C (Jupiter), Fourth movement

Johann Sebastian Bach: "Brandenburg Concertos"
Gioacchino Rossini: "William Tell Overture" (finale)
Ludwig van Beethoven: Symphony No. 7 in A-major, Third
    movement
————. Symphony No. 5, Fourth movement
Manuel DeFalla: "Ritual Fire Dance" (from *El Amor Brujo*)

Suggestions to assist in moving away from a depressed mood.

Popular Music Suggestions (CD, tape, or album)

Paula Abdul: *Forever Your Girl*
B-52's: *Cosmic Thing*
B: Tribe: *Fiesta Fatal!*
Babyface: *Tender Love*
Badfinger: *Straight Up; Greatest Hits; No Dice*
The Bangles: *Greatest Hits*
The Beach Boys: *Endless Summer; Pet Sounds; Good Vibrations*
    (boxed set); *20/20; Sun Flower*
The Beatles: *With the Beatles; Please Please Me; A Hard Day's
    Night; Beatles for Sale; Help!; Rubber Soul; Revolver; Sergeant
    Pepper's Lonely Heart's Club Band; Let It Be; Abbey Road; The
    Beatles Live at the BBC*
Big Brother and the Holding Company: *Cheap Thrills*
David Bowie: *Let's Dance*
The Moody Blues: *Seventh Sojourn; A Question of Balance; Days of
    Future Passed; Time Traveler* (5-CD boxed set)
Blur: *Blur*
Tracy Bonham: *The Burdens of Being Upright*
Allman Brothers: *Eat a Peach; Brothers; The Fillmore Concerts*
The Darling Buds: *Erotica*
Kevin Burke: *Kevin Burke's Open House: Hoof and Mouth*
The Byrds: *Twenty Essential Tracks from the Box Set*
Fine Young Cannibals: *The Raw and the Cooked*
Cheap Trick: *Live At Budokan*
The Doobie Brothers: *The Captain and Me; Greatest Hits*
The Cars: *Greatest Hits*
Inner City: *Big Fun*
The Dave Clark Five: *The History of the Dave Clark Five*
Culture Club: *Colour by Numbers*

Bad Company: *Run With the Pack; Bad Company*
The Commitments (*Original Motion Picture Sound track*): Vols. 1 & 2.
Elvis Costello: *Girls, Girls, Girls; Get Happy*
Marshall Crenshaw: *Life's Too Short; Marshall Crenshaw*
Sheryl Crow: *Tuesday Night Music Club; Sheryl Crow*
Black Crowes: *Shake Your Money Maker; Three Snakes and One Charm*
Dion: *The Road I'm On—A Retrospective;; Yo' Frankie; Bronx Blues; The Columbia Recordings*
The Eagles: *Hotel California; On the Border; Desperado; The Eagles*
Gloria Estefan: *Into the Light; Abriendo Puertas; Let it Loose; Greatest Hits; Destiny*
Melissa Etheridge: *Brave & Crazy*
John Denver: *The Rocky Mountain Collection*
The Doors: *The Best of the Doors*
Elvis Presley: *The King of Rock and Roll: The Complete 50's Masters* (boxed set)
Pink Floyd: *Dark Side of the Moon*
John Fogerty: *Centerfield*
————. *Blue Moon Swamp*
Peter Gabriel: *Shaking the Tree*
Marvin Gaye: *What's Going On?*
Spice Girls: *Spice*
Gladhands: *La Di Da*
The Flaming Groovies: *Groovies Greatest Grooves*
Van Halen: *1984*
George Harrison: *Cloud Nine; George Harrison*
Buddy Holly: *From the Original Master Tapes*
Crowded House: *Crowded House*
Michael Jackson: *Off the Wall; Thriller*
Billy Joel: *Greatest Hits; Piano Man; The Stranger; Street Life Serenade*
Elton John: *Goodbye Yellow Brick Road; Madman Across the Water; Elton John; Elton John: To be Continued* (4 CD boxed set)
Rickie Lee Jones: *Pop Pop*
Janis Joplin: *Pearl; Kozmic Blues*
Chaka Khan: *Life is a Dance*
Carole King: *Tapestry*

The Gipsy Kings: *The Best of the Gipsy Kings*
The Kinks: *Remastered (3 CD boxed set)*
Patti LaBelle: *Be Yourself*
Cyndi Lauper: *She's So Unusual; Twelve Deadly Cyns*
Huey Lewis & The News: *Time Flies . . . The Best of*
John Lennon: *Double Fantasy; Imagine; Rock 'N Roll; Collection*
Fleetwood Mac: *Rumours; Fleetwood Mac*
Bob Marley & The Wailers: *Legend*
Paul McCartney: *Choba B CCCP; Ram; McCartney; Red Rose Speedway; Band on the Run; Venus and Mars; All the Best; Unplugged; Flaming Pie*
Roger McGuinn: *Back from Rio*
John (Cougar) Mellencamp: *American Fool*
Alanis Morissette: *Jagged Little Pill*
Van Morrison: *Astral Weeks; Moondance; Too Long in Exile; The Healing Game*
Oasis: *(What's the Story) Morning Glory?; Definitely Maybe*
Tom Petty: *Full Moon Fever; Greatest Hits; Wildflowers*
The Police: *Message in a Box; The Complete Recordings* (4-CD boxed set)
The Pretenders: *Singles*
Deep Purple: *Machine Head*
Bonnie Raitt: *Collection; Nick of Time*
Credence Clearwater Revival: *Chronicle (Two Volumes)*
Linda Ronstadt: *Mad Love; Greatest Hits (Two Volumes)*
Rush: *Moving Pictures*
Todd Rundgren: *Something/Anything; Anthology*
Santana: *III; Abraxas; Caravanserai*
Bob Seger & The Silver Bullet Band: *Greatest Hits*
Lynyrd Skynyrd Band: *Gold & Platinum*
Ella Baila Sola: *Ella Baila Sola*
The Spongetones: *Beat & Torn; Oh Yeah!*
Squeeze: *Singles; East West Story*
Cat Stevens: *Buddha and the Chocolate Box; Catch Bull at Four*
Rod Stewart: *The Mercury Anthology*
Bruce Springsteen: *Born to Run; Born in the U.S.A.; The Wild, The Innocent & The E-street Shuffle; The River*
The Rolling Stones: *Exile on Main Street; Beggar's Banquet; CD Singles Collection: The London Years (4 CD boxed set); Let it Bleed*

James Taylor: *JT; Flag; Hourglass*
George Thorogood: *Live*
Traffic: *Smiling Phases*
U2: *Pop; Joshua Tree*
Stevie Ray Vaughn: *Couldn't Stand the Weather; Soul to Soul*
Paul Weller: *Wildwood; Paul Weller; Stanley Road; Heavy Soul*
The Traveling Wilburys: *Volume 1*
Stevie Wonder: *Natural Wonder; Songs in the Key of Life; Innervisions; Talking Book*
XTC: *Oranges & Lemons, Skylarking; Nonsuch*
Crosby, Stills, Nash & Young: *Deja Vu*
Neil Young: *Freedom; Decade; Harvest; Harvest Moon*
Warren Zevon: *The Best of*
ZZ Top: *Eliminator; Greatest Hits*

Willing To Try Some Alternative Suggestions?

Belly: *Star*
Blur: *Blur*
The Boo Radleys: *Wake Up*
Cast: *All Change*
Velvet Crush: *In the Presence of Greatness; Teenage Symphonies to God*
The Diggers: *Mount Everest*
The Spin Doctors: *Pocket Full of Kryptonite*
Fountains of Wayne: *Fountains of Wayne*
The Grays: *Ro Shambo*
Gin Blossoms: *New Miserable Experience; Congratulations I'm Sorry*
Greenday: *Dookie*
Dave Mathews Band: *Under the Table and Dreaming; Crash*
The Iguanas: *Nuevo Boogaloo*
Sonny Landreth: *Blues Attack; South of I-10*
The Lemonheads: *Come on Feel*
Live: *Throwing Copper; Secret Samadhi*
Morphine: *Good; Cure for Pain*
Sam Phillips: *Martinis & Bikinis*
Phish: *A Live One*
The Spent Poets: *The Spent Poets*
The Posies: *Frosting on the Beater*

R.E.M.: *New Adventures in Hi-Fi; Green*
Ride: *Tarantula: Carnival of Light*
Rusted Root: *When I Woke*
Semisonic: *Great Divide*
Kula Shaker: *K*
The Smithereens: *Blown to Smithereens*
Matthew Sweet: *Girlfriend; 100% Fun; Blue Sky on Mars*
Sugarplastic: *Bang, The Earth is Round*
Supergrass: *I Should Coco*
Yo La Tengo: *Painful; Fakebook*
Weezer: *Weezer*

Suggested General "Greatest Hit" or Anthology Compilations

Various: *Growing Up Too Fast: The Girl Group Anthology*
Londonbeat: *The Beat is Back*
The Temptations
The Four Tops
The Supremes
The Shirelles
Martha and the Vandellas
Marvin Gaye
Sam & Dave
Sly and the Family Stone
Curtis Mayfield
The Stray Cats
Chuck Berry
Little Richard
Three Dog Night
The Bangles
Mitch Ryder and the Detroit Wheels
The Rascals
Eddie Cochran
Gene Vincent
Jr. Walker and the All Stars

Additional Reading

For additional reading regarding how music may affect moods, you may refer to the following articles:

T. G. Bever, "A Cognitive Theory of Emotion and Aesthetics in Music," *Psychomusicology*, 1988, 7, pp. 165–175.

R. Brim, "The Effect of Personality Variables, Dogmatism and Repression-Sensitization Upon Response to Music," *Journal of Music Therapy*, 1978, 15, pp. 74–87.

H. J. Devlin and D. D. Sawatzky, "The Effects of Background Music in a Simulated Initial Counselling Session with Female Subjects," in *Canadian Journal of Counselling*, 1987, 21, pp. 125–132.

G. Groeneweg, E. A. Stan, A. Celser, L. MacBeth, M. I. Vrbancic, "The Effect of Background Music on the Vocational Behavior of Mentally Handicapped Adults," *Journal of Music Therapy*, 1988, 25, pp. 118–134.

M. Martin, "On the Induction of Mood," *Clinical Psychology Review*, 1990, 10, pp. 669–697.

K. McDermott, "Music Soothes," *The Magazine of Case Western Reserve University*, 1988, 1, p. 40.

P. O. Peretti, "Changes in Galvanic Skin Response as Affected by Musical Selection, Sex, and Academic Discipline," *Journal of Psychology*, 1975, 89, pp. 183–187.

M. R. Pignatiello, C. J. Camp and L. Rasar, "Musical Mood Induction: An Alternative to the Velten Technique," *Journal of Abnormal Psychology*, 1986, 95, pp. 295–297.

V. N. Stratton and A. H. Zalanowski, "The Effects of Music and Paintings on Mood," *Journal of Music Therapy*, 1989, 26, pp. 30–41.

M. H. Thaut, "The Influence of Music Therapy Interventions on Self-Rated Changes in Relaxation, Affect, and Thought in Psychiatric Prisoner-Patients," *Journal of Music Therapy*, 1989, 23, pp. 155–166.

2

COMFORT IS AN ILLUSION CREATED BY NOT-KNOWING.
KNOWING ALL, WE CEASE TO GROW, GROWING,
WE ENCOUNTER PAIN. PAIN LEADS TO MOVEMENT, MOVEMENT LEADS
TO EMPTINESS, MAKING ROOM FOR GROWTH.
OPENNESS LEADS TO CHANGE. EMBRACE OPENNESS.

Pain

*It is a fact that the way to individual self-discovery often leads
through suffering. . .*[1]

In my life, I have never experienced anything as painful as watching
my young, once robust father, dying a slow, agonizing death. On
September 14, 1980, my beloved father finally died after losing a two
year bout with cancer.

One night in particular, shortly before he passed on, I sat by his bed
in utter frustration, trying to come up with some "magical solution" that
would somehow quell his incurable, irreversible pain. I recall that he had
music—the opera which he loved so much—playing in the background
which felt, in my state of helplessness, irritating to the point of annoyance.
"Do you want me to turn that music off?" I asked. "No!" he replied, somehow summoning the strength to sound explicit while at the same manag-
ing to enlighten me, "Don't you see," he said, "as long as I can hear the
music I know that I'm alive, and if I'm dead, and I can still hear it, then
death can't be so bad." He was 50 years old.

---

1. Peter Michael Hamel, *Through Music to the Self* (Shaftesbury, England: Element Books, 1986), p. 10.

Being alone with one's pain may increase concentration on painful feelings, decrease pain tolerance, and increase subjective pain experiences.[2]

"No pain, no gain." In the '90s, it's a good thing that most trainers and athletic instructors have abandoned that horrific phrase and belief system. Pain-free, our bodies sing, flowing melodically. In pain, those sounds become discordant cries for help.

Out of our sufferings, we should learn something.[3]

Obsessing over chronic pain can, and often does, essentially take over a suddenly chaotic life. When suffering from chronic pain, the energy that goes into worrying about the source of our discomfort could be otherwise applied to productive daily situations. Senses lie awake like hidden shadows with sharpened claws. In chronic pain, we spend enormous amounts of time feeling for every twinge, spasm, or sensation that may help in our "self-diagnosing" the "true cause" of the pain. Hopefully, that one magical piece of information will assist our physician, surgeon, or physical therapist to once and for all help us be rid of it. Sitting through a movie in a theater turns into an endurance marathon. Interesting lectures become stifling, social encounters suffocating. Tolerance hits bottom, and a simple request from a friend may sound like an unreasonable demand. Minimal irritations appear affixiating, mild distractions intolerable. We are on the edge, and the noises inside our head seem to scream in incessant turmoil. We become aliens within our own bodies. Dancing with the pain we feel trapped, as if helplessly spinning in a downward spiral.

It's time, as we used to say in "pre-CD" times, to "change that record."

The following story serves to illustrate the efficacy of music in attenuating pain. In a recent article, Jane Edwards describes an incident where Ivan, a 12-year-old boy hospitalized with burns to his right leg and genitalia, was to undergo a painful and anxiety provoking "debridement bath." In describing this procedure, Edwards indicated that "the child is placed in a bath of water after having the bandages and dressings removed. The dead skin on and around the burn site is then removed with sponges." Using music as a therapeutic adjunct, Edwards, accompanied by a guitar,

2. Hamid Hekmat and James Hertel, "Pain Attenuating Effects of Preferred Versus Non-preferred Music Interventions," in *Psychology of Music,* 1993, 21, 2, pp. 163–173 (pp. 170–171).
3. Thich Nhat Hanh, *Peace is Every Step* (New York: Bantam, 1991), p. 103.

selected the song "A Little Help from My Friends," by the Beatles, to try and alleviate the pain of the debridement procedure. [4]

> When I began to hum the tune, "A Little Help from My Friends," Ivan lifted up his right arm and gave a "thumbs up" signal. A little later he said, "you are singing beautifully." At the end of the bath, which must have taken about 20 minutes, but could have taken longer, Ivan told me that he had felt no pain during the bath. He had been imagining himself lying on his bed at home listening to the radio. He expressed amazement that he hadn't been aware of the nurse touching him during the procedure.[5]

Edwards indicated that the music was able to address immediate needs, helped to rally the psychological resources (through imagery and entrainment) Ivan required to "get through" the experience, provided a sense of security and safety, and provided a bridge from distress and resistance to relaxation and calm. Overall, Edwards said that "music can provide a focus for the child away from the pain and discomfort and provide comfort and psychological support." [6]

> This state in which music holds the brain's attention may explain why listening to music can block pain. Pain and tension are intimately connected; pain leads to tension, which leads to pain. Soothing music can short-circuit this pain cycle, which is why some dentists use Beethoven or Bach as a kind of aural anesthesia.[7]

GREGORIAN CHANTS, MEDIEVAL TROUBADOURS, RENAISSANCE MASSES, BAROQUE ORATORIOS. PAINLESS ORDER BECOMES STAGNANT, PAINFUL DISORDER LEADS TO CHANGE. WITH PAIN COMES RENEWAL, TRANSITION, REGENERATION. PAINLESS, THE MIND REMAINS INERT, THE HEART, DORMANT,. THE SPIRIT, BARREN. DEFINING TIME, MUSIC FREES SOULS, CAPTURES AND SURRENDERS HEARTS, COLORS THE MIND, HURLS THE SPIRIT INTO THE INFINITE.

---

4. Jane Edwards, "You are Singing Beautifully: Music Therapy and Debridement Bath," *The Arts in Psychotherapy,* 1995, 22, 1, pp. 53–56 (p. 53).
5. Edwards, "You are Singing Beautifully," p. 54.
6. Edwards, "You are Singing Beautifully," p. 54.
7. William Poole, *The Heart of Healing* (Atlanta: Turner Publishing, 1993), p. 135.

I spend an average of three hours a day (seven days a week) caring for chronic back and neck injuries. For years, my regimen has included yoga in the mornings, swimming every evening, weight training three times per week, and a combination of ice and moist heat treatments as often as I get the opportunity. Actually, this injury has forced me into the American fitness regime. As an adjunct to my workouts, music is indispensable. It not only provides rhythmic motivation and a pace-setting, continuous energy boost, but also helps to basically eliminate psychological noise (mental "shoulds and oughts" that interfere with the here and now) during my workouts.[8]

MAKING MUSIC, OR PLAYING IT, IS TAKING
RESPONSIBILITY FOR ONE'S INTERNAL AND
EXTERNAL ENVIRONMENTS.

Pain Elimination/Reduction

Music can help eliminate pain by serving as an imaginary sanctuary—a safe haven—from pain. It helps reduce stress and tension, and elicits relaxation. It triggers endorphins, and helps our minds create sound images so we can temporarily escape into a "painless world" sheltered by the imagination. Music functions as an "interpreter," translating pain "waves" (sensations) into healthy, "sound" energy or vibrations.

○

EXERCISE 3:
Pain Elimination/Reduction

*Whenever you feel there is pain, you take that breath with the sound.
It will soothe you. It will give you an inner massage where no
healers' hands can go. No acupuncturists' needle can pierce at that
very membrane because you know where it hurts.*[9]

---

8. See Psychological Noise, page 281.
9. Joan Allekote and Marsha Maslan, "Sri Karunamayee: An In-Depth Interview," *Open Ear*, 1996, 1, p. 8. Sri Karunamayee is responding to a question from Joan Allekote.

Pain is a symptom of disharmony. For the purposes of this exercise, "pain" can be viewed as a series of sounds—or vibrations—sending messages to the brain indicating something is wrong in a particular part of the body. These pain messages can be heard as an alarm alerting us to a particular state of dissonance somewhere in the body. The purpose of this exercise is to achieve physical and mental harmony by converting the pain vibrations into vibrations of comfort, ease, and relief.

1. Select (instrumental) music with soothing, or relaxing qualities of approximately 20 to 30 minutes in duration.[10] Choosing the best musical background to accompany this, or any activity which uses music as adjunct, is as relative and personal as the pain experience itself.

2. Find a comfortable, relaxing place where you can sit or lie, and play the music, perhaps through a portable device (CD player, cassette deck). Headphones would be preferable whenever possible as these help isolate us from extraneous sounds and they engulf us within a "musical blanket."

3. Begin your relaxation regimen by starting a slow, natural rhythm of diaphragmatic (i.e., "belly") breathing.[11]

4. Once you feel relaxed, allow your awareness to go directly to the source of your pain (lower back, head, sinuses, neck). Allow yourself to focus on the *exact* location of the pain.

5. Once you have pinpointed its *exact* location (to the best of your ability) use your imagination to examine the various aspects of the pain. "Look" at its size, shape, and form. In your mind, try to define and describe its characteristics as well as you can. Is it jagged or circular, pulsating or constant? Look at its texture. Is it smooth or rough? Can you attribute a color to it?

6. Once you have determined the above characteristics of the "pain," use your imagination and begin to translate the pain vibrations into *sound* vibrations. What does the pain *sound* like? Is it high-pitched and piercing? low, deep, heavy and dull? jarring and discordant? Do the pain vibrations "echo" or resonate to other parts of your body? Once you have tuned into the "sound" emitted by the pain, you can now begin to modify those pain "sound waves," or energies, into calm, flowing, harmonious vibrations.

10. See Soothing Musical Menu, page 55, Meditation Musical Menu, page 230, Altered States Musical Menu, page 241, or Chanting Musical Menu, page 345, for a few suggestions.
11. See Breathing, page 333.

7. At this point, begin to quietly and naturally imagine yourself breathing in the soothing music as it flows all around you. With each breath you take, imagine the soothing, healing sounds being inhaled deeper and deeper into your body until they reach the pain, itself.

8. Once the music reaches the pain, imagine the sound vibrations completely engulfing the pain. In your mind's eye, "see" the musical resonance slowly but efficiently dismantling the pain. "Watch and listen" as the pain vibrations are disassembled into dozens—then hundreds—then thousands—of tiny particles surrounded and embraced by the music's melody.

9. As you breathe out, begin to actively visualize the dismembered pain particles and molecules being smoothly breathed out of your body by waves of sound. Continue to listen to the rhythm and pulse of the music carrying the diluted pain waves out of your body. Watch these pain waves disappear as the pulse of the music continues flowing and swaying them further and further into the infinite distance.

   Continue the "breathing-in" of music, visually dismantling the pain, and breathing out the pain fragments until you feel comfortable that every bit of the disintegrated pain is completely out of your body.

10. Once the pain is out of your physical body continue to breathe in the cleansing, clearing, natural, massaging, and healing sounds of the soothing music. Allow your inner awareness to visualize the ameliorating sounds entering the area where the pain once was. Imagine the musical vibrations cleaning and sweeping the rejuvenated area with its rhythms. "Watch" and listen to the melody as it nourishes and purifies the relieved area. As the music ameliorates and revives the area, feel and observe the restorative, invigorating, and regenerative effects these musical echoes are having inside your body.

11. If at any point during this "cleaning" ritual you encounter any remnants of new, or left-over, pain, continue your rhythmic breathing and your sound inhalations ("inhaling" the musical melody), and allow the sound waves to gently "escort" the pain out of your system.

12. Once you feel that the music has completely and successfully restored your "sound" health to the afflicted area allow your mind and body to relax. Lie back and continue to enjoy the soothing sounds of the music until the selection(s) complete their cycle. As you relax, allow yourself the

awareness that you, and not "the pain," are in control of your life. Even when the music stops playing, your brain and body retain a perfect "acoustic imprint" of the memory of the music. At this point, you would most benefit from letting go of any concerns, fears, or negative images relating to the pain and allowing the resonating musical echoes to pulsate throughout your body, continuing the healing cycle throughout the remainder of your day.

13. You can repeat this exercise as often as desired. Throughout the exercise remember to allow the natural flow of your rhythmic breathing so mind and body can achieve the harmony you need to eliminate the pain, and heal the body.

Additional Reading

For further reading on the effects of music on pain you may refer to:

M. G. Linoff and C. M. West, "Relaxation Training Systematically Combined with Music: Treatment of Tension Headaches in a Geriatric Patient," *International Journal of Behavioral Geriatrics*, 1983, 1, pp. 11–16.

M. S. Rider, J. Floyd and J. Kirpatrick, "The Effects of Music, Imagery, and Relaxation on Adrenal Corticosteroids and the Re-Entrainment of Circadian Rhythms," *Journal of Music Therapy*, 1985, 22, pp. 46–58.

3

Self-Esteem

*Our outer world reflects our world within. The conditions
around us reflect how we feel about ourselves.*[1]

When we are so afraid of following our inner rhythms that we settle for external ones, we call this insecurity. We are born with
access to the essence of all music, and we spend the rest of our lives searching for inner harmony while we sort through external noises. This is called
personal validity.

I treated a remarkable case of low self-esteem some time ago. At the
age of 6, twin brothers Jamal and Jaime became the innocent victims of
their parents' destructive marriage. After seven years of on and off separa-
tions, the boys' mother was granted a divorce from the boys' chronic alcoholic father. Following a lengthy custody battle, the mother received custody of Jamal and remained in their home town. Jaime, meanwhile, moved
away with his father.

During the next few years, the identical twins' upbringing took two
distinctively different paths. Living with his mother, Jamal was the lucky
recipient of unconditional love, support, and a nurturing acceptance which
provided him with a strong, solid base of self worth. Shortly after the

---

1. Diane Dreher, *The Tao of Inner Peace* (New York: HarperCollins, 1991), p. 51.

divorce, the boy's mother pursued a life-long ambition of attending night school, earning a degree and securing a rewarding position in her field. While in school, she met a kind, gentle man with whom she fell in love. Three years after the divorce she married this caring, supportive man who in turn became a positive male role model for Jamal.

Throughout school Jamal, encouraged and supported by both his mother and stepfather, excelled in sports, academics, and intercurricular activities. A middle class family with a combined average income, they nonetheless managed to provide Jamal with "nothing but the best." After high school graduation, Jamal went on to college. There, he excelled at various sports, had a fulfilling social life, and was highly active in both school- and community-based activities. Graduating with honors, Jamal went on to graduate school and eventually received a degree in engineering.

Years later, the twin brothers, who had maintained an on-off relationship through the years, showed up at my office at Jamal's insistence. By that time, Jamal had become the top engineer, and vice-president, of a highly respected international firm. His hobbies included skiing, golf, kayaking and writing research articles. He was happily married and actively involved with his wife and three children who were following closely in his footsteps.

Jaime, in the meantime, had grown up in spite of his father. Shortly after the divorce, the father, a successful and fairly wealthy attorney, had begun what would be a life-long pattern of inflicting blame, guilt, and degradation upon his young son. Fatherly lectures later recalled by Jaime revolved around the theme of personal rejection, where the young boy would be constantly reminded that he was unwanted by the mother only to be rescued by an unappreciated father. Beyond setting impossible standards that Jaime could never hope to fulfill, the father resorted to devaluing any sort of forward movement accomplished by his intimidated and degraded son. Essentially, Jaime was blamed for everything in their lives. The divorce, the drinking, the ensuing abuse, were all somehow Jaime's fault.

Shortly before the divorce, an intellectual assessment (obtained from school records) had revealed that the twins were almost identically matched in their mental capacities. Falling within the superior range of intelligence, their primary strengths were in mathematics. According to his feared father, however, Jaime was inadequate at *everything*. While Jamal was receiving praise, support and encouragement back home, Jaime—living in a nearby town—was being humiliated, punished, and discouraged. Feeling abandoned and neglected, Jaime failed to develop the internal strength or confidence necessary to pursue healthy relationships, become involved in outside pursuits, or—most importantly—believe in himself. Feeling inadequate, he was unable to develop a sense of belonging, trust, or reliance in himself or his dormant abilities. Rather than respecting his father, Jaime feared him.

After graduation, Jaime continued to work at a local department store where he had worked throughout high school. Although he graduated with A's and B's Jaime was convinced he was not smart enough for college. Years later, after two failed attempts at marriage, Jaime—now in his 30s—enrolled in night school and managed to graduate from a local community college with a two-year degree. Hampered by his lack of self-confidence and shattered self-identity, he was turned down after several interviews and settled for eventually becoming "one of the assistant managers" at the old department store. He had no interest in athletics, never participated in any collegial, parochial, or community activities, had no close friends, and had no hobbies beyond watching TV. He had no children and no one special in his life.

Over the years, the twin brothers had managed to maintain a sporadic, mostly long-distance relationship. As time went by, however, Jamal realized Jaime's downward spiral, and became involved in his brother's impaired life. Concerned about Jaime's chronic low self-esteem, Jamal convinced his twin to accompany him to therapy.

Upon entering my office Jamal appeared years younger than his identical twin. He seemed taller, trimmer, and impressively robust. He flashed a charming, engaging smile and communicated through comfortable body language, direct eye contact, and a firm handshake. His eyes radiated with confidence and his voice was deep, sonorous, and evoked a sense of warmth. He was a likable person, the type who lights up a room. He exuded balance, success, harmony.

Although the same height and of similar weight, Jaime appeared inches shorter, heavier, and in grave need of conditioning. He had a listless, forced smile, slouched, avoided eye contact, and offered a frail, lifeless handshake. While Jamal was radiant and full of life, Jaime *looked* old. He dressed old, wore unappealing glass frames, sported an unseemly haircut, spoke in a dull whisper, and was the walking epitome of "worn and tired." While Jamal appeared to be in charge of life, Jaime seemed defeated by it. In the music world, Jamal was the equivalent of a star performer; Jaime was the guy who would have no idea how to even get tickets to his own brother's concert. Remarkably, Jamal, who had seen his father only sporadically between age 6 and his father's death twenty odd years later, remembered him distinctly. Jaime, on the other hand, who had lived with his father, had only a faint recollection of this abusive and uncaring man.

In therapy, Jaime described himself as an impostor, "a fake." Everything he had accomplished had, in his opinion, been by coincidence. Good things had just happened to him, bad things were his fault. Even his affirmations were laced with disclaimers such as, "I'll try that, but it won't work out." His self-statements were filled with self-denying phrases such as, "That's not me," or, "I'm just not very smart." Discussions referring to social or interpersonal affairs were equally deprecating: "I'm a pretty boring person," "I don't blame her one bit for leaving me." References to future possibilities were consistently disqualifying: "I'll never amount to anything," "I don't handle change very well," "Things just don't work out for me." Even compliments such as, "That's a nice sweater," would be rejected or taken as sarcastic put downs: "I know it makes me look fat, it was just the first thing I grabbed!" His favorite expressions seemed to be, "I should . . . (be taller, thinner, stronger, smarter, further along, etc.)," "I'm sorry," and "Something is wrong with me." Overall, his worldview was riddled with doubt, dejection, and insecurity. He was inflexible, rejected minor challenges, and was generally afraid of life.

One of the few things Jaime actually enjoyed was music. Growing up, he had developed a particular affinity to the soft-pop group "Bread," while his favorite songs included the very melancholic "Aubrey," "Everything I Own," and "Diary." The lyrics in each seemed to reflect autobiographical accounts of his painful life.

Throughout much of his life, Jaime was faced with the cruelty of an emotionally (and physically) abusive father who "injected" injurious, almost crippling messages, seriously damaging his self-identity. Along the way, the father also succeeded in implanting "emotional buttons," or points of high sensitivity, which he could push or trigger whenever he felt the need to undermine his son and activate his misery. Long after the father passed away, his malicious influence lingered, impairing Jaime's life and stunting his hidden potential. These "buttons," inserted long ago, were now well in place and there for the world—including Jaime—to "push" and activate. Each push of the button would remind Jaime of his incompetence, his barren life, and his imperfect existence. Much as catchy "song hooks" function to trigger underlying emotions, these subversive tunes (the negative messages) seemed to echo relentlessly, haunting Jaime whenever they were activated.

Our goals in therapy included assisting Jaime in activating his inner resources, impacting growth to help him develop inner confidence, and helping him to recognize and acknowledge his self-value in order that he may eventually begin to more effectively take care of his basic needs. Part of our approach consisted of erasing his old, damaging "playlist" of dysfunctional tunes and replacing these with more adaptive, harmonious self-statements. In other words, we attempted to convert his "internal critical balladeer" into a more empathic messenger who could positively affect the detrimental tunes resounding within him.

MUSIC ENABLES THE OBSERVING SELF TO REACH
NEW LEVELS OF AWARENESS WHILE PROVIDING
THE GUIDING STRUCTURE FOR INNER,
PERSONAL EXPLORATION.

Exercise 4 (page 42) is very similar to the one we used to help Jaime establish boundaries while deleting the old "dysfunctional tunes." This exercise helped him begin the journey into self-healing.

Music can energize people; it helps us cleanse our minds. Music, therefore, can be instrumental in helping us:

- Alter our thoughts and reprogram old, "dysfunctional tunes," or negative messages;
- Modify our beliefs and attitudes, allowing us to perceive, and believe, our value as human beings;
- Begin setting realistic and achievable goals;
- Counter psychological noise, which in turn clears the way to help us reexamine self-imposed expectations, as well as to challenge internal and external assumptions;
- Move toward modifying inner messages, particularly those shrouded in "shoulds" and "musts," or self-defeating, no-win quandaries;
- Eliminate the dissonant, negative, and self-destructive dialogues haunting our minds;
- Let go of guilt feelings, unresolved angers, resentments, and destructive self-images we may be harboring;
- Let go of false standards which represent our own misperceptions of others' thoughts about how one "should," or "ought" to be;

- Examine and rid ourselves of unrealistic, self-imposed standards that can manifest in anxiety, hostility, and/or depression, and result in a poor self-image.

[With rhythm] [i]t is like a dream of flying; it is so easy to soar. One feels as if one could lift oneself by one's bootstraps. The pattern once grasped, there is an assurance of ability to cope with the future.[2]

Throughout the following exercise remember that this is *your* musical. You are the author, the composer. In your visualizations *you* are the lead singer, the star performer, the hero or heroine.

O

EXERCISE 4:

Self-Enhancing: Changing Noise to Harmony

The most painful thing is to think that there's something wrong with me, *and that nobody else is having the trouble I am. That's not true, of course.*[3]

1. Select a piece of (instrumental) music with lively (or inspirational), up-tempo, motivating qualities of approximately twenty minutes in duration.[4]

2. Find a comfortable, relaxing place where you can play your music. Use a CD player or cassette deck. If possible, use headphones to help isolate you from extraneous sounds and to help you submerge into the stimulating musical vibrations.

3. Begin your relaxation process by starting a slow, natural rhythm of diaphragmatic (i.e., "belly") breathing.[5]

2. Carl E. Seashore, *Psychology of Music* (New York: Dover, 1967), p. 142.
3. Charlotte Joko Beck, *Every Day Zen: Love and Work* (New York, HarperCollins, 1989), p. 56.
4. See Inspirational Musical Menu, page 48. Also, see Stimulating Musical Menu, page 20, and Letting Go Musical Menu, page 259.
5. See Breathing, page 333.

4. Allow the music to clear your mind of negative thoughts and inner assumptions (I "should" be more relaxed, I "ought" to be better at this by now," "why" is this so hard for me?"). In other words, *let go* of any expectations of what you "should" be feeling, "ought" to be doing, or "must" accomplish during this session.[6]

5. As the music flows, try and envision yourself in a difficult situation which would typically threaten your self-image (talking before an audience, going through an interview, asking for a raise, arguing for a better grade on a term paper, convincing someone of the worth of a product). Another approach may be to imagine yourself confronted by your greatest fear regarding your self-identity ("I know I'm not good enough and now they are all going to find out what an impostor I truly am!").

If the above attempt begins to feel too overwhelming, return to the deep breathing and allow the music to help wash away any images that evoke anxiety or discomfort. Once you begin to feel more comfortable, either begin again, with a less threatening image, or try and return to the previous imagined situation. If this continues to feel too uncomfortable at this time, put the exercise aside and try again tomorrow, or return to it whenever you feel ready to resume your imaginary journey.

The painter must achieve a harmony within before portraying it without.[7]

6. Seeing yourself in this difficult situation, allow your inner self to tune-in to your "internal critical balladeer." Listen to these little songs inside your mind which seem to constantly remind you that you are "an impostor," "a loser," "a failure," or will "never amount to anything!" Those resounding echoes inside your mind only serve to remind you that "*everyone* you know seems to be doing better than you," that you "*never* say or do the right thing." Select the *one* primary critical lyrical message which you need to focus on and focus on the heAr and now.[8]

Keep in mind that balance is the path to the self. Listen to the music of your inner mind and dance to the inner rhythm. Be aware of your self as a vibrating being, a microcosm of the pulsating universe. As you nurture your inner nature, you can yield to the sound that evolves.

6. For those of you unfamiliar with these terms, see Shoulds, page 311, Whys, page 303, and Expectations, page 293.
7. Dreher, *The Tao of Inner Peace*, p. 77.
8. See Affirmations, page 325, for a number of song titles that may serve to trigger positive, forward moving "lyrical messages."

7. Select up-beat, stimulating music—or songs with positive messages—to energize you and help counter your negative self-statements. The main objective is to minimize, disrupt, or eliminate any negative psychological noise that is keeping you from thinking rationally and objectively.[9] Following our inner rhythm, we seek without anticipating, reach without extending, know without learning, flow without hesitation. Inner music brings out the neglected aspects of the self.

8. As the songs and music help you to transform the mental images, begin to challenge the validity of your critical messages. "Am I truly *incapable* of learning new material? Do I really blow *every* opportunity? Is it feasible that I *always* say the wrong thing?"

> Living the Tao means becoming more aware of our own patterns and harmonizing with them.[10]

9. Listen to yourself. With a mind more calm and clear, use thought-stopping techniques to help you to stop, listen, and tune in to your internal, resounding negative "song-hooks" ("I am *truly incapable* of..., I blow *every* opportunity, I am *always* wrong").[11]

10. Activate your inner composer to help you to rearrange your internal "lyrics" and turn your "internal (soap) opera" into a more realistic, more objective musical, where you are the author, conductor, and performer.

> To everyone, the sound which comes through themselves is the most assuring thing.[12]

Focusing on the issue at hand, the *heAr and now*,[13] allow yourself the objectivity to compose more realistic lyrics as you assess the *present* situation. The above messages may be replaced with more positive, proactive self-statements such as:

- Throughout my life I have learned an enormous amount of material and am *fully capable* of continuing to learn new things.

9. See Stimulating Musical Menu, page 20, or Letting Go Musical Menu, page 259, for musical suggestions.
10. Dreher, *The Tao of Inner Peace*, p. 36.
11. See Thought Stopping, page 329.
12. Sri Karunamayee to Joan Allekote and Marsha Maslan, "Sri Karunamayee: An In-Depth Interview," *Open Ear*, 1996,1, p.7.
13. See HeAr and Now, page 243.

- I *often* take advantage of opportunities as they arise.
- Although I *sometimes* make mistakes, I have a lot to offer, and so I'm willing to take risks.

Again, the key here is to *not* allow past issues or mistakes to affect the present condition (stay in the heAr and now!); don't allow future catastrophizing; and don't allow internal or external "shoulds, musts, oughts and whys" to conflict the situation *at hand*. As Carl Seashore said, "[R]hythm is never rhythm unless one feels that he himself is acting it."[14]

11. While allowing the music to *passively* stimulate your positive energies, *actively* visualize yourself comfortably *succeeding* at your goal. Depending on the particular issue at hand, visualize yourself relaxed, organized, confident, assertive, focused, etc.

> When you receive a compliment, take it in by saying, "Thank you, I appreciate that." To demur on a compliment is to put yourself down.[15]

Here are some suggestions that you may consider while rearranging your "dysfunctional inner tunes," or harmful messages:

- Visualize yourself successfully moving along your path one small step at a time. Keep each goal simple, realistic, to the point, direct and attainable. Concentrate on coping with each situation, one at a time, to the best of your ability. HeAr and now. (Are you doing the best that you can, heAr and now? If not, what can you *realistically* do to make things better, move issues along, help things to move *forward* for yourself?)
    A healthy, adaptive, and more rational statement may take the form of: "Up to this point, I have done the best I could with what I've had. It is up to *me* to stay at this level or try and improve my situation to the best of my *present ability.*"

- Hear yourself saying and doing the "right" things. Each time you manage to do or say the "proper" thing, you will feel increasingly more capable of succeeding with each situation that arises. On the other hand, on those occasions when you "slip up" and say the wrong thing, you will be

---

14. Seashore, *Psychology of Music*, p. 142.
15. Chungliang Al Huang and Jerry Lynch, *Thinking Body, Dancing Mind* (New York: Bantam Books, 1992) p. 143.

better able to put those inevitable situations in perspective, shake the incident off, and move on with your life. Our inner music instills a source of power. It transforms the way we feel, the way we experience our own existence or identity.

• Think of yourself accomplishing your goal and later acknowledging the positive consequences and benefits. In your mind, "hear" yourself being congratulated, thanked, rewarded, praised or complimented. As an "encore," take your visualization one step further and imagine yourself dealing with similar *future* situations even more comfortably, confidently, and successfully than the one before.

• Allow yourself reasonable and realistic flexibility in dealing with new, unusual, awkward and difficult situations. For example, if you have never driven in a particular city before, be flexible and realistic enough to understand that, if you get lost, it does not mean that you "have failed" in your quest to find your proposed destination. Replace the "I'm hopelessly inept with directions" with "I know that finding my way around is not one of my strengths so it's just going to take me a little longer to find this place!"

• Think of yourself minimizing—or eliminating—unrealistic demands on yourself. If you have never played a saxophone or violin before in your life, realize that you will have to struggle for a while until you begin to feel comfortable playing the instrument. Be in the heAr and now, concentrate on each bit of *progress* you manage to make, rather than focusing on the mistakes.

• Visualize yourself avoiding the tendency to bring up false, interfering emotions such as self-pity, pride, or depression. Say you just lost at a card game. This does not mean you "are a loser," deserve to be pitied, "should" feel terrible about yourself, or even that you need to question the mystical, underlying meaning as to *why* you lost. It simply means you lost at a card game. Period. This time around, it was the other person's turn.

• Listen to your inner dialogues and use this opportunity to adapt more healthy, adaptive, and rational self-statements:

"I lost at a card-game, but gained another learning experience";

"I may have lost this time around but I had a good time playing and spending time with friends";

"What did I learn from this round that may help me with future strategies?"

"If I'm going to get this upset at playing cards maybe I can find a less distressing way to spend my Friday evenings."

Music nurtures the natural order of things. It does not compete, it does not compare, it does not complain, or explain. A spiral process, it flows through past, present and future. Blending, but not forcing, bonding, but not joining, balanced, it effects balancing. As such, music continues its dance in accord with the Tao.

Be realistic about your present, available resources. For example, you find yourself comparing your home to your neighbor's larger, more splendid home. Does this more elegant home make you a failure in life? Doubtful. How did your neighbor come to afford this marvelous home? An inheritance? Money awarded following some form of loss or natural disaster? Has the neighbor worked, slaved and saved longer, making more sacrifices than yourself? Did the neighbor get an early break, an earlier, more expedient financial start? Is your neighbor in debt? Perhaps your neighbor has taken greater risks, or is simply more skilled at playing the market! Again, *what difference do the "whys" make?!*

Let go of the whys—*"Why* does everyone in this neighborhood have a better house than ours?" Let go of the shoulds—"We *should* be doing so much better than this by now!" Regardless of the "reasons," what *in reality* does your neighbor's accomplishment say about your own? Most likely, nothing!

What is it about *yourself* that is *choosing* to compare yourself with your neighbor? Would not simply enjoying your own successes and achievements be a much healthier way to spend your weekend? Further, the fact that your neighbor is willing to invest time and money converting modest abodes into celestial mansions will increase *your* property value!

A healthy, adaptive, and more rational statement might be: "It's unproductive and self-defeating to rate and compare myself to anyone else. Everyone lives in a different reality with different antecedents and in different situations." Or, more simply, "Boy, great house! I love their wrap-around porch!" Beyond that, *let it go,* and return to working on your own life.

If you find yourself returning to negative, self-demeaning thoughts, try thinking back to previous accomplishments. Give yourself credit for what you have achieved, *without comparison* to anyone else. Remember, *everything is relative.* Think of the positive qualities you have, what you mean to others such as family, friends, and co-workers.

Finally, never forget that *you create your own reality.* So, while realistically allowing yourself the latitude to make some mistakes along the way, *always conclude your visualization successfully and positively.* Remember, this is *your* musical. You are the composer. In your visualization *you* are the lead singer, the star performer, the hero. Never the victim.

The same tone sounds different to ten thousand people. Each person hears what needs to be heard at that moment. Some cry, some laugh, some fall asleep, some are indifferent. Some remain where they are, others travel far away, in distance and in time. Those who understand are filled, the mindful feel empty. Enjoy without understanding. Relax before the need arises. Teach, by becoming harmonious with learning. Learn, by flowing with the rhythm within the teaching. Allow people to solve their own personal mysteries. Trust the sound of simplicity. Be amazed at an ordinary beat. Follow the echo of your own footsteps.

In each of us is something Special, and that we need to keep.[16]

♪

Musical Menu 4
Inspirational Music

Classical Music Suggestions

> Sir Neville Marriner: "Mozart in the Morning"
> Akiko Ebi, Hiroshi Koizumi & Tomoko Kato: "Music of Hikari Oe"
> Erich Kunzel, Cincinnati Pops Orchestra: "Time Warp"
> Frederick Renz, Early Music Ensemble (Pre-1600 music): "Instanpitta!"
> John Philip Sousa: "Stars & Stripes Forever"; "Washington Post March"
> Major Rodney Gashford, Band of the Grenadier Guards: "Stirring Marches of the USA Services"
> Franz Schubert: "Rosamunde" Overture

16. Benjamin Hoff, *The Tao of Pooh* (New York: Penguin Books, 1983), p. 65.

Dmitri Shostakovich: "Symphony No. 5," Second movement
Richard Wagner: "Lohengrin: Prelude to Act III"
George Frideric Handel: *Messiah:* "Hallelujah Chorus"
Bedrich Smetana: "The Moldau"
Various Orchestras: "Fireworks for Orchestra"
Squirrel Nut Zippers (Dixieland Jazz): "The Inevitable Squirrel Nut Zippers"
Eugenia Zukerman & The Shanghai Quartet: "Music for a Sunday Morning"

New Age Music Suggestions

Wally Badarou: *Words of a Mountain*
Eko: *Future Primitive*
Herb Ernst: *Dreamflight III*
Joyce Handler: *Reflections of Hope*
Great Lake Indians: *Honor the Earth Powwow*
Carole Isis: *You Are the Diamond*
Ottmar Lievert & Luna Negra: *Borrasca*
Music of Nature: *Yellowstone*
Shanghai Chinese Traditional Orchestra: Chinese Feng Shui Music: *Tiger; Phoenix*
Paul Speer & Leroy Quintana: *Shades of Shadow*
John Tesh: *The Games*
Various Artists: *By the Rivers of Babylon: Timeless Hymns of Rastafari*
Yanni: *Out of Silence*

Additional Reading

For further reading on the effects of music on various areas related to self-esteem, you may refer to the following research articles:

H. J. Devlin and D. D. Sawatzky, "The Effects of Background Music in a Simulated Initial Counselling Session with Female Subjects," *Canadian Journal of Counselling*, 1987, 21, pp. 125–132.

R. Brim, "The Effect of Personality Variables, Dogmatism and Repression-Sensitization Upon Response to Music," *Journal of Music Therapy*, 1978,15, pp. 74–87.

B. L. Harper, "Say It, Review It, Enhance It with a Song," *Elementary School Guidance and Counseling*, 1985, pp. 218–221.

M. Priestley, "Music and the Shadow," *Music Therapy*, 1987, 6, pp. 20–27.

L. Summer, "Guided Imagery and Music with the Elderly," *Music Therapy*, 1981, 1, pp. 39–42.

M. H. Thaut, "The Influence of Music Therapy Interventions on Self-rated Changes in Relaxation, Affect, and Thought in Psychiatric Prisoner-Patients," *Journal of Music Therapy*, 1989, 23, pp. 155–166.

C. A. Smith and L. W. Morris, "Differential Effects of Stimulative and Sedative Music on Anxiety, Concentration and Performance," *Psychological Reports*, 1977, 41, pp. 1047-1053.

4

Stress

*Having found your rhythm, listen for the silence. Within the silence,
find your strength, having found the center, return to the child. Find
peace within the noise, restfulness within the anxiety, harmony
within conflict, symmetry within confusion.*

Angelique was having problems feeling safe in her room at night. She
was 4. One night too many, she had risen from her bed in the middle of the night, walked into her (single) mom's room, and climbed beside
her in bed. Angelique's mother, a 34-year-old speech therapist, indicated
she was "at her wit's end" with her young daughter's irrational nightly
fears.

Each night, at bedtime, Mom would read Angelique one of her
favorite stories, kiss her good night, and tuck her in for the night.
Moments after the little girl would fall asleep, her mom would leave the
room. However, after a while, Angelique would awaken and begin to feel
anxious, to "hear noises," and to "start thinking bad things." During therapy, we found that Angelique's fears, as well as the "noises," were rooted
in her imagination and her fears of being left alone in her room at night.
Initially, I suggested that the mother play soothing music in the background to help lull Angelique to sleep. The music tapes which were being
used by Angelique's mother—Victorian music box tunes—had proven
very successful for most of the children whom I had encountered in simi-

lar situations. In addition, it was one which Angelique was very enthusiastic about and actually requested as her "favorite."[1]

Taking advantage of what we knew to be helpful (the story readings and the Victorian music-box tapes) I suggested to Angelique's mom that she begin a routine of reading the stories *in conjunction* with the music as it played softly in the background. From the first night, this combination worked beautifully, except for one flaw. At first, Angelique would fall asleep—as usual—during the story reading, lulled by the music and the comfort of her mother's voice. When the tape ran out, however, the young girl would eventually awake and they would be back to square one.

With one minor modification, the purchase of a dual-direction cassette deck (i.e., one which plays one side of the tape, then proceeds to play the opposite side continuously), the mother's problem was finally resolved. While helping to lull the child to sleep, the music had served to "block out the (psychological) noises," while also providing enough continuous support to allay Angelique's fears.[2]

> The image Lao Tzu offers of rivers flowing to their destinations
> calms anxiety. We do not have to worry about whether a river
> goes north, south, straight, or takes innumerable twists and
> turns. The river will eventually find its home in the sea.[3]

Stress is a normal, natural, healthy, and unavoidable part of life. Actually, there are two different types of stress. There is "good" stress ("eustress") which helps keep us attentive, motivated, and alert to events as they unfold around us. Then there is "bad" stress ("distress") which disrupts our daily lives and can often result in physical illness. Change is one of the main causes of stress (transition from job, school, or living environments; personal loss; additions to the family; chronic illness; retirement). However, distress can also result as a reaction to numerous other "negative" (financial burdens, overwhelming responsibilities) or "positive" life events (marriage, promotion, vacation). It all depends *how* we perceive the event, and *what* we do to deal with it.

Sound Idea

Each day, as you step out into
the world, seek harmony.

---

1. See page 210 for a list of music-box tune selections.
2. See Psychological Noise, page 281.
3. Greg Johanson and Ron Kurtz, *Grace Unfolding* (New York: Bell Tower, 1991), p. 91.

Here are ten easy ways we may choose to use to deal with stress:

1. *Relax.* Take breaks. Breathe. Go for walks. Listen with a smile.

2. *Practice positive self-statements.* Avoid negative self-talk. Practice thought stopping.[4] Concentrate on thinking rationally and realistically. Build support systems. Practice being positive and optimistic and visualize success and happiness.

3. *Practice Discipline.* For many of us, having organization in our lives is the cornerstone of feeling centered. While being organized feels good, it also helps to give us a sense of completion, control, and balance which radiates to other aspects of our daily responsibilities. Practice discipline. Take the time to structure your daily routines without overwhelming yourself. Be realistic about your resources and reasonable about your limitations. Try to give yourself plenty of time to get things done as often as possible.

4. *Recognize unnecessary, unhealthy competitive patterns.* Focus on *your own* priorities. Everything in life is not dictated by first place finishes. Most of the time "winning" a personal or social debate (or discussion) does not earn you awards, trophies, or a gold medal. Set realistic, attainable goals. Break large projects down into smaller tasks. Avoid arguments and unnecessary confrontations.

5. *Incorporate healthy habits.* Sensible, balanced, nutritional diets help to provide a lot of the natural resources we need to prevent and ward off stress. Alcohol, tobacco, excessive caffeine, and non-prescription drugs restrict blood flow and help to trigger stress. Incorporate a healthy, positive mind set. Be assertive and *act* on things, rather than simply *reacting* to them.

6. *Externalize.* Talk out your feelings, frustrations and concerns with a trusted friend. Entertain yourself. Socialize. Communicate your feelings and ideas objectively and positively. Learn to accept what you cannot change.

7. *Exercise.* Take time out regularly, as often as it is feasible and realistic, to work out. Whenever possible, engage in exercise or sports activities *which you find pleasurable and motivating*. Pursuing an exercise regimen because it

---

4. See Thought Stopping, page 329.

is "enjoyable" makes it a lot easier to instigate and maintain than trying to force yourself to pursue a tedious and boring routine simply because it is "good for you!"

8. *Let go.* Practice patience. Give in once in a while. How important is the event which is causing this stress? How will it *realistically* impact your life tomorrow? Next week? Five years from now? Is it truly worth worrying about? If so, organize your options and act accordingly. If not, recognize it, accept it, then let it go. Life's too short. Welcome change. Rid yourself of damaging relationships whenever possible. Clear your mind periodically. Accept your feelings. Be flexible and adaptable. Listen to the messages underneath life's difficulties and disappointments and hear the opportunities for growth.[5]

9. Follow the various suggestions presented throughout this book, particularly those under the sections on Relaxation, Mantras, Affirmations, Letting Go, Exercise, Breathing, and Chanting.

10. Find a quiet, comfortable place, and treat yourself to *at least* twenty minutes of *undisturbed*, soothing music (preferably with the added benefit of headphones). See the Soothing Musical Menu at end of this section for music suggestions.

If you feel you have done your best, but feel you need further assistance or support, seek professional help.

Some of the outcomes of stress, or tension, include physical pain, depression, anger, procrastination, sleeplessness, and the inability to relax. The corresponding sections in this book discuss these areas individually, in more extensive detail, and offer exercises on how to deal with each one.

If we do not untie our knots when they form, they will grow tighter and stronger.[6]

---

5. See Letting Go, page 249, and Growth and Change, page 125.
6. Thich Nhat Hanh, *Peace is Every Step* (New York: Bantam Books, 1991), p. 65.

♪

MUSICAL MENU 5
Soothing Music (Rhythmic Synchronicity)

The following selections are all largo movements from string concertos by Baroque composers. They are suggested as generally soothing selections recommended for use with relaxation or learning/reading situations. These are ideal for arranging sequentially for the purpose of attaining a state of calm, relaxing rhythmic synchronicity.

Vivaldi: "Concerto in C for 2 flutes and strings," Largo movement

———. "Concerto in D minor for 2 oboes and strings," Largo movement

———. "Concerto in C for 2 oboes, 2 clarinets, and strings," Largo movement

———. "Concerto in G major for flute," Largo movement

———. "Concerto in D minor for viola and lute," Largo movement

———. "Concerto in G major for oboe and bassoon," Largo movement

———. "Concerto for mandolin, strings, and continuo," Largo movement

———. "Concerto for lute, strings and continuo," Largo movement

Telemann: "Concerto in E minor for recorder and flute," Largo movement

———. "Concerto in D major for flute and strings," Largo movement

———. "Concerto in D for horn, strings and continuo," (a) Largo movement

———. "Concerto in D for horn, strings and continuo," (b) Largo movement

———. "Concerto in D major for 2 horns, strings, and continuo," Largo movement

Bach: "Air on a G String from Suite No. 3 in D."

Locatelli: "Concerto Grosso in C minor," Largo movement
Merdacante: "Concerto in E minor," Largo movement

New Age Music Selections

General musical selections recommended for attaining states of peace and relaxation (CDs, tapes, or albums)

Acoustic Research Series: *Healing Music* (4 CD set).
Aeoliah: *Angel Love* (Synthesizers, piano, chimes, voices)
————. *Angel Love for Children* (Bells, flutes, voices)
Stephen Bacchus: *Pangea* (Flutes, Tibetan bells, tabla, oboe)
Bindu: *Zenrise* (Acoustic guitar, with some flute, keyboards, percussion)
Jim Chappell: *Nightsongs and Lullabies* (Piano, with harmonica, oboe, cello, flute, and background female voice)
John Coltrane: *Ballads* (Saxophone)
Rusty Crutcher: *Machu Picchu Impressions* (Natural sounds with flute, synthesizer, and light percussion backgrounds)
Ken Davis: *Tai Chi Music*
Gover Dhan: *Inner Tai Chi*
Enya: *Watermark* (Voices, synthesizers, percussion)
————. *Shepherd Moons* (Some vocal, some instrumental)
Dean Evenson: *Ocean Dreams* (Ocean waves with harp, flutes, whale and dolphin sounds, and synthesizer)
Cesara Evora: *Cabo Verde*
Scott Fitzgerald: *Bamboo Waterfall* (Water sounds, with wind-bells, chimes, piano and bamboo flute backgrounds)
————. *Dreamland* (Ocean waves and falling rain, with piano and synthesizer backgrounds)
Barolk Folk: Any selection
Kay Gardner: *A Rainbow Path* (Synthesizers)
Dexter Gordon: *Ballads* (Saxophone)
Paul Horn: *Inside the Taj Mahal*, Vols. 1 & 2 (Flute)
David and Steve Gordon: Any selection
Daniel Kobialka (Violin music with various backgrounds):
Fragrances of a Dream
————. *Going Home Again*
————. *When You Wish Upon a Star*

————. *Timeless Motion*
————. *Afternoon of a Fawn*
————. *Dream Passage*
————. *Oh, What a Beautiful Morning*
————. *Rainbow* (compilation)
————. *Velvet Dreams* (compilation)
————. *Celtic Guitar*
Larkin: *O'Cean* (Flute, backed by ocean waves and synthesized drones)
David Lanz: *Cristofori's Dream* (Piano, with strings, percussion, and guitar)
Kevin Locke: *Dream Catcher* (Native American)
————. *Keepers of the Dream* (Native American)
Chris Michell: *Serenity*
R. Carlos Nakai (Native American flute music): *Canyon Trilogy*
————. *Desert Dance*
————. *Earth Spirit*
————. *Carry the Gift,* with William Eaton (Guitar, harp guitar, and lyre)
————. *Changes*
————. *Cycles*
————. *Island of Bows*
————. *Journeys*
————. *Jackalope*
————. *Sundance Season*
————. *Weaving*
Willie Nelson: *Stardust; Spirit*
Terry Oldfield: *Zen* (The search for enlightenment)
Gary Prim & David M. Combs: *Beautiful Thoughts* (Piano, with synthesizer background)
Rachel's: *Handwriting Up*
————. *Music For Egon Schiele*
Michel Rubini: *Secret Dreams* (Synthesizers, with harp and guitar)
Steve Roach: *Structures from Silence* (Synthesizers)
Mike Rowland: *The Fairy Ring* (Piano with synthesized strings)
Stephen Rhodes: *Music for Healing*
Searles and Yslas: *Dream of the Troubador*
Ravi Shankar: *In Celebration: Highlights; Chants of India*

Jon Shore: *Tibetan Memories: Music of Tibetan Bells and Synthesizers*

John Singer and Paul Hurst: *Moonlit Castle* (Japanese shakuhachi, bamboo-flute)

Judith Lynn Stillman: *Piano Silhouettes* (Piano)

Eric Tingstad and Nancy Rumbell: *Pastorale*

Various Performers: *Baroque Music for Guitars*

———. *Music for Lute, Guitar & Mandolin*

Stuart Weber: *Evening in The Country* (Guitar)

———. *Hired Man's Dream* (Guitar)

Kate Williams, with the Sylvan String Orchestra: *The Fairy Ring Suite*

George Winston (Solo piano music): *Autumn; December; Summer; Forest*

———. *Winter into Spring*

Paul Winter: *Canyon* (Soprano saxophone with ambient sounds, French horn, guitar, cellos, keyboards, and percussion)

Popular Music Suggestions (CDs, tapes, or albums)

Bread: *Anthology of Bread*

The Carpenters: *1969-1973*

Classics IV: *Greatest Hits*

Cowboy Junkies: *The Trinity Session*

Donovan: *Sutras*

Gloria Estefan: *Mi Tierra*

Pink Floyd: *Meddle*

Patti Griffin: *Living with Ghosts*

Nancy Griffith: Any album, CD, or tape

The Innocence Mission: *Glow*

Rickie Lee Jones: *Naked Songs*

———. *Ghosty Head*

Sonny Landpeth: *Blues Attack*

Lush: *Spooky* or *Split*

Pentangle: *The Collection*

Tom Petty: *Wildflowers*

Madeleine Peyroux: *Dreamland*

Linda Ronstadt: *Winter Light,* or *Cry Like a Rainstorm, Howl Like the Wind*

Mazzy Star: *Halah,* or *Among My Swan*
Santana: *Caravanserai*
Slowdive: *Just for a Day,* or *Souvlaki*
Cat Stevens: *Classics*
B. J. Thomas: *Greatest Hits*
Charlie Watts: *Long Ago & Far Away*
Neil Young: *Harvest* or, *Harvest Moon*
XTC: *Skylarking*

5

Anger

*The Aikido Move: Confronted by emotional noise, respond with
silence. Confronted by dissonant emotions, respond by centering.
Confronted by defensiveness, respond with nonresistance.
Confronted by hostility, respond with harmony.*

Although anger is a normal reaction to many real life situations, and
a healthy sign of adjusting to change, the way in which we deal
with frustrations and other anger-inducing events determines whether the
end-result will be healthy or unhealthy.

About two years ago, 14-year-old Frank, an extremely bright, only
child, was brought in by his mother. She was seeking help for what she
described as "uncontrollable anger." According to Frank's mom, her son
had been displaying "fits of rage" from about age 5, two years before she
divorced his abusive father.

To date, a number of approaches to deal with Frank's destructive
behaviors and defiant attitude had proven completely unsuccessful. In
addition to being expelled from a number of schools, including a military
academy, Frank had also been kicked off various sports teams due to his
unprovoked, violent behavior. Having refused counseling in the past,
Frank's presence in my office was the result of a court mandate which
offered counseling in lieu of time at a detention center.

Although the first couple of visits were somewhat difficult, with Frank exhibiting oppositional and defensive behaviors, something occurred during his third visit which changed the course of our relationship, as well as the direction of Frank's life. Upon Frank's arrival he noticed a guitar case sitting in a corner of my office. Although he did not ask about it directly, it was impossible not to notice his obvious interest in the instrument.

"Do you play?" I asked.

"No," he replied, "What kind is it?"

"It's a Rickenbacker..." I said, "12-string, vintage '64, I just took it in to have the neck adjusted . . . would you like to look at it?"

"Sure!" he said, eyes opening wide and an unforeseen softness illuminating his young face. For a moment, Frank dropped his guard and allowed his true, inner sensitivity to shine through. He immediately fell in love with the guitar. He looked at it, felt it, caressed and stroked it for the remainder of the session. It was the first time, he said, he had ever held a musical instrument.

Up to that point, this had been about the most in-depth conversation we shared. Before long, Frank and I were involved in an honest, heart-to-heart discussion of rock music, accentuated by his total shock that not only was I well versed in modern music, but that I had basically grown up on stage, playing classic rock and roll. During the session, Frank revealed his deep love for music in general and heavy metal in particular. For years, his secret ambition had been to learn to play the guitar and become a rock musician. Our unprecedented musical connection suddenly provided an excellent forum so we could establish a positive working relationship.

At first, Frank discussed his enjoyment of "power" songs—those replete with loud, violent lyrics which seemed to reflect the incessant turmoil he felt inside. On the following visit, however, Frank's mood and attitude were completely different. Though portraying his typical tough, almost menacing aura—as usual—Frank opened the hour with a discussion on ballads. The softer feelings and gentler messages typically portrayed through those songs, it seemed, were what he had wanted all along. At some time, over the course of the years, however, Frank had somehow created and nurtured a rough, angry image. Attacking whenever he felt threatened had become his normal mode of dealing with the world. Frank's reaction to his youthful vulnerability created such a hardened personality mask that he was no longer able to be responsive to his own sensitivity.

During that session, Frank asked how long it usually took to learn to play the guitar. A couple of weeks later, after some encouragement, and his mother's assistance in purchasing a Fender Telecaster guitar, Frank began to take lessons and quickly learned the major power chords that frame most rock and heavy metal music. Simply "holding a guitar," Frank revealed, made him feel good, and somehow peaceful. Motivated by the music, after learning just three major chords, Frank began to compose his own songs, which he proudly brought in during our weekly sessions. From the start, his very basic songs seemed to function as a direct channel so he could express his underlying feelings of rage and abandonment. Before long, and with continued practice, the songs provided a conduit for him to process, explore, and extend his inner needs without feeling threatened about expressing his sensitivities.

A year after his first lesson, Frank's violent outbursts, his trademark for so many years, had almost completely disappeared. According to his mother, getting the guitar had been "like a religious experience" for him. He would spend hours in his room either practicing alone, or playing along with his favorite CDs. As his musicianship improved, his songwriting soon began to expose deeply rooted fears and terrifying images which provided excellent material for us to pursue in therapy. Within a few months, music had provided this "angry" boy a voice for his inner sensitivities and a healthy, positive channel for his turmoil. During this time, Frank, who had just entered a new high school, had also begun to "hang out" with a different group of kids. The fact that they did not know "the old, tough Frank" provided a perfect opportunity for him to hone a completely new image. This new identity, Frank revealed, was now that of a "cool, deep and sensitive artist," and he loved it.

Sound Idea

(Boomerang Karma)
Next time you have the urge to
respond with a negative or hurtful
comment, replace it with
something positive.

Common Causes of Anger

1. *Anxiety*. When our stress level is up, and we feel unduly worried, concerned, or "trapped," we may react as if anger is the only way out.

2. *Low Tolerance*. When we are tired, and our resources seem depleted, we are much more likely to react with exasperation. When we are suffering from chronic pain, our ability to deal with daily situations is significantly impeded; our tolerance levels drop remarkably and we may become hypersensitive. The inability of others to relate to our situation or understand our pain often and naturally gives rise to anger.

3. *Frustration*. Frustration usually arises, and escalates to anger, when we are prevented from pursuing or finishing a particular task; when we encounter failure or defeat; or when we are misunderstood, or not given a fair chance or hearing.

4. *Hypersensitivity*. Being overly sensitive to someone's teasing and playful, but annoying, provocations, or hearing something that stirs up unrelated, but sensitive or hurtful, past memories, will frequently trigger angry or even violent responses.

5. *Psychological noise*. Daily stress often results in our feeling mentally cluttered or confused, and unable to think clearly or rationally. Feeling frenzied or agitated by too many mental or emotional events echoing in our minds at the same time can easily result in "noises" being externalized in the form of anger.[1]

6. *External Irritations*. Bothersome nuisances, such as a neighbor's barking dog or our own children's blaring music is often quite vexing. Also, disappointing events such as rain ruining a planned outing will likely lead to anger responses.

7. *Abuse*. Abusive behaviors can come in many forms including physical, mental, or emotional abuse. These enraging violations often lead to our feeling humiliated, or result in personal degradation to our character, damaging our self-image.

8. *Escalating arguments*. When situations are taken out of context, drawn from irrelevant past events, overgeneralized, or irrationally exaggerated,

---

1. See also Psychological Noise, page 281.

interactions can quickly lead to confrontation and turn into turbulent arguments.

9. *Injustice.* Unjust infringements that give rise to expressions of wrath can include unfair treatment, being taken advantage of, being placed in double-bind or no-win situations, or various forms (gender, sexual, racial, ethnic, religious, age, class) of prejudice, bias, or harassment.

10. *Impatience.* You want things done now, immediately. Your package was supposed to arrive today, but it never arrived. You're waiting to hear from a prospective employer about a job decision but "the call" does not seem to ever come. Like the ones discussed above, these irritating situations generate a sense of restlessness and can all be common triggers to indignant responses.

TUNING INTO INTERNAL HARMONY
SILENCES EXTERNAL NOISES.

Dealing with Chronic Anger

Tao people express what the Chinese call pu shih,
accepting all that comes in the rhythm of life[2]

We are often involved with frustrating life situations which give rise to anger. Sometimes, however, it is unfeasible, irrational, or inappropriate to express those feelings directly. For instance, most of us have been involved in incidents when we've known that—regardless of how we handle the situation, for whatever reason—expressing our anger will simply get us nowhere. This may happen even when we are careful to express ourselves in an assertive and detached manner. It may happen even though we avoid being judgmental or blaming anyone. It may happen even though we are clear and succinct, or understanding of the other person's feelings or situation.

    If you are dealing with feelings of chronic anger, Exercise 5 on page 67 is designed to help you release those feelings in the safety and privacy of your home. Knowing that you have this outlet available will give you

---

2. Diane Dreher, *The Tao of Inner Peace* (New York: HarperCollins, 1991), p. 113.

the opportunity to express those feelings of frustration in a positive and healthy way, rather than "swallowing" them, or allowing them to magnify and develop into something worse than they already are.

1. *Keep it in the heAr and now.* As the anger-evoking situation is taking place, recognize it as such. Do not drag up events from the past regardless of how relevant they may be to the situation at hand. Keep it in the present. This is what is happening *right now.* Period.[3]

2. *Breathe.* Take a deep breath and try to replace your angry thoughts with a counteracting mantra which is relevant to the situation. This may be something very basic like: "I am calm," "Relax," "Breathe," or "This will be over in a few minutes." It may also be something more practical such as, "I need this job," "This person is a jerk, just let her talk," "This is so unimportant in my life," or "This is it, I'm taking care of this matter this afternoon."[4]

3. *Thought Stopping.* When the confrontation is over, practice thought stopping to try and put it out of your mind for the time being. To the best of your ability, put it "on hold," or "on the back burner," and, if feasible, tell yourself you are going to address the situation later. If you know that pursuing this issue is not appropriate, wise, or feasible, or you know it will simply do no good to push it (e.g., unfair boss in enmeshed system, or political situation) do your best to "let it go" at least for the time being.[5]

4. *Get Away.* If at all possible to get away for an hour or so, do it *now* and move on to the following exercise. If you can't get away from your present responsibilities at the moment, or find you cannot successfully "let it go" naturally, then do your best to put the issue on hold, and remind yourself that you are going to release it later on in a healthy way through one or more of the methods suggested in Exercise 5.

Sound Idea

The best time to hear their weakness
is when they speak of their strengths.

---

3. See HeAr and Now, page 243.
4. See Breathing, page 333, and Mantric Sounds, page 339.
5. See Thought Stopping, page 329. Also see Letting Go, page 249.

EXERCISE 5:
Letting Go of Chronic Anger

The kind of anger that hurts people is when we smile sweetly and underneath we're seething. [6]

1. *Take some time.* When you get home, take approximately twenty to thirty minutes during which you will not be disturbed. If that is not feasible, make a formal request to be left alone for that period of time. Be open and considerate with the uninvolved people around you who may be trying to be supportive. If nothing else, let them know that you've had a tough day, and do not want to discuss it right now, and that you need some time to be alone. Be aware of the fact that *they did not cause your problem* and that attacking them will only result in more negativity and additional issues. Keep in mind, of course, that the quicker you can release your feelings of anger and frustration, the better.

(2) *Pick out some "angry music."* As soon as you get the opportunity, select a number of songs or music, which, to you, *sound* just about the way that you *feel*. These songs, or music, should be up-tempo and loud, and have other characteristics or elements which may otherwise reflect the energies you are feeling (energized, stimulated, aroused) or which seem to "feel the way you do" (agitated, restless, frustrated, confused, annoyed, irritated, furious, enraged) at the moment. Other suggestions would include songs with empowering or motivating lyrics that would assist you in moving through, or beyond, your anger or frustration. The point is to *match your feelings to the music.*[7]

3. *Act it out.* Once you are alone in your safe place, turn up the volume and resign yourself to completely surrendering to the music. During this time, in your privacy, allow yourself to release your feelings of anger and frustration. If you have a song with lyrics which touches on issues similar to the ones you are dealing with, then play that tune, and sing along with it, loud, and heartily! If not, then allow yourself to release, discharge, and dis-

---

6. Charlotte Joko Beck, *Every Day Zen: Love and Work* (New York: HarperCollins, 1989), p. 12.
7. See Music for Dealing with Anger, page 73, for a number of musical suggestions.

miss your negative and harmful energies through jumping, shouting, screaming, singing, or dancing free of inhibition.

If you feel uncomfortable with the suggestion for "acting it out," insert your music tape or CD into a portable stereo, put on your headphones, and go for a long, brisk walk. While allowing the music to set your walking tempo, allow it also to help dislodge the feelings of anger from your mind, helping you to process the situation with a clearer, more cleanly energized mind.

4. *Get "in sync" with the music.* The purpose here, of course, is to cleanse your soul from the negative vibrations of anger and frustration. As your vibrations merge and bond with those of the music, surrender your feelings of anger to the driving beat. Feel them dissipate more and more with each note, each measure, each chorus, each melody, each song. As you purge yourself of this unnecessary ire, allow the music to bring you back to balance, to harmonize you. Allow the steady rhythms to get you back "in sync,"[8] so that you can go on with what is truly important in your life.

5. *Log it into your "acoustic memory."* From that point on, the knowledge that you are able and fully capable of truly taking control, and that you have the availability of this anger-releasing tool at your disposal, will help empower you. You'll learn to feel more comfortable with these confrontations. Eventually you will be able to recognize those situations when "taking control" and "letting go" are important.[9]

According to the Tao, what matters is not the situation,
but the way we perceive it.[10]

---

8. See Rhythmic Synchronicity, page 275.
9. See Acoustic Memory, page 291.
10. Dreher, *The Tao of Inner Peace,* p. 5.

EXERCISE 6:

Diverting Another Person's Anger

*Taoism is based on rhythm and flux, on the natural, the
unconventional, the freedom-loving detachment from worldly things.*[11]

When someone else is communicating with you through a veil of anger or
frustration there are several approaches, or stances, which are typically
helpful.

1. First and foremost, try to get an idea of what the person seems to expect
from directing this anger at you. Is this a formal complaint? An accusa-
tion? Is the person simply venting? Does this person merely need someone
to *listen* at this moment? Remember that, very often, when a person vents,
he or she is not seeking answers, suggestions, or solutions. What is needed
at that moment is a caring, responsive *listener*. Listen for the "what," rather
than the "why."[12]

2. Be considerate of the other person's feelings.

3. Be attentive to the other person's point of view.

4. Listen calmly and objectively.

5. Avoid taking the issues presented personally. Too often the person
speaking in anger says things he or she doesn't really mean.

6. Make reflective and sympathetic statements ("I hear what you are saying," "That must be really frustrating," "I can understand why you are
angry.").

7. Listen for the underlying cause of the anger (i.e., how valid is this angry
reaction and what, if anything, can you realistically do to help alleviate
this person's frustration?).

11. J. C. Cooper, *Taoism, The Way of the Mystic* (London: HarperCollins, 1990), p. 35.
12. See Whys, page 303.

As the angry person's level of communication begins to escalate some of the more direct approaches you can try may include one of the following:

1. Taking deep breaths;

2. Keeping the focus on the heAr and now;

3. Avoiding "sinking down" to their level (i.e., do not stoop down to personal insults or blaming);

4. Being direct (i.e., continue bringing the conversation back to the point, or heart of the matter);

5. Avoiding antagonistic silence (i.e., giving the person the "silent treatment" is often perceived as a passive-aggressive taunt and can heighten the anger);

6. Avoiding the portrayal of a sense of superiority (i.e., an anger confrontation is not a good time to let the other person know you perceive yourself as superior).

CENTERED, THE STUDENT FINDS IN EACH NOTE AN
ENTIRE SYMPHONY. STRAYING FROM THE CENTER,
THE NOTES ARE LOST IN A SYMPHONIC DIN.
USEFUL KNOWLEDGE BECOMES WASTED POTENTIAL
UNLESS ONE IS CENTERED.
WHEN CLOSE TO THE EDGE,
RETURN TO THE CENTER.

EXERCISE 7:

The Angry Troll: Dispelling Anger through Silent Humor

It is best if we do not listen to or look at the person whom we consider to be the cause of our anger. Like a fireman, we have to pour water on the blaze first and not waste time looking for the one who set the house on fire.[13]

The following exercise, to be used when someone else is directing anger at you, is a take off on the "performance anxiety" technique which calls for an inhibited speaker to visualize the audience either naked, or as if they were all sitting before you in their undergarments. The essence of this approach is to imagine the angry person *singing* his or her anger. Throughout this, however, keep in mind that breaking into laughter will only worsen the situation!

1. As the person's voice begins to rise, and the anger begins to escalate, try and imagine what he or she would sound like if music were accompanying the anger.

2. As you listen, try and pick out any musical characteristics evident within his or her frustration. Some of these may include pitch, timbre, texture, rhythm, and, of course, volume.

3. Imagine what the message being conveyed would sound like if it would suddenly begin to rhyme. Could the anger be somehow interpreted into a rap song?

4. Visualize the person in full operatic garb, standing on a decorated stage, acting out these lines in various voices. How would this sound if it were coming from a soprano? Baritone? Tenor? As an alternative, what sort of "music video" would do justice to this person's "tirade"?

13. Thich Nhat Hanh, *Peace is Every Step* (New York: Bantam, 1991), pp. 57–58.

5. As you listen, try and tune in to the harmony underneath this person's frustration. As you listen, remember what it felt like the last time *you* were angry. Remember, try and hear your own familiar melody in this person's "song."

6. Finally, and *very importantly,* do not forget that this exercise is based on *silent,* internalized humor. The last thing you want to do when confronted with an angry person is allow this type of *internal* processing to manifest itself *outwardly* as a smile or laughter, which may further provoke, or magnify, the person's fury!

> *Music is a ". . . heaven-sent ally in reducing to order and harmony*
> *any disharmony in the revolutions within us . . ."*[14]

THOUGH IT CAN BE WRITTEN,
MUSIC CANNOT BE CAPTURED.
BELONGING TO EVERYTHING,
IT OWNS NOTHING,
ALWAYS GIVING, NEVER TAKING,
UNNOTICED, UNEXPLAINED, IT BENEFITS EVERYONE.
MUSIC EVOKES WHAT HAS ALWAYS BEEN,
HELPING US TO COME TO TERMS WITH OURSELVES.

---

14. Plato, *Timaeus and Critias,* Desmond Lee, trans. (London: Penguin, 1977), p. 65.

♪

MUSICAL MENU 6
Music for Dealing with Anger

Classical Music Suggestions

Hector Berlioz: "Symphonie Fantastique" (Finale)
Gioacchino Rossini: "William Tell Overture"
W. A. Mozart: "Symphony No. 41 in C" ("Jupiter"), fourth
  movement
Ludwig Van Beethoven: "Third movement, Symphony No. 7
  in A major"
————. "Fourth movement, Symphony No. 5"
Manuel DeFalla: "Ritual Fire Dance," from *El Amor Brujo*
Rimsky-Korsakov: "Flight of the Bumble-Bee"
Johann Sebastian Bach: "Toccata, Adagio & Fugue in C major"
Gustav Holst: "Mars," from *The Planets*

Popular Music Suggestions (Individual songs)

The Beatles: "Helter Skelter," or "Revolution," from *The Beatles*
  (AKA "The White Album")
The Neville Brothers: "Sons and Daughters," from *Brother's
  Keeper*
Pink Floyd: "Another Brick on the Wall," "Run Like Hell,"
  "The Trial," from *The Wall*
The Jam: "The Modern World," from *Greatest Hits*
Janis Joplin: "Down on Me," from *In Concert*
John Lennon: "Mother," or " Well, Well, Well," from *Plastic
  Ono Band*
John Lennon with The Plastic Ono Band: "Cold Turkey," from
  Live Peace in Toronto, 1969
Paul McCartney: "Angry," from *Press to Play*
The Police: "Oh My God," or "Mother," from *Synchronicity*
Bonnie Raitt: "Real Man," from *Nick of Time*
The Who: "Won't Get Fooled Again," from *Who's Next?*
XTC: "Dear God," from *Skylarking*

Neil Young: "Rockin' in the Free World," from *Freedom* (two versions with different tempos!)

Neil Young & Crazy Horse: "F*!#in' Up," from *Ragged Glory*

Popular Selections (CDs, tapes, or albums)

Artists United Against Apartheid: *Sun City*
The Clash: *The Clash; London Calling; Give 'em Enough Rope*
Elvis Costello: *This Year's Model; My Aim in True*
Tracy Chapman: *Tracy Chapman*
Joy Division: *Closer*
Husker Du: *Land Speed Record*
Peter Gabriel: *Peter Gabriel*
Marvin Gaye: *What's Going On?*
J. Geils Band: *Rage in a Cage*
Iggy & The Stooges: *Raw Power*
The Jam: *Greatest Hits*
John Lennon and The Plastic Ono Band: *Plastic Ono Band*
Metallica: *Kill 'em All*
Randy Newman: *Trouble in Paradise*
Graham Parker & the Rumour: *Howlin Wind; Squeezing Out Sparks*
The Sex Pistols: *Never Mind the Bollocks, Here's the Sex Pistols*
The Ramones: *The Ramones*
R.E.M.: *Document*
The Rolling Stones: *Exile on Main Street; Black and Blue; Goats Head Soup*
RUN D.M.C.: *RUN D.M.C.*
U2: *War; Boy; October*
Was (Not Was): *What's Up Doc?*
The Who: *Who's Next; Tommy; Meaty, Beaty, Big & Bouncy*
Neil Young: *Rust Never Sleeps*
Sonic Youth: *Daydream Nation*
Led Zeppelin: *Led Zeppelin* (4CDs, tapes, or albums)

Willing to Try Some "Alternative" Selections? (Individual songs)

Beck: "Loser," from *Mellow Gold*
Tracey Bonham: "Mother Mother," from *The Burdens of Being Upright*

Coolio: "Gangsta's Paradise," from *Gangsta's Paradise*
Curve: "Wish You Dead," from *Doppelganger*
Green Day: "Chump," or "Basket Case," from *Dookie*
Juliana Hatfield: "A Dame with a Rod," from *Become What You Are*
Alanis Morissette: "You Oughta Know," from *Jagged Little Pill*
Public Image Limited: "Angry," from *Happy*
XTC: "Don't Lose Your Temper," from *Black Sea*

Alternative Selections (CDs, tapes, or albums)

Alice in Chains: *Face Lift; Alice in Chains*
60 Foot Dolls: *The Big 3*
Hole: *Live Through This*
Live: *Throwing Cooper; Secret Samadhi*
Rage Against the Machine: *Evil Empire*
Nine Inch Nails: *The Downward Spiral*
Nirvana: *Smells Like Teen Spirit*
Sex Pistols: *No Future U.K.?*
Smashing Pumpkins: *Pisces Iscariot; Mellon Collie & the Infinite Sadness; Siamese Dream*
Tricky: *Pre-Millennium Tension*
Pearl Jam: *Vitalogy, Ten, No Code*
U2: *Achtung Baby*

Additional Readings

For further reading on how music may affect anger or other similar emotions you may refer to the following books and articles:

H. J. Devlin and D. D. Sawatzky, "The Effects of Background Music in a Simulated Initial Counselling Session with Female Subjects," *Canadian Journal of Counselling*, 1987, 21, pp. 125–132.

B. L. Harper, "Say It, Review It, Enhance It with a Song," *Elementary School Guidance and Counseling*, 1985, pp. 218–221.

T. B. and A. R. Roberts, "The Effects of Different Types of Relaxation Music on Tension Level," *Journal of Music Therapy*, 1984, 21, pp. 177–185.

S. Nielzèn and Z. Cesarec, "On the Perception of Emotional Meaning in Music," *Psychology of Music*, 1981, 9, pp. 17–31.

Sheila Ostrander and Lynn Schroeder, *Superlearning* (New York: Dell, 1979).

6

Sleeplessness

*The isle is full of noises, sounds and sweet airs, that give delight and
hurt not. Sometimes a thousand twangling instruments will hum
about mine ears, and sometime voices that, if I then had waked after
long sleep, will make me sleep again.* [2]

The term sleeplessness, as used in this section, will refer to those situations when a person's inability to sleep (problems initiating sleep, random awakenings throughout the night, being unusually tired upon awakening), regardless of the time period, leads to marked physical, mental, or emotional discomfort, sometimes disrupting daily activities. (Note: If your condition of sleeplessness persists for longer than two weeks, begins to cause significant concern or to interfere with daily functioning, you are strongly advised to consult with a licensed psychologist, or physician, before attempting these exercises.)

The following case illustrates a condition of sleeplessness.

In forty-three years Lelia had never experienced sleep problems. Her sleeping patterns commonly followed the same pre-organized, structured rhythms as other aspects of her life. For their second honeymoon, Lelia and her husband fulfilled a promise they had made to themselves twenty-three

---

1. Alexander Pope, "The Dunciad," Book I, lines 92-93, in John Bartlett, *Familiar Quotations* (Boston: Little, Brown & Co., 1909), p. 331.
2. William Skakespeare, *The Tempest*, Act III, in *A Dictionary of Musical Quotations*, Ian Crofton and Donald Fraser, eds. (New York: Schirmer Books, 1985), p. 138.

years earlier. After their children left the nest, they would splurge and take a two-week vacation in England. Although both partners were extremely enthusiastic about this dream trip, it had special significance for Lelia, whose ancestry was rich with English tradition.

As Lelia had expected, she was unable to "sleep a wink" during their seven hour trip over the Atlantic. Last-minute planning would surely keep her up throughout the flight. Either way, she was too excited to sleep. Arriving at Heathrow airport early the following morning Lelia was wide awake, pulsating with adrenaline and raring to get started. After a fun-filled, highly stimulating first day when everything happened to go "exactly as planned," the couple retired to their room, "completely exhausted." Lelia, however, experienced her second consecutive night of sleeplessness.

The next two nights followed almost identical patterns. Meticulously planned, festive days followed by increasing weariness over her inability to fall asleep. As she reported later, the act of drifting off seemed to become a cue that would alert her to awaken, at times even causing her to quickly sit up in bed and shake her head as if to shock herself awake. Each passing day, Lelia became increasingly more frustrated and exhausted. She would sleep "maybe a few minutes" during the night, force herself to "rise when the sun came up, stumble through that day's planned activities, and then proceed to drift throughout the day half-asleep." Although she was unable to fall asleep at night, she found herself easily and quickly falling asleep in the trains, buses, ferries, museums, concert halls, restaurants and basically any other place that was not included in the sleeping itinerary.

After three basically sleepless nights Lelia tried over-the-counter sleeping pills which she obtained at a local pharmacy. These worked well the first night during which she was finally able to gain a normal night's sleep. The second night, however, her inability to sleep returned in spite of the pill, and, come daylight, and time for their scheduled itinerary, Lelia spent a horrific day fighting off the pill's effects. It was as if the pill's sleep-inducing effects had been put on hold throughout the night. After that experience, she threw the remaining pills away. Having spent the day drifting in and out in a half-drugged state, she was again unable to fall asleep that night.

This remarkably frustrating bout with sleeplessness endured throughout their "dream trip" in spite of Lelia's dauntless resourcefulness in searching for a "cure." During those two weeks the couple tried switching rooms (although their room and beds were reportedly warm and comfortable), changing hotels, buying two different special pillows, not ingesting any caffeine (including chocolate), and returning to their room to try and sleep at different times of the day as well as night. Alcohol did not come into the picture as they were both non-drinkers.

During the trip, Lelia even purchased a self-help book which provided additional suggestions including deep breathing, progressive relaxation, autogenic exercises, affirmations, thought stopping, getting up during the night and "doing something boring," doing nothing stimulating before bedtime, visualizations, praying, crying, talking about it, not talking about it, drinking warm milk and herbal teas, leaving the TV on as well as the radio, wearing earplugs (although there were no disturbing noises present), and even counting sheep. *Nothing* worked.

By the end of their vacation, Lelia and her husband were depressed and glad to be coming back home. Their dream journey had been completely ruined. Apparently, Lelia's anxieties and fears about the *possibility* of something going wrong, or the potential of something outside of their control disturbing their pre-fabricated schedule, had simply destroyed their holiday. It was basically a self-fulfilling prophecy.

The problem, however, did not end there. Once the consumed couple arrived home the nightmare continued. Two weeks later, a haggard Lelia arrived at my office referred by her physician who had found no medical problems or precipitating psychological conditions, such as anger or depression. Lelia simply could not sleep during her sleeping time (regardless of when or where that was) but could barely stay awake otherwise (i.e., during her non-sleeping times). Her work suffered and, even worse, she was finding herself drifting off while driving her car.

Lelia's somnambulistic pattern, which had begun during her first night in England, was described as follows: she would go to bed, begin deep breathing, close her eyes, then her mind would begin racing. After a while, she would begin to toss and turn, open her eyes and look at the clock. It was fifteen to twenty minutes later. She would then either turn over and remain in bed, or get up and read, watch something on TV, or simply stare at the wall for a while, during which she would become more frustrated "knowing" that she would not be able to fall asleep. Eventually she would "convince herself that she was becoming sleepy," return to bed, begin deep breathing and attempt thought stopping[3] and other cognitive techniques. The bed would feel good, her body worn and tired, but then her mind would again begin to race. She indicated that even though her "eyelids would close due to sheer exhaustion," in her mind they "appeared to be wide open," as if she were actually "staring through her eyelids at the ceiling."

3. See Thought Stopping, page 329.

By the time Lelia made her initial visit to my office she was very dis-
traught and quite dubious of behavioral or cognitive approaches, as she felt
she had already tried them all without success. She was adamantly opposed
to being referred for medication and my suggestion for hypnosis was
rejected as she "did not trust it." She, instead, wanted "something different" that would work. Consequently, we decided to put together a special
program that would address Lelia's disturbed sleeping patterns from a
fresh and creative perspective. Incorporating a multimodal approach I
designed a special audio tape which I titled "The Spiral Sojourn."[4] This
tape aimed to at least minimize, or hopefully eliminate, the "psychological noise"[5] which was apparently functioning as anxiety provoking
thoughts triggered by her fear of sleeplessness.

Rather than overdubbing the tape with precategorized soothing
music, as most patients prefer, we chose to tape the "Spiral Sojourn" exercise without incorporating a musical background so Lelia would be free to
play the tape in conjunction with different sound backdrops of her own
choosing. I suggested she use a sound (or white noise) screen together with
the taped exercise. An extra advantage of having the "white noise" separate from the audio tape was that she was able to regulate each volume
independently. (For the "sound screen" she used a common house fan and
days later purchased a commercially available "white noise," or masking
machine.)[6]

That night, with the help of a well-structured sequence including
deep breathing, thought stopping, and progressive relaxation, Lelia fell
asleep while listening to *The Spiral Sojourn*, accompanied by the sound
screen, or white noise masking element. Three months after her initial
visit, she was still using this approach successfully. During that time she
suffered sleeplessness on only two occasions: one, the night before her
daughter's wedding; the other, the night before a major qualifying professional exam. Aside from those two nights, Lelia's days and nights seemed
to be back in harmony again.

> While the bee with honeyed thigh,
> That at her flowery work doth sing,
> And the waters murmuring,
> With such consort as they keep,
> Entice the dewy-feathered sleep.[7]

4. See The Spiral Sojourn, page 361.
5. See Psychological Noise, page 281.
6. The reader may refer to Psychological Noise for a discussion on "white noise" and masking, page 281.
7. John Milton, "Il Penseroso," lines 142–147 (1632), in Crofton and Fraser, *A Dictionary of Musical Quotations*, p. 138.

Before you proceed with the Sound Sleeping Exercise 8 (page 82), you need to consider whether one, or more, of the following may be underlying, or disrupting, your usual sleeping patterns, or leading to sleep deprivation. The above also pertains to dependency on alcohol or drugs, or sleeping disorders such as Narcolepsy (brief bouts of deep sleep which occur daily), Sleep Terror Disorder (abrupt awakening from sleep beginning with an alarming scream), or Sleep Apnea (gasping for air while snoring). If you suspect any of these symptoms, they should be discussed with your physician or a licensed psychologist.

1. How much caffeine (coffee, teas, soft drinks, chocolate, and certain vitamins), or other stimulants (even sugar, and some vitamins), have you consumed throughout the day? Perhaps you may try cutting down, or cutting off, your caffeine intake (at least for seven hours, but preferably longer, depending on your sensitivity to the substance) before bedtime.

2. Are you taking naps, of any length, during the daytime? If so, these may be affecting your night sleep. If possible, save your sleep, catnaps and all, for bedtime. In addition, try and keep your bedtime consistent, with as little variation as possible.

3. Are you performing any vigorous, or stimulating activities[8] before bedtime? These may include active (working out, stimulating conversations, beginning a project that excites you or gets you wound up) or passive (planning projects which "rev-up" your mind, listening to energetic music, reading an exciting book) activities. For at least one to two hours before retiring to bed try and find something. monotonous, tedious or dull to do. Find something to do that would "put anybody to sleep"!

4. Has your bed somehow become a sort of secondary (or primary) office, work space, or "hang-out" lounge? Think of your bed (and bedroom) as a "temple of respite." Keep food, phones, TV, sedentary work, hobbies, etc., away from your bed in particular and bedroom in general.

5. If you feel you may be suffering from a medical or psychological problem which has not been addressed, you need to consult with your family physician, or a licensed psychologist.

> Why rather, sleep, liest thou in smoky cribs,
> Upon uneasy pallets stretching thee,

8. Sex is an exception.

And hush'd with buzzing night-flies to thy slumber,
Than in the perfumed chambers of the great,
Under the canopies of costly state,
And lull'd with sound of sweetest melody?[9]

O

EXERCISE 8:

Sound Sleeping

1. Turn on either a "white noise" machine (air purifier, house fan, air-conditioning unit, or any other commercial "sound-shield" unit designed to block out extraneous sounds), or a tape of continuous *soothing* music of your choice. As you make your musical selections, try and select music which you would not ordinarily listen to at other times. Select music—whatever it is—to be played specifically for the purpose of helping you to relax and get to sleep. Further, play your "sleeping" music only in the room where you wish to sleep and only during that time. Paying attention to these details will intensify the contextual cuing[10] effects of the music, as well as help you to associate (i.e., conditioning) the sounds of this particular music (or "sound masking" unit) with sleeping. (See Soothing Musical Menu, page 55, and Meditation Musical Menu, page 230 for a number of musical suggestions.)

2. Whatever music (or white-noise source) you choose, tell yourself that this particular method, tune, or approach will provide the cue you need to assist you in drifting off to sleep. Approach each act leading to your bedtime in an almost ritualistic manner. With each task (inserting the tape, turning the machine on, selecting a comfortable volume, taking off your robe, fluffing your pillow, climbing into bed, setting your alarm, pulling the sheets or blanket over yourself, taking off your glasses, turning off the light) serving as yet another cue to remind you of *how relaxing and comfortable* this entire procedure is.

For example, you may consider telling yourself: "The day is over and the only responsibility I have in this world, at this time, is to rest, and relax. Whether I fall asleep or not, I will still be able to rest and repose.

---

9. William Skakespeare, *Henry IV*, Part Two, Act III, in *A Dictionary of Musical Quotations*, p. 138.
10. See Contextual Cuing, page 287.

The mere act of lying in bed, doing my deep breathing, and not having to be out and about taking care of anything else until morning will be comforting, restful, and relaxing." Wording your "affirmation" in this manner will take away some of the pressure and assist you with "being" rather than "trying to be"[11] relaxed.

3. If you have the tendency to look at your clock to see just exactly how long you *haven't* been sleeping, take it out of the room, or cover the face. If your clock doubles as a wake-up alarm unit, turn it around so that you can no longer see the time. Turn off the lights, lie down on your bed (floor, couch, mat or other comfortable place), close your eyes and begin you "deep breathing," diaphragmatic breath routine.[12]

4. Consciously tell yourself that it is now "time to become deeply relaxed." When thoughts begin to intrude, whatever they are, passively acknowledge them and quietly remind yourself that you will return to dealing with those issues when you awake in the morning.[13]

5. As you attempt to relax, your mind may begin to play tricks on you. After all, it is your brain that is setting this whole thing up, and your brain usually lets your mind know what it's up to. Some of these mind tricks may include catastrophizing ("I'll *never* get to sleep again as long as I live"), "shoulding" ("I *should* be able to sleep, what's wrong with me?"), "whying" ("*Why* can't I get to sleep . . . let's see, it's probably because . . ."), problem solving ("Now that it's nice and quiet, it's a good time to think about the specifics of my daughter's wedding"), negativizing ("I have *no control* over anything in my life and this is just another example of that").

If thoughts (psychological noises) continue to intrude, there are a number of ways through which you may try to counteract them.

- Continuously return to your slow, diaphragmatic breathing. This alone will serve to relax you automatically, and it will help to quiet and occupy your mind.

- Try to visualize the word "breathe" ("relax," "peace" or any other word which you may associate with being very restful

---

11. See Being Versus Trying to Be, page 261.
12. See Breathing, page 333.
13. See Thought Stopping, page 329.

across the inside of your forehead. As your mind wanders, continue returning to the word, again, then again. You may also
try slowly "sketching" the word within your mind, letter by
letter (B...R...E...A...T...H...E...). This will serve as a cue to
remind your body what it needs to be doing and your mind
that it's time to close shop for the night. It is usually best to
avoid using the word "sleep" as this, at times, seems to provide
extra psychological pressure at a time when you need as little
stress as possible.[14]

• While continuing your breathing, passively allow your
mind and body to "hitch a ride" with either the soothing music
or the white noise. If your background consists of soothing
music, your mind and body will eventually begin to rhythmically synchronize[15] with the musical tempo, becoming slower,
more regular, and more calm. As this occurs, passively listen to
the music, allow your thoughts to merge and blend with the
sounds, and let them dissipate into the night, each thought
escorted out by it own corresponding musical note.

6. If you have chosen a "white noise" machine to serve as acoustic background, focus your attention on the constant drone of the sound and literally listen to the avalanche of sound as it seemingly sucks out, and then
envelops, your thoughts, like a warm, soft, furry blanket. As you breathe,
watch your thoughts as they slowly and helplessly give up control to the
unyielding, resounding murmur of the "white noise," while it accompanies your mind to a place of complete repose.

7. If you continue to have problems drifting off after twenty minutes or so,
you may elect to consider the following time-tested technique. If your
mind chatter (psychological noise) continues to interfere, suggest to yourself that, if you are unable to sleep, you have *the option* of getting up and
tackling some of those tasks which you may have been neglecting or
putting aside for a while. The trick here, however, is twofold. First, be sure

---

14. Other words which work quite well for a lot of people are "hush," aum," or "calm." In using these
words you may choose to stretch out the "...shhhhh..." in "hush," or "...mmmmm..." in "aum" or
"calm." For a lot of people, this practice functions to help drown out "psychological noise," while at
the same time providing a soothing internal vibration that helps "massage" the mind. For more on this
topic, see Psychological Noise, page 281.
15. See Rhythmic Synchronicity, page 275.

to choose a task that you find particularly *unappealing or dreadful*. Second, remind yourself that, should you *choose* to pursue such a task, you may stop at any time, return to bed, and begin the above exercise all over again. The last thing you want to do is place any additional pressure on yourself. In this manner, if you don't sleep, you would have finally caught up on those awful, dreaded duties. If you *do* fall asleep, this will help you to be well rested the following morning, and therefore better able to read about Procrastination (page 133).

> *There is sweet music here that softer falls*
> *Than petals from blown roses on the grass,*
>
>   . . .
>
> *Music that gentlier on the spirit lies,*
> *Than tired eyelids upon tired eyes;*
> *Music that brings sweet sleep down from the blissful skies.*[16]

Sound Idea

Invest in some "sleepy time music" for your children. Some suggestions:
Various Performers: *Sweet Dreams*
Linda Ronstadt: *Dedicated to the One I Love*
Music Box Tunes

---

16. Alfred Lord Tennyson, " The Lotos Eaters" (1833), Choric Song, lines 1, 2, 5-7, in *A Dictionary of Musical Quotations*, p. 138.

7

Control

If you are standing by a river and a leaf floats by,
you have your choice of following the leaf with your eye
or keeping your attention fixed in front of you.
The leaf floats out of your line of vision.
Another leaf enters...and floats by.[2]

One of the most frustrating things in life is lack of control. However, how much control *do* we have? Not only over external events and situations, but over our own thoughts, feelings and—sometimes—even our behaviors? There are theories which expound that childhood events dictate what type of individuals we will become, that these events inevitably shape our personalities. Others propose that our thoughts, feelings, and behaviors are determined by our surrounding environments. Still others suggest that we are simply at the mercy of other people such as our teachers, bosses, repair persons, telephone operators (directly), marketing ploys, and organizations, such as governments, big industry, large businesses, and manufacturers of various products (indirectly).

> [W]e feel as though we did this all because we wished to, because we craved it, because we were free to do it, because we were able to do it.[3]

1. Diane Dreher, *The Tao of Inner Peace* (New York: HarperCollins, 1991), p. 66.
2. Ram Dass and Paul Gorman, *How Can I Help?* (New York: Alfred A. Knopf, 1985), p. 101.
3. Carl E. Seashore, *Psychology of Music* (New York: Dover, 1967), p. 142.

Like with most things, it all depends on how we choose to look at it. Or, *listen* to it. According to Social Learning Theory,[4] if we can identify what things affect us, and how, we can then look at the options we have, and choose to act on the situation in order to improve it for ourselves.

> Empowering through music enables us to do something, something which we otherwise might not be able to undertake. The musical empowerment enables us *to permit* ourselves, to give ourselves permission, to be transformed.[5]

There are a number of ways we can gain a sense of control. Use any of the following suggestions.

1. *Focus on the present*. Listen to what is happening around you, heAr and now.[6]

2. *Follow through with plans*. The longer we stick to fulfilling our goals, the better the chance to see them come to fruition (e.g., if you truly want to become a good cellist you need to, among other things, find a good cello teacher, be committed to practicing, and sacrifice a few other things in your life).

3. *Accept your limitations*. Everyone cannot become a *great* cellist! Acknowledge your positive gains and reward yourself for small advances. If you need to, remind yourself of things you do well, your special talents or abilities, and put cello playing in proper perspective.

4. *Consider your viable alternatives*. Rather than focusing on things over which you have no control (e.g., the music they play on the radio), switch your consciousness to things over which you do (switch the station, choose the tapes or CDs you want to play in your car and bring them along).

5. *Remove yourself from the situation*. If you don't like the music in a club, leave! If you want to take further control, ask the manager what other types of music they have scheduled over the following weeks and make suggestions. If their musical taste is not to your liking, suggest some alternative, more appealing choices for them to consider. If they reject your suggestions

---

4. For further reading on Social Learning Theory see A. Bandura, *Social Learning Theory* (Englewood Cliffs, NJ: Prentice-Hall, 1977).
5. R. J. Stewart, *Music, Power Harmony: A Workbook of Inner Forces* (New York: Sterling, 1990), p. 14.
6. See HeAr and Now, page 243.

and show no interest in providing your type of music, then don't go back to that club and find one where they play more of what you like.

6. *Be assertive.* Without being aggressive, if you are not happy with the music being played at a friend's home during a visit, politely request they change it, or simply ask if they have anything by "whomever (some act you may prefer)" that they could play instead. If you happen to have some of your own music, say, in your car, you may ask if they have heard "the latest by . . ." (whatever artist you happen to have in your car) and ask if they would like to have a listen.

7. *Accept you cannot change the situation and ride it out.* If "Music theory" is a *required* course, one you need to graduate, try and find *something* in the class, course, or subject matter itself that can motivate you to stay awake long enough so you can pass the course, graduate, and go on with your life.

8. *Be okay with not always having to have everything your way.* You and some friends are at a club where they happen to be playing music you don't care for. Rather than trying to manipulate the others to leave with you, or be miserable, you can focus on other, more positive aspects of the evening, try and find something intriguing or positive about the music, or become an amateur psychologist and try to analyze why anyone in their right mind would compose, play, or want to listen to such drivel!

9. *Strive for structure and discipline in your life.* The more effectively you control your time, the better you will be able to control your life.

10. *Try positive affirmations.*[7] When the situation demands that you be in control, tune in to some positive self-statement, such as "I can do this!" or "I'm in control!"

11. *Give up control.* Accept that it's impossible to always be in control. Actually, the responsibility of anyone having to be in control over everything all the time would be too overwhelming for anyone. Take a break. Let someone else take over. By doing this you are actually gaining control of yourself.

12. *Yield to expertise.* No one is an expert at everything. Regardless of what it is, sooner or later you will run into people who can do some things bet-

7. See Affirmations, page 325.

ter than you. Let it go. Yield to their expertise and learn from the experience. If you can do this, you are indeed exercising self-control.

THE PROCESS OF MAKING SOUNDS
INVOLVES A SENSE OF CONTROL.
MAKING SILENCE INVOLVES A SENSE OF
LETTING GO OF THAT CONTROL.

EXERCISE 9:

Giving Up Control: Letting Go

This exercise is designed to help us feel more comfortable with giving up
control.

> Becoming mindful has to do with letting go of ambitions to
> control, solve problems, or achieve something.[8]

1. If possible, select a time when you know you are going to be completely alone at home. If that does not seem feasible, likely, or even possible,
then find a place where you can be alone and undisturbed for at least fifteen to twenty minutes. This may be someplace out in the country, a basement, or any other secluded area in your office or home.

2. Select a number of songs, or music, which you know well and which you
feel will elicit feelings of abandon, surrendering, or letting go. This may
be something which, during your childhood or (extended) adolescence,
made you feel "wild," "uninhibited," or simply very excited.[9]

3. Once alone, turn up the volume and resign yourself to completely surrendering to the music. During this time, in your privacy, allow yourself

---

8. Greg Johanson and Ron Kurtz, *Grace Unfolding* (New York: Bell Tower, 1991), p. 13.
9. See Inspirational Musical Menu, page 48, Letting Go Musical Menu, page 259, Stimulating Musical
Menu, page 20, Music for Dealing with Anger, page 73, Big Band selections, page 160, and random
selections on pages 177-182.

to renounce all social etiquette, resign all propriety, discharge your ideas of appropriateness, and dismiss all modesties.

4. The purpose here, of course, is to *let go*. Let go of what you perceive as proper, normal, or seemly behaviors. Surrender to your internal beat, release your natural rhythms, yield to your inner pulse, feel the surge and give in to the urge, go with the flow . . . palpitate, undulate, vibrate![10]

5. Once you have been able to accomplish the above, you will know that you have broken through some of your former inner barriers. From that point on, simply knowing that you are able and fully capable of relinquishing control will help you to feel a little better, and more comfortable, with accepting those situations of which you simply need to let go. Knowing you are capable of letting go in such a manner will be helpful in a number of ways. For one, you will have experienced how good it felt to do so. Second, you will have a sense of *how* it is done. Third, if you are unable to let go at the exact moment you need to, due to any number of circumstances, you can always "keep it under your belt and let it all out" once you get home.

> [R]egardless of how we *feel*, we always have some control over what we *do*.[11]

MUSIC OBEYS, BUT DOES NOT CONFORM.
IT FOLLOWS, BUT DOES NOT COMPLY.
INFLUENCES, BUT DOES NOT CONTROL.
DIRECTS, BUT DOES NOT COMMAND.
ATTEND TO HARMONY,
YIELD TO INNER RHYTHMS,
SERVE THE TAO.

---

10. Please refer to section IV-4, Letting Go, page 249.
11. William Glasser, *Control Theory: A New Explanation of How We Control Our Lives* (New York: HarperCollins, 1984), p. 45.

Additional Readings

For additional reading regarding how music may affect the sense of control, you may refer to the following books or research articles:

L. M. Bailey, "Music Therapy in Pain Management," *Journal of Pain & Symptom Management*, 1986, 1, pp. 25–28.

Albert Bandura, *Social Learning Theory*. Englewood Cliffs, NJ: Prentice-Hall, 1977.

M. H. Thaut, "The Influence of Music Therapy Interventions on Self-rated Changes in Relaxation, Affect, and Thought in Psychiatric Prisoner-patients," *Journal of Music Therapy*, 1989, 23, pp. 155–166.

H. Wadeson, "Art therapy" in *The Newer Therapies*, S. Abt and I. Stewart, eds. New York: Van Nostrand, 1982.

8

Relaxation

To hear your inner music, be silent.

Relaxation techniques have been found to be significant in helping to increase the body's immune system, increase self-esteem, improve concentration, generate spontaneity, and enrich creativity. In addition, regular practice of relaxation techniques helps decrease anxiety, tension, stress, panic attacks, anger, fear, and other negative emotions and reactions to our environment. In itself, relaxation helps us return to a natural state of attunement and harmony with nature. In effect, while being relaxed, it is impossible to be tense, anxious, upset, or otherwise disquieted. As a result, a state of relaxation is essential in self-healing, centering, and effective visualization.

The power of music to induce, or enhance, deep states of relaxation has been strongly supported by scientific research studies dating back to the early 1800s. These earliest findings on the physiological effects of music are discussed in an article dating back to 1923 by Diserens where he presents findings by Gretry (1813), Couty and Charpentier (1874), and Dogiel (1880).[1] A few years later, Hyde (1924) was among the first to study cardiovascular, pulse rate, and blood pressure responses to music. From her experiments, she concluded that people are typically affected both psychologically and physiologically by music which is harmonic and rich in tone.[2] This type of music, she concluded, seems to benefit the cardiovascular system, influence muscle tone, enhance endurance, and aid digestion. From that point on, a large number of scientific researchers have substantiated her findings, and found that music effectively instills, or enhances a state of peace, calm and relaxation.

Some findings have indicated that listening to "soft music" is just as effective as progressive relaxation, or autogenic techniques in reducing anxiety,[3] that it enhances,[4] or surpasses,[5] the relaxation effects of EMG biofeedback. Published scientific studies by other experts indicate that music helps to minimize reactions to stress,[6] reduces tension,[7] lowers one's pulse rate,[8] and effectively minimizes anxiety while enhancing relaxation.[9-11]

Finally, a number of additional studies have indicated that the effects of "soothing" music are particularly effective in reducing "state" anxiety[12] and alleviating tension, stress and daily frustration.[13-16]

1. C. M. Diserens, "Reactions to Musical Stimuli," *The Psychological Bulletin*, 1923, 20, pp. 173–199.

2. I. M. Hyde, "Effects of Music Upon Electrocardiograms and Blood Pressure," *Journal of Experimental Psychology*, 1924, 7, 213–224.

3. S. B. Reynolds, "Biofeedback, Relaxation Training, and Music: Homeostasis for Coping with Stress," *Biofeedback and Self-Regulation*, 1984, 9, pp. 169–179.

4. J. P. Scartelli, "The Effect of EMG Biofeedback and Sedative Music, EMG Biofeedback Only, and Sedative Music Only on Frontalis Muscle Relaxation Ability," *Journal of Music Therapy*, 1984, 21, pp. 67–78.

5. Reynolds, "Biofeedback, Relaxation Training, and Music: Homeostasis for Coping with Stress," pp. 169-179.

6. Helen L. Bonny, "Music and Healing," *Music Therapy*, 1986, 6A, pp. 3–12.

7. B. L. Wheeler, "The Relationship Between Musical and Activity Elements of Music Therapy Sessions and Client Responses: An Exploratory Study," *Music Therapy*, 1985, 5, pp. 52–60.

8. C. Webster, "Relaxation, Music and Cardiology: The Physiological and Psychological Consequences of Their Interrelation," *Australian Occupational Therapy Journal*, 1973, 20, pp. 9–20.

9. W. B. Davis and M. H. Thaut, "The Influence of Preferred Relaxing Music on Measures of State Anxiety, Relaxation, and Physiological Responses," *Journal of Music Therapy*, 1989, 26, pp. 168–187.

10. S. Hanser, S. Larson, and A. O'Connell, "The Effect of Music on Relaxation of Expectant Mothers During Labor, "*Journal of Music Therapy*, 1983, 20, pp. 50–58.

11. M. G. Linoff and C. M. West, "Relaxation Training Systematically Combined With Music: Treatment of Tension Headaches in a Geriatric Patient," *International Journal of Behavioral Geriatrics*, 1983, 1, pp. 11–16.

Overall, the consensus in these and many other scientific research findings is that music plays a significant part in enhancing or bringing about the relaxation process. It helps individuals attain deeper and more satisfying states of calmness, peace, contentment, and tranquillity.

> [I]t is possible to notice a single thought, sensation, or situation arise, but not get totally lost in identifying with it. We observe the cloud but remain focused on the sky, see the leaf but hold in vision the river. We are that which is aware of the totality. And our skills develop with practice.[17]

In order to get the greatest benefit from relaxation exercises, it is suggested that these be performed *daily*, at *least* twenty (but preferable thirty) minutes per day. If possible, doing *two* twenty to thirty minute sessions each day is preferable and helps to *more than double* the effects of our efforts.

At first, some people may react by thinking that "twenty minutes to just lie there and relax" may be too much of a personal commitment. However, if you can, just take a moment right now and think about how much time you spend each day in other things which you could easily eliminate, or modify, in order to adopt and develop a life-enhancing and ultimately lifesaving habit.

ALTHOUGH MUSIC CANNOT CHANGE THE SEASONS,
IT CAN ALTER THE WAYS WE PERCEIVE THEM.

---

12. "State" anxiety concerns a particular, transitory emotion which can be aroused or depressed according to the situation.

13. S. L. Curtis, "The Effect of Music on Pain Relief and Relaxation of the Terminally Ill," *Journal of Music Therapy*, 1986, 23, pp. 10–24.

14. L. K. Miller and M. Schyb, "Facilitation and Interference by Background Music," *Journal of Music Therapy*, 1989, 26, pp. 42–54.

15. J. P. Scartelli and J. E. Borling, "The Effects of Sequenced Versus Simultaneous EMG Biofeedback and Sedative Music on Frontalis Relaxation Training," *Journal of Music Therapy*, 1986, 23, pp.157–165.

16. B. L. Schuster, "The Effect of Music Listening on Blood Pressure Fluctuations in Adult Hemodialysis Patients," *Journal of Music Therapy*, 1985, 22, pp.146–153.

17. Ram Dass and Paul Gorman, *How Can I Help?* (New York: Alfred A. Knopf, 1985), pp.108–109.

Music as a Relaxation Cue

Even if your schedule makes it *absolutely impossible* to practice these exercises on an ongoing, daily basis, what you may want to try at this point—for the time being—is to sacrifice something else in your life for a few weeks until you are able to develop your very own basic relaxation "feel" or "mode." Once your body and mind are in tune with the relaxation response, this book provides techniques to help you learn how you may use music backgrounds and personal visualizations to elicit those same relaxation responses and achieve harmony and tranquillity as you carry on with your daily activities.

Sound Idea

At least once, for a moment each day,
take time to be in the stillness of silence.

The following "progressive relaxation/music breathing" exercise is designed to help us to become accustomed to a music-enhanced progressive relaxation technique, become comfortable with progressive relaxation, deep breathing and visualization, and develop a relaxation response to musical backgrounds which, with practice, should become automatically cued[18] and easily induced through the simple process of deep breathing and/or exposure to your chosen musical background(s). Further, with extensive, long-term practice and the presence of these musical cues you will eventually become better able to induce your "relaxation response" by simply using deep breathing to cue or activate the relaxation associated with your "acoustic memory."[19]

As long as your mind is silent,
it is open to endless sounds.
The more it is agitated,
the less it will be open to listening.

---

18. See Contextual Cuing, page 287.
19. See Acoustic Memory, page 291.

EXERCISE 10:
Reducing Stress

This exercise uses music as an adjunct to relaxation. It should be thought of as consisting of three parts, lasting about a total of thirty minutes.

Listening to or participating in music can restore a person.[20]

Part 1. Before you formally begin this exercise, allow the music to simply play for about five minutes. As it plays, feel the music setting the soothing vibrations that you wish to be surrounded by. Allow yourself to become "rhythmically synchronized"[21] to this harmonious environment. Use this time to simply "be"[22] with the music, allowing it to allay, and "massage" you with its soothing vibrations.

Part 2. The exercise itself should take about twenty minutes.

Part 3. The final five minutes should function as a final opportunity for you to "breathe out" any remaining stress or tension you may have and to allow your internal self to become "rhythmically synchronized" to the external world.

1. Choose thirty minutes of music you find particularly soothing. (Refer to the Soothing Musical Menu, or Soothing Musical Rhythmic Synchronicity Menu, pages 55–59.

2. Find a quiet, comfortable place where you will not be disturbed and where you can sit, or lie, undisturbed for the duration of the exercise.

3. Take care of your sound environment (disconnect telephones, turn off personal pagers, inform others in the house that you wish to remain undisturbed, etc.).

4. Begin playing your selected music.

20. Anthony Storr, *Music and the Mind* (New York: The Free Press, 1992), p. 122.
21. See Rhythmic Synchronicity, page 275.
22. See Being, versus Trying to Be, page 261.

5. Spend a few moments (three to five minutes) becoming rhythmically synchronized to the external, soothing environment.

6. Begin the following exercise. (For your convenience, this exercise may be taped using your own preferred musical background(s) as a personal backdrop to your relaxation exercise.[23]

> Close your eyes.
> Breathe...
> Visualize your body as a hollow drum.
> Breathe in...Breathe out...Let go.
> Allow the sound to enter through the soles of your feet.
> Breathe in the sound...Breathe out the noise...Let it go.
> Allow your breathing to settle to the cadence of the sound.
> Allow your mind to find comfort in the rhythm of the sound.
> Breathe in...Breathe out...Let go.
> Feel the sound reverberating through the soles of your feet. Let
>   go.
> With each pulse, feel the sound pulsating away all tension.
> Breathe in...Breathe out...Let go.
> Follow the sound as it rises up through your feet.
> Each beat vibrates away all tension from your feet.
> Breathe in...Breathe out...Let go.
> Follow the sound as it vibrates up through your ankles.
> Feel the sound reverberate away any tightness.
> Breathe in...Breathe out...Let go.
> Follow the sound vibration up through your calves, through
>   your lower legs.
> Feel it resonating through your leg bones, massaging away all
>   feelings of stress.
> Breathe in...Breathe out...Let go.
> Visualize the sound moving upward, through your thighs.
> Feel and hear the high-pitched, stressful vibrations in your
>   lower body dropping to a lower key...feel the vibration with-
>   in your legs becoming slower, and slower...Breathe
>   in...Breathe out...Let go.
> Allow the sound to flow up through your pelvis and genital
>   area...

23. Refer to Motivating the Mind, page 201, for suggestions on making an instructional tape using background music.

Feel the vibrations resounding within the hollowness of your
pelvis, your buttocks, your abdomen...
Breathe in...Breathe out...Let go.
Feel the soothing sounds resonating throughout your lower
back, up through the spinal column...listen to the alleviat-
ing sound as it spirals through each vertebra, relaxing each
one, one by one, moving upward...
Breathe in...Breathe out...Let go.
Breathe the sound through your hollow body,
Feel the sound fluttering upward through your rib cage, listen
to it as it thaws away all pressure.
Breathe in...Breathe out...Let go.
Allow your inner ear to follow the sound upward into your
chest.
Listen to the sound waves echoing through the emptiness of
your chest cavity...
Breathe the sound up into your shoulders.
Feel the vibrations entering and caressing every molecule with-
in your shoulders.
Listen to the sound as it ameliorates the stiffness...
As it assuages the strain.
Breathe in...Breathe out...Let go.
Follow the soothing echoing of the sound up into your throat.
There, feel the soothing sound resounding within your throat.
Watch it as its pulse dissolves all rigidity.
Breathe in...Breathe out...Let go.
Listen to the sound resonating upward and through the empti-
ness of your facial cavity.
Follow the murmur of the comforting sound as it softens your
facial muscles.
Feel the vibrations massage your jaw.
Feel them enter deep into your chin, and thaw away all tension.
Breathe in...Breathe out...Let go.
Listen as the tenseness yields to the pulsing of the music.
Watch the stress spiraling out of your body in the form of
sound waves.
Breathe in...Breathe out...Let go.
Feel the tension within your mouth and tongue, allow your
mouth to relax, and visualize the music echoing through
your mouth cavity.

Watch the sound bounce off your palate, your teeth, listening
to the softening, hear the yielding.

Feel the sound waves resonating the area around your eyes.

Allow the tension around your eyes to relax to the sound waves.

Breathe in...Breathe out...Let go.

Feel the sound waves resonating the area around your eyes.

Allow the tension around your eyes to relax to the sound waves.

Breathe in...Breathe out...Let go.

Inhale the soothing sound.

Feel the cavities within the nose open and welcome each
inhalation of the soothing melody.

Listen as the sounds enter the face and rise upward into your
forehead

Breathe in...Breathe out...Let go.

Feel the pressure within your forehead dissipate with each pulsating breath, with each soothing note...

Allow the strain within your scalp to abate with each sound of
your breath.

Welcome the music as it enters your mind.

Breathe in the comfort of the music.

Breathe out the noise, watch the noise as it quiets into silence.

Breathe in the restful tone.

Breathe out anxiety, watch anxiety fade.

Breathe in the tranquillity within the sound.

Breathe out all turmoil, watch turmoil evaporate.

Breathe in the alleviating melody.

Breathe out all negative thoughts, watch thoughts being
released.

Breathe in the allaying harmonies.

Breathe out all tenseness, watch tenseness vanish.

Breathe in the calming tempo.

Breathe out the burdening emotions, watch negative emotions
calming.

Breathe in the easing rhythms.

Breathe out confusion, watch confusions clear and fade away.

Breathe in consolation.

Breathe out annoyance.

Breathe in the sound of peace.

Breathe out irritation.

Breathe in calming vibrations.

Breathe out turmoil.
Breathe in the music.
Allow your mind to drift to the pulse.
Allow your mind to drift with the pulse.
Allow your mind to drift with the pulse.

6. As the soothing music continues to play, allow yourself a few moments to become "rhythmically synchronized" to your external environment.

7. Do not forget that, whenever you need to access the feelings of relaxation promoted by this exercise, you may simply use the music you played during the exercise to help "cue" that sense of relaxation.

Throughout this book, there are a number of other ideas that relate to using music to instill and promote a sense of relaxation. Among these are some that are less structured or formal than the more traditional progressive relaxation exercise discussed here. You may want to refer to Chanting, Meditation, Toning, Thought Stopping, Breathing, Mantric Sounds, or the chapters in Part Four.

Additional Readings

For additional reading on how music may affect relaxation the following research articles and book chapter are suggested:

W. Gantz, H. M. Gartenberg, M. L. Pearson and S. O. Schiller, "Gratifications and Expectations Associated with Pop Music Among Adolescents," *Popular Music and Society*, 1978, 6, pp. 81–89.

R. P. Greenberg and S. Fisher, "Some Differential Effects of Music on Projective and Structured Psychological Tests," *Psychological Reports*, 1971, 28, pp. 817–818.

H. Hope, "Music has Charms," *Nursing Mirror*, 1971, 132, 40–41.

H. Hunter, "An Investigation of Psychological and Physiological Changes Apparently Elicited by Musical Stimuli," *Psychology of Music*, 1974, 2, pp. 53–68.

J. A. Jellison, "The Effect of Music on Autonomic Stress Responses and Verbal Reports," in C. K. Madsen, R. D. Greer, & C. H. Madsen, Jr. (eds.), *Research in Music Behavior: Modifying Music Behavior in the Classroom*, (New York: Teachers College Press, 1975), pp. 235-271.

P. D. Peretti and K. Swenson, "Effects of Music on Anxiety as Determined by Physiological Skin Responses," *Journal of Research in Music Education*, 1974, 22, pp. 278-283.

S. J. Rohner and R. Miller, "Degrees of Familiar and Affective Music and Their Effects on State Anxiety," *Journal of Music Therapy*, 1980, 17, pp. 2–15.

J. A. Stoudenmire, "A Comparison of Muscle Relaxation Training and Music in the Reduction of State and Trait Anxiety," *Journal of Clinical Psychology*, 1975, 31, pp. 490–492.

PART TWO

PERSONAL ISSUES

Music reminds us that life is a dance.

9

WHAT WAS THE FIRST SOUND YOU EVER HEARD?
WAS IT THE SOUND OF YOUR MOTHER'S HEARTBEAT?
OF YOUR OWN HEARTBEAT?
YOUR MOTHER'S VOICE?
MUSIC TAKES US BACK TO THE BEGINNING.

Memory Recall

What's the name of that song?!

The *Star Wars* soundtrack. The "Tonight Show" theme. Your favorite news channel. ESPN. Sit-com theme songs weekly alerting us that "I Love Lucy," "Bewitched," "M*A*S*H," "Cheers," "Friends" were (or are) on their way. And what about the sounds of birds heralding spring? A baby's voice. A purring cat. A microwave timer. A dentist's drill. A barking dog. A passing train. An ambulance in the distance. A car's engine turning over . . . or not! Laughter. Weeping. Rain. Holiday tunes. A neighbor's lawn mower. The silence of a snow covered morning. What memories are evoked by the soundtracks of *your* life?

Music, when soft voices die, vibrates in the memory.[1]

Most of us have at least one special song that serves to trigger otherwise forgotten memories. A timely musical piece that just "happened to be playing" at that special moment when we had a particular experience. The

---

1. Percy Bysshe Shelley, from "To ____," in *A Dictionary of Musical Quotations*, Ian Crofton and Donald Fraser, eds. (New York: Schirmer, 1985), p. 149.

moment may have had a certain degree of significance, such as a first kiss, an argument, a spin in a brand new car.

In memory everything seems to happen to music.[2]

The coincidence of that particular song playing (or sound occurring) at that precise moment has served to indelibly imprint that positive, negative or even neutral experience into your acoustic memory.[3] In the future, that music (or sound) will serve to activate that special, emotional memory, much like a family snapshot briefly returns us to the birth of a special occasion. The episode will be somehow captured as an auditory photograph, an audiograph. After a while, it's like having our own set of personal music videos.

ONLY THROUGH MUSIC CAN WE HEAR THE PAST,
ENJOY THE PRESENT, AND COMPOSE THE FUTURE.

When a musical piece is composed, it reflects its composer's world— his/her thoughts, feelings, or psychological state—at that moment in time. Those feelings, transposed into music—a translation of an otherwise elusive emotion—lives on in the composition. Later on, through the music, we are able to not merely hear, but at some level at times feel the emotions being processed by the composer, from our own personal perspective. Each time the music is played, those emotions are freed, and we are free to make those emotions our own. Once seized from the imagination, and introduced into our auditory world, the music is captivated like a genie in a bottle. Allowed out, it can sometimes become our slave, sometimes our master.

MUSIC FREEZES IMAGES INTO RECOLLECTIONS AND RELEASES
RECOLLECTIONS INTO IMAGES. AS CHILDREN, WE DREAM OF BEING
ADULTS. AS ADULTS, WE DREAM OF HAVING BEEN CHILDREN.
ALONG THE PATH, MUSIC SHAPES US—AS WE CREATE IT—IN
ACCORDANCE WITH OUR OWN REALITIES. THE CHILD IS
TRANSFORMED INTO AN ADULT, WHILE THE ADULT RETAINS THE CHILD.

2. Tennessee Williams, in *The New International Dictionary of Quotations*, Hugh Rawson and Margaret Miner, eds. (New York: E. P. Dutton, 1986), p. 171.
3. See Acoustic Memory, page 291.

In my emotional mind, The Beatle's "Paperback Writer" is an auditory mnemonic, contextual cue,[4] or affective trigger to the summer of '66 . . . Overhill Lake, Glen Allen, Virginia. The emotional memories unleashed by that song are so powerful that even thirty years later, a mere few seconds of its powerful chords, irresistible drum beat and perfect resonating harmonies and I'm fourteen again. The parking lot, the ascending entry ramp, the snack bar, the descending ramp, the sand, the crowds, the towering diving board, the rescue platform at the center of the lake, the hordes of bikini-clad girls, the competition . . . they all surround me once again . . . in blaring stereo.

SOMETIMES, YOU PLAY THE MUSIC
JUST TO TASTE THAT KISS ONCE AGAIN.

We express both our personal and our group identity through music at different stages in our lives. . . . The songs can be used again to evoke memories of the emotional context of these times.[5]

Music has very powerful cuing effects. Whenever music is associated with a particular moment, event, or personal experience, the listener can attach very private imagery, feelings, or personal meaning to that particular piece of music. Later, through the music, one is capable of reexperiencing a mental and emotional representation of the *essence* of the moment when it was first heard. Once the music has been contextually cued to a particular musical moment, once that "audiograph" is taken, it will tend to act as a melodic mnemonic, returning the listener to that emotional moment that still resonates within our very core, frozen in audible time.

BEFORE, THE MEMORIES WERE DIFFERENT.
LATER, THE MEMORIES WILL CHANGE. LIKE FINGERPRINTS, OR
SNOWFLAKES, NO TWO MEMORIES ARE EVER THE SAME.

4. See Contextual Cuing, page 287.
5. Leslie Bunt, *Music Therapy: An Art Beyond Words* (New York: Routledge, 1994), pp. 158–159.

EXERCISE 11:
Spiral Sojourn through Musical Memories

Music can contain the paradox, ambivalence and intense passion
often associated with traumatic experience. It can act as bridge for
time travel, containing past, present, and future simultaneously while
still exemplifying the flow of process.[6]

After a powerful experience how clearly do you remember the dialogue? In recollecting the memory, do you search for the meaning underlying each word, or simply savor the melody of the moment?

Select eight to ten songs from a particular period you wish to recall. For instance, if you wish to remember something from your "15th summer" and you were born in 1950, you would want to select songs which were particularly popular during the summer of 1965, those "top-40," popular songs which they played on the radio twenty-four hours a day. If you cannot recollect any songs from a particular period you would like to recall, you can quickly refresh your memory by visiting your library, book, music, or record store and inquiring about books which would provide such information ("Seventies Hit Parade," "Popular Music from the Eighties," "Music from the Fifties," "Top 100 Tunes of 1965," etc.). For a quick musical excursion of some of the top songs stretching over five decades (the '30s through the '70s) see the Time Travel Musical Menu, page 145.

Another, more direct alternative, would be to select one or more songs which, to you, hold a particular association to a personal event in your past. This may be a song which you shared with a high school sweetheart, one that you associate with a specific moment or incident, or one which you feel may evoke feelings from a particular time in your life.

Having selected the song(s), find a comfortable place and initiate your "Spiral Sojourn."[7]

---

6. Stephanie Volkman, "Music Therapy and the Treatment of Trauma-Induced Dissociative Disorders," *The Arts in Psychotherapy*, 1993, 20, 3, pp. 243–252 (p. 25).

7. See Spiral Sojourn, page 361.

As you descend, or ascend, in your "time traveling journey," allow the music background to serve as your pilot, and to function as your internal guide, leading you to the place and time you wish to rediscover.

Throughout this exercise, allow yourself to be transported by the music. By releasing expectations and conscious efforts, the cuing effects of the music will gently escort you back through time and to your destination, releasing long-lost images, feelings, and ideas.

Once you begin to encounter and recollect familiar impressions you once experienced, simply allow yourself to "be there"[8] and "flow" with the experience. Rather than "acting" on the feelings and thoughts being triggered, passively place yourself in the role of "recipient" or "observer," viewing, feeling, and listening to whatever images are evoked by the music. In this manner you will be able to revisit with yourself at any moment in history, and dance with the echoes that linger deep within your mind.

THE MORE WE LISTEN, THE MORE THERE IS TO HEAR.

---

8. See Being Versus Trying to Be, page 261.

Additional Reading

For further reading on the effects of music on memory, the following articles are suggested:

R. P. Bowman, "Approaches for Counseling Children Through Music," *Elementary School Guidance and Counseling*, 1987, 19, pp. 284-291.

Cora L. Diaz de Chumaceiro, "What Song Comes to Mind: Induced Song Recall: Transference/Countertransference in Dyadic Music Associations in Treatment and Supervision," *The Arts in Psychotherapy*, 1992, 19, 5, pp. 325-332 (p. 325).

M. Priestley, "Music, Freud and the Port of Entry," *Nursing Times*, 1976, 1940–1941.

10

Time Management

Viewed in the context of human behavior, time is organization.[1]

Concentration of any sort obliterates time.[2]

Time, our worlds revolve around it. We waste a lot of it wishing we had more; there never seems to be quite enough. While we're children, time seems to move at a snail's pace. As we age, the clock seems to speed up. While children seem to think of tomorrow as "the distant future," for teenagers the coming weekend seems like a lifetime away. By the time we reach maturity five, ten, or even twenty years ago seems like only yesterday! Regardless of our age, however, our commonalties converge when it comes to weekends which tend to disappear much faster than any other two days of the week. Our vocabularies are replete with time-honored statements, such as "Where has the time gone?" "I wish I had more time . . . " "It's that time again," etc. We are praised for "being on time," receive awards for "running faster" than our competition, and get extra credit in sections of some tests for "finishing quickly."

Yesterday's world moved very fast. Today's moves a lot faster. Tomorrow's . . . well, we will all need much more proficient cognitive

---

1. Edward T. Hall, *The Dance of Life* (New York: Doubleday, 1983), p. 138.
2. Hall, *The Dance of Life*, p. 180.

processors, and laptops, to assimilate all of the incoming data. There is no time and so we need a quick analysis. People become exasperated by the slowness of microwaves and fast food lines. We demand larger amounts of memory from our hard drives, and more sophisticated hard drives to accommodate infinite volumes of audio and graphic capabilities. Copy machines move too slowly, faxes do not come through fast enough. Access codes and numbers to personal pagers and portable phones seem to get longer, taking too long to redial. Traffic speed lanes don't move fast enough. Even major sports continue to adapt new rules to help speed up the games. Popular tunes get faster, and rhythms more complex and intricate. Placed in unfamiliar surroundings, or around unfamiliar people, we tend to draw from our past to "fill in the blanks." It tends to even become a (conscious or unconscious) competition, "I can name that tune on . . . *one* note!"

Although all of us share the same world, we inhabit different realities. We have different jobs that take up different amounts of time; we pursue individual responsibilities, hobbies, and activities that exhaust our hours and days at different rates. While some people work a few hours and make a lot of money, others work a lot of hours and make little money. There may be little justice in the world, but there is even less time. However, regardless of who we are, and what we do, the mechanics of time are exactly the same for each of us. Regardless of how rich, important, or famous someone may be, an hour still lasts sixty minutes, a day twenty-four hours, and a week seven days. This never changes, time is forever in control. As such, the only choice we have is to try and manage the time we have to the best of our ability.

Some objectives of time management include the following:

1. *Setting priorities.* Clarify your sense of short (paying monthly bills), medium (painting the front porch) and long-term (finishing your first novel) goals.

2. *Establishing a hierarchy of low to high priority tasks.* Take the time to outline well thought out, educated decisions placing the focus on your *high* priority tasks. As often as possible, *begin* with *high* priority tasks and work your way *down*.

3. *Creating realistic schedules.* It is impractical—if not impossible—to think of driving from New York to California in one day. Break large, involved projects into smaller, realistically "do-able" segments. Dividing tasks into

reasonable steps makes them more manageable, mentally, emotionally, and physically.

4. *Maximizing resources.* Conserve your energies. Learn to delegate. Set up orderly filing systems. Discipline yourself to "fit in" small tasks between larger ones. Remember, you can do six "five minute" tasks in half an hour.

5. *Developing effective and productive habits and routines.* How essential is it to socialize with everyone you pass along the way to the photocopy machine? Do you truly need to watch the rerun sitcoms? Are you using your phone as a communication device or a mode of long-term psychoanalytic therapy?.

6. *Being flexible.* Find harmony within your environment. Adjust or modify your daily needs and responsibilities in a realistic and comfortable fashion so that you can realistically react to, and take time for, the unexpected.

7. *Setting realistic expectations.* If you are catering a party for one hundred guests or making airplane reservations to fly to Florida during the holidays you better give yourself plenty of time for the arrangements.

8. *Acknowledging and accepting personal limitations.* If you are a slow reader simply accept that you are *not* getting through *War and Peace* or *Ivanhoe* in one evening and plan accordingly.

9. *Learning the difference between "wasting time" and "taking a break."* This is highly relative to each situation and individual. What may seem like "taking a break" to you may seem like "wasting time" to someone else. Generally, if you are lying around and *feeling guilty about it,* you're probably wasting time, if you're lying around and *feeling good about it,* you're probably taking a break.

10. *Setting Limits.* Be assertive about your own needs. Set boundaries, be gentle, but firm. We need to take care of ourselves before we can afford the energy to take care of others.

11. *Allowing yourself a reasonable and realistic amount of time for each planned activity.* Set a comfortable pace, or tempo, and follow the beat of your own internal music. If you must guess, err in giving yourself *extra* time for

activities (if you suspect that spring cleaning will take five to six hours, give yourself six to seven, you can always find something to do with an extra hour). It's usually better to have time left over, than not enough time.

12. *Allowing time for things beyond your control.* Learn to dance with the rhythms of each day—traffic flow, weather, decisions which involve other people. Always allow time for that "unknown" floating variable (long lines at the bank or the airport, lack of parking spots, stalled train blocking your path). Remember, everyone marches to the beat of a different drummer.

13. *Rewarding yourself for accomplishments, regardless of how small they may be.* Routinely reward yourself by at least mentally and emotionally acknowledging small achievements and any sort of forward progress you accomplish.

14. *Taking time to recharge each day.* Take a walk. Lie out on a hammock, or recliner, and read a good book, a few pages per day. Meditate. Exercise. Listen to music. Sit back and enjoy a sitcom or two. Laugh.

15. *Letting go.* So you made a mistake. Learn from it, let it go, and move on. Nobody is perfect, even you.[3]

> It is extraordinary and paradoxical that the very activities that are most rewarding and satisfying are those in which time is experienced as passing with extreme rapidity or in which the sense of time has been lost completely.[4]

The following exercises offer various ideas on how music can be utilized to enhance our time management skills.

---

3. See Letting Go, page 249.
4. Hall, *The Dance of Life*, p. 148.

○

EXERCISE 12:

Time Management through Music

This exercise is designed to encourage us to use different length tapes to function as time compartmentalization devices. It also introduces basic ideas on how to use music to make the best use of our time.

1. Decide how much time you *realistically* have, and *reasonably* need to complete a project.

2. Select music which will help *you* to set the proper, desirable rhythm or tempo to help you flow with the *process* of fulfilling your task ("soothing" music to study, "stimulating" music to set your work pace, "masking" music or "white noise" to help block out extraneous noises and distractions and help with focusing).[5]

3. Selecting the proper background music helps us to move along or set our work rhythm by:

- Helping us to set a desired pace while conserving energy (see Soothing Musical Rhythmic Synchronicity Menu, page 55);
- Making us feel more energized and stimulated (see Stimulating Musical Menu, page 20);
- Keeping us focused and alert;
- Creating a pleasant environment (select from Meditation Musical Menu, page 230, or Soothing Musical Menu, page 55);
- Instilling positive time distortion (use any music mentioned above, depending on which you prefer, or refer to Altered State Musical Menu, page 241, or Letting Go Musical Menu, page 259;

---

5. See Stimulating Musical Menu, page 20, Soothing Musical Menu, page 55, and Psychological Noise and Masking, page 281.

- Evoking inspiration (see Inspirational Musical Menu, page 48);
- Blocking out "psychological noise"[6] (again, refer to any of the above menus depending on which type of music/pace you desire);
- Setting a steady tempo.[7]

4. Using favorite music pieces (or drawing from selections in the sections suggested above), make tape compilations using tape lengths to fit your time schedule (a 90-minute tape for a 1 1/2 hour workout; 60-minute tape for a meditation, relaxation, or visualization session; a 120-minute tape for a 2-hour project, etc.). By creating these tapes you will know exactly how much time has passed, and how much there is left, before you need to move on to your next activity. Although it will take time initially to create these tapes, the time invested will substantially pay off in the long run.

Time away from a loved one moves at a snail's pace, while a rendezvous is over before you know it.[8]

O

EXERCISE 13:

Using Music to Speed Your Pace

By imposing order, music ensures that the emotions aroused by a particular event peak at the same moment.[9]

Whenever you find yourself with a limited amount of time to complete a particular task, surround your environment with a stimulating music background to set, and help maintain, a desired and energetic pace.

1. Choose a music background which happens to be "right for you" at the time, one which sets the desired, energetic pace *for the task at hand,* that *you* find enjoyable, and that helps *you* to feel stimulated.

6. See Psychological Noise, page 281.
7. See Rhythmic Synchronicity, page 275.
8. Hall, *The Dance of Life*, p. 146.
9. Anthony Storr, *Music and the Mind* (New York: The Free Press, 1992), p. 30.

Deciding on the proper music will improve the chances that the music will, through the processes of Entrainment[10] and Rhythmic Synchronicity:

- Provide a comfortable working tempo;
- Tend to minimize monotony, giving you the perception that time is "going faster" than it actually is;
- Help you to better concentrate on your task, keeping away distracting thoughts and enhancing your ability to do a better job in less time;
- Provide a more attractive working ambiance;
- Function as a motivational factor;
- Help you to focus on the heAr and now;[11]
- Help generate a positive attitude.

Mood and psychological states have an incredible effect upon the experience of the passage of time.[12]

O

EXERCISE 14:

Using Music to Slow Your Pace

Music structures time; and some musicians claim that, for them, this is music's most essential function.[13]

When faced with a task that requires intense concentration, attentive focusing, and extreme care, you may want to surround yourself with a soothing or relaxing musical background to help maintain the desired slower pace.

1. Choose a music background which happens to be "right for you" at the time, one which sets the desired, slow pace for the task at hand, one you find enjoyable, and that helps you to feel relaxed, but yet alert.

10. See Entrainment, page 317.
11. See HeAr and Now, page 243.
12. Hall, *The Dance of Life*, p. 145.
13. Storr, *Music and the Mind*, p. 184.

Again, deciding on the proper music (for you) will improve the chances that the music will provide the same benefits as mentioned above, as well as evoking a sense of relaxation, relieving tension, clearing and relaxing the mind, increasing your sense of control, and enhancing creativity and artistic expression.

Sound Idea

Tick tock, tick tock
Set your pace to a musical clock.
Try Joseph Haydn's
Symphony # 101 in D major
("The Clock"),
Second movement.

11

Grief and Loss

*When we are grieving, a certain piece of music can move directly
into that grief, deepening, defining, and expressing it in inexplicable
ways. It brings us to an acknowledgement and acceptance
of our grief.*[2]

Grief is a natural response to loss that can be normally experienced by anyone and which can result in a wide range of emotions. Although reactions to loss can vary greatly, most people experiencing a grieving situation share certain similar emotional patterns. At first, we may experience shock or numbness, denying that the loss actually occurred. Secondly, perceiving the loss as "unfair," or "unjust," we may feel powerless, and experience an emotional release in the form of anger—toward ourselves or others for not preventing the loss—and crying. Third, guilt or depression may be experienced. Although the guilt is typically related to situations beyond our control, we may fall into the trap of blaming ourselves for "not being there" or for having "unfinished or unresolved issues" related to the loss.

Depression, another normal and natural reaction to a loss, may take the form of loneliness, helplessness, emptiness, and intense sadness as we

1. Anthony Decuir, "Trends in Music and Family Therapy," *The Arts in Psychotherapy*, 1991, 18, pp. 195–199 (p. 196).
2. Joanne Crandall, *Self-Transformation Through Music* (Wheaton, IL: Theosophical Publishing House, 1986), p. 41.

recognize the extent of the loss. The depression may at times also involve feelings of remorse, isolation, and—in the case of a loved one's death—confronting our own mortality. Finally, the mental, physical, and emotional stress often experienced may sometimes affect our immune system, resulting in a number of physical ailments (exhaustion, nausea, insomnia, headaches, colds, hypertension).

The following case illustrates how music was instrumental in assisting one particular individual with getting through her personal grief.

Jean, a 36-year old, divorced social worker, came to me a year after losing her mother to an unprecedented heart attack. An only child, she maintained a close relationship with her mother who lived over twelve hundred miles away. Their bond had grown significantly stronger from the time that Jean's father abandoned the family years earlier for a younger co-worker.

Before coming to me, Jean had attempted a number of approaches (medication, psychotherapy, journaling) in attempts to get in touch with her loss and deal with her unyielding depression more effectively. She had even attempted to run a "grief" group herself, with the hope that this would help her to better deal with her own grieving. To date, however, each of her attempts had proven unsuccessful. Confounding her loss, Jean, a helping professional herself, felt a sense of shame for "not being able to handle a situation similar to that for which she typically helped her own clients." In effect, in addition to her own personal pain and loss, she now began to feel "like an impostor" in her professional practice. Further, she felt constantly fatigued, irritable, and was having serious problems getting out of bed in the morning, concentrating, and finding motivation in general.

After a couple of sessions, I suggested that Jean make a list of a number of songs which reminded her of her mother. Tunes which, for some reason or another, had an emotional connection within their relationship. During our third session, Jean brought in a list of twelve songs, all of which had some emotional importance in relation to her daughter-mother connection. Later, she was successful in locating nine of these tunes on audio cassette tape at her local music store. My suggestion at that point was for Jean to take some time during the following few nights, find a comfortable space in the privacy of her home, disconnect all phones, and allow herself the opportunity to spend that time passively listening to these tunes. Her only "assignment" other than listening to the music was to "flow with the feelings triggered by the songs," and to write—or "journal"— these feelings down if she found that to be helpful.

During our very next session Jean indicated that, at first, she had felt a certain trepidation about playing these songs, feeling they would be emotionally loaded. Having moved beyond that hurdle she reported that "the moment the first tune began to play" she experienced a powerful cathartic event, and was "finally able to truly cry about her loss." Her grieving had effectively begun. Over the following few nights, She continued to play the tunes during which times she was finally able to compose a detailed, expressive letter which helped her begin to purge herself of the feelings of loss that she had been harboring for over a year. The music, as she began to realize, was effectively triggering her previously buried feelings.

With each subsequent visit over the following few weeks, Jean happily reported that not only had her depressive mood begun to lift, but that with each passing week thoughts of her mother were increasingly accompanied by fond, happy memories. Although at times the songs continued to elicit feelings of sadness, they also provided a sense of comfort and relief whenever she felt the need to emotionally process her grief. The anger and sorrow she felt during all that time had begun to dissipate. A few weeks later Jean returned for a follow-up session, indicating she felt that her professional work was significantly benefiting from her therapeutic experience, and she felt that she was on her way to once again becoming a fully functioning, happy individual.

Exercise 15:

Using Music to Trigger Emotional Responses

This exercise may elicit some very powerful emotions and should be done only at the individual's discretion. It can be used to help trigger emotions related to loss, processing the loss, and moving on.

1. You may want to pursue this exercise either alone, or with another person, or group of persons, who may share similar emotions associated with the present loss.

2. For the initial part of this exercise, select one or more musical piece(s) which have particularly touching, or emotional meanings for you and/or

has a special connection to the loss object. For the second part of the exercise select a number of soothing, relaxing tunes with positive overtones. (See Soothing Musical Menu, page 55, and Bonding with your Depressed Mood Musical Menu, page 19.)

3. Perceive this exercise as an opportunity for a "moving" experience, one which will assist you in moving *through* your present emotional state and into one of acceptance of the loss.

4. As the music plays, feel its power activating and deepening whatever feelings you are presently experiencing in relation to the loss (grief, loss, sadness, anger, etc.).

5. As these feelings are triggered, actively feel their intensity flowing through you. As this occurs, allow yourself to express any painful feelings, thoughts, and memories you have which relate to the loss. These may involve crying, talking with someone whom you trust, or even hollering out loud if this is the reaction which is elicited. If you feel like expressing yourself physically, act out your frustration or anger by striking a soft, safe, or otherwise unbreakable object, such as a cushion or large pillow.[3]

6. Having given yourself the opportunity to experience and process the emotions related to the loss, switch to the second set of musical selections, the ones chosen for their soothing, comforting, and positive feel.

7. As you [and your friend(s)] listen to this second set of musical selections, gradually switch your conversation so that it reflects a more positive, hopeful, and optimistic tone. During this time, it may be helpful to acknowledge the loss, discuss your fears and limitations, recognize that you will allow yourself and others "whatever time is needed" to process the loss, and acknowledge the need and availability of personal and professional support systems which are potentially available (grief support groups, professional counseling, individual or group grief therapy). Use this opportunity to acknowledge and discuss whatever positive aspects you may remember connected to your loved one, to bond with, and share, loving memories.

---

3. If you begin to feel nauseous, dizzy, or otherwise ill, cease the exercise immediately and initiate a deep breathing and relaxation exercise (see Breathing, page 333, and Relaxation, page 93). If you feel comfortable with attempting the exercise at a later time, you may choose to return to it at your own discretion. However, if you feel the emotions are too powerful or overwhelming, you should seek professional assistance in dealing with this particular grieving experience.

8. At this point you may also choose to make a commitment to yourself to work on improving your own life and becoming more aware of those important people in your life whom you may have been neglecting. Some personal goals may include asking for and accepting help (personal or professional) as needed, getting plenty of rest and taking care of yourself and your own personal needs and responsibilities, or making an effort to stay healthy by eating a balanced diet, exercising, and avoiding any potentially harmful substances such as alcohol, tobacco, and non-prescription drugs.

When we are deeply in touch with the present moment, we can see that all our ancestors and all future generations are present in us.[4]

EMOTIONS AND THOUGHTS
BEAT IN THE HEART,
RESIDE IN THE MIND,
DIE WITH THE BODY.
TRANSFORMED INTO MUSIC,
EMOTIONS AND THOUGHTS
ECHO IN THE HEART,
RESONATE IN THE MIND,
LIVE ON FOREVER.

4. Thich Nhat Hanh, *Peace is Every Step* (New York: Bantam, 1991), p. 73.

Additional Reading

For further articles referring to the use of music as an adjunct to help in dealing with grief and loss see:

T. G. Bever, "A Cognitive Theory of Emotion and Aesthetics in Music," *Psychomusicology*, 7, 1988, pp. 165–175.

L. B. Meyer, *Emotion and Meaning in Music* (Chicago: University of Chicago Press, 1966).

A. N. Whitehead, *Symbolism: Its meaning and effect* (New York: Capricorn Books, 1969).

12

Growth/Change

The heart you can depend on; the mind is always changing.[1]

*No matter how tightly we cling to the familiar, the
only constant in life is change.*[2]

The Tao of music seeks no audience, yet it reaches everyone. Timeless, it defines the times. Intangible, it is felt by everyone. Desired by all, it is nonetheless indescribable. Perceived, it can never be seen. Savored, it has never been tasted. And so music follows The Way, fickly finding myriad forms, through ageless paths, and countless cultures, while the Tao of music remains unchanged. As C. J. Beck said in *Every Day Zen*, ". . . there is nothing in the universe but change."[3]

Familiar music provides us with a sense of control. We can hum the melody, sing the lyrics, interpret its underlying meanings. Beyond that, while playing music on our stereos we can exercise further control by raising, or lowering, the volume. Regulating the bass or treble. Adjusting our equalizer or any other "effects" we may have connected to our stereo system. "For the human being, alone and afraid, an orderly universe is reassuring. . . . Music is the reflection and the expression of that order. . . . As

---

1. Edward T. Hall, *The Dance of Life* (New York: Doubleday, 1983), p. 102.
2. Diane Dreher, *The Tao of Inner Peace* (New York: HarperCollins, 1991), p. 60.
3. Charlotte Joko Beck, *Every Day Zen: Love & Work* (San Francisco: HarperSanFrancisco, 1989), p. 37.

we experience music, we feel our connection with a world of design and order."[4] Be okay with change, growth. Delve into the mysterious. Try something new. "Music not only reflects the evolution of life; it is one with the process of growth and change."[5]

Just recently, while attending a major psychological conference, I ran into an old friend and mentor. Ed, who happens to be a wonderful musician, is a clinical psychologist who specializes in working with adolescents and college students. During our brief time together I had the opportunity to ask Ed how it is that, after thirty-five years in our field, he is still able to relate to—and establish relationships with—these highly mercurial populations.

Ed's reply was quick and simple, "Music!"

According to Ed, keeping up with emerging musical trends is a sure-fire way to keep up with the constantly emerging legions of young people with whom he interacts. "Listening to popular music," he insists, "gives you a far more accurate, up to the minute idea of where the kids' hearts and heads are at than watching TV, reading the papers, or even attending workshops and professional conferences! . . . It all comes down to a matter of communicating with people and being able to change, grow and adapt to changing times."

> [R]eal progress involves growing and developing, which
> involves changing inside, but that's something the inflexible
> Backson is unwilling to do.[6]

As I have found in my own practice, contemporary music is an excellent barometer of change. It defines and reflects the times. In effect, keeping up with "kids' new music" is tremendously helpful in raising our awareness of where young people as a group stand in terms of their social, political, sexual, philosophical, and emotional levels. On the other hand, by asking individuals what type of music they typically listen to, or prefer, we can gain a fairly accurate idea of what stage of development they are in at the moment.

"When I started out as a very young, inexperienced counselor in the fifties," Ed indicated, "I often found myself at a loss as what to talk about

4. Joanne Crandall, *Self-Transformation through Music* (Wheaton, IL: The Theosophical Publishing House, 1986), p. 27.
5. Crandall, *Self-Transformation through Music*, p. 28.
6. Benjamin Hoff, *The Tao of Pooh* (New York: Penguin Books, 1983), p. 104.

with my adolescent clients. Sooner or later, we would begin to discuss music and it usually proved to be an excellent ice breaker." In effect, it seems that being a musician provides a definite advantage when working with people in general, and with adolescents in particular. According to Ed's estimations, "about 90 percent of the kids are very involved in music of one type or another, and while about 50 percent play an instrument, it seems almost the other 50 percent would *like* to play one!"

Having something in common with another individual is imperative in establishing a trusting and lasting alliance. Even if one's taste in music is at the opposite extreme of the person one is dealing with, the mere fact of having a mutual passion for music can help to establish a certain affinity between the parties involved. If there is no ground where the parties can relate, the relationship, if ever established at all, will likely be short-lived and tends to feel shallow and superficial. Although it may not provide an experience of "rhythmic synchronicity,"[7] a shared passion for music in general will often lead to a type of closeness which is misunderstood by those for whom music may be dismissed as inconsequential.

> In the beginner's mind there are many possibilities, but in the expert's there are few.[8]

Our musical preferences can serve as a fairly good mirror of our personalities, worldviews, or states of mind. A teenager who prefers classical music, for example, will often exhibit a distinctively different attitude from one who strongly prefers rock. One who can't decide between the two will typically present a fairly complex character. Likewise, an individual preoccupied with protest songs will usually reflect a completely different state of mind from someone enamored with romantic ballads. For the most part, as our "heAr and now" preferences in music change, so do our emotional states.

So does Ed listen to modern music? "Sure! Listening to different types of music is just like listening to different types of people. Some you like a little more, some a little less. Some you can relate to, others you can't. But if you listen close enough there's something unique and interesting about everyone, there's always something to learn." At home, however, Ed prefers to go home and surround himself with classical jazz. "In the end," he stated, "you always want to be with the one you love."

---

7. See Rhythmic Synchronicity, page 275.
8. Shunryu Suzuki, *Zen Mind, Beginner's Mind* (New York: Weatherhill, 1983), p. 21.

A GENERATION WITHOUT ITS OWN MUSIC
IS LIKE A BEING WITHOUT ITS OWN SOUL.

With the aid of music (therapy) individuals are able to "literally hear their own self coming into being. If human survival is concerned with a repertoire of flexible coping responses to both external and internal demands, then in the playing of improvised music may be heard the creative way in which a person meets those demands."[9]

Change Engendering Growth

We live in a world of no boundaries. Music reflects that world most accurately when it is allowed to flow and evolve as life itself evolves.[10]

Quite often, when we are encountered by a change in our lives, we begin to feel the fears and concerns associated with the emptiness which may result. Rather than perceiving the inevitable laws of change as an *opportunity* for personal growth and transformation, we instead grieve over the loss (our old neighborhood, job, partner, childhood friend, old car or home, seeing a child off to college, retirement) we are about to face. One positive approach to facing the many inevitable changes in our lives is to relate it to other changes we have experienced in our past.

For instance, take a moment and look back at issues and life situations you had in your past, which you eventually outgrew, which passed on, which turned out to be "not as bad as expected!" During those transitions, what did you learn? In particular, you may want to focus on particular struggles you encountered as a child, or adolescent. Those things which seemed truly important during those stages of development. Those awkward first dances, the awful haircuts, a lost football game, a broken date, a "D" (or "F!") on a test. Was the pain truly endless? Was the situation actually unbearable? Was is really worth the wear and tear on your nerves? The anxiety, the stress, the depression, the worries, the aging? Or

---

9. David Aldridge, "Physiological Change, Communication, and the Playing of Improvised Music: Some Proposals for Research," *The Arts in Psychotherapy*, 1991, 18, 1, pp. 59–64 (p. 64).
10. Crandall, *Self-Transformation through Music*, p. 29.

were these situations merely *challenges?* Opportunities for maturation, personal expansion, *growth?*

Another point you may want to consider is that, in spite of popular opinion, pain and struggle do not have a monopoly on growth and change. Looking back through your life's passage, you can probably identify just as many situations when comfort and pleasure elicited as much personal growth as conflict and life's random irritations. Throughout your development, you can likely identify instances when peace, resolution, and conformity enacted as much forward movement as frustration, conflict, and rebellion. Of course hard work effects changes in our lives. But, in moderation, so does sitting back and watching your path as it unfolds before you. Some may call this contemplation. Many times silence and patience enable positive change much more rapidly, and effectively, than action and reaction. In the long run, it simply comes down to balance, to getting in tune with the rhythm of things as they develop and unfold all around us.

> Curiosity asks one question and nature asks her ten. One degree of rhythmic perception acquired becomes a vantage ground from which we may approach higher levels, and each of these in turn traversed leads to higher vantage grounds, level after level, vista after vista.[11]

Perceived as forward movement, growth can be seen as life's dance. As with any type of dancing, it (growth and change) flows much more easily if, as we change and grow, we dance (rather than struggle) to the music which surrounds us, following our inner rhythms and striving for harmony.

On the other hand, there are certain attitudes, or approaches, to ongoing situations which actually stunt growth, or create unnecessary barriers and obstacles on the path to harmonious change.

For instance, trying to look ahead *through* pessimism is much like trying to crash through a steel-reinforced, cement barrier. It is much easier to think optimistically, study the situation, and *take the path of least resistance.* Rather than worrying, approach the issue at hand from a problem-solving perspective. Recognize our limitations. Exercise our option to let go. Instead of holding on to, and recycling negative attitudes, find a positive angle. Adopt an optimistic stance. See change as a challenge, an opportunity for growth, a good excuse for an adventure. In life, there's always room for more memories.

---

11. Carl E. Seashore, *Psychology of Music* (New York: Dover, 1967), pp. 144–145.

[P]leasure in making music and joy in the creative process act
as motivators toward overcoming the fear of self-expression,
exposure and change.[12]

If you don't feel like dancing, rest. If you don't like the "song" which is
playing, play a different tune. If it is outside of your control, be patient,
soon life will change it for you. Also, recognize when you have the option
to either change the music yourself, make suggestions, or simply let it
play. Likewise, recognize and accept those situations when those options
are not available. When "they" play a tune you like, enjoy it to its fullest
in the heAr and now. Finally, if the music playing is not something you
would have necessarily chosen, give it a chance, listen to it. If you still
don't like it, let it go. Either way, you have just experienced something
new and different in life.

> Music connects us with our essence which is movement and
> vibration. As we listen or play, we feel the flow, the movement
> within and around us, the utter transitoriness of life. . . . As we
> proceed on the journey of transformation, we may use music at
> every stage, helping us to move, flow, open, surrender.[13]

EXERCISE 16:
Creating New Memories

{W}e continue to evolve through our choices.[14]

This exercise uses music to assist us in an imaginary "time-travel journey"
where we may visualize various aspects of projected growth and positive
change in our lives.

Music as a tool for flowing with change, and enacting growth, can
help us to understand evolving, ever-changing social, emotional, and
philosophical themes. It can elicit varying emotional points of view, initi-

---

12. Diane Snow Austin and Janice M. Dvorkin, "Resistance in Individual Music Therapy," *The Arts in Psychotherapy*, 1993, 20, 5, pp. 423–430 (p. 428).
13. Crandall, *Self-Transformation through Music*, p. 92.
14. Dreher, *The Tao of Inner Peace*, p. 63.

ate movement, maintain a balance between transitional stages, and provide "contextual cues" for holding on to old memories, as well as helping us realize newly emerging concepts and ideas. Music also helps us maintain a sense of optimism and positivity, blocks out resonating fears and irrational concerns, provides a soundscape to accompany personal growth, and can serve to anchor us to the heAr and now, keeping us focused in our way along evolving paths.

1. Select musical selections which denote feelings of inspiration and movement. (See Inspirational Musical Menu, page 48, and Stimulating Musical Menu, page 20.)

2. Lie down, close your eyes, initiate deep breathing. During this exercise you will have total control of this (imaginary) life transition. You will be the architect and composer of your own reality. Surrendering to the flow, you will also take an active part in the process.

3. In your mind's eye, tune in to a clear image of the adventure in which you are about to embark. As the music plays, listen to your inner self as it verbally describes this opportunity to fulfill an unresolved dream, meet new people, share new experiences, create new memories. If you ever needed an excuse to "do something different," here it is!

4. As you listen to yourself depicting the details of your approaching transaction be specific, clear, and above all, positive and optimistic about how it is all *going to work out.* As you continue your breathing, feel and visualize a "smiley face" (a positive grin) outlined across your face. Visualize yourself undergoing the various changes you wish to make. With the music as your "time-traveling companion," focus only on positive, forward moving consequences. Obstacles as challenges. Conflicts as new opportunities for growth and movement. Difficulties as adventurous encounters with reality which, in itself, will continue to evolve.

5. Riding in the safety, flow, and comfort of the musical rhythms, visualize yourself five years from now, looking back at all the changes which have occurred and transpired. Again, feel and "see" the "smiley face" sketched across your face. Looking back through your transformation and period of development listen to yourself in the heAr and now describing the flourishing which you experienced during those five quick years. Hear the satisfaction of the maturation process, the pride in having taken control of your passage and having created the reality of your life's flow.

6. Having actualized your positive metamorphosis, allow the music to bring you back to the present moment. As you allow yourself to return to the actual reality of embarking on your new adventure, allow the feelings elicited by the feel of the music to become part of your acoustic memory.[15]

From this point on, as you begin your dance along the path to creating your future realities, you need only close your eyes and—for a brief moment—take a deep, replenishing breath and allow your acoustic memory to cue you back to the flow and harmony accompanying you on your special journey.

One with the Tao, music is expressed through the ten thousand things. Mastery is attained through genuine commitment, perfection never reached. Comfort flows after years of hard work, flawlessness is never attained. Accept the search, abandon the struggle, by becoming one with one's instrument, the self echoes the Tao.

OPEN YOUR HEART, BE MINDFUL,
HOLD NO EXPECTATIONS. "TRUTH" TWISTS AND TURNS.
MUSIC ADAPTS BECAUSE IT IS FLEXIBLE, IT ADJUSTS
BECAUSE IT BENDS. BE FOREVER YOUNG.
WHEN REACHING AN ENDING,
LOOK FOR A NEW BEGINNING.

---

15. See Acoustic Memory, page 291.

13

Procrastination

Do it! Let's Get Off Our Buts.[1]

Regardless of what brings people to psychotherapy, they unsuspectingly always bring their own solutions. As clinicians, a great deal of our work is spent helping patients clear the static (psychological noise) that keeps them from harmonizing with life and with themselves. In effect, when Sally and her mother came to see me for their initial visit, with each question they unknowingly brought resolution. All that was needed was some fine-tuning.

Sally had a dilemma. She was 14, loved alternative music, and had a strong preference for expensive CDs. However, she was—according to her parents—"too young to work outside the home" and lacked the money to pay for the steady barrage of new releases. She also had a second problem: her mom hated this music.

Fortunately, Sally's mom also had a dilemma (solution). She worked weekends and did not have the time to clean their home and so relied on hiring an outside person to come in and clean on a regular basis. On the

---

1. John-Roger and Peter McWilliams, *"Do It! Let's Get Off Our Buts"* (Los Angeles: Prelude Press, 1991).

other hand, she felt that this was a task which could easily be done by Sally who could benefit by "learning the worth of a dollar" while getting used to the idea of the likeliness of this future responsibility. Mom, however, found it "impossible" to motivate Sally—a "professional procrastinator"—to do things which were not fun, such as helping around the house. Also, much to Sally's dismay, Mom did not believe in giving her daughter an allowance, but felt that money should be earned. In other words, Mom had the money which Sally needed, while Sally had the time to fulfill her family's needs. Time to make a deal.

As is true with most compromises, both parties usually have to learn to give and take. With me serving as consultant, Mom and Sally created a "formal" behavioral contract in my office which generally included the following compromises:

- Mother and daughter agreed to a specific, weekly time frame for Sally to clean the house as well as a fair, mutually agreed upon hourly rate. Sally could also earn bonuses for extra work (cleaning the oven, doing minor repairs, ironing curtains, cleaning out screens, washing windows, dusting light bulbs, etc.).
- Sally would perform her work duties as scheduled *without procrastination*. If she procrastinated or began to slack off on her work she would be "fired," and her mother would rehire their house-cleaner.
- Sally could use her hard-earned money toward purchasing her alternative music.
- Sally could play the music at any volume she desired while she cleaned the house. (Her mom was not at home during that time anyway.)
- Sally would be allowed to listen to her music in the privacy of her room, with controlled volume, when the other family members were home.
- The contractual agreement would be discussed and reviewed as necessary during future (biweekly) office visits.

A few weeks later, after some minor fine-tuning of secondary issues, both Sally and her mom found that not only was the deal working to everyone's benefit, but that a lot of this alternative music actually sounded a lot like mom's own classic rock. In effect, during later sessions, Sally confessed that she actually liked a lot of her mom's classic rock music which *she* felt sounded like minimalistic alternative music. After this revelation, daughter and mother began to share each other's music, which served to function as an unprecedented emotional bridge, opening up new paths of communication between the two.

> When you're fully present, fully aware, you can make the most
> of every moment. The Tao is here and now.[2]

Throughout our lives, most of us fall prey to the traps of procrastination. Following are a few suggestions on processing and progressing through these inevitable situations.

1. *What is underlying the procrastination?* Before actually starting on breaking through your procrastination barriers, you may need to zero in on the basic issue which is underlying your problem.

- Is it perfectionism? If so, this issue needs to be addressed, preferably through professional assistance from a local licensed clinician.
- Is the task at hand feasibly attainable? Realistic? If not, then acknowledge the fact that you are faced with an unrealistic task or demand, and go back to square one (what are some reality-based alternatives?).
- Does the enormity of the problem feel overwhelming? If so, can it be broken down into smaller pieces, or spread out over time? Can it be approached from a different, more realistic angle?
- Is this project something within your capability or field of expertise? If not, would it be more practical, or beneficial, to have it delegated, assigned to—or shared with—a colleague? Should it be contracted out to a specialist?
- Is it an assigned project, part of your work responsibilities? If this is something you are getting paid for, and have no interest in doing, but need to do to "keep your job," then come to terms with the fact that the sooner you begin, the sooner it will be done. They wouldn't call it work if it were all fun!
- Is what you need to do unclear? If so, get clarification.

---

2. Diane Dreher, *The Tao of Inner Peace* (New York: HarperCollins, 1991), p. 22.

- Are you afraid of the potential end result being evaluated by others? If this is the case, you need to come to terms with the fact that you will never be able to control others' subjective evaluation of your work. The only thing you can do is *your* best, and then move on.

- Are you physically or mentally unable to carry out this task? If this is at the root of your problem you need to take charge of the situation and take appropriate steps to either delegate the project, abandon it and move on to something else, or explain to the person in charge that—due to your limitations—you are actually unable to fulfill this requirement.

- Are you afraid of success? Could it be that the fear of succeeding at something unusually important may be holding you back from pursuing completion of this task or project? Is this something which is providing so much joy in your life that you may be afraid of carrying it through to completion, that, once you are done, your life will once again feel empty, unexciting or without purpose? If you feel one of the above may be underlying your delays, it may be helpful for you to come to terms with this awareness and allow yourself to experience the thrill of completion, which will free you for the challenge of embarking on a new task or direction.

- Are you waiting for something "magical" to happen? Maybe it will. But, in the meantime, it's up to you to create your own reality. One never knows what may summon the magic to actually manifest.

2. *Is the task actually do-able?* If you decide that your procrastination involves something you are indeed *capable* of doing, and need to get done, you may consider taking the following approach:

- Take a minute or so, take a few deep breaths, close your eyes, and visualize yourself sometime in the future with your project *already accomplished.*
- Visualize how you feel, having *completed* your task.
- Look at the *finished* work, "touch" it, feel the sense of pride and relief which comes from having actualized your goal.
- That done, open your eyes and return to the heAr and now. Drawing from the above visualization, ask yourself what

exactly it is that you need to do to begin, carry through, and bring your task to actual fruition.

3. *If the task is within your capability, then* make realistic decisions, taking into consideration the size of the job, and the amount of time you can (or are willing to) *practically and realistically* put into your project. Then, break the project down into small "do-able" parts, outlining the actual sequence of steps you need to follow within your time frame in order to attain timely, but reasonable completion. Finally, if you have been avoiding the work, come to terms with the fact that you are ready to take responsibility to carry this project through.

4. *Using music as a tool to break through procrastination.* You may use music to help you deal with procrastination in a number of ways. Used properly, music can help:

- Provide a pleasant ambiance to look (or listen) forward to;
- Tune out otherwise disruptive "psychological noise";
- Provide a pleasant, yet moving environment;
- Enhance concentration on your task (see Centering, page 223);
- Keep you grounded in the present (see HeAr and Now, page 243);
- Stimulate and trigger the release of natural endorphins;
- Trigger, and or maintain, motivation (see Training through Entrainment, page 157);
- Establish and set a desirable rhythmic pace, or work tempo (see Rhythmic Synchronicity, page 275);
- Provide "companionship" during your work (see Companionship, page 173);
- Appropriate a sense of discipline and time structure that helps you feel as if time is going by more quickly (see Time Management, page 115).

Each day before you embark on your task, you may need to select the type of music you feel will provide the proper background to accomplish your goals for that day. For instance, if you need to maintain a slow, but steady pace, choose soothing, relaxing music with a steady beat to help guide and set your working tempo while keeping you alert. A faster work pace will call for more upbeat, stimulating music. In either case, the stimulating rhythms underlying the music will help to stabilize concentration, and set the pace, as long as it is music that you enjoy.

With regard to appropriating a time schedule, if you know the time you will be able to spend on the project, the music can serve as a pleasant timer or "alarm clock" to alert you to approximately how much time has gone by. At the same time, it will be providing you with unobtrusive company while creating the illusion that time is going by more quickly and helping your work to flow much more effortlessly.

Finally, even if the work you are procrastinating seems dull, uninteresting, and "colorless," a good, generic selection of music backgrounds can add a sense of variety, satisfaction, and pleasure to almost any task. While functioning as passive entertainment, the option of music can help you to look forward to beginning your task, add colorful diversity to monotonous routines, and supply an entertaining sense of diversion—and even fantasy—to otherwise tedious responsibilities.

Later, now will get in the way.

○

EXERCISE 17:
Beating Procrastination

Use this exercise to start, maintain, and complete a dreaded task, such as cleaning the house, or doing any chore you are avoiding.

1. To the best of your ability, try and calculate how long the job will take. This will keep you from having to stop during the middle of your task to search for additional music later.

2. Select a number of musical selections which correspond to the amount of time you estimate your task will take to complete, *plus one hour*. For example, if you think the house cleaning will take five hours, put aside about six hours worth of music. The reasons for this include unplanned interruptions and most people's tendency to *under*estimate the length of a planned task. (Here's where a multiple CD changer comes in quite handy!).

Be innovative. Be adventurous, make it fun. Select music that you have not listened to in a long time, but have been longing to hear. Choose music in accordance with your needs. Remember, everyone has the tendency to rhythmically synchronize to a sound environment. If you play slow music, you will more likely work slowly, and more meticulously. If you surround yourself with music of a faster pace, it serves to set your pace accordingly. For example, if you need to polish the silverware, slow, soothing music may be in order. Cleaning out the attic, on the other hand, may require more stimulating, energizing tunes. For energizing selections see Stimulating Music, page 20, or Inspirational Music, page 48. For more relaxing musical selections see Soothing Music, page 55. To help create an entrainment ambiance, working up from "warm up," through stimulating, and into "cool down," see recommended selections on page 160ff.

Go out and purchase some stimulating, up-beat music that will help to rhythmically synchronize you to your work pace. Think of it as money you would otherwise pay to a house-cleaner. The average cost of hiring someone to clean a home typically runs approximately $50-$75 for five hours ($10-$15 per hour). You can buy a lot of music for that much money. Treat yourself! Also, if you "treat yourself" in this manner every few times you clean the house, your music library will soon be the envy of the neighborhood!

3. *Plan ahead.* Stack the music selections (CD's, records, tapes) beside your stereo. This will serve to get you started in the "mode" of getting things structured, organized, and in order.

4. *Visualize the finished goal.* Once you get started, aim for the finish line. The most difficult part of accomplishing (dreaded) tasks is getting started. The toughest part is usually that initial hurdle. The process of thinking about, and physically selecting the music serves to "cue" you to the fact that you have, indeed, *already begun* your task. Once you have started, the music will help generate and maintain steam.

5. *Enjoy the process.* Having begun, find enjoyment in what you are doing.

CREATE NEW MEMORIES, NOW.

14

Aging

*The Tao of music cannot be learned, it is inherent in each of us.
Without expectation we are born to its rhythm, live within its
harmony, and ultimately return to its resonating nature.*

Some of the biggest and most significant catalysts of the aging process
include stress, worry, anxiety, depression, low self-esteem, lack of exercise, and weakened, vulnerable immune systems. By counteracting, minimizing, or eliminating any or all of the above with the help of music we
may help to slow down, or even reverse the aging process. Ageless, music
connects ancient and modern, defining the rhythmic beat of each generation. Spiraling, it creates a harmonious path, translating chaos into inno-
vation. Stimulating the imagination, it creates inter-generational connections and cross-cultural bridges. Borrowing from youth gone by it helps to
determine the future, while describing the past. Turning dreams into
memories, music pervades all. It is forever young.

Music therapy is particularly beneficial to the elderly. Coupled
with gentle exercise, listening to music relieves pain and promotes motion in a way that exercise alone cannot do.
Neurologist Oliver Sacks recounts how some patients with
Parkinsonism and other brain diseases respond to music in

truly extraordinary ways: "One sees Parkinsonian patients unable to walk, but able to dance perfectly well, or patients almost unable to talk, who are able to sing perfectly well." Sacks describes one patient who sat virtually motionless except when she sat down at the piano, where she at once developed fluidity and grace. Listening to Chopin—her favorite composer—would cause an increase in her measurable brain activity from coma-like slowness to near-normal levels.[1]

The following exercise is designed to use music as an alternative to help motivate and encourage us to pursue a hobby or activity which we have long forgotten or neglected. It suggests using music to enhance visualization of an actual, desired activity thus helping you in creating that reality and eventually bringing it to fruition.

O

EXERCISE 18:

Rejuvenation through Music

This can be done by anyone who considers him or herself to fall within the ranks of the "mature adult."

> *As children, we whistle a simple tune and feel the wonder.*
> *As we age, we whistle that simple tune,*
> *and our wonderment returns.*

1. Select a number of musical compositions which take you back to a time when you felt "young," alive, and energetic. These may be tunes from your youth—childhood, adolescence, 20s, 30s, or any other time in life when you heard a song that made you feel particularly energized. (See Musical Menu 7, page 145, to rekindle musical memories spanning over five decades!)

2. As you listen to the music, sit back and contemplate some activities or hobbies which were once, in your opinion, just beyond your grasp, and

---

1. William Poole, *The Heart of Healing* (Atlanta: Turner Publishing, Inc., 1993), pp. 134 -135.

which you may have been unable to pursue due to any number of limitations. These obstacles could have included job responsibilities, a chronic illness, raising children, caring for a loved one, or pursuing other hobbies or activities. Some examples may include golf, skiing, mountain climbing, deep sea fishing, motorcycling, scuba diving, snorkeling in the tropics, playing music in a small combo or symphony orchestra, singing in your church choir, going on an exotic vacation, or any other reality-based activity that is within your potential and possible grasp.

3. Taking into consideration your present well-being, financial status, and time constraints, select one—or more—of the above hobbies or activities which you would still like to pursue. If you cannot think of any such hobbies or activities from your past, or feel unable to pursue the one you would prefer, spend as much time as you need exploring any *available* possibilities that may be within your capability and which are of present interest to you. Be adventurous, but be realistic. If you are unable to come up with anything on your own, consult your "inner guide"[2] with regard to any potential ideas or suggestions.

4. At first, select a hobby, activity, or adventure which is simple, attainable, and appealing to you in the heAr and now.[3] Later, as you become increasingly comfortable with your newly-found "fountain-of-youth," you can begin to expand your horizons at your own discretion.

5. Having decided on a hobby or activity to pursue, select a few musical compositions which have special meaning or significance in *your* life. Play this music as background as you initiate a "Spiral Sojourn" and take a musical journey to your "special place."[4]

6. Upon entering your "special place" allow yourself to blend and flow with the music. As the music plays, feel yourself becoming charged and energized by the music. Visualize yourself actually "breathing in" the rejuvenating vibrations emanating from the musical compositions.

7. As you listen to the music, imagine your ideas becoming realized much like the different aspects of the music pull together to create a perfect harmony. As your mind "dances" to the beat, feel the rhythms as these res-

2. See Inner Guide, page 371.
3. See HeAr and Now, page 243.
4. See the Spiral Sojourn, page 361, and Your Special Place, page 367.

onate within the very marrow of your bones and echo in the recesses of your mind. Imagine yourself flowing with these rhythms as you begin to visualize taking part in your selected hobby or activity.

8. As you visualize yourself deeply involved in the actual process of pursuing the hobby or activity you've selected, feel the music reinvigorating your body and refreshing your mind. Listen to yourself sing or "hum along." If you feel the urge, allow your body to respond by snapping your fingers or tapping your hands or feet as they keep the beat or follow the rhythm to the music. Flow.

9. As musicians perform, they tap into energies from their inner core and transpose these energies into musical vibrations through their instruments. Drawing from the vigorous energies being translated into musical vibrations by the performers, feel yourself resonating with vitality, endurance, and energy. Visualize yourself in full health, happily and actively concluding work on your hobby or activity.

10. Conclude the visualization by imagining yourself looking forward to returning to work on this project or activity in the near future. If you choose to move on to other projects or adventures, visualize yourself actively planning to begin work on those fresh, new endeavors.

11. Having empowered yourself through the help of music and visualization, you may now begin to use these same music backgrounds as a catalyst to help you bring some of these images to fruition in your daily life.[5]

Being one with the Tao seasons change, while the harmony of our world remains. That which in winter sleeps, in spring awakens. What rests in fall, in summer strives. Stray from the Tao, and seasons lose their rhythms. Disharmony becomes the norm. Music inspires as it relaxes, it expands while moving inward, lifts without touching, pulls without reaching, beckons without voices, conquers without doing. By simplifying the mystical, music adorns the path.

---

5. For a review on how these encoded musical cues may be automatically accessed during future endeavors, please refer to Acoustic Memory, page 291.

[M]usical activities are preserved while other cognitive functions fail. Alzheimer patients, despite aphasia and memory loss, continue to sing old songs and to dance to past tunes when given the chance.[6]

GOOD MUSIC AGES WELL.

♪

MUSICAL MENU 7
Top Songs of the '30s

"When Your Hair Has Turned to Silver"
"Happy Days Are Here Again"
"On the Sunny Side of the Street "
"Little White Lies"
"I Got Rhythm"
"Dream a Little Dream of Me"
"Good Night Sweetheart"
"Stardust"
"Brother, Can You Spare a Dime?"
"Night and Day"
"Stormy Weather"
"Smoke Gets In Your Eyes"
"Did You Ever See a Dream Walking?"
"Anything Goes"
"Lost in a Fog"
"You're the Top"

"I Get a Kick Out of You"
"Cheek to Cheek"
"On the Good Ship Lollipop"
"The Way You Look Tonight"
"It's De-Lovely"
"Pennies From Heaven"
"Once in a While"
"September in the Rain"
"Good Night, My Love"
"My Reverie"
"Heigh Ho"
"Ti Pi Tin"
"You Must Have Been a Beautiful Baby"
"Sunrise Serenade"
"Moonlight Serenade"
"If I Didn't Care"

6. David Aldridge and Gudrun Aldridge, "Two Epistemologies: Music Therapy and Medicine in the Treatment of Dementia," *Arts in Psychotherapy*, 1992, 19, 4, pp. 243-256 (p. 252).

♪

MUSICAL MENU 8
Top Songs of the '40s

"The Woodpecker Song"
"I'll Never Smile Again"
"When You Wish Upon a Star"
"Frenesì"
"Tonight We Love"
"Chattanooga Choo Choo"
"Intermezzo"
"Maria Elena"
"This is Worth Fighting For"
"The White Cliffs of Dover"
"Don't Sit Under the Apple Tree"
"Tangerine"
"White Christmas"
"That Old Black Magic"
"Don't Get Around Much
     Anymore"
"Paper Doll"
"Mairzy Doats"
"I'll Be Seeing You"
"Besame Mucho"

"It Had to Be You"
"Don't Fence Me In"
"It's Been a Long, Long Time"
"Accentuate the Positive"
"Sentimental Journey"
"Oh! What It Seemed to Be"
"Let it Snow!"
"Personality"
"The Gypsy"
"Peg O' My Heart"
"For Sentimental Reasons"
"Linda"
"Buttons and Bows"
"I'm Looking Over a Four Leaf
     Clover"
"Nature Boy"
"A Tree in the Meadow"
"Some Enchanted Evening"
"Cruising Down the River"
"I Can Dream, Can't I?"

♪

MUSICAL MENU 9
Top Songs of the '50s

"My Foolish Heart"
"Bewitched"
"Goodnight Irene"
"Mona Lisa"
"Frosty the Snowman"

"Too Young"
"Because of You"
"Hello, Young Lovers"
"Tennessee Waltz"
"If"

"Slow Poke"
"Wheel of Fortune"
"Kiss of Fire"
"Glow Worm"
"How Much is That Doggie in the Window?"
"Your Cheatin' Heart"
"Ebb Tide"
"Stranger in Paradise"
"Young at Heart"
"Three Coins in the Fountain"
"Sh-Boom"
"Mister Sandman"
"The Ballad of Davy Crockett"
"Unchained Melody"
"Cherry Pink and Apple Blossom White"
"Rock Around the Clock"
"Love is a Many-Splendored Thing"

"Heartbreak Hotel"
"Moonglow"
"Love Me Tender"
"Whatever Will Be, Will Be"
"Love Letters in the Sand"
"Tammy"
"All Shook Up"
"April Love"
"The Purple People Eater"
"Peggy Sue"
"Volare"
"All I Have to Do Is Dream"
"It's All in the Game"
"The Chipmunk Song"
"Smoke Gets in Your Eyes"
"Come Softly to Me"
"Mack the Knife"

♪

MUSICAL MENU 10
Top Songs of the '60s

"Theme from A Summer Place"
"Cathy's Clown"
"Itsy Bitsy Bikini"
"Save the Last Dance For Me"
"Are You Lonesome Tonight?"
"Tossin' and Turnin'"
"Hit the Road, Jack"
"Take Good Care of My Baby"
"Moon River"
"Peppermint Twist"
"I Can't Stop Loving You"
"Sherry"

"I Left My Heart in San Francisco"
"He's So Fine"
"Sukiyaki"
"More"
"Blue Velvet"
"Dominique"
"I Want to Hold Your Hand"
"She Loves You"
"Hello Dolly"
"People"
"A Hard Day's Night"
"Oh, Pretty Woman"

"I Feel Fine"
"Downtown"
"Goldfinger"
"King of the Road"
"Yesterday"
"Help!"
"Satisfaction"
"A Taste of Honey"
"The Shadow of Your Smile"
"Strangers in the Night"
"The Ballad of the Green Berets"
"Michele"
"Somewhere My Love"
"Winchester Cathedral"
"This Is My Song"
"It Must Be Him"

"To Sir With Love"
"Gentle On My Mind"
"Love Is Blue"
"Honey"
"This Guy's In Love With You"
"Hey Jude"
"Those Were the Days"
"Wichita Lineman"
"Traces"
"A Boy Named Sue"
"Aquarius/Let the Sunshine In"
"Jean"
"Raindrops Keep Fallin' On My Head"
"Leaving On a Jet Plane"

♪

MUSICAL MENU 11

Top Songs of the '70s

"Bridge Over Troubled Water"
"Let it Be"
"Everything is Beautiful"
"Close To You"
"We've Only Just Begun"
"Fire and Rain"
"Something "
"It's Impossible"
"Where Do I Begin?"
"It's Too Late"
"Baby, I'm a Want You"
"American Pie"
"Without You"

"Alone Again (Naturally)"
"The First Time Ever I Saw Your Face"
"Dueling Banjos"
"Tie a Yellow Ribbon Round the Ole Oak Tree "
"And I Love You So"
"Loves Me Like a Rock"
"Time in a Bottle"
"The Way We Were"
"The Entertainer"
"Annie's Song"
"I Honestly Love You"

"My Eyes Adored You"
"Angie Baby"
"Have You Never Been Mellow?"
"Feelings"
"Wildfire"
"I Write the Songs"
"Fifty Ways to Leave Your Lover"
"Silly Love Songs"
"Muskrat Love"
"After the Loving"
"Evergreen"
"When I Need You"

"How Deep Is Your Love?"
"Just the Way You Are"
"We'll Never Have to Say Goodbye
   Again"
"Bluer Than Blue"
"Three Times a Lady"
"Time Passages"
"You Don't Bring Me Flowers"
"Crazy Love"
"Lead Me On"
"You're Only Lonely"

Sound Idea

Remember, whenever you need a
psychological, vibrational, or rejuvenating
boost, you have the ability to trigger this vitality and motivation through exposing yourself to
the music of your youth.

Additional Reading

J. David Boyle, Glenn L. Hosterman, & Darhyl S. Ramsey, "Factors Influencing Pop Music Preferences of Young People," *Journal of Research in Music Education*, 1981, 29, 1, pp. 47-55 (pp. 54-55).

Alicia Clair Gibbons, "Popular Music Preferences of Elderly People," *Journal of Music Therapy*, 24, 1977, pp.180–189 (p. 188).

David S. Smith, "An Age-Based Comparison of Humor in Selected Musical Compositions," *Journal of Music Therapy*, 1994, 31,3, pp. 206–219 (p. 206).

———. "Preferences for Differentiated Frequency Loudness Levels in Older Adult Music Listening," *Journal of Music Therapy*, 1989, 36, 1, pp. 18–29 (p. 28).

15

Physical Exercise and Music

*Aside from making exercise more pleasant, allowing you to stay with
your exercise program, it (music) keeps you from getting tired and
enables you to push harder with less effort. It also regulates your
breathing and promotes better muscle coordination.*[1]

The courting, dating, engagement, and marriage of music to sports,
or exercise, have become so intertwined that in recent times it has
become difficult to think of one without the other. After all, music—as
colorful vibrations—encourages movement, or dancing. Exercise, on the
other hand, is very much like art in motion, or, again, dancing. And dancing, like exercise, can be performed with a partner, along with a group or
alone.

> The effect which music has upon repetitive physical actions is
> predominantly rhythmic. . . . Breathing, walking, the heart-
> beat, and sexual intercourse are all rhythmical aspects of our
> physical being.[2]

Can you imagine a modern day aerobic exercise class without a music background? A military parade in the absence of a drum corps setting the
pounding pace with their marching cadence? Halftime during a college
bowl game without the band? The world of sports is rich with historic and

---

1. Stephanie Merritt, *Mind, Music and Imagery* (New York: Penguin Books, 1990), p. 106.
2. Anthony Storr, *Music and the Mind* (New York: Free Press, 1992), p. 33.

stereotypical sounds which are, invariably, inseparable from the sport, itself. For instance, it is difficult, if not impossible, to think about a table tennis match without the simple "musical cadence" of the ball, "ping-ponging" back and forth across the table. The soft, but yet powerful popping "thuds" of tennis balls as two rhythmic players exchange smooth, sweeping motions answering each other's challenging strides. The indistinguishable "sweet crack" of a baseball bat meeting a 92 mph fastball on a fresh spring day. Or, if the batter misses, the "thump" of 92 mph cowhide finding a temporary home in the catcher's thick, cushiony leader mitt. The roar of a powerful car engine dispatching into high gear as it thunders across the speedway. The desperate breathing and grunting of two runners edging each other as they rapidly approach the finish line. The "swish" of a basketball passing effortlessly through the net. Or the eerie echo of a basketball being dribbled in an large, empty gym. The explosive burst of a capacity football crowd when the home team scores the "go ahead" touchdown. The sound of "music," in effect, is relative to the heAr and now.[3]

> [C]hoosing the right music becomes more complex than having the pitch or frequency levels correspond to the swiftness or slowness of your movements. Other factors to be considered are the amount of concentration, grace, and skill your sport or exercise requires, the level of self-awareness and self-esteem needed on your part to perform well, and whether or not you need to avoid high-intensity stress or be motivated by its presence.[4]

Kate Gfeller, a professor from the University of Iowa, conducted a study which examined the attitudes of young adults (ages 18 to 30) regarding their musical preferences and attitudes when used in conjunction with aerobic fitness activities. Her study found that ". . . 97% indicated that music made a difference in their class performance. Specifically, musical style (96%), tempo (96%), rhythm (94%) and extramusical associations evoked by music (93%) were the musical components most effective in aiding aerobic activity. Ninety-seven percent of the subjects responded that music improves mental attitude toward the activity, while 79% indicated that music aids in pacing, strength, and endurance."[5]

---

3. See HeAr and Now, page 243.
4. Barbara Anne Scarantino, *Music Power: Creative Living through the Joys of Music* (New York: Dodd, Mead, 1987), p. 88.
5. Kate Gfeller, "Musical Components and Styles Preferred by Young Adults for Aerobic Fitness Activities," *Journal of Music Therapy*, 1988, 25, pp. 28–43 (p. 28).

Other findings from her study indicated "music benefits activity, both in terms of increasing motivation and in helping to set the pace of exercise; the use of preferred music is essential, as matching the music to the peoples' tastes tends to facilitate active focusing on the activity; music selected should provide the appropriate rhythm to properly pace and coordinate the movements required by the activity; the music should evoke 'pleasant extramusical associations' such as images found in the movies 'Rocky' or 'Fame,' in which the characters triumph over adversities; the aerobic activity 'should optimally begin and end with stretching and warmup, with gradually reduced activity at the close.'"[6]

If you feel that you need a *reason* to exercise, feel free to choose one (or several) from the list below. The "why," as discussed in other sections of this book, is often of minor relevance.[7] As in many other situations, the *what* (exercise you choose), *where* (you do it), *when* (you take the time), and *how* (you execute your program) is what is truly important.[8]

Reasons to Exercise

Exercise has been found to be effective in:
- Improving muscle tone;
- Reducing insomnia;
- Rejuvenating our immune systems;
- Improving digestion;
- Stimulating blood flow and vascular circulation;
- Regenerating skeletal joints;
- Clearing our minds and enhancing levels of concentration;
- Building up stamina and reducing fatigue;
- Decreasing cholesterol levels;
- Lowering blood pressure;
- Strengthening our hearts and lungs;
- Generally "cleaning out" our mental, physical, emotional systems;
- Strengthening our respiratory systems;
- Preventing coronary heart disease;
- burning calories and helping to prevent obesity;

6. Gfeller, "Musical Components and Styles Preferred by Young Adults for Aerobic Fitness Activities," p. 41.

7. See Whys, page 303.

8. Before altering your regular activity level, especially if you have a medical condition or any other concerns with regard to initiating an exercise program, it is strongly suggested that you consult with your family physician.

- Dispelling muscular tension;
- Increasing self-esteem and confidence;
- Helping to lift depression;
- Reducing anger and frustration;
- Lessening anxiety;
- Increasing our bodies' metabolic rates;
- Refreshing the body and mind, increasing alertness and tolerance;
- Helping one to simply "feel good!"

How Can Music Help?

There are a number of ways you can use music to enhance and enliven an exercise program. The energy that music generates can motivate you to get started, to maintain your desired rhythmic page, and to regulate your personally-selected program intensity. While it blocks extraneous noise with more desirable sounds, music will also automatically transform otherwise tedious tasks into recreational activities, making your exercise programs a welcome part of each day. In addition, studies indicate that music can further enhance physical activities by effectively lowering blood pressure, regulating breathing, and helping to align mind-body coordination. Preselected musical backgrounds can be programmed to function as timers, setting the desired duration of personalized exercise programs. Finally, the time you invest on your exercises provides an ideal opportunity for either listening to old tunes you have long neglected, or experimenting with some of those new sounds you've heard so much about.

> When we value our bodies and listen to them more closely, we become more connected to ourselves and to the world around us.[9]

Stephanie Merritt's excellent book, *Mind, Music and Imagery*, discusses how conductors of large orchestras "live much longer than the average person. Even in their seventies and eighties they are healthy and well-balanced." According to Ms. Merritt, "Conductors, leading their orchestras, constantly move their arms above their heads, releasing the tightness in their necks and shoulders and exercising their heart muscles. This is among the best forms of aerobic exercise for your heart. The circulation and metabo-

9. Greg Johanson and Ron Kurtz, *Grace Unfolding* (New York: Bell Tower, 1991), p. 54.

lism of these conductors get greater stimulation than with any other kind of exercise. At the same time, they are taking in the full, rich sounds and vibrations of the music throughout their whole being."[10]

Earlier this year, Daphne, the owner of two local private health spas, stopped by my office seeking a consult with regard to enhancing the soundscape of her exercise facilities. During our initial visit, Daphne echoed a growing awareness shared by a rapidly increasing number of health facility directors with whom I have spoken. In essence, they firmly believe that providing the right musical ambiance in their health and fitness centers is as important as equipping it with the best training machinery; furnishing it with spacious, comfortable surroundings; and providing well-trained, courteous employees. Although she had personally attempted to program the music backgrounds for her health spas, she was running into a number of complications. Among the common complaints; the *same* music at the *same* volume was reportedly too loud/quiet, too fast/slow, or too modern/old fashioned.

One of Daphne's facilities, while conveniently located in a central suburban location, was designed to accommodate children, teens, adults and the elderly. The other facility was located across the street from a major university campus and mostly frequented by a college-age crowd. In effect, Daphne's primary problem was that she was trying to please too many different segments of the population with the same type of music. First, she had tried subscribing to a local, "canned" musical format from a local radio station. Predictably, the music proved too generic for the diverse groups of people to whom her health centers catered. Second, she tried programming the music herself. The problem with that, she quickly deduced, was that—before long—she fell into the trap of either playing music *she* wanted to hear, or trying to please each individual request. As she stated later, she felt like a "band taking requests!"

Although, because of the demographics involved, I suggested approaching the two spas as distinct entities, there were similar things we tried in each. First, in democratic fashion, we gave the members the opportunity to make their own choices. For each general area (running track, teen lounge, cardiovascular center, Nautilus room, free-weight area, relaxation lounge, fitness rooms) we provided every current member with a "musical menu" survey which offered various alternatives. Their choices— available through the subscription service at the local radio station— included "classic rock" (music from the '60s and '70s), top forty (whatev-

10. Merritt, *Mind, Music and Imagery,* pp. 118–119.

er popular tunes were in the charts at that time), jazz, country/ western, rhythm and blues, big band, alternative, heavy metal, new age, world beat, a mix (all of the above mixed at random), or silence (no music). Although, luckily, the different music types were available through the radio station, an alternative would have been to create a small library of compilation tapes such as those described in the section on "Entrainment" (see page 317).

Second, those enrolled in special, time-limited classes (Tai Chi, volleyball, yoga, water aerobics) voted on the music they would like to have playing throughout the duration of their program's tenure. Third, "personal theme days" were offered to those in the special classes whereas different people in the group were encouraged to bring their own tapes or CD's. Group participants were offered the option of signing up for these "theme days" on the first day of class. The choice of how to handle the music formats (group voting vs. signing up for "theme days") for these time-limited sessions was ultimately left to the individual instructors. This particular option proved very successful, as it supplied further motivation to those enrolled in the classes, while adding a sense of surprise and diversity to each class.

Fourth, a separate, individual meeting with the aerobics instructors generated an excellent series of entrainment tapes all of which contained warm up, progressive routines and cool-down music. In addition, different tapes were prepared for beginning, intermediate, and advanced level classes. Fifth, individuals in enclosed areas (racquetball courts, tanning beds) were given the opportunity of selecting their own music and volume while they occupied those rooms. Finally, for the children's (babysitting nursery) center we compiled a small library of both soothing and stimulating music which ranged from classic rock and baroque to Disney soundtracks and prerecorded nursery rhymes.

Once the music had been voted on, and the volumes set, complaints dropped significantly. Before long, feedback from both employees and members alike began to be increasingly expressed in the form of praise, commendation, and helpful recommendations. The combination of giving the members a certain amount of control[11] over their sound environment, and playing music which provided a better corresponding "fit," proved tremendously successful.

11. See Control, page 87.

EXERCISE 19:
Training through Entrainment

The purpose of this exercise is threefold. It is designed to provide a period of warm up, sustained performance, and cool-down.

Entrainment, of course, can be used to modify our present, existing mental and physical state in any direction. For the purpose of an exercise program, we can use entrainment music sequences to help our bodies and minds to "get into" the warm-up period, initiate and stimulate our active work-out, and help achieve a smooth, and comfortable cool-down period, maximizing the mental, emotional and physical benefits from our exercise programs.

Selecting the Music

The choice of the musical piece to be used by beginners requires careful thought and is more difficult than may appear on first consideration.[12] The music you select for this exercise will be determined by the level of exercise you wish to pursue. This may range from low, to moderate, and up into high intensity aerobics. Basically, aerobic exercise serves to strengthen our large muscle groups and cardiovascular system, and it enhances physical stamina. Some aerobic exercises include swimming, jogging, cross-country skiing, rowing, bicycling, fast-paced walking and, of course, dancing.

Low intensity exercise, although not as active and physically demanding as aerobic exercise, also increases physical strength and agility. Some of these exercises include moderate walking, stretching, yoga, tai-chi, and weight-lifting or body sculpting.

1. *Making your selections.* Before creating your entrainment tape, or selecting your entrainment music background, you need to determine your starting point, your mental and physical state *prior* to initiating your exercise program. Having determined your relative starting point, you can then begin to work up, and then down, from there.

---

12. Roberto Assagioli, *Psychosynthesis* (New York: Penguin, 1982), pp. 253–254.

2. *The warm-up period*. For all three exercise levels (slow, moderate, or high) your warm-up period should consist of at least ten to fifteen minutes of music with a moderately slow and steady pace. This should be music which has a moderately invigorating effect, and motivates you to begin getting mentally and physically ready to begin your exercise program.

If your exercise program consists of a low intensity workout your "sustained performance" selections should consist of music in which the *tempo* is slightly more vigorous than your warm-up selections. By using music as background for your exercise program, you have the additional advantage of selecting the number of selections which can be formatted to correlate exactly with the amount of time you wish to spend on this main portion of your workout (a "musical timer!").[13]

In effect, while preparing the selections to accompany you throughout your workout, you are also setting a "time-marker" to keep you abreast of how far along you are during each of your exercise sessions. During each period, the level of intensity you choose, and which can be regulated by the musical beat or tempo you select is, of course, relative to each individual. Before you begin, you need to make a personal decision regarding which tempo feels "just right" for *you*. Your "cool-down" selections should reflect a similar tempo to the "warm-up" music, but should have more of a "winding-down," calming, or relaxing "feel" or associations than those chosen for the warm-up. Again, that "feel" is relative to each person. Entrainment music sequence examples, including warm up, sustain (regular and high intensity) and cool down are provided at the end of this section.

3. *The active period: Sustained performance*. For the aerobic exercises you will want the total length of your "sustained performance" selections to dictate the amount of time you wish to spend on this main portion of your workout (if you wish to exercise vigorously for thirty minutes, choose a music sequence that will last that period of time). After your initial warm-up, you will need to significantly pick up the background tempo of the music to one which is more stimulating.

The music pulse for this active exercise period should be quite lively, dynamic, and energetic, motivating you to activate your inner resources and externalize your energies. The general "feel" and intensity of the musical tempo should always reflect *your* personal preference and relative level

13. See Time Management, page 111.

of physical capability and endurance. Throughout this exercise you have the luxury of functioning as director, choreographer and engineer—as well as performer—within your own musical adventure.

4. *The "cool-down."* The "cool-down" period should consist of ten to fifteen minutes of music which "wind-down," decelerating in terms of pulse and activity. The selections for this very important portion of your aerobics training should be approached to reflect a less agitated, quieter, and temperate state of being. Rather than entraining you "down," this sequence should culminate in helping you to achieve a state of "relaxed alertness."

As explained in the "Entrainment" section of this book, the most efficient way to approach this musical adjunct to exercising is to create your own "exercise entrainment tapes" in a way that will reflect your typical, personalized work-outs. In this manner, after an initial minor investment in time preparing your first tape, you can continue to enjoy the benefits of your own "musical scores" whenever you are ready for your next "performance." Further, by creating a number of tapes using different types of music of different styles (jazz, pop, alternative, rock, country) and tempos (high energy, medium pace, alternating rhythms), you can guarantee for yourself a growing library of "entrainment exercise" tapes that will help to keep away monotony while adding a colorful diversity to your exercise regimens.

Be aware of the contact between your feet and the Earth. Walk as if you are kissing the Earth with your feet.[14]

---

14. Thich Nhat Hanh, *Peace is Every Step*, (New York: Bantam Books, 1991), p. 28.

♪

Musical Menu 12

Entrainment Sequence: Big Band

Warm Up:
> Harry James: "Ciribiribin"
> Glen Miller: "A String of Pearls"

Sustain:
> Glen Miller: "In The Mood"
> Duke Ellington: "Take the 'A' Train"
> Woody Herman: "Woodchopper's Ball"
> Count Basie: "One O'Clock Jump"
> Tommy Dorsey: "Opus One"
> Charlie Barnet: "Skyliner"
> Stan Kenton: "Taboo"
> The Hi-Los: "Rockin Chair"

Sustaining High Energy:
> Bob Crosby: "South Rampart Street Parade"
> Sy Oliver: "Well, Git It"
> Benny Goodman: "Let's Dance"

Cool Down:
> Ink Spots: "If I Didn't Care"
> The Mills Brothers: "Paper Doll"

♪

Musical Menu 13

Entrainment Sequence: '60s Pop

Warm Up:
> Lovin' Spoonful: "Daydream"
> The (Young) Rascals: "A Beautiful Morning"

Sustaining Performance:

    Lovin' Spoonful: "Do You Believe in Magic"
    Sly and The Family Stone: "Dance To the Music"
    ————. "I Want To Take You Higher"
    Tommy James and the Shondells: "Mony Mony"
    Wilson Pickett: "In The Midnight Hour"
    ————. "Land of 1,000 Dances"
    ————. "Funky Broadway"
    The (Young) Rascals: "Good Lovin'"
    ————. "Come On Up"
    ————. "People Got To Be Free"
    ————. "See"
    Mitch Ryder and the Detroit Wheels: "Jenny Take a Ride!"
    ————. "Little Latin Lupe Lu"
    ————. "Shake a Tail Feather"
    ————. "Devil With a Blue Dress/Good Golly Miss Molly"
    ————. "Sock It To Me Baby"
    Spencer Davis Group: "Gimme Some Lovin'"
    ————. "I'm A Man"
    Them: "Gloria"

Cool Down:

    The (Young) Rascals: "Groovin"
    ————. "Love is a Beautiful Thing"

♪

MUSICAL MENU 14

Entrainment Sequence for Limited Budgets

The following three albums are filled with moderate to high level tunes that can be arranged to provide excellent aerobic exercise routines in two different styles. Each album also has at least one tune that can be used as a warm up/cool down tune.

    Fine Young Cannibals: *The Raw and The Cooked.* '80s pop.
      Dance music. Steady driving beats and catchy melodies.
      Use song #9, "As Hard As It Is," for both your "warm up"

and "cool down" and arrange (or program) the remainder of the album as a moderate to high energy 40-minute work out.

The B-52's: *Cosmic Thing*. Dance music. Again, steady driving beats, and very catchy melodies. '80s pop. Use song #10, "Follow Your Bliss" as your warm up/cool down and arrange (or program) the other nine songs in any sequence to fit your desired intensity and sustain levels. Total album length: just over 47 minutes.

Elastica: *Elastica*. '90s pop. Alternative dance music. Moderate to high energy beats with catchy melodies. Try using songs #8, "Indian Song," #6, "Hold Me Now," and #7, "S.O.F.T." for your warm up/cool down and arrange (or program) the other thirteen songs in any progression you choose to reflect the level of intensity you desire. The entire album is just over 40 minutes in length.

Other popular albums that can be used in this manner include Cyndi Lauper's *She's So Unusual*, and Michael Jackson's *Bad*, or *Thriller*.

Various Orchestras: *Power Classics*. High energy classical masterpieces. Box compilation of five CDs, or cassettes, totaling 5 hours 14 minutes.

For additional stimulating and soothing music suggestions, see pages 20, and 55.

PART THREE

SOCIAL ISSUES

Even silent movies had music.

16

Improving Communication

A melody is like a marriage of notes—each note dependent on
another for harmony. While one note rests, another ferments, where
one leads, another follows. Committed to harmony their union
depends on clear communication.

Communication is the essence of all successful relationships. "In all communication the signal that transmits the information is a major determinant of the interpretation of the message by the receiver."[1] Scientific evidence has demonstrated that music serves as an efficient signal in communicating emotional messages. Take the emotion out of a message and you might as well be imparting information or sharing your data base in Morse code. Based on findings gathered from a series of experiments, researchers have proposed that music provides a powerful means of increasing receptiveness and bridging discrepancies between any two individuals.[2] In other words, it helps us to bond with one another. According to other studies, multidimensional, non-verbal characteristics in music (which stimulates right-brain processing) help to cross through linear, verbal communication channels.[3] In short, music helps us to get beyond ver-

---

1. S. Nielzèn and Z. Cesarec, "On the Perception of Emotional Meaning in Music," *Psychology of Music,* 1981, 9, pp. 17–31 (p. 7).
2. See K. A. Brydon and W. R. Nugent, "Musical Metaphor as a Means of Therapeutic Communication," *Journal of Music Therapy,* 1979, 16, pp. 149–153.
3. See H. L. Bonny, "Music and Healing," *Music Therapy,* 1986, 6A, pp. 3–12.

bal barriers, helping to enrich the meaning behind our intended messages at emotional, psychological and thinking levels.

WITHOUT RESORTING TO
LOGICAL REASONING OR ARGUMENT
MUSIC DOES NOT SEEK TO PERSUADE, CONVERT, OR OVERCOME.
RATHER, IT EMBRACES ALL THINGS EQUALLY.

A number of studies have indicated that background music can be quite helpful in initial, stressful encounters, making music an ideal adjunct when a situation calls for approaching someone for the first time, or for socializing in uncomfortable environments. Similar studies have also indicated that soothing background music can be very helpful in encouraging increased verbal communication.[4] Simply, the evidence seems to indicate that music facilitates the relationship building process.

> Facilitating communication among family members seems to be the most common use of music in family treatment. The nonverbal nature of music and the other arts makes them well-suited to accomplish the task of promoting non-threatening and relaxed communications among family members.[5]

Regardless of the type of relationship (collegial, professional, romantic, social, familial) there are certain attributes which are essential to successful communication. Active listening (being genuinely involved in what the other person is saying), for instance, is paramount. A lot of people can effectively "tune-in" to sitcoms and daily soap operas, quickly becoming totally encapsulated by the script and character plot. When involved in the midst of an *actual*, real life "soap-opera" in face-to-face encounters, however, they suddenly switch to a number of automatic techniques. Some of these are problem-solving or advice giving ("What you *should* do . . ."), internalizing or personalizing ("I would *never* do that!"), competing ("Oh, really, *my* daughter was doing that by the time she was 2!"), prejudging

---

4. See V. N. Stratton and A. H. Zalanowski, "The Relationship Between Music, Degree of Liking and Self-Reported Relaxation," *Journal of Music Therapy*, 1984b, 21, pp. 184–192; and V. N. Stratton and A. H. Zalanowski, "The Effect of Background Music on Verbal Interaction in Groups," *Journal of Music Therapy*, 1984a, 21, pp. 16–21.
5. Anthony Decuir, "Trends in Music and Family Therapy," *The Arts in Psychotherapy*, 1991,18, 3, pp. 195–200 (p. 199).

("It's obvious this person has never had a *real* job!") or defensiveness ("Now . . . *I* never said that!").

Focusing and concentrating on what is actually being said are essential cornerstones of clear communication which we often take for granted. Daydreaming ("I would look *so* good in a convertible!") and future planning ("And *after* I mow the lawn I need to . . . ") are typical examples of what gets in the way of "being"[6] with others as they share their lives through communication. Along those lines, being "in the heAr and now"[7] (in the moment) is indispensable. There is nothing worse than being caught off-guard—thinking of whether we remembered to program our VCR, for instance—while someone is waiting for an empathic response on a personal dilemma they just shared with us! Spontaneity adds color to communicating, while, letting go of expectations[8] (refraining from finishing the other person's sentences, or trying to guess or predict what they may be about to say), is surely easier than trying to read another person's mind.

GIVING A SPEECH, OR CARRYING ON A CONVERSATION, WORDS HAVE LITTLE VALUE IF THERE IS NO HARMONY WITHIN THE MESSAGE.

In musical terms, communication can also be perceived as "harmonizing" with the other person. It's about "getting in sync," and establishing a common pulse, or rhythm, with your "dancing" partner. Along those lines, we may choose to think of it as being involved in a dance where the lead is constantly shared, flowing back and forth between the two communicators. You may have heard of the by now common advice in public speaking situations to "visualize a naked audience." A metaphor I share with my patients to help them to let go of the struggling often involved in person-to-person interactions is to visualize, or feel themselves, involved in a tug-of-war. In other words, "let go of the rope and stop competing!" For instance, while someone is telling you about their exciting trip to "the shore" this past summer it's best not to interrupt them to let them know how wonderful Maui was during *your* summer vacation!

In addition to background music's ability to help "set the pace" during casual conversations, it can also help to enhance our listening and bonding sensitivities.

6. See Being Versus Trying to Be, page 261.
7. See HeAr and Now, page 243.
8. See Expectations, page 293.

Music, like speech, involves the processing of sequentially presented elements, the organization of these elements into larger
more meaningful patterns and the recognition of these patterns
despite variations in how they are produced (e.g., different
speakers or instruments).[9]

Among other communicational factors affected by music, soothing background music in particular increases our general impression of the person
with whom we are engaging. For my doctoral dissertation, for example, I
designed a study to evaluate whether preselected music would serve to
improve the communication between two individuals, a client and a counselor, during an initial encounter. Research very strongly supports the
notion that the first session between any two individuals is extremely
important in terms of one making a lasting impression. Assessing whether
a music background could in any way enhance such a first impression, particularly between two strangers in what is, for many people, an uncomfortable situation, would tend to suggest that such music would provide a
very powerful adjunct in such situations.

As predicted, findings from my study indicated that a soothing
baroque musical background tends to *significantly* increase the participants' perception of expertness, attractiveness, and trustworthiness for one
another. In addition, the largo movements from string concertos which I
selected as the background music for my study also tended to strongly
influence the individuals' perceptions of smoothness, depth, arousal, and
positivity during the interactions, as well as helping to reduce their anxiety. By the end of the sessions, the counselors, as well as the clients
involved in the study, almost unanimously indicated that the music had
proven extremely effective in helping them feel at ease, comfortable and
quite positive during these initial meetings.[10]

Drawing from the above findings and observations, I often prescribe
regular music listening sessions to patients who have difficulty in listening, focusing, or processing information while communicating with others. Typically, problems with communication are often closely related to an
inability to listen to what the person is saying (rather than trying to guess
ahead), remaining in the present (rather than thinking what you need to
do later, or what this person is "probably going to say" based on what

9. Barbara Morrongiello, "Effects of Training on Children's Perception of Music: A Review," *Psychology of Music*, 1992, 20, 1, pp. 29–41 (p. 38).
10. John M. Ortiz, *The Facilitating Effects of Soothing Background Music on an Initial Counseling Session*, unpublished doctoral dissertation, The Pennsylvania State University, 1991d.

he/she has said before), and "being" (flowing, rather than, for instance, *trying* to find some mutual ground) with the other individual.

Sound Idea

Listen, and trust your ability
to hear.

EXERCISE 20:

Listening and Communication Enhancement

1. Select a block of about twenty to thirty minutes sometime during your day when you will not be disturbed.

2. Pick out a few musical selections—enough to fill the time selected above.

3. Accept the mind-set that, during those twenty to thirty minutes, *your only responsibility will be to become completely involved with the music and its components.*

4. As you sit, or lie, comfortably, place an emphasis on the following goals:

- Being with the music—lyrics, instruments, or melody, the choice is yours— rather than "trying" to hear something specific;
- Remaining in the heAr and now;
- Listening (see Educating the Ear, page 213).

As you "practice" listening, being, and being present with the music, allow yourself to flow with the music. Hear it as it is, the whole, as well as the sum of the parts. Allow yourself to experience the moment. With practice, the sessions will help you to develop a keener sense in those three very essential areas of communication.

> *Through balance, music bridges cultures. Inherent in all that there*
> *is, it celebrates diversity. It knows no ethnicity, caters to no race,*
> *honors all ages, respects both genders. It prays to no religion, intuits*
> *no philosophy. It sympathizes with all creeds, and synchronizes with*
> *time. Having no ego, music exists in accordance with the Tao.*

Music has also been called the universal language. It is often frustrating when we cannot verbally communicate with individuals who speak languages different from our own. Sometimes, due to cultural differences, it is quite difficult to convey desired images or information with people from other lands, or who have cultural or ethnic backgrounds distinctively different from our own. Music seems to have the ability to transcend those barriers and bridge the gaps that exist with verbal communication.

Presently, with the growing emphasis on various types of world music, many of us are reaping the endless benefits of experiencing other cultures through the rhythms, beats, and melodies from remote, exotic places. Our contemporaries in places such as South America, Africa, China, Japan, and other areas physically remote from our own have for years been "turned on" to our culture via American music. More recently, however, it seems that the time has arrived when these cultures are now effectively communicating the essence of their cultures to us through their own musical roots.

Music is an endless quest for harmony; war is an endless quest for peace; rhythm is an endless quest for stillness; diversity is an endless quest for unity. Readers are encouraged to review the following sections for additional suggestions in helping to facilitate communication: Relationships, page 177, Centering, page 223, Letting Go, page 249, and Clearing the Mind, page 267.

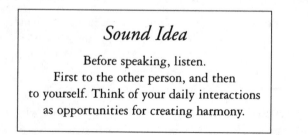

Sound Idea

Before speaking, listen.
First to the other person, and then
to yourself. Think of your daily interactions
as opportunities for creating harmony.

Additional Reading

For further reading on how music affects communication, the following articles and books are suggested:

R. Brim, "The Effect of Personality Variables, Dogmatism and Repression-Sensitization Upon Response to Music," *Journal of Music Therapy*, 1978, 15, pp. 74–87.

L. Bunt, V. Wren and D. Pike, "Music Therapy in a General Hospital's Psychiatric Unit—An Evaluation of a Pilot Eight Week Programme." *Journal of British Music Therapy*, 1987, 1, pp. 22–28.

M. Priestley, "Music and the shadow," *Music Therapy*, 1987, 6, pp. 20-27.

W. W. Sears, "Processes in Music Therapy," in E. T. Gaston (ed.), *Music in Therapy*, (New York: Macmillan, 1968), pp. 116–136.

P. K. Shehan, "Student Preferences for Ethnic Music Styles," *Contributions to Music Education*, 1983, 9, pp. 21–28.

V. N. Stratton and A. H. Zalanowski, "The Effects of Music and Paintings on Mood," *Journal of Music Therapy*, 1989, 26, pp. 30–41.

K. Swanwick, "Can There Be Objectivity in Listening to Music?" *Psychology of Music*, 1975, 3, pp. 17–23.

17

Now in tune, now out of tune, now too
sharp, now too flat. Now consonant, now
dissonant, now in union, now in conflict.
Each of us is but a single note in the
symphony of life.

Companionship

*A melody is like a friend without jealousy, without reservations,
without expectations. Unconditionally, a melody can be a selfless ally
when we're happy, a crutch when we're sad.*

Throughout the course of our lives, we may often hear the words, "I just want to be left alone." How many times, however, have we heard the sentiment, "I just want to be lonely?" The word "lonely" is generally defined as "being without company," or "being cut-off from others." Being "alone," however, is defined as being "separated from others," an objective fact which involves "being by oneself."

At different points during our lives, most of us experience both "loneliness," and "aloneness." One may be all alone (without anyone else around) in a large, empty building, and feel completely comfortable. On the other hand, one may be in the middle of a New Year's party, riding a float surrounded by thousands during a parade, or be sitting in the midst of 60,000 at a sports event and feel extremely lonely, desolate, forlorn.

In general, loneliness can result from either external circumstances (moving to a new environment, beginning a new job, retirement, divorce) or internal issues (poor social or communication skills, low self-image, shyness, fear of rejection). Being alone, on the other hand, can result from choice (wanting time for yourself), or from an inability to find or maintain mature relationships.

In either case, this chapter presents various ways in which music can be used to alleviate feelings of loneliness and to provide us with pleasant and diverse companionship when (being) alone.

[L]istening to music makes us aware of important aspects of ourselves . . . music makes us whole again.[1]

Using Music to Help Transcend Loneliness or Aloneness

1. *Music takes the stillness out of silence.* Silence is generally associated with emptiness, solace, or loneliness. Music provides an ambiance of energy. By occupying that space where silence created a void, music can add a sense of aliveness.

2. *Music moves.* Music increases body metabolism, alters muscular energy, and reduces physical fatigue. With its energizing rhythms, it motivates us to move out of our frozen existence. Music arouses our inner pulse and entices us to find synchronicity[2] with external pulsing vibrations. It challenges us to dance with our aloneness. On the other hand, it can often serve to motivate us to "move out of our present shell," energizing us to step out into the world and pursue new adventures. Go out and listen to a good jazz band, attend a symphony, invite a friend to a dance.

3. *Music inspires.* As artists, inspirational melodies and tantalizing rhythmic patterns challenge our minds and stir our emotions. Released from silence, musical vibrations are translated into radiant colors, quenching a thirsting canvas.

4. *Music enhances visualization.* Music is to our auditory senses what color is to vision. Music is auditory colors. It's what colors sound like when we listen. It is impossible to be alone when the mind is enriched with its own creativity.

---

1. Anthony Storr, *Music and the Mind* (New York: The Free Press, 1992), p. 147.
2. See Rhythmic Synchronicity, page 275.

5. *Music helps to increase concentration and generate creativity*. For the writer, the notes, resonating in grammatical form, begin to appear filling page after page of that previously unwritten book.

6. *Music flows*. Once released, whether from the heart, an instrument, or a written score, music does not "try." It simply *is*. In its presence, we have the propensity to follow along. To merge and pour forth, to flourish.

7. *Music is timeless*. While keeping us firmly grounded in the present, music accompanies us as we visit the past, and moves us to unfurl the future that spreads before us.

8. *Music cleanses the mind*. By bringing us to the heAr and now,[3] and arousing mental, physical and emotional movement, music unbinds us to move out of stagnating, negative, and self-defeating moods and move on with our lives. Soothing, it slows the mind, allowing it to regenerate, which rejuvenates the body, and arouses the emotions.

9. *Music frees us*. Alone with our music we can be Mozart, Bach, Beethoven, the Beatles, Barbara Streisand, Elvis, Madonna, Capurso, Kiri Te Kanawa, The Supremes, The Temptations, Neville Marriner, Boyz II Men, Mariah Carey, or any other performer or conductor who has ever lived, playing a solo, making a recording, or conducting an orchestra to an audience of millions.

10. *Music can provide us with goals*. Music gives us a solid reason, and ample motivation, for learning to dance. Try out, even for a minor part, in a small, local play. Take lessons on an instrument you always dreamed of playing. Take voice lessons. Join your church choir. Go and perform at a local coffee shop, or entertain at a family gathering during the holidays. Start working on increasing a comprehensive music collection.

Finally, although feelings of loneliness can be turned into a positive (it can motivate us to become more active, take control of our lives, initiate change) they can also lead to sadness, depression, isolation, or alienation. This is a sense of being which is often described as emptiness, or hollowness. As an instrument of nature, next time that you perceive that sense of being hollow, remember that without the hollowness of open spaces most

---

3. See HeAr and Now, page 243.

instruments would be merely blocks of wood, skin, metal, glass, string, or otherwise inert materials. When feeling lonely, or alone, music will always provide a warm, trusting, dependable companion. It quickly, and pleasantly, reminds us that harmony is a state of mind.

Sound Idea

Next time you make plans to take a long trip, don't forget to include your favorite tapes or CDs. They're great company and will help to keep you awake.

18

IF NOISE AND SILENCE CAN CO-EXIST,
THEN SO CAN WE.

Relationship Issues

*Fortunately, there is the other kind of person: the one who is always
in sync, who is such a joy, who seems to sense what move you will
make next. Anything you do with him or her is like a dance.*[1]

We have already learned that effective communication is the cornerstone of most, if not all, successful relationships. In general, the difference between a relationship either failing or flourishing usually revolves around the level and quality of communication that exists between the parties involved. It is not surprising, then, that one of the most typical problems found among relationships stems from discordant, or dis-harmonious communication.

There are a number of ways in which music can be used to help develop, improve, and maintain positive, comfortable relationships by enhancing communication. For example, music helps to sharpen listening as well as focusing skills, both of which are prerequisites for clear communication. By developing, and maintaining, a heAr and now orientation and enhancing our listening sensitivities music also helps to efface old, distracting messages, improving our ability to cue in to the "lyrics" (or words) within the "song" (or message). In addition, by exposing us to the rich universe of rhythms and tempos used by different people, music serves to bridge social, cultural, and even economic gaps between people. In a sense, by improving

---

1. Edward T. Hall, *The Dance of Life* (New York: Doubleday, 1983), p. 163.

our ability to discern differences in intonation and other aural characteristics underlying our communication styles, music can help us to tune into the "harmony" or "dissonance" that accompanies any given interaction.

> A single tone by itself is not a melody. Only as it exists with other tones different from itself does a melody emerge.[2]

When involved in a relationship, regardless of its nature, there are several goals which we need to keep in mind.

• *Actively listen.* Listen with attention, openness and interest. Without judgment, prejudice, or expectation.[3]

• *Focus on the moment.* Listen in the present. HeAr the *now.*[4] Do not allow noise and messages from the past, or fears about what may or may not happen in the future, to affect what your partner is trying to convey at *this moment.*

• *Be empathic.* Make a concentrated effort to understand the other person's perspective or situation. Ask yourself how you would like to be treated if the roles were reversed. Listen in the same way you would like to be listened to.

• *Refrain from projecting.* As you feel the urge to interrupt, actively replace that urge with the cue to "breathe," or "listen." Avoid blame, sarcasm, or threats, as these will only force your partner into a defensive stance. Also, be aware of impulses to externalize, or project, your anger or frustration and convincing yourself that they are coming from the other person.

• *Echo a sense of caring and understanding.* Validate the other person's feelings and concerns by "echoing" back their message as you understand it. Let the other person know that you are hearing what is being said by acknowledging the message with a confirming response ("Just *hearing* the type of day you've had leaves me exhausted," or "You sound angry!").

• *Ask for clarification.* If unsure of what your partner is attempting to communicate, subtly and calmly ask for clarification of anything you don't

---

2. Joanne Crandall, *Self-Transformation Through Music* (Wheaton, IL: Theosophical Publishing House, 1986), p. 19.
3. See Educating the Ear, page 213 and Expectations, page 293.
4. See HeAr and Now, page 243.

understand. Ask for specific examples while avoiding "all or none," negatively phrased, and "always/never" statements ("You *never* do anything around the house!"). Rather, re-compose your messages more positively; "I *appreciate* that you always do the dishes and the laundry . . . " and specifically " . . . but I could really use your help *transporting the children* and *paying the bills*!").

• *Strive for harmony.* As you communicate your thoughts, feelings, and point of view, actively and consciously strive for harmony. Be positive. Take responsibility for your thoughts and feelings. Use "I" statements while being clear and specific about your needs ("I just want to be hugged right now"). The more sensitivity you show toward other people's feelings the more comfortable they will feel disclosing of themselves or making themselves available to you.

> We hold these truths to be self-evident, that all men and
> women are created equal . . . [5]

• *Shun false promises.* Attempt to find a harmonious, mutual solution to any discordant issue or situation without promising something you cannot, or will not, deliver.

• *Avoid conflict.* Remain aware that your goal is to achieve a peaceful and harmonious accord. Try to avoid unnecessary conflict or a negative escalation of the pressing situation. Inner music can be shared, but never compared.

• *Voice your feelings and thoughts: clarity is paramount!* If you are feeling unduly angry or depressed at the moment, and feel unready to listen openly and objectively, take a deep breath and communicate the fact that "this is not a good time" to discuss the situation at hand. Indicate you need some time for yourself and try to give a *clear* idea as to when it may be a better time to bring up the issue.

• *Practice.* Duets require more practice than solos.

> There can be no meaning in life without deep relationship,
> just as there can be no song without melody.[6]

5 Elizabeth Cady Stanton, from *Declaration of Sentiment*, First Woman's Rights Convention, 1848, in *The New International Dictionary of Quotations*, Hugh Rawson and Margaret Miner, eds. (New York: E. P. Dutton, 1986), p. 343.
6. Crandall, *Self-Transformation Through Music*, p. 20.

Sound Idea

Share a smile,
hear the harmony.

EXERCISE 21:

Enhancing Listening Sensitivity

Music can act as a transformer of shared meaning.[7]

A relationship, like a melody, cannot be simplified. Dissect the notes, and
you lose the essence. A melody is greater than the sum of its tones. In
searching for the heart of the melody, one finds the melody itself is the
heart.

1. Select, or purchase, a number of musical pieces which you may have
been wanting to hear for some time. Having made your selections, plan to
play the same pieces a number of times over a period of a few nights.

2. Take some time over the next few weeks (thirty minutes a night, at least
two or three nights per week, but preferably more often) to just *listen to the
music.*

3. Upon first hearing, allow yourself to flow with the music without anticipation or expectation[8] of where the melody may go, or what the lyrical
message of the song may be. Listen openly, and objectively.

4. After your initial exposure to the piece, begin exploring various listening experiences. At first, you may simply listen to the song or composition
while actively trying to hear something new and fresh. This may involve
listening for particularly interesting changes or nuances in melody or "hidden" messages in the lyrics which you may have missed the first time
around.

---

7. Leslie Bunt, *Music Therapy: An Art Beyond Words* (London: Routledge, 1994), p. 73.
8. See Expectations, page 293.

5. During a future hearing, try and *focus* on something *different* from what you heard the first couple of times. This may simply involve following the string or rhythm section. While consciously focusing on particular aspects of the music, actively and consciously allow the other musical components to play on, while you focus on the instrument(s) or component(s) you selected.

6. At another time you may choose to pick out a single voice, or instrument, and do your best to follow that single element throughout the entire piece. While attempting this exercise, notice how difficult it is to not allow other instruments or components of the music to "contaminate" your concentration.

7. The next time you listen to the piece attempt to listen from a stance of deeper emotional awareness. Try and hear the emotions that the composer, or performer, attempted to get across on this piece. Have you ever felt feelings similar to those conveyed by this music? Have you ever been in situations when this music could have provided a "perfect" soundtrack? Can you imagine times when you could have (emotionally) composed this very piece yourself?

8. Continue following the above patterns with the various selections you have chosen, and, in time, continue adding fresh new selections. To move further, and develop a keener sensitivity and listening acuity, once in a while you may choose to explore distinctive types of music. Each time you listen to these musical pieces *approach the experience as an adventure*. A rare opportunity to marvel in the richness of distinctive cultures, or to share feelings experienced and expressed by other individuals with whom you will very likely never have personal contact (the musicians, singer, composer).

Following these exercises will help you to develop basic listening and concentration skills, maximize your ability to remain "in the present," and develop patience. They will also help to relax you while exercising your mental capacities. With practice, not only will your abilities and sensitivities to listen, focus, and understand others be enhanced, but you will also be enriching your own personal musical universe.

IN BETWEEN THE SONG AND THE MEMORY,
BETWEEN THE MUSIC AND ITS PERCEPTION,
BETWEEN THE RHYTHM AND THE DANCE,
THERE IS THE TAO.

Additional Reading

For further reading on how music may affect relationships, you may refer to the following articles:

P. V. Glassford, "Staff Experimental Relaxation Group," *Australian Occupational Therapy Journal*, 1972, L9, pp. 51–54.

J. S. Goldman, "Toward a New Consciousness of the Sonic Healing Arts: The Therapeutic Use of Sound and Music for Personal and Planetary Health and Transformation," *Music Therapy*, 1988, 7, pp. 28–33.

T. B. Logan and A. R. Roberts, "The Effects of Different Types of Relaxation Music on Tension Level," *Journal of Music Therapy*, 1984, 21, pp. 177–185.

19

I LOVE, THE MELODY IN YOUR VOICE,
THE SOUND OF YOUR LAUGHTER,
THE RHYTHM OF YOUR WAYS,
THE BEATING OF YOUR HEART.
YOU, ARE MUSIC TO ME.

Romantic Intimacy

*On every level of life there is rhythm and entrainment. . . . During
relationships when two people are "in love" they appear to pulsate together.
When immersion into the pulse of love is interrupted with arguments
the couple always goes out of phase.*[1]

So powerful are the sensual/sexual powers of music and rhythm that
puritans throughout the ages have attempted to denounce and sup-
press it by affiliating it with negative and even satanic influences. The following particularly interesting attempt at condemnation, written in 1933
by Cyril Scott, is an excellent example. While aiming to deprecate its
effects, it instead serves to support the exquisite aphrodisiac powers of
music in general, and jazz in particular:

> Whereas at one time women were content with decorous flir-
> tations, a vast number of them are now constantly preoccupied
> with the search for erotic adventures, and have thus turned sex-
> ual passion into a species of hobby. Now, it is just this over-
> emphasis of the sex-nature, this wrong attitude towards it, for
> which Jazz-music has been responsible. The orgiastic element
> about its syncopated rhythm, entirely divorced from any more

---

1. John Beaulieu, *Music and Sound in the Healing Arts* (New York: Station Hill Press, 1987), p. 81.

exalted musical content, produced a hyper-excitement of the nerves and loosened the powers of self-control. It gave rise to a false exhilaration, a fictitious endurance, and insatiability resulting in a deleterious *moral* and physical reaction.[2]

More recent writings, however, have suggested more rational and objective perspectives:

> The effect of jazz syncopation is primarily sexual: the beat somehow ties in with the rhythm of sexuality in man and woman. In fact, hard, loud, relentless pulsation also has a similar effect. . . . Such rhythms actually possess the capacity to force the subtle energies of the body downward into this region of the anatomy, therefore increasing the outpouring into the bloodstream of sexual hormones.[3]

Making Musex

In many ways, the arts of making love and making music appear almost inexorably linked. While providing a feast for indulging the senses, both activities involve rhythm, passion, and delicate timing. Both offer unique opportunities for self-expression, adventurous experimentation, intimacy, and unbridled inspiration. As they each replenish and deplete, frustrate and delight, excite and mollify, both activities provide fertile ground for escape through private or shared fantasies. In addition, both music-making and lovemaking provide a forum through which we can improve our performance through practice and a growing awareness of ourselves as sexual, as well as musical, instruments.

Following are a number of factors you may consider in using music as an ideal tool to enhance romantic, or intimate, interludes.

• *First:* ask yourself *what* it is that you want the music to add to your romantic, sexual, or lovemaking experience. Is it intimacy? inspiration? increased potency? endurance? enhanced sensitivity? establishing a particular rhythmic pulse? passion? removed inhibitions enabling you to better communicate your fantasies? helping to set the mood for clear, open, and straight communication?

2. Cyril Scott, Music: *Its Secret Influence Throughout the Ages* (York Beach, ME: Samuel Weiser, 1958), p. 142.

3 David Tame, *The Secret Power of Music* (Rochester, VT: Destiny Books, 1984), p. 199.

- *Second:* select music possessing the emotional character to help you fulfill your sexual fantasies. A musical aphrodisiac. Turn to the Romantic Magic Nightclub Musical Menu on page 194 for music suggestions.

- *Third:* approach each sexual experience as an adventure, allowing the music to serve as your guide.

- *Fourth:* allow the music to serve as a constant, resonating cue to help you to enjoy the *process* of the sexual adventure, rather than simply aiming for the end result (orgasm).

- *Finally:* think of your lovemaking as an opportunity to make "musex."

Using music as a catalyst, draw from musical related images and associations to set a creative scenario for your special evening. For instance, you may imagine your lovemaking as a symphonic concert. You are the conductor, and your partner is the orchestra. Your sensations are the audience . . . arouse them!

WELCOME EACH VIBRATION WITH YOUR SKIN,
LISTEN WITH EVERY CELL OF YOUR BODY.

In a second scenario, you are the maestro. Here, your partner's body becomes a delicate and sensitive instrument. Just as a virtuoso performer can draw a limitless variety of sounds and vibrations from a musical instrument, an impassioned lover can liberate a universe of sounds, desires, and sensations from a willing recipient. Take turns being the instrument.

From another perspective, you can select from a universe of musical types and varieties to create the proper ambiance, or environment, and enhance the initiation, unfolding, and realization of your innermost sexual pursuits and desires.

YEARN FOR THE RHYTHM OF TWO BODIES,
BECOMING ONE, SENSELESS TO THE SOUND,
SILENCED BY THE HARMONY, BEATING TO ONE PULSE,
MINDFUL TO THE MELODY OF THE TAO.

Indian ragas, for instance, typically begin with a soft stroke, a caress, a gentle tease. Then slowly, steadily, and sensuously the music builds up to an arousing interplay of ascending and descending patterns ornamented with the slides, trills, and echoes that resonate with sexual passion, potency, and endurance. As it deepens, impassions and excites, the movement between the notes begins to throb with deep emotion. The intensifying counter-rhythms and haunting drones kindle the body and entrance the mind, generating motions and emotions which build up to a frenzied climax. Having discharged its energies, the music finds unimpeded resolution.

HAVING BECOME ENTRANCED
LOVE WITHIN RHYTHM,
RHYTHM WITHIN LOVE,
TWO ARE ONE WITH THE TAO.

The Magic Nightclub

O, My Luve 's like a red, red rose,
That's newly sprung in June;
O My Luve 's like the melodie
That's sweetly played in tune.[4]

The "Magic Nightclub" is an opportunity for you and your partner to have a night *in*. An intimate "club" within your own home where romantic forays into unexplored (or explored) intimate adventures occur on a regular basis. It is designed to provide any number of creative, "get away" private adventures with all the comforts of home. With a little imagination, and the proper music soundtrack(s), you can create an array of magical evenings within the safety, warmth, and security of your own home. Although the setting for the "Magic Nightclub" is typically your own home, one of the special benefits of these self-designed intimate romantic escapades is that you can take them on the road! In other words, reservations for a "Magic Nightclub" can be made anywhere—be it a motel room,

4. Robert Burns, "My Love is Like a Red Red Rose," lines 1–4, in *The New International Dictionary of Quotations*, Hugh Rawson and Margaret Miner, eds. (New York: E. P. Dutton, 1986), p. 159.

summer cottage, ski lodge, or your own living room. Once you are at "the club," you are there for the night.

A visit to the magic nightclub means no traffic, no parking, no tipping, no stumbling strangers, no unwanted cigarette smoke, no crowds, and no waiting in line. It means you can dress up, down, or not at all. At the "club," you play the music you choose, at the volume you like. Although dancing is optional, the loosening of inhibitions through rhythmic movements is encouraged. Eating and drinking, also optional, can be as exotic as your imagination (and budget) allows. Since there is no driving home after a "night in," plans for designated drivers are not necessary.

One of the most popular "Magic Nightclub" adventures among my patients has been "theme night." On theme nights one places a particular emphasis on providing every practical detail to set the mood for a special event. This past summer, for instance, one of my patients held a beach theme "magic club" night: she and her husband wore bathing trunks and bikinis and played Beach Boys' music. I have worked with several couples who have relived their wedding night using as their soundtrack the same songs they played at their wedding, or during their honeymoon. Some have chosen to further recreate the event by literally returning to their original honeymoon site and making reservations for their "magic nightclub" there. Another one of my couples played "British pub," playing traditional Celtic tunes and going as far as purchasing a dart board, imported beer and cheeses, and baking kidney pie! Yet another couple held an "Iberian night" and went as far as renting traditional Spanish costumes, playing Spanish music, buying a piñata and special ordering a paella! As you can see, "Magic Nightclub theme nights" are the adult equivalent of playing "dress up." It's an opportunity to indulge ourselves.

Finally, actually, there *is* no finally! With music as background, images become more vivid, senses more intensified, and creativity is engaged. With the "Magic Nightclub," the possibilities are endless! Two imaginations are better than one.

> Temple dancers in ancient cultures, be they female or male, were able to arouse intense sexual energy. . . . They were trained intensively to draw upon spiritual archetypes and forces, giving them outer physical expression through their own bodies, and transferring and arousing energies within others through the power of music and movement.[5]

5. R. J. Stewart, *Music, Power & Harmony: A Workbook of Music and Inner Forces* (New York: Sterling, 1990), p. 76.

To assist you with your romantic forays, a number of "mood adjuncts" are suggested.

1. *Music.* The reader is referred to the Romantic Magic Nightclub Musical Menu at the end of this section. Generally, your featured entertainment can be provided by Mozart, John Coltrane, Ravi Shankar, Gregorian monks, Pearl Jam, or The Smashing Pumpkins. The choice is yours. Further, with the money you save by staying in you can slowly but surely amass an impressive musical catalog which can serve to provide countless "Magic Nightclubs" in the future. With theme nights, one night you can be in a blues club listening to Dexter Gordon. The next night you can be entertained by Franz Liszt as he regales you in a private concert with his "Liebestraum (Dream of Love)."

But is music an aphrodisiac? That probably depends on how you listen . . . to yourself. According to Barbara Anne Scarantino, for instance, "Before structured music ever came into existence, musical tones and rhythms were used by primitive cultures, primarily to attract a mate."[6] Ms. Scarantino adds:

> The heavy percussion instruments, such as the bass drum, influence our emotions by arousing our base passions. And the sound vibration of the electric bass guitar, with its very low frequency levels powerfully amplified, acts as a sexual stimulus because it resonates right at the "crucial point" between the thighs. The drum and the bass guitar combined offer a musical aphrodisiac that has popularized popular music more than any other element.[7]

Regarding jazz music, Ms. Scarantino suggests:

> [T]he pulsations and syncopations of jazz music are also sexually arousing. With its primitive African roots, syncopated jazz rhythms (with the accent *off* the beat in four-quarter time) induce high physical and emotional energy and, in an attempt to release these tensions, the body just has to move (with activity centered primarily around the loins). This lower chakra (energy center) stimulation results in an outpouring of sexual

6. Barbara Anne Scarantino, *Music Power: Creative Living through the Joys of Music* (New York: Dodd, Mead & Company, 1987), p. 49.
7. Scarantino, *Music Power*, pp. 39–40.

hormones and a desire to fulfill sexual impulses as soon as possible. In some instances, people may even lose control.[8]

2. *Attire.* Suggesting any particular attire (costumes, uniforms, outfits) would be similar to recommending a particular type of wine. These are all relative! Suffice it to say that the "Magic Nightclub" provides ample opportunity for you and your partner to be creative. While silk, satin, suede, furs, and pearls work best for some people; cotton, denim, leather, and costume jewelry may work best for others. On the other hand, this is your opportunity to bring out those lacy boots, top hats, Easter bonnets, tiaras, spiked heels, loin cloths, and "Zorro" type masks which have been collecting dust in your closet. If you never had the opportunity to wear a cheerleading outfit or football uniform this could be your chance! If you are having a "theme night," dress accordingly; after all, you would not wear the same outfit to a classical concert that you would to a jazz club.

3. *Beverages.* Optional and relative. While fine wines and champagne work for some, hot cocoa or exotic teas may better help to set the stage for others. Whether alcohol fits into your game plan or not, try expanding your refreshment repertoire; there are beverages out there (alcoholic or not) for everyone. Did you know there are drinks called "Sex on the Beach," "Screaming Orgasms," and "Gin and Sin"? Invest some money on a drink mixers' guide. Sample and explore.

4. *Food.* Popular lore lists a number of culinary aphrodisiacs (oysters, ginseng, turtle eggs, bananas, asparagus, chocolate, vanilla); scientific research, however, has not found any aphrodisiac powers among these foods. Basically, if you are planning on drinking alcohol you should balance your liquid refreshments with a nutritional buffer. If you are planning on having sex, you may want to limit your pre-sex eating to something light such as appetizers, salads, or hors d'oeuvres. Save the large, fancy meals (or the pizza) for *after* sex. It's also fun to have sweets around. Bakery store pastries or other elegant desserts add extra enticement to a well rounded evening.

5. *Incense.* Something subtle. According to Diane Ackerman, some scents do seem to have aphrodisiac-like qualities:

> Musk produces a hormonal change in the woman who smells it. As to why floral smells should excite us, well, flowers have

8. Scarantino, *Music Power*, p. 50.

a robust and energetic sex life: A flower's fragrance declares to all the world that it is fertile, available, and desirable, its sex organs oozing with nectar. Its smell reminds us in vestigial ways of fertility, vigor, lifeforce, all the optimism, expectancy, and passionate bloom of youth. We inhale its ardent aroma and, no matter what our ages, we feel young and nubile in a world aflame with desire.[9]

When scent shopping, then, let your nose be your guide.

6. *Candles.* Dripless. Use every safety precaution.

7. *Massage oils.* Be aware of your sheets, carpet, rugs, furniture, and clothing; oils can get messy. Keep a towel handy. In addition, in today's market there are many flavored and scented oils so, depending on your preferences, be aware of taste (and calories).

8. *Window shades.* Keep these down. This is *your* show, not your neighbors'.

9. *Telephones and personal pagers.* Off. If you have an answering machine turn the monitor volume *off* and unplug the phone; you don't want to spend the finest moments of your romantic evening wondering who that call may have been from. Listen to your messages later.

10. *Lights.* If candles are not for you, and you choose electric lighting, keep these dim. Colored lights, particularly blue or red, help to set a sensuous, seductive mood.

11. *Day (night) of the week.* Although any night (or day) of the week, or weekend, is fine, nights when neither of you has to get up too early the next morning work best. The fewer time restrictions or limitations the better. This is your time for adventurous love making. *Be* there.

12. *Make a date.* Whichever day/night you choose, make a date. Send out an invitation, formal or informal. Sometimes a simple expression ("I want you; how about tonight?") written with marker on an index card can be more effective than an elaborate, embroidered poem written inside a $5.00 store-bought card. A romantic note arriving in the mail the next morning, either at home or at the office, is a nice touch. These can serve as cues to trigger the feelings aroused during your special evening well after the

9. Diane Ackerman, *A Natural History of the Senses* (New York: Random House, 1990) p. 12-13.

main event takes place. Be innovative, send a telegram, fax, e-mail, or, if your budget allows, flowers.

13. *Communicate.* Take turns. Discuss your plans, setting, and particulars with your partner. Write out and exchange romantic menus, listing your preferences and daily specials. Be equal partners. Equality, respect for each other, and sharing control and responsibility for your special evening can be as erotic as the *Kama Sutra.*

14. *Do not set yourself, or your partner, up.* To the best of your ability, leave out aspects of your evening that may set you up for disappointment. Some of these may include how the evening "should" or "must" turn out, *any type* of expectations, and "why" you are doing whatever it is you are doing.[10] What is important is what you are doing, where it is taking place, at what time (when), and how you are going to go about it.

15. *Experiment.* Be adventurous. Think variety, diversity. Expand your (horizontal and vertical) horizons. Even if the setting for your "Magic Nightclub" is always the same place your routines are only limited by your imagination. Wear a three-piece, "power suit" one night, and a silky bathrobe the next. Dining on caviar one evening can be followed by egg rolls the next. Try different wines, after all, each "Magic Nightclub" experience is a special occasion. Surround yourself with different musical environments. While jazz (Dexter Gordon), romantic (Chopin), classical (Mozart) or new age (George Winston) may fulfill some folks' needs, others may prefer Marvin Gaye, Frank Sinatra, Billie Holiday, Van Morrison or Boyz II Men to establish a more enticing and seductive acoustic soundtrack for their night in. Remember, the night is about ambiance and movement. Use whatever it takes to help establish the desired "rhythmic synchronicity."[11]

This part of the "Magic Nightclub" evening is merely the first half of your night in. Although some couples are content with ending their romantic foray there, most prefer to utilize these preparations as an overture to the second half of their evening.

> [R]hythm and love may be viewed as part of the same process. People in general don't sync well with those they don't like and they do with those they love.[12]

10. See Shoulds, page 311, Whys, page 303, and Expectations, page 293.
11. See Rhythmic Synchronicity, page 275.
12. Edward T. Hall, *The Dance of Life* (New York: Doubleday, 1983), p. 165.

EXERCISE 22:

The Magic Nightclub

Here you use entrainment[13] music as adjunct to the overture, main show, coda and encore.

1. Begin your sexual adventure with a number of musical selections which set the mood for your intimate overture (inducing arousal). The ambiance created should vibrate with warmth, trust, and feelings of closeness. Enjoy the process. Allow it to unfold as a flirtatious interplay of rhythmic and melodic dialogue.

2. Having set the initial mood, escalate the pulse of the evening with selections which you and your partner find sensual in character. These should function as catalyst to taunt the flesh and tease the mind, serving as background stimulation for sexual foreplay. Remain aware of the process. This is happening heAr, and now. Listen to it, hear it, *you* are creating this reality.

3. As you enter the carnal gates of sexual intimacy, allow the music to guide and glide you through whatever passages of passion your desires provoke. As the beat of the tempo sets your pace, allow the rhythms to escort you through the uncharted mounds, peaks, and crevices in your path. See yourself as an explorer, a pioneer. If at any point you lose track, or allow linear thinking to get in your way, simply return to the music, flow, and allow it to escort you to and through your chosen path.

4. Allow the music to seduce and transform you into a seducer. Flowing with the process, hear the music which is being created by the vibrations of your merging bodies. Release your body and allow your unobstructed flesh to listen to the messages conveyed within the dance.

5. As your bodies swell, the mind spirals, and emotions explode, feel the resonance of your bodies merging, blending, fusing into one. And, if just

13. See Entrainment, page 317.

for a brief moment, allow yourself the rapture of total awareness, of complete abandonment.

6. Taste the melody of your intimate encounter. And, as your bodies quell, savor the ecstasy of the moment, bathe in its echo. Embrace in harmony.

THE TAO OF MUSIC
CAN BE FOUND AT THAT MOMENT
WHEN LIPS, IN A GENTLE KISS, MEET APERTURE...
WHEN FINGERS, STROKING STRING,
AWAKEN SOUND FROM ITS SILENT STILLNESS...
WHEN BREATH, RELEASED AS TENDER SIGH,
SOARS THROUGH WOODEN CAVERNS,
FINDING FREEDOM IN EVERY OPENING...
WHEN HANDS, SENSING DESIRE,
CARESS THE RESONANCE OF THE FLESH.

♪

MUSICAL MENU 15
Romantic Magic Nightclub

Suggested CDs, Tapes or Albums

William Ackerman: *Imaginary Roads*
Tori Amos: *Boys for Pele; Little Earthquakes*
Fiona Apple: *Tidal*
Rafael Aragon: *Passion*
Anita Baker: *The Songstress; Rapture*
Tony Bennett: *MTV Unplugged*
Toni Braxton: *Secrets; Toni Braxton*
Bobby Brown: *Don't Be Cruel*
Peabo Bryson: *The Peabo Bryson Collection*
Jonathan Cain: *Piano With a View*
Mariah Carey: *Daydream*
Natalie Cole: *Unforgettable, With Love; Stardust; Take a Look*
John Coltrane Quartet: *Ballads*
Celine Dion: *Unison; Falling Into You; The Colour of My Love;
    Celine Dion*
The Commodores: *Best of*
D'Angelo: *Brown Sugar*
Endless Love: *Great Motown Love Songs*
Enigma: *MCMXC, a.D.; The Cross of Changes*
Enya: *The Memory of Trees; Watermark; Shepherd Moons*
Gloria Estefan: *Mi Tierra; Destiny; Greatest Hits; Hold Me, Thrill
    Me, Kiss Me*
Cesaria Evora: *Cabo Verde*
Terrence Farrell: *Love Songs for Guitar*
Roberta Flack: *The Best of Roberta Flack: Softy with These Songs*
Marvin Gaye: *I Want You; Let's Get it On; Here My Dear;
    Vulnerable; Midnight Love*
Hector Ivan Garcia: *Ecos de Amor (Songs of Romance)*
Dexter Gordon: *Ballads; Go; Dexter Calling; Our Man in Paris*
Govi: *Passion & Grace*
Michael Gray: *Emergence*
Al Green: *Greatest Hits; Anthology*

Pedro Guerra: *Tan Cerca de Tì*
Enrique Iglesias: *Enamorado Por Primera Vez; Vivir; Enrique Iglesias*
Julio Iglesias: *Volver; Tango; Crazy; 1100 Bel Air Place*
Al Gromer Khan: *Mahogany Nights*
Al Gromer Khan & Kai Taschner: *Black Marble & Sweet Fire*
Brian Keane: *Suleyman the Magnificent*
K. D. Lang: *Ingènue*
Madonna: *Something to Remember*
Johnny Mathis: *All About Love; 16 Most Requested Songs*
Maxwell: *Maxwell's Urban Hang Suite*
Boyz II Men: *Cooley High Harmony* or *II*
Luis Miguel: *Nada es Igual*
Van Morrison: *Enlightment; The Healing Game; Too Long in Exile; Best of*
Anne-Sophie Mutter: *Romance*
Narada Artists: *Romance Music for Piano*
Willie Nelson: *Stardust; Spirit; Greatest Hits*
Heather Nova: *Oyster*
Laura Pausini: *Las Cosas Que Vives*
Emile Pandolfi: *Once Upon a Romance*
Madeleine Peyroux: *Dreamland*
Nina Postolovskava: *Romantic Piano*
Gary Prim & David M. Combs: *Beautiful Thoughts*
Ike Quebec: *Blue & Sentimental; Soul Samba;* or *The Art of Ike Quebec*
Bonnie Raitt: *Nick of Time*
Stephen Rhodes: *Venus*
The Righteous Brothers: *Greatest Hits*
Joshua Redman: *Freedom in the Groove; Moodswing;* or *Joshua Redman*
Steve Roach & Robert Rich: *Soma;* or *Strata*
Gabrielle Roth & The Mirrors: *Initiation; Ritual; Totem; Trance;* or *Tongues*
Linda Ronstadt: *Frenesì; with Nelson Riddle and His Orchestra*
Sade: *Love Deluxe; The Best of Sade*
Jon Secada: *Amandolo; Jon Secada; Amor; Heart, Soul & A Voice*
Paul Simon: *Negotiations & Love Songs*
Frank Sinatra: *Love Songs; Sinatra's 80th, All the Best; The Reprise Collection*

Rod Stewart: *If We Fall in Love Tonight*
The John Tesh Project: *Sax by the Fire*
UB 40: *Labour of Love; Promises & Lies*
Dawn Upshaw: *Forgotten Songs; Dawn Upshaw Sings Debussy*
Luther Vandross: *Your Secret Love; The Night I Fell in Love; Never Too Much*
Glen Velez: *Assyrian Rose*
Andrew Lloyd Webber: *Love Songs*
Ben Webster (with Strings): *Music for Loving; The Warm Moods; Soulville*
George Winston: *Forest*
Yanni: *Reflections of Passion*

The following menus are suggested for achieving rhythmic synchronicity within an ambiance of soothing sensuality.

Classical/Romantic Individual Selections

George Gershwin: "Rhapsody in Blue"
Franz Liszt: "Liebestraum"
Maurice Ravel: "Bolero"; "Daphnis and Chloe"
Franz Schubert: "Serenade"; "Die Schone Mullerin" (Der Neugierige); "String Quartet in C Minor"
Ludwig van Beethoven: "Moonlight Sonata"; "Für Elise"
Rimsky-Korsakov: "Scheherazade Suite"; "Song of India"
Claude Debussy: "Afternoon of a Fawn" (Prelude); "Clair de Lune"; "La Mer"; "Nocturne"
Anton Dvorak: "Four Romantic Pieces" (Larghetto); "Fifth Symphony, Second movement"
Delius: "Hassan" (Intermezzo & Serenade)
Igor Stravinsky: "The Rites of Spring"
Rachmaninoff: "Symphony No. 2" (Adagio)
Peter I. Tschaikovsky: "Waltz of the Flowers"; "Violin Concerto" (Canzonetta); "Panorama," from *Sleeping Beauty*
Wieniawski: "Violin Concerto No. 2" (Adagio-non troppo):

Individual Selections by Nat King Cole

"Embraceable You"
"Unforgettable"

"The Ruby and the Pearl"
"That's All"
"Stardust"
"That Sunday, That Summer"
"On The Street Where You Live"
"L-O-V-E"

Big Band, Individual Selections

Artie Shaw: "Begin the Beguine"
Tommy Dorsey: "I'm Getting Sentimental Over You"
Glenn Miller: "Moonlight Serenade"
Claude Thornhill: "Snowfall"

Jazzy Blues: Saxophone, Soothing-Sensuous Individual Selections

Dexter Gordon

Six CD Box Set: "The Complete Blue Note Sixties Sessions,"
   or,
"Darn that Dream"
"Don't Explain"
"I'm a Fool to Want You"
"You've Changed"
"Guess I'll Hang My Tears Out to Dry"
"Body and Soul"
"As Time Goes By"
"Sophisticated Lady"
"Easy Living"
"Stairway to the Stars"
"Still Time"
"Ernie's Tune"
"For All We Know"
"Cry Me a River"
"Tenderly"
"Don't Worry About Me"
"I Should Care"
"Someone to Watch Over Me"
"Stardust"

Ben Webster

"Tenderly"
"That's All"
"Come Rain or Come Shine"
"Old Folks"
"You're Mine, You!"
"Do Nothing Till You Hear From Me"
"Chelsea Bridge"
"Love's Away"
"Soulville"
"Star Dust"
"I Got it Bad and that Ain't Good"
"Prelude to a Kiss"
"John Brown's Body"

Ike Quebec

"Just One More Chance"
"Brother Can You Spare a Dime"
"Heavy Soul"
"I Want a Little Girl"
"Blue and Sentimental"
"Don't Take Your Love From Me"
"Blues for Charlie"
"Count Every Star"

John Coltrane

"The Night We Called it a Day"
"Naima"
"I'll Wait and Pray"
"Central Park West"
"Everytime We Say Goodbye"
"Equinox"
"Original Untitled Ballad" (To Her Ladyship)
"Say It (Over and Over Again)"
"You Don't Know What Love Is"
"Too Young to Go Steady"
"I Wish I Knew"
"What's New"
"Nancy (with the Laughing Face)"

Frank Morgan

"In a Sentimental Mood"
"Bessie's Blues"

Kenny G.
Frank Sinatra
Johnny Mathis
David and Steve Gordon

Using the Entrainment Techniques suggested in Appendix B (page 317), choose from among the many releases from these artists, and, allowing your sensuality to serve as your guide, create your own.

20

TAKE THINGS IN STRIDE. LIKE PLAYING A SCALE,
ONE NOTE AT A TIME.

Motivating the Mind

*It (rhythm) makes us play, young and old. It determines the form of
play, in large part. Through play it leads to self-realization by
serving as an ever-present incentive for practice.*[1]

Recently, reports released by the College Board indicated that students enrolled in music appreciation courses prior to taking their SATs (Scholastic Aptitude Test, which functions as a primary tool used by most colleges and universities in their admission requirements) scored an average of sixty-one points higher (verbal), and forty-six points higher (math) on their exams over those not involved in these classes. Additionally, students with a background in taking music lessons scored fifty-one points higher (verbal) and thirty-nine points higher (math) than those without musical training.

Music helps to enhance spatial reasoning, or the ability to perceive visual objects accurately, to develop imagery and to distinguish between different available options. Music is also significantly effective in helping to induce relaxation. Since anxiety often gets in the way of clear thinking, the use of music to reduce tension is extremely effective in improving concentration and retention of learned material. Since the release of the book

---

1. Carl E. Seashore, *Psychology of Music* (New York: Dover Publications, 1967), p. 145.

Superlearning, by Ostrander and Schroeder,[2] numerous educators and researchers have found the use of largo movements from string concertos by Baroque composers to be extremely effective adjuncts in the learning and retaining of information. Apparently, the use of this soothing, and calming music (with tempos of four beats to the measure, and averaging about sixty beats per minute) serves to at once relax and alert the mind, setting a steady, comfortable rhythm by which the learner can better integrate the material.

Overall, Baroque music has been found to be significantly effective when compared to other forms of music in terms of inducing "alpha states" (i.e., a sense of relaxed alertness accompanied by feelings of well-being) in the listener.[3] When compared to other music types, Baroque music has also been found to be very relaxing, extremely predictable and perceived as soothing almost universally.[4] Studies have even indicated that, when asked to select the "most soothing" music selections, the "four top most predictable" selected are usually baroque compositions (e.g., Bach, Telemann).[5]

BYPASSING WRITTEN OR SPOKEN LANGUAGE,
MUSIC TRANSCENDS ALL CONCEPTS. RISING ABOVE THOUGHT,
IT EXCEEDS UNDERSTANDING.

Throughout my clinical career, I have had ample opportunity to serve junior high, high school, college-age and returning adult students. Through these contacts my opportunities to suggest techniques for enhancing learning, studying, and reading methods have been—needless to say—quite copious. Beyond suggesting the typical, more traditional cognitive and behavioral learning approaches used among my peers, I have in addition recommended the extremely effective use of background music as an adjunct.[6]

2. Sheila Ostrander and Lynn Schroeder, *Superlearning* (New York: Dell, 1979).

3. Ostrander and Schroeder, *Superlearning,* 1979.

4. H. J. Devlin and D. D. Sawatzky, "The Effects of Background Music in a Simulated Initial Counselling Session with Female Subjects," *Canadian Journal of Counselling,* 1987, 21, pp. 125–132.

5. H. Hunter, "An Investigation of Psychological and Physiological Changes Apparently Elicited by Musical Stimuli," *Psychology of Music,* 1974, 2, pp. 53–68.

6. Two books I regularly and highly recommend in this area are J. J. Gibbs, *Dancing With Your Books: The Zen Way of Studying* (New York: Plume, 1990), and Sheila Ostrander and Lynn Schroeder, *Superlearning* (New York: Dell, 1979).

Blending rhythm, beat, and melody, the Tao of music merges mind, brain, body, and spirit. The whole then becomes a union, the union, a whole. The ways in which music can be applied as an adjunct to learning situations seem to be limited only by our imagination. For example, used as a soothing background, music helps to clear the mind of "psychological noise," or information overload from thousands of competing thoughts, images, ideas, and concerns which clutter and sometimes overwhelm our minds. While unobtrusive, music reduces stress and anxiety by facilitating relaxation and eliminating uncomfortable silences. By blocking out unwanted external noises, music can serve to improve concentration and return our attention to the heAr and now. More directly related to learning, music enhances focusing, energizes, and increases alertness. All together, these characteristics are instrumental in helping us to better establish, and maintain, a comfortable rhythmic pace by which to read, learn, or otherwise study. In addition, while providing a creative form of time management, music helps to create a pleasant environment while providing a sense of inspiration. In general, then, carefully selected music—used appropriately—will significantly help to motivate, unclutter, and stimulate the mind.

For students interested in memorizing (or learning) the hundreds (or thousands) of word lists available as preparation for SAT, GRE, or other similar examinations I suggest the following exercise.

◯

EXERCISE 23:
Using Music to Memorize Word Lists

A style of music which we have never before heard, and now hear for the first time, may open our minds to an entirely novel feeling or way of looking at the world. A stirring, patriotic song during wartime can encode, unify and intensify the thoughts of an entire nation. And in combining words and music, many concepts can be encoded as never before.[7]

For this exercise you will need *two* music sources (one to play music and the other for recording) at least one of which must have recording capa-

---

7. David Tame, *The Secret Power of Music* (Rochester, VT: Destiny Books, 1984), p. 149.

bilities. The number of blank tapes you will need will be relative to the
number of words you wish to learn, and the speed at which you record
them. The amount of background music you use depends on the amount
of musical variety you wish to have serving as your background.

MUSIC HELPS TO OCCUPY OUR RIGHT HEMISPHERIC CHANNELS.
WHILE SPEAKING VOICES OR READING ARE
PROCESSED BY THE LEFT HEMISPHERE OF OUR BRAINS,
THE MUSIC ENGAGES THE RIGHT.

• Find a quiet place where you have access to both playing and recording
music (CD or record player, cassette deck, etc.).

• Prepare your preferred, chosen background music.[8] The music suggested for this exercise is the same type of soothing, Baroque music suggested
as "soothing Music" (see Soothing Music, page 55). Depending on your
personal preference, you may prefer to try different types of soothing music
(see Soothing Music, page 55, or Meditation Music, page 230), or even
stimulating music (see Stimulating Music, page 20, or Inspirational
Music, page 48).

• Prepare the word lists you wish to memorize.

• Insert a blank tape into your second tape recorder.

• Begin to play your chosen background music at a low to moderate volume. Note: Before you begin to actually record the word lists for posteri-
ty, make sure you do a trial run to make sure that the volume levels of the
background music versus your voice volume, reading the word lists, is to
your liking and satisfaction. You will want the soothing music barely
audible, setting a soothing, "cushiony" backdrop to your word lists. Your
voice, by contrast, should be clear and distinctively in the foreground,
making it easy for you to be able to hear the word lists (or whatever else
you may want to tape for memorization) and their definitions without any
difficulty.

---

8. See Choosing Music, page 355.

• With the music playing in the background, begin to slowly and rhythmically read the word lists, and their definitions, into the recording tape at a pace which feels comfortable for you. Although this will take quite a while, and quite a few blank tapes, I have found the end result, if done properly, is almost always impressively effective.

First of all, the mere act of reading the words and their definitions aloud helps us to integrate them. Second, reading them while the background music plays helps to clear the mind, set the reading/breathing pace and tempo, and integrates the meanings even deeper than reading them without the music. Third, having recorded all of your lists, you can now play them back ad nauseam! Many patients have related that, as they prepare for the exams, they listen to these tapes while driving, flying home, lying out in the sun, exercising, showering, cleaning their apartments, ironing, gardening, and even while drifting off to sleep! A number of patients have even indicated that they allow the tape to play, in a "continuous loop" mode, while they sleep throughout the night! If you don't have the desire, or time, to make the above tapes then you may want to try simply playing the music as background each time you study the words. Either way, the benefits of using the background music are typically quite remarkable!

When things are arranged rhythmically our ability to learn and remember them is vastly improved. As has been indicated, "the rhythm need not be conspicuous to be effective. It need not be objective. It need not be conscious. At best it is a habit."[9]

Almost unanimously, the feedback I have received regarding the use of background music has been absolutely fascinating. For instance, law students have found it extremely helpful when preparing for their L.S.A.T.s, while attorneys searching for cases used in litigation have found it reduces the tedium of these lengthy processes. Having found music to be highly effectual in preparing for their M.C.A.T.s, medical students have later turned to music backgrounds while studying physiology and human anatomy. Even later on in their careers, I have spoken with surgeons who continue to use music regularly while performing surgery. Some, believing that music has great healing powers, go as far as asking their patients which music *they* prefer, and incorporate *patients'* preferred music during surgical procedures!

Chemistry and physics students memorizing lengthy tables and mathematical formulas have come back after highly exacting exams relat-

9. Seashore, *Psychology of Music*, p. 140.

ing the relaxing and advantageous effects that music as adjunct had on their studies and final results. Other people I have consulted within my practice who have found this technique useful have included realtors, nurses, hairdressers, mechanics, electricians, and x-ray technicians. In essence, anyone involved in any profession that requires learning or memorization for licensing, certification, qualifying, or any other type of examinations will benefit from adapting background music as adjunct to their studying/reading/learning approaches.

> There are also problems connected with mood changes, and what may be relaxing on one day may irritate the next.[10]

Unexpected feedback on individual musical preferences, or types of music which individuals have found useful or helpful, has been fascinating as well as, at times, quite surprising. For instance, a number of teens have related how heavy metal, or rap music helps them relax and concentrate on their studies. A number of college students have likewise returned after my suggestion to try some relaxing music to communicate how serviceable industrial, alternative, techno, or jazz fusion tunes have been in helping them get through the semester. Attempts to analyze *why* certain types of music work for specific individuals, or groups of individuals, isn't as important as ascertaining *what* music works for each individual *in which* instances (*when*), and at which situations and settings (*where*).

At the other end of the spectrum I hear from "old timers" who have found that my suggestion that they try music "from their period" has proven crucial in renewing their interests to learn, read, and study material which they had long ago abandoned. Among my favorites, however, are the many mothers who report how music-box tunes,[11] and baroque music, seem to have a remarkable effect on helping to cultivate their children's reading habits.

> [W]e look back and connect various pieces of music with significant life events.[12]

However, everything is relative. I cannot emphasize enough how important *individual preferences* are to making the magic work.

---

10. Leslie Bunt, *Music Therapy: An Art Beyond Words* (London: Routledge, 1994), p 186.
11. See end of this section for some music-box tune suggestions.
12. Bunt, *Music Therapy*, p. 158

EXERCISE 24:
Improving Learning Skills

This exercise will help you use music to enhance concentration so you can relax, pace, integrate material, and block psychological noise that may interfere with study, reading, or just regular learning skills.

As for all exercises presented throughout this book, you are always the best judge as to what music has which effects for you personally. In effect, the "best" music to read, learn, or study by is always that which best works for you. The most anyone outside of yourself can do is offer suggestions. In general, however, when it comes to reading, learning, or studying, research has found that the majority of people tend to benefit most from music that evokes a sense of calm or relaxation (however, "relaxing" music is relative to each individual). General benefits of music perceived as "soothing" are quite varied and include improved attitude, stress and anxiety reduction, lower blood pressure and pulse rate, setting a comfortable pace, and enhanced concentration. The following exercise will present two slightly distinct scenarios.

The first (2a) allows you full freedom in choosing and precategorizing your own "soothing" music selections. The second (2b) suggests the use of Baroque music as an adjunct to your learning regimen. Baroque music is suggested based on the vast amount of existing scientific data which validates its effectiveness in these (academic enhancing, learning, studying, reading) situations. For further and more in-depth exploration of the benefits of Baroque music in this area, the reader is referred to the book *Superlearning*, by Ostrander and Schroeder,[13] and to scientific research articles by Nielzen and Cesarec,[14] Hunter,[15] Devlin and Sawatzky,[16] Ortiz,[17] Logan and Roberts,[18] and Wapnick.[19]

13. Ostrander and Schroeder, *Superlearning*, 1979.
14. S. Nielzèn and Z. Cesarec, "On the Perception of Emotional Meaning in Music," *Psychology of Music*, 9, 1981, pp. 17–31.
15. H. Hunter, "An Investigation of Psychological and Physiological Changes Apparently Elicited by Musical Stimuli," *Psychology of Music*, 1974, 2, pp. 53–68.
16. Devlin and Sawatzky, "The Effects of Background Music in a Simulated Initial Counselling Session with Female Subjects," 1987.
17. John M. Ortiz, *The Facilitating Effects of Soothing Background Music on an Initial Counseling Session*, Unpublished Doctoral Dissertation, Pennsylvania State University, 1991d.

The universality of music depends upon basic characteristics of the human mind; especially upon the need to impose order upon our experience.[20]

1. Select a 90 to 110 minute audio cassette tape.

2a. Select enough "soothing" musical selections, of your choice to fill your tape (if you wish to use the same music for both sides you only need 45 to 50 minutes worth of music).

2b. Select a large number of *baroque musical compositions*[21] from either your private collection, local library or university to make your own tape compilation. "Baroque" music is that composed from the period approximately between 1600-1750. Some of the most famous and renowned composers from that era include; Bach, Vivaldi, Corelli, Telemann, Scarlatti, Buxtehude, Pachelbel, Purcell, and Handel. Largo selections from string concertos by these composers are strongly suggested, and should be used whenever possible.

3. Select the *largo* movements from each of the Baroque pieces in each music source (cassette tape, LP, CD, DAT, etc.) and tape these movements in sequence, filling your tape. Be careful to monitor your recording levels very closely, particularly when recording these largo movements from different sources. You want to make sure that the overall level of your learning/reading/studying tape does not rise and fall in volume, as this would be disruptive and detrimental to creating the desired background musical ambiance. In other words, as you are recording from one source to the next, *keep a close eye on your recording meters!*

4. Once you have enough material to fill one side of the tape, you may choose to use the same selections to fill the second side. If you have extra material you can fill the second side with fresh largo movements from your collection of string concertos. As long as you are careful to closely moni-

18. T. B. Logan and A. R. Roberts, "The Effects of Different Types of Relaxation Music on Tension Level," *Journal of Music Therapy*, 1984, 21, pp. 177–185.

.19. J. Wapnick, "A Review of Research on Attitude and Preference," *Bulletin of the Council for Research in Music Education*, 1976, 48, pp. 1–20.

20. Anthony Storr, *Music and the Mind* (New York: The Free Press, 1992), p. 64.

21. See Rhythmic Synchronicity Menu, page 55, for specific selections recommended for creating a compilation "learning" tape as described above.

tor and regulate the volume levels, you can mix and match your musical sequence as desired.

5. Gather all your study materials and take them into your favorite study area.

6. Although the volume at which you play your music background is up to your discretion, the recommended, or suggested, volume is 45 to 50 decibels. This means that the music should be barely audible in the background. Here you need to play with different volumes until you find the right one for you and your needs or preferences.

As research has shown, using "soothing" music as background while studying helps minimize, or eliminate, psychological noise, as well as block out unwanted extraneous sounds. This type of music background can be very effective in enhancing your ability to focus, relax, and pace yourself so you can integrate the material much more comfortably. By taking the time to create a personal "Learning Music" library, you will be able to return to access the music's many benefits time and time again. So, in making your selections, take your time—experiment—and, above all, enjoy the process!

HAVING LEARNED,
THE STUDENT CAN TEACH OTHERS.
HAVING STUDIED,
THE LEARNED CAN THEN UNDERSTAND.
IN THE ABSENCE OF KNOWLEDGE, OR UNDERSTANDING,
THE SAGE MOVES WITH THE TAO.

♪

Musical Menu 16
Music-Box Tune Suggestions
(CDs, TAPES, ALBUMS)[22]

Rita Ford Collection: *Musical Box Dances: Favorite Victorian Dances*

Rita Ford Collection: *Music Box Opera: Opera Excerpts Played on Music Boxes*

Christopher Light and David Kraehenbuehl: *The Ultimate Music Box (Vols. 1 & 2)*

Rita Ford Collection: *Music Box Tunes for Children*

Sound Idea

Each day learn a new word.
Just for the sound of it.

---

22. This music is available from The Musical Heritage Society, Inc., 1710 Highway 35, Ocean, NJ 07712.

Additional Reading

For further reading on the effects of music on learning, you may refer to the following:

H. L. Bonny, "Music and Healing," *Music Therapy*, 1986, 6A, pp. 3–12.

R. Brim, "The Effect of Personality Variables, Dogmatism and Repression-Sensitization Upon Response to Music," *Journal of Music Therapy*, 1978, 15, pp. 74–87.

S. H. Burleson, D. B. Center, and H. Reeves, "The Effect of Background Music on Task Performance in Psychotic Children," *Journal of Music Therapy*, 1989, 26, pp. 198–205.

G. Groeneweg, E. A., Stan, A. Celser, L. MacBeth, M. I. Vrbancic, "The Effect of Background Music on the Vocational Behavior of Mentally Handicapped Adults," *Journal of Music Therapy*, 1988, 25, pp. 118–134.

J. P. Scartelli and J. E. Borling, "The Effects of Sequenced Versus Simultaneous EMG Biofeedback and Sedative Music on Frontalis Relaxation Training," *Journal of Music Therapy*, 1986, 23, pp. 157–165.

C. A. Smith and L. W. Morris, "Differential Effects of Stimulative and Sedative Music on Anxiety, Concentration and Performance," *Psychological Reports*, 1977, 41, pp. 1047–1053.

S. B. Stainback, W. C. Stainback, and D. P. Hallahan, "Effects of Background Music on Learning," *Exceptional Children*, 1973, 40, pp. 109–110.

A. L. Steele and H. A. Jorgenson, "Music Therapy: An Effective Solution to Problems in Related Disciplines," *Journal of Music Therapy*, 1971, 8, pp. 131-145.

D. E. Wolfe, "The Effect of Interrupted and Continuous Music on Bodily Movement and Task Performance of Third Grade Students," *Journal of Music Therapy*, 1982, 19, pp. 74–85.

21

How To Listen: Educating the Ear

In other people we hear what help they really require, what license they are actually giving us to help, what potential there is for change. We can hear their strengths and their pain. We hear what support is available, what obstacles must be reckoned with.[1]

Music can be used in a number of ways to help enhance our listening skills. Aside from the characteristics that help us focus and concentrate, music educates our ears by increasing our receptivity and sensitivities to our sound environments. Following are a number of suggestions that may be used to assist us in raising sound awareness and increasing reasoning abilities, generally helping us to think and react more clearly and effectively.

Sound Suggestions

1. *At this moment, this sound/music is all there is.* If you are in a situation where you need, choose, or are expected to listen, actively tell yourself that, at this moment—while you listen—you have nowhere else to go, no other responsibilities, nothing else to do. At this moment, during this time, nothing else matters, nothing exists outside of *you and the sounds* that you are listening to.

---

1. Ram Dass and Paul Gorman, *How Can I Help?* (New York: Alfred A. Knopf, 1985), p. 112.

2. *Listen unconditionally, without expectations.*[2] As you listen, allow yourself
to release all manner of anticipation, judgment, or expectation regarding
what the sounds themselves or the essence of their underlying meanings
may be. Attend to the music/sounds simply as "music/sound," without
labels or description (fast/slow, loud/soft), without comparison to other
music, sounds, or noise, without preconceived ideas of how it should or
should not sound. Detach yourself from any "whys" or even "hows" (how
or why are these sounds occurring?) and "where" (they are coming from)
for this exercise, and simply remain aware of "what" you are hearing. For
further focusing on the heAr and now,[3] once you are in tune to the "what"
of the sound allow your awareness to expand to the "when" the sounds are
taking place (i.e., *now!*). Hearing always involves filters. Before you begin
listening, make sure that yours are clean. Without prejudice, opinion, pre-
conception, expectation, or judgment. Just . . . listen.

3. *Hear them now, listen to them later.* As irrelevant thoughts intrude ("psychological noises" unrelated to the task at hand), allow them to pass, and
recognize that you will return to those later. In social conversation the content is secondary in importance. It is the listening that is essential. The
answer is not in the hearing, but in the listening. When being questioned,
listening is the answer. Listening is the answer to all questions.

4. *Call on your inner silence.* Allow your mind to be still. Remember the
silence that rests within your inner core. When the mind is muddled by
thoughts, listen for the silence. Hear the message of the beating heart.

5. *Detach from the self, attach to the sound.* Detach yourself from any preconceived notions, ideas, or feelings you have toward the sound source (type
of speakers, instruments, musicians, mode of sound reproduction). Put
aside personal preferences and judgments ("This orchestra is only average"), expectations ("This exercise will improve my listening skills immediately!"), discriminations ("That sounds like a trumpet, I wish I had chosen something to listen to without trumpets!"), biases ("I wish I had those
$1,000 speakers now, they would sound so much better!"), or anticipations
("I just 'know' someone is going to knock on the door any moment now!").
Listen effortlessly. Flow with the sound. Without resistance, you will hear
the message. In conversation, thinking interferes with listening.

2. See Expectations, page 293.
3. See HeAr and Now, page 243.

Expectations hinder understanding, anticipation obstructs the process, projections lead to misinterpretations. When in the orchestra, perform. When in the audience, listen. In life, be mindful, emotions cloud the intellect.

6. *Listen to others* (as you would like them to listen to you). Allow yourself to "become one" or merge with the sound source. If you were these sounds how would you like to be listened to? When you speak, or perform, how do you prefer to be received? Listened to? Heard? When others speak, listen to the rhythm of their breath, the expression of their affect, the melody in their voices, the sound behind their thoughts. Regard words as limitations to self-expression.

7. *Listen, heAr and now*! Listen in the heAr and now. Don't listen based on comparisons with things you have heard in the past, or hope to hear in the near future. Just listen to the sounds being emitted in the present moment. Do not allow anything outside of your listening pleasure to steal the beauty and richness of the moment's experience. When listening, be there. You will never need to return.

8. *Offer timely and appropriate feedback*. Encourage the speaker's flow with detached and open-ended responses ("Yes, I see . . . ", "Then what happened . . . ?" "And then what . . . ?" "So, how did it turn out . . . ?"). Remain objective and attentive to the persons' needs and confirm their messages (e.g., "Sounds clear to me!" "I hear what you're saying!"). These serve to assure the speaker that one is present, openly receptive, caring, sensitive, interested, non-judgmental and understanding. If something is unclear, do not hesitate to ask for clarification. When in doubt, check back with the speaker to make sure that you are understanding the meaning of thoughts being conveyed and feelings being expressed. Only through rhythm can we communicate. Only through harmony can we relate. Only by listening can we understand.

9. *Body language*. "Listen" to the body's communicative rhythms. As you listen, remain aware of the speaker's physical proximity, facial expressions, eye contact, physical contact, social distancing, tense versus calm vibrations, and voice tone. Is the "feel" of the tone happy or sad? Loud and agitated or quiet and calm? Clear or muddled? Welcome each vibration. Listen with every cell of your body.

10. *UNlistening*. While listening, *UN*listen. To "UNlisten," listen uncritically, without expectations, associations or interpretations of what is being—or may be—said. Listen from an external frame of reference (i.e., with attention to the speaker's subjective reality). Listen from the speaker's perspective, without superimposing your own.

While hearing "what" is being said (the "lyrics"), listen for the underlying and surrounding "hows" (the production, arrangement), or the *manner* in which the message is being conveyed. Is the speaker impassioned? Defensive? Is the speaker asking for solutions or just merely in need of dispelling tension without actually searching for an answer? The best way to listen is to ignore your own inner noise.

11. *Absolve from resolving*. Detach your ego. As you listen, remain empty. Be comfortable with silence. Do not fall into the trap of trying to say the right thing, resolving presenting issues, coming up with alternative options, or relating how you would be dealing with the situation at hand. Each and every situation is completely relative to the individual and the moment. Let go, and simply listen. If the person does request answers to personal problems, or seems to be seeking solutions to ongoing issues, it's often best to remain attentive, empathic, and kindly suggest they speak with a professional who may better help them through the maze of their personal situations.

LISTENING MEANS YOU HAVE TO GIVE UP CONTROL.

EXERCISE 25:

Listening

The primary purpose of the following exercises is to help educate our ears and minds. The exercises are also designed to help enhance our present-moment focusing capabilities, particularly as these pertain to listening to music, lectures, social chatter, or casual conversation. They can be practiced by listening to music, voices, or any other sounds. The words "sound" and "music" are used interchangeably.[4]

1. *Rediscovering your past.* Rediscover and explore a type of music you have not heard in quite some time (a particular classical piece, an old folk song, a tune from adolescence). As you listen, listen for something you never noticed before. Something positive. Something negative. What feeling is the tune bringing up? Frustration? Angst? Joy? Sadness? Nostalgia? Excitement? Can you recall the last time you identified with those feelings?

Since thoughts interfere with consciousness, the music helps us to experience the Tao by (bypassing conscious thought) transcending our awareness beyond the cognitive realm (or, by dissolving the ego).

2. *Fine tuning to your environment.* Next time you walk into a department (or any other type of) store, tune in to the background music. The store's soundtrack. In your opinion, what is the purpose behind the music being played? Is it there to try and stimulate us? To relax and slow us down? Is it meant to help us to acclimate and feel at ease with the surroundings? Is it working? If this were *your* store, what sort of music would *you* program?

WHEN LISTENING,
BE AWARE OF THE NOISE.

---

3. *Observing sound.* If you work out at a gym, and there is music playing (it's a very rare gym if there's not!) try and detach yourself from the music. Tune in to how the others there are reacting to the different tunes being played. Make note of how their reactions, movements, and tempos change and alter with the different beats and rhythms. Are their workouts becoming synchronized to the music?

> *Listening to music, the listener becomes the creative force. Composing without doing, hearing without thinking, playing without performing, dancing without moving, music and listener become one within the Tao.*

---

4. For an excellent book in this area, I highly recommend Robert Harris, *What to Listen for in Mozart* (New York: Simon & Schuster, 1991).

4. *Subliminal listening.* As you watch an advertisement on TV, a commercial, become actively aware of the background (or foreground) music being played. Does the feel—or theme—of the music in any way resonate with the public's "need" to buy that particular product? Does associating the music with the product somehow motivate or entice *you* to rush out and purchase their product or is it "turning you off" to their product?

> *What are you listening to?" asked the young child.*
> *"I am listening to the silence between the notes," replied the sage.*

5. *Movie magic.* As you watch a movie, try and imagine what the picture would seem like without the background score. Would the music-less picture have the same effect? Would the absence of the background music alter the cadence or feeling being projected? Would a different score, in your opinion, have a "greater" or "lesser" effect?

> *Performers play, and audiences listen. Entertainers perform, and*
> *crowds dance. When the sage plays, people are silenced.*

6. *Synchronizing sounds.* While watching a dance scene from a movie, or music video, turn the sound off for a moment and watch intensively. Once you feel you have tuned in to the rhythm of the dancers, that you have rhythmically synchronized[5] to their movements, turn the sound back up and note how closely—or not—your auditory image fits, or does not fit, the actual soundtrack.

> [Sounds] do not explain themselves; sounds reveal themselves.[6]

Bonus exercise: Turn on your TV and turn the volume all the way down, or to "mute." Now, "surf" the channels until you find a music video or see people dancing. Based on the people's movements, try and imagine what the music sounds like. After a few moments, turn the sound up and listen to how "in tune" you were.

7. *Oh say can you hear . . .* ? Put on a patriotic record, tape, or CD. Close your eyes and LISTEN to it. What's patriotic about it? What images does it elicit in your mind? In your opinion, where and how did your personal images relating to that music originate?

---

5. See Rhythmic Synchronicity, page 275.
6. John Beaulieu, *Music and Sound in the Healing Arts* (Barrytown, NY: Station Hill Press, 1987), p. 15.

> The way we appreciate sounds is through listening. When sounds are listened to—and not merely "heard"—they become music.[7]

8. *Acoustic memories.* Do you have your own theme music, or musics? Your own soundtrack(s)? (Every sitcom has one!) If so, how did these originate or come to be? How did they earn their place in your life? Can you recall the first time you heard what is now *"your* soundtrack?" *What* was going on at that moment? *Where* were you? *When* was it? *Who* else was there with you—physically, mentally or spiritually? *How* was the connection between you and your theme music originally established? Does this music still have the same impact on you as it did at that original moment?

> The reassurance does not come from the words themselves, of course, but from what the words represent. It comes if the person indeed *feels* heard. It may not be that a particular story from one's life is so important. But sharing it is a way of being together—heart to heart.[8]

9. *Traveling in time.* Listen to a piece of music from your childhood. What memories does it elicit? Can you visualize how old you were when you first heard it? How did you, or your significant others, look? What was it about that particular piece of music, or moment, which made it special in your mind? (See the Time Travel Musical Menu, pages 145–149, for a quick jaunt over fifty years of top melodies.)

Sound Idea

Think of a single, pure tone, echoing
endlessly through time. Listen to it
disappear in the distance. Following it with
your inner ear, let it take you where it may.

---

7. Beaulieu, *Music and Sound in the Healing Arts*, p. 13.
8. Dass and Gorman, *How Can I Help?*, p. 113.

Additional Listening Suggestions

• Be genuine in your gestures and responses.

• Tune in to people as individuals—as each person *is* at that moment, not as they "were" last time you spoke, not as you think or feel they "are," or "may be," not as you think they "should" be.

• To the best of your ability, remain non-judgmental. Accord the person the care and respect you desire for yourself.

• Be aware of internal influences. Remain aware of your own anxieties, state of mind, and prejudices. Remain aware of how your psychological noises and personal echoes may be transposing what is being said.

• Be aware of external influences. Be clear about your limits; set boundaries. Listen to your inner pulse. Be assertive about issues, or areas, you may feel uncomfortable discussing (politics, religion, personal or sexual matters, spiritual ideologies, particular fears or anxieties).

• Be aware of "filters." What, or how something is being said always resonates through the person's individual characteristics and numerous other factors such as cultural, social, or ethnic backgrounds.

• Listen to the need that resonates within each person's voice.

• Be aware that the true meaning of the message extends beyond the words. It lies within the melody, the pitch, and the volume of the content which is being expressed.

> "I *am* listening . . . " "You *better* listen . . . " "You *should* be listening . . . " "You *never* listen . . . " "*Listen* to me . . . "

Listening is a process, not a goal, nor a means to an end.

Sound Idea

Before singing, breathe.
Before responding, listen.

PART FOUR

SPECIAL ISSUES

*I envy the child for the myriad sounds
about to be discovered.*

22

Centering (Silence)

*When all else fails, remember
you have the right to remain silent.*

Over the past few years I have noticed a steady increase in the number of people who approach me with an interest in "centering," or "achieving inner balance." Whether this interest is posed by individuals in therapy, attending my workshops, or during casual conversations, their questions about this balancing of the mind, body and spirit—or any combination thereof—is basically the same: "How can I become centered?"

What is centering? To me, being centered refers to having a sense of inner calm, a central tranquillity, a private serenity, being at peace with oneself.

Regardless of anyone's personal definition or interpretation of this term, each one of us needs to find his or her own manner of becoming centered. For me, I have found it easiest to become centered by playing an instrument. And so, my answer to "What's a good way to become centered?" is typically a simple question, "Do you have an instrument?" Not necessarily if you play one, but do you simply *have*, or at least *have access to* a musical instrument?

I have met a lot of very skilled musicians who can quickly reach a point of rooted placidity by blissfully submerging into their instrument.

As they reach that point of inner sanctum, of becoming one with their preferred instrument, an unsuspecting passerby may wander by and find it almost impossible to leave the area. Often, just being near someone who is centered will, in itself, seem to have a calming effect. It just feels good.

I happened to experience such a temporary state of bliss during a concert at Bucknell University's chapel a few years ago. The Tibetan flutist Nawang Khechog was regaling the audience with a blend of his harmonic chanting and mastery of an Australian Aboriginal woodwind instrument known as a didgeridoo. Although the sounds he created through his instruments were just short of sublime, his proficiency appeared to be secondary to the deep silence that resonated from within the nucleus of his passion. For a few moments, it felt as if the entire audience vibrated within a common hub.

> It's as if we could breathe into the trees and make them speak. We hold a branch in our hands, blow into it, and it groans, it sings.[1]

It is a given that most of us are not as skillful at playing the didgeridoo as Master Khechog. However, I have worked with a large number of individuals who have no musical knowledge, or even minimal musical ability, but who have achieved a highly satisfying sense of inner peace, or centeredness, with the aid of various musical instruments. The approach is, in true Taoist style, quite basic and simple. It has to do with "being," rather than "trying to be." With "letting go," rather than "doing." With being heAr, now, rather than worrying about earlier, or later.[2]

EXERCISE 26:
Sound Convergence

Through a musical experience we can empty our minds by passing self-consciousness and maybe, just for a moment, recognize our focal point.

If you have access to a piano, try the following:

1. Sit at the piano and choose a note, any note that "sounds good," or that

---

1. Diane Ackerman, *A Natural History of the Senses* (New York: Random House, 1990), p. 225.
2. See Being versus Trying to Be, page 261, Letting Go, page 249, and HeAr and Now, page 243.

happens to feel particularly pleasing. Select a tone in your instrument that happens to resonate with your particular vibrational need at the moment.

2. Having found the right note, gently place your finger on it. Close your eyes, and breathe regularly, and naturally. With your finger (or thumb) on the selected note press down on the key and hold it.

3. As the piano string reverberates, simply listen to the sound until it is no longer audible.

4. As you hold your finger down on the key, feel the emerging oscillations as these quiver up your finger, through your arm, and up into your body.

5. Continue to stroke the same piano key, to play the same note, until you are able to follow the emerging vibrations into your very core.

6. Continue to resound (i.e., play) this note until it escorts you to what you feel is a place of inner serenity, a place of internal tranquillity where silence is so deep that it actually drowns out all other sounds.

If you do not have access to a piano, a similar exercise can be practiced on almost any other instrument. I have found that some of the more conducive, as well as readily available ones seem to be chimes, drums (or other percussion instruments), guitars (or other stringed instruments), organs (or other keyboard instruments), and various brass or wind instruments including a simple harmonica, a wooden flute, or a penny whistle.

The Tao of music is, by one definition, a balance. Like anything else, it involves the duality of yin and yang. Positive cannot be without negative. Sound cannot be without silence.

Silence

Is sound the absence of silence, or is silence the absence of sound?

The center of all sound is silence. All sounds rise from and lead back to silence. Listening is the art of discovering silence. Silence is the key to the many adventures the world of sound has to offer. Through silence we are truly safe and free. We know the beginning and we know the end.[3]

3. John Beaulieu, *Music and Sound in the Healing Arts* (New York: Station Hill Press, 1987), p. 17.

Silence is all around us, within and without us. All sounds come from silence. All sounds end there. Anytime you hear a sound—any sound—you are merely experiencing the temporary leakage of the collective universe of sounds which abound within silence. Throughout life, you are constantly discovering ways to release these various sounds from within their silent sanctuaries. Pluck an "A" note on a guitar string, for instance, and the vibrations act as a key to release that particular sound ("A") from what, a moment ago, was pure silence. As soon as the vibrations die out, the "A" note immediately recedes into the "silent universal," remaining dormant until it is once again reawakened.

> Silence is crucial for giving space and significance to a sound
> and can almost be regarded as an element in its own right.[4]

Sounds, like everything else in our world, are fleeting and temporary. Their ephemeral nature makes their presence, and our quest for them, ever more alluring. Strike a drum head, and listen as the delicately proportioned vibrations generate the precise amount of energy necessary to release the familiar "thump" from the "silent universal."

Throughout nature, everything has its own special "key" which, when activated properly, will release its own special sound from silence. The ocean waves are constantly, relentlessly, on an endless mission to release their fury on their perennial destination—the shore, releasing their inimitable sound upon the silent beaches. Birds are capable of releasing small, but enviable sound rainbows from the silent ambiance of any environment that surrounds them. Each bird species holds its own sound key, capable of releasing a sound unlike any other. Breeze uses every nook and cranny it can find—every slightly opened window sill, every loose shingle, every leaf—to release the startling sounds of nature. Do not be afraid of silence; simply listen.

Sound Idea

Today, as you meander through your daily
activities, temper every sound with a time out,
a dose of silence. Balance. Thirst makes one
appreciate a sweet taste of water that much
more. Seek at-one-ment.

---

4. Leslie Bunt, *Music Therapy: An Art Beyond Words* (London: Routledge, 1994), p. 51.

EXERCISE 27:

Finding Your Center

Centering, or balancing of the self, begins with silencing . . . and ends with silence.[5]

1. Choose an instrument to which you have access, and play one single note. Listening closely, follow it to absolute resolution. As the tone fades, become actively aware of your inner sounds, your breathing, pulse, and heartbeat.

2. While breathing, and focusing on the heAr and now, listen to how your inner nature pulls and pools together your inner resources.

3. If you do not have an instrument handy, use anything else which will make a sound; a glass, a wooden piece of furniture, a box, an empty canister, or simply hum. Play with the "instrument" until you obtain a sense of connectedness with it. This may take a few seconds, or several minutes, so simply continue to liberate the sound and follow it until you feel you are relating, bonding, or joining with it.

4. Once you find that point of connectedness, begin to breathe in—or to incorporate—the sound, itself. Using the tone as your focal point, follow its echoing resonance into the depths of your inner being. Follow its echo image into the nucleus of your mind. Feel the vibrations as these penetrate your bone marrow. Follow the sound waves with your inner ear, and hear them converge within the midst of your intuition, the core of your personality.

5. As the music plays, feel it spiraling inward. As you spiral within the music, and the music spirals within you, allow your inner ear to locate the stillness of the silence which lies at that point exactly between your internal noises, and the external sounds. Attending as the vibrations inherently cancel each other out, feel the sense of atonement. Vibrations stabilized, tune into that inner space of silence where rests the essential nature of your

5. See Rhythmic Synchronicity, page 275, and Psychological Noise, page 281.

equilibrium, that inner stillness which, as in water, lies just beneath the surface.

Bonus Exercise: Take a "balancing break," an internal "musical massage." Select a particularly soothing, meditative musical piece. Find a quiet, and comfortable place. If possible, use headphones to help isolate yourself from any external distractions or unwanted sounds. Allow your mind to flow with your selected music as it guides you within, toward your center. To the best of your ability, follow the spiraling melodies as they guide you through cavernous paths . . . circling inward, unfurling your thoughts . . . centering.

♪

Musical Menu 17
Centering Music

Gabrielle Roth and The Mirrors: *Ritual*
Tony Scott: *Music For Zen Meditation*
R. Carlos Nakai: Any selection
George Winston: Any selection
Steven Halpern: *Spectrum Suite*
Paul Horn: *Inside the Taj Mahal* (Vol. 1 or 2)
Ludwig Van Beethoven: "Moonlight Sonata"
The Benedictine Monks of Santo Domingo de Silos: *Chant*
Hans de Bach: *Gong Meditation*
————. *Singing Bowl Meditation*
Rainer Tilmann: *The Purity of Sound*
Barramundi: *Didgeridoo: Music for Meditation*
Shanghai Chinese Traditional Orchestra: *Chinese Feng Shui Music: Tortoise*

Centering, inner balancing, or achievement of personal harmony is not necessarily achieved through meditating in the Himalayas, chanting at the Taj Mahal, or levitating in an Egyptian pyramid. By following the exercises suggested above, and below, we can incorporate the "essence" of spiraling toward our inner core. Having acquired that basic ability, we can continue to practice, and achieve, a sense of balance or harmony while washing dishes, vacuuming the carpets, dusting furniture, paying bills, watching television, raking leaves, gardening, conversing with a friend, going for a stroll, waiting in line at the grocery store, or even, yes...inching our way through heavy traffic! By practicing centering in these, and other similar situations, we can each choose to practice "harmonizing" as a daily routine, conditioning ourselves to react, or *not* react to—and interact with—the realities posed by our daily environment.

○

EXERCISE 28:

Centering through Music

Our core is most readily reached by emptying our minds of theories and turning our awareness inward toward present experience.[6]

1. Begin by taking a moment to listen to what your heart, body, and mind are telling you.

2. According to how you feel at this very moment, select a piece of music that reflects your *present* state as closely as possible. For instance, if you are feeling calm and relaxed, play a very soothing piece and listen to it as it brings you to the center of your internal spiral. For a number of musical ideas, turn to the "Meditation Musical Menu" at the end of this section. (See also, Soothing Musical Menu, page 55.)

3. Feeling anxious, angry or "wired?" Play a very raucous, or even irritating or annoying piece (if *that's* how you feel!) and follow *that* to resolution. The point is to find a musical piece that will help you to bond, merge, or get in touch with HOW you feel, right *heAr*, right *now*. (See Stimulating Musical Menu, page 20.)

4. If your mind is resounding with "psychological noise", you need to match your internal vibrations to the sound of your external environment. Quell the internal noises, neutralize the echoing tensions, bring the raving, chattering voices to reticence. Silence the cacophony, the poundings of internal discord. In this manner, it's not so much "thought stopping" as

---

6. Greg Johanson and Ron Kurtz, *Grace Unfolding* (New York: Bell Tower, 1991), p. 12.

"thought releasing," letting go! (See Music for Dealing with Anger, page 73, and Music for Letting Go , page 259.)

With regular practice any one of us can increase our ability to achieve a sense of "centering" regardless of *what* we are doing. The key is *to do*, *what we do*, with full awareness, remaining fully conscious of the moment, and in accordance to *how* we are doing it.

♪

Musical Menu 18
Meditation Music
(CDs, tapes, albums)

Hans de Bach: *Chakra Meditation*
Chaurasia: *Flying Beyond*
Dik Darnell: *In the Presence of Angels*
Brian Eno: *Thursday Afternoon*
Ferraro & Howard: *Himalayan Nights*
Fumio: *Meditation*
Randall Gray: *One Hand Clapping*
Al Gromer Khan & Amelia Cuni: *Monsoon Point*
Dennis Keene: *Voices of Ascension: From Chant to Renaissance*
Mischa Misky & Pavel Gilivov: *Meditation*
Jon Mark: *Land of Merlin*
David Naegelle: *Temple in the Forest*
Karma Moffett: *Tibetan Soft Bowls*
The Power of Movement: *Trance 1*, & *Trance 2*
Coyote Oldman: *In Medicine River*
————. *Tear of the Moon*
Ali Jihad Racy: *Ancient Egypt*
Steve Roach: *Quiet Music*
Ravi Shankar: *In Celebration* (4 CD box set)
Tony Scott: *Music for Zen Meditation*
Dr. Jeffrey Thompson: *Egg of Time*
Valley of the Sun Artists: *The Eternal Om*
Various Performers: *Ringing Clear: The Art of Handbell Ringing*

See also Mantric Musical Menu, page 342.

Music Sources

A number of additional Meditation, Chanting, and Mantra audio selections can be obtained from the following companies.

The Hanuman Foundation
524 San Anselmo Ave., Suite 203
San Anselmo, CA 94960

Pacific Spirit
Whole Life Products
1334 Pacific Avenue
Forest Grove, OR 97116

Insight Recordings
P.O. Box 700
San Jacinto, CA 92383

Omega Institute for Holistic
    Studies
260 Lake Drive
Rhinebeck, NY 12572-3212

ISHK Book Service
P.O. Box 176
Los Altos, CA 94022

Living Arts
P.O. Box 2939
Venice, CA 90291-2939

Sounds True
735 Walnut Street
Boulder, CO 80302

Samuel Weiser
Box 612
York Beach, ME 03910-0612

23

Creativity

A fly can't bird, but a bird can fly.[1]

How often do we hear the expression, "I'm just not creative enough!"? And, in response, how often do we, through reflex or habit, *agree* with this "observation" ("Yeah, neither am I!")?

A lot of us perceive of "creativity" as something which is almost magical. A celebrated specialty reserved for others by the supreme lords who bestow those wondrous powers at the instant of conception or the moment of our births. Leonardo's Mona Lisa, now *that* was creative! How about Bach's "Brandenburg Concertos"? Genius! As is Michelangelo's exquisite sculpture of David. And what of Handel's "Messiah," Beethoven's "Ninth Symphony," or Mozart's "Eine kleine Nachtmusik"? Now *those* were innovative! And let's not forget the writings of Shakespeare, Wordsworth, Hemingway, and Poe. Aesop's Fables, Grimm's Fairy Tales, "Alice's (in Wonderland) Adventures through the Looking Glass." How about the ideas of Freud, Jung, Einstein, and Maslow? Or, how about more recent, contemporary phenomena such as Stephen Hawkings' theories, The Beatle's *Sgt. Pepper's Lonely Hearts' Club Band*,

---

1. Benjamin Hoff, *The Tao of Pooh* (New York: Penguin Books, 1983), p. 39.

Pink Floyd's *The Wall*, and Marvin Gaye's *What's Going On?*; Disney's and Spielberg's movies, Bob Kane's "Batman"; Siegel and Shuster's "Superman"; Charles Schulz' "Peanuts," Bill Watterson's marvelous "Calvin and Hobbes," and Scott Adam's "Dilbert." Creativity at its finest!

But is creativity only that which can be associated with the arts? How about fabulous architecture such as the Taj Mahal, the Eiffel Tower, the Roman Baths? And what of earth-shaking inventions, such as the printing press, the light bulb, the airplane, the automobile, modern computers, MRI scanners, or the laser? Or historical documents such as the Declaration of Independence, the Magna Carta, and Lincoln's Emancipation Proclamation? Therefore, is creativity a quality that abounds only within the realm of genius?

Not really. In actuality, creativity and intelligence (or IQ), are not directly correlated. Although basic intelligence is necessary before we can express ourselves creatively, people can be highly intelligent without being highly creative and vice versa. Another factor is our culture's lack of incentive for developing creativity among many of our educational systems. Rather than rewarding creativity, most academic institutions—from the primary through the graduate level—tend to discourage (right brain) artistry, imagination, and creativity, while encouraging (left brain) logical, rational thinking and linear, traditional processing and memorization. Having directed this very question to school administrators, the reply I typically receive is that "creativity is hard to teach or grade." A reply which, in itself, tends to lack any degree of creativity or imagination.

For me, creativity can be defined as our ability to use whatever is available to fill a need, pass the time, and generally make the best of whatever talents or abilities we have. Coming up with something that is helpful or useful in some way to oneself or others. In everyday terms coming up with quick or efficient ways of shoveling snow, raking leaves, mowing the lawn, washing dishes, getting through the laundry, arriving at a destination on time while avoiding annoying traffic, or keeping our homes clean and orderly are essentially as creative, and often more practical, than being able to produce architectural masterpieces or great works of art.

Ordinary people, doing ordinary things, are often unaware of their high levels of creativity. My grandfather Paco's comic routines, my grandmother Fina's sewing, my mom's meals, my father's baseball tales; now *those* were creative! Creativity is at work among families with six children sharing one bathroom. It thrives in individuals with average intelligence who surprise everyone, including their school counselors, by graduating with an "A" average. It resonates among families with two or more teenage children and one car. It is the stuff of those persons who see opportunities where others see only obstacles, of children who stumble upon an old cardboard box and see a sleigh, or entrepreneurs who hear news of a market deficit and foresee a rising trend.

One of the most creative individuals I ever met arrived at my office in the guise of an 82-year-old woman. Beaming with energy, Charlotte made an appointment to discuss "her life's passages," and gain deeper insights into the psychodynamics of her personal world. Years back, in her mid-40s, Charlotte, an extremely gifted seamstress, was diagnosed with arthritis. At the time, her physicians reluctantly informed her that her condition was very serious, and that, before long, she would have to abandon the wonderful hobby which had served as her life's signature. To Charlotte, sewing was her life's mission, the thing she could do better than anyone else in the family. Beyond being "what she was known for," in her mind, sewing was "who she was."

Immediately after being diagnosed with arthritis, her doctors placed the saddened Charlotte on medication, and referred her to physical therapy. Although her therapeutic exercises were somewhat helpful, Charlotte found them tedious and boring. In her judgment, the medical community had basically "put her out to pasture," assigning her the role of "old lady" without having the slightest idea of who she was, or what her talents meant to her, and her family. Regardless, she continued her sewing in spite of increasing pain and rapidly diminishing fine dexterity and eye-hand coordination.

A few months later, while Charlotte sat at home watching a musical concert on television, she noticed that the hand movements being exhibited by a harpist were quite similar to those encouraged by the physical therapists. The following day, Charlotte made a number of calls, eventually locating a harp teacher. Welcomed as the instructor's oldest student, Charlotte, who liked music but who had no previous musical training or former desire to learn to play a musical instrument, began her tutorial. Almost immediately, Charlotte related, she "felt the harp's healing powers vibrating through my hands." The more she played the better she felt, and the more fluid and effortless her hand motions became. Before long, she had begun to regain her former coordination and hand dexterity. In Charlotte's words, it was not only the plucking and stroking of the harp strings which was therapeutic, but also the whole vibrational experience gained by holding the resonating instrument close to her body that seemed to have incredible healing and energizing effects.

The effects gained through this musical experience extended far beyond Charlotte's rejuvenated abilities as a dexterous seamstress. Once Charlotte started becoming "more intimate" with music as a whole, she began to see a connection between people and the music they preferred. "You know how people start to look like their dogs?" she asked, "Well, I think they also look and feel like the music they listen to!" As a result of this observation, the new and improved Charlotte developed an amazingly innovative approach to her sewing.

Feeling invigorated and motivated by the music, she gave in to long-standing community requests and extended her sewing practice to outside of her own family circle. Charlotte had two simple requests for those who sought her services. First, they had to meet her personally whenever they placed their orders. Second, they had to provide her with samples of their favorite music while she worked on their garments. "Their vibrations are the same as the music they like," she related, "By listening to their music while I work, their vibrations come out of the stereo, through me, and into the garments. It's like magic!"

Just as "magical" were both the end results and the feedback that Charlotte received from her customers. No one could understand how, after meeting a customer for only a few minutes, this woman was able to personalize each garment so distinctively, capturing, as they described, "the spirit" of what they wanted. After fifty years of limiting her skills to creating beautiful, ornate apparel for her family, she creatively developed a way to personalize strangers' garments based on the vibrational feel of their musical preferences. Before long, there weren't enough hours in the day for Charlotte to keep up with the local demands, much less for those which started to come from customer's distant relatives and surrounding communities. Luckily, she remained centered enough to set limits and restrict herself to certain types of work and a comfortable work schedule. That was thirty-two years ago. To this day, Charlotte, at 82, continues to play the harp, develop new insights and create wonderful works of art for a lucky few.

> What is universal is the human propensity to create order out of chaos.[2]

Throughout our lives, we spend significant amounts of time attempting to find a sense of structure or discipline. Almost relentlessly we search for "whys," "solutions," "meanings," and "purposes." Against all odds, we struggle endlessly to create order from the chaos, to find substance within the void. We yearn for harmony and symmetry to assist us in defining our

2. Anthony Storr, *Music and the Mind* (New York: Free Press, 1992), p. 64.

realities. Eventually, all of this "trying" rapidly drains our energies, motivation and creative juices.

So what would happen if we simply allowed ourselves the luxury of taking a few minutes each day to regenerate our resources? To take the opportunity to listen to what is deep, very deep inside ourselves, unimpeded from discipline or structure? To relish in the silence of the void and feel absolutely comfortable, and at peace, with the chaos that surrounds us?

Although music can be used as a unique and powerful tool to promote order and structure, it is just as effective in providing an escape from reality and escorting us into temporary mental and emotional retreats where we can be safe from the demands of the external world. Guiding us through, and beyond, our inner "psychological noise," it can also assist us in bypassing, and transcending, our self-imposed fears and limitations.

> Music takes your mind to another place and allows it to wander freely and unencumbered.[3]

The objective for the following exercise is to assist in freeing you from any anchors that bind you to past or present worries or concerns, as well as helping you disengage from self-imposed future limitations or expectations. To assist you in this exercise, you may want to select either music with which you have little or no association (i.e., do not select music which may tend to stir up old images, or which you are well-acquainted with), or music you find particularly interesting or intriguing (i.e., this may be "world beat" music with uncommon elements from exotic lands such as Asia, the Middle East, or Africa, or perhaps tunes with instruments to which you are unaccustomed to hearing, perhaps Indian sitars, Tibetan bells, a hurdy gurdy, or aeolian harps; for fascinating sounds from ancient times you may also enjoy Gregorian chants, as well as Celtic music or tunes from the Middle Ages or the Renaissance). In effect, this presents an excellent opportunity to experiment with new or unusual music, or to tune in to that special soundtrack you have been saving for a special occasion.

> The joy of Tao is many things, but most of all a realization that we're part of something larger than ourselves, a pattern of infinite beauty that flows within us and around us.[4]

---

3. Barbara Anne Scarantino, *Music Power: Creative Living Through the Joys of Music* (New York: Dodd, Mead & Company, 1987), p. 159.
4. Diane Dreher, *The Tao of Inner Peace* (New York: Harper Collins, 1991), p. 118.

EXERCISE 29:

Enhancing Creativity

{L}istening to music that paints pictures in your mind of far-off
places or exciting romantic adventures will fill you with
new inspiration.[5]

1. Prepare either a pad and pen, or a portable cassette recorder with a fresh tape and batteries. Retire to a quiet, comfortable place where you may sit or lie down for twenty to thirty minutes without being disturbed.

2. Make a musical selection that you feel will be particularly inspiring or motivational, something you believe may serve to awaken your muse and stimulate your creative juices. (For some suggestions, see the Altered States Musical Menu, page 241.)

3. Before beginning your creative musical sojourn, close your eyes, initiate deep breathing, and remind yourself that you are about to embark on a journey where there are no rules, expectations, "shoulds," or limitations.[6]

4. The act of "letting go"[7] is particularly essential for this exercise. As you allow the musical images to unobstruct your path, remind yourself that wherever it appears, there you'll follow. Along the way, listen to how the music releases you from boundaries, providing you access to the archetypal patterns encoded in the vastness of the cumulative unconscious.

5. Turn on your music and initiate a "Spiral Sojourn"[8] technique.

6. Throughout your creative journey, pay attention to any sensations or images that may appear. As the music emancipates, and then intensifies your inner images, feel them merge, shape, and bond with your emotional character.

---

5. Scarantino, *Music Power*, p. 159.
6. See Expectations, page 293, and Shoulds, page 311.
7. See Letting Go, page 249.
8. See Spiral Sojourn, page 361.

7. Having reached your "special place"[9] remain open to colors, shapes, sizes, textures, scents, tastes, and of course sounds that you may encounter. As these appear, feel yourself flowing and dancing with them. Again, feel yourself completely surrendering to the music.

8. As the music unbinds your "inner guide," listen to cues, clues and suggestions that provoke deeper exploration into the invisible realms that surround you. Remember that here, in your special place, your ability to look into the invisible is vivified, so observe. Your yearnings to hear the inaudible are realized, so listen.

9. As you enter deeper into your inner worlds, flowing amidst the sound waves, feel yourself soaring through the silence of the spaces between the notes. As you enter this hollowness, find yourself in a very private place where you may encounter the core of your vibrational being. Within this place, all physical laws are dismissed, and all ideas unhampered. Here, at last, is that long lost space where you vibrate in stillness and dance in the silence. It is from this deepest of all places that you may stimulate new memories and gather the seeds of new impressions.

10. Having spent the time you need with your "inner guide," once again re-enter the rhythmic structure of the music and allow the musical patterns to support and lift you back to the world of resonance and dissonance, harmony and discord. Upon exiting the Spiral Sojourn and returning to the "heAr and now,"[10] take the time to immediately write or dictate onto a tape every thought, feeling, idea, or impression which you gathered from the inner guide at your "special place."

11. Even upon returning to the "real world," remind yourself not to lose the sights and sounds generated from your innermost images. As always, remember that this is a place where you are always free to return, whenever you want to and as often as you wish. All you need to do to return there is allow your "acoustic memory"[11] to trigger the descent back through the Spiral Sojourn, releasing your mind from expectations, and opening your mind to the harmony that abounds within the chaos.

12. Having returned from your musical "Spiral Sojourn," you may choose to surround yourself with a stimulating, soothing, meditative, or inspira-

9. See Special Place, page 367.
10. See HeAr and Now, page 243.
11. See Acoustic Memory, page 291.

tional music background that will provide the proper ambiance to moti-
vate work on a personal creative project. See corresponding Musical
Menus: Stimulating Music, page 20, Soothing Music, page 55, Meditation
Music, page 230, and Inspirational Music, page 48.

Sound Idea

Buy . . . rent . . . borrow a foreign language
audio tape (record, CD). As it plays, listen to
the music of the voices, the rhythms, tones,
textures, the melody, pitch, tempo. Without
trying to understand, listen.

♪

Musical Menu 19
Music for Altered States
(CDs, TAPES, ALBUMS)

Prem Das: *Journey of the Drums*
Michael Danna: *Skys*
Dead Can Dance: *Spirit Chaser*
Farzin: *In a Far Away Land*
Robert Gass & On Wings of Song: *Shri Ram*
Philip Glass: *Koyaanisqatsi*
Randall Gray: *One Hand Clapping*
Michael Harner: *Drumming for the Shamanic Journey, vol. 1*
David Hykes & The Harmonic Choir: *Harmonic Meetings*
Larkin: *O'Cean*
Gabrielle Roth and the Mirrors: Any selection
Steve Roach, Michael Stearns & Ron Sunsinger: *Kiva*
Steve Roach, Stephen Kent & Kenneth Newby: *Halcyon Days*
Shanghai Chinese Traditional Orchestra: *Tortoise; Phoenix; Serpent; Tiger* (Chinese Feng Shui Music)
Runestone: *Mysteries*
Various Artists: *The Tree of Life* (Persian Music)

24

LIKE LIFE, EACH MUSICAL COMPOSITION
HAS A BEGINNING, AND AN END.
WHAT TRULY MATTERS IS WHAT
WE CHOOSE TO DO
DURING THE INTERVAL.

HeAr and Now

*Any individual moment in the music has had a past and is prelude
to a future. Our success as listeners consists in our increasing ability
to hear each moment in a wider context.*[1]

Music is timeless. We compose, play and listen to it in the present, listen forward to it in the future, and remember it in the past. Although life as we know it can only occur in the present moment it seems that we try our hardest, consciously and unconsciously, to avoid the inevitable "here and now." As a result, we are usually so distracted by our concerns over what occurred "in the past" and how we can make amends "in the future" that we are rarely aware of the fact that we are living "now," in each and every present moment. Masters of disguise, distractions attack us in either positive (success, joy, entertainment, humor, laughter, revelry) or negative (anxiety, worries, fears, pains, itches, disappointment) forms. These distractions bombard our every waking moment, and are so omnipresent that the only choice we have is to acknowledge them ("Yes, there they are!") and then make the *conscious* decision to concentrate on what we are involved in at the moment.

1. Robert Harris, *What to Listen for in Mozart* (New York: Simon & Schuster, 1991), p. 131.

> [W]hen you're no longer thinking ahead, each footstep isn't
> just a means to an end but a unique event in itself.[2]

Not long ago, I had the pleasure of working with Nancy, a woman who
"never had enough time." A married, 48-year-old mother of two, Nancy
reported being happily married but unhappy with life in general. Early
during our first session, Nancy indicated that for as far back as she could
remember she had been unable to enjoy anything. She felt that she was
"aging too fast," and that "the world was passing her by."

As we proceeded with her initial session, it became quickly apparent
that Nancy found herself struggling to provide me with some very basic,
run of the mill information about herself. Her mind, she indicated, had the
tendency to wander. At one point during our conversation I asked her
where her mind was at the moment. "Well . . . here!" she replied, rather
defensively. Having gained her attention, I took this opportunity to further clarify my point by asking her "where she was *in time*." Her first
response was to quickly introduce me to her favorite phrase, which was "I
don't have time for this!" After pondering for a moment, however, Nancy
agreed that, as I talked, she had found herself drifting in time. In fact, she
had spent the past couple of minutes worrying about how congested the
traffic would be on the way home after our session (the future), mentally
replaying a morning conflict she had experienced with a co-worker (the
past), wondering what she would wear to work the next day (the future),
and feeling guilty that she had "wasted" an hour the evening before watching a television special (again, the past). She affirmed that her mind "did
this all of the time" and staunchly believed she lacked any control over
these occurrences.

As we delved deeper into Nancy's daily pattern, it became increasingly apparent that she did, indeed, spend much of her time in the future
or the past, either trying to foretell and pre-empt events that may occur or
dwelling over incidents she "should" have handled more effectively in the
past. She wasted enormous amounts of energy, she revealed, "expecting"
things to happen and trying to predict "why" events would or would not
occur, or "why" they had or had not occurred. For Nancy, it seemed, there
was no now. Only then, and later.

During later sessions, Nancy began to realize just how extensive and
deeply imbedded her avoidance of the present seemed to be. Whenever her

---

2. Robert Pirsig, *Zen and the Art of Motorcycle Maintenance* (New York: Morrow, 1976).

children visited, she would waste most of her time wondering how long it would be before they would visit again. As soon as they left, she would worry whether they had enjoyed themselves, and wondered what else she could have done, said, or served, that could have increased their pleasure and comfort. Rarely, if ever, she remembered what had taken place during the actual visit. At the office, Nancy—a professional career woman who insisted she loved her job—would spend most of her day thinking about what there was to do at home in the evening. She would then spend the evenings thinking about what she had left unaccomplished at the office and how she would take care of it tomorrow. When on vacation, Nancy disclosed she would waste her time either worrying over whether this would be their last vacation together, trying to live up to previous outings or pressing to make up for events they had not shared together in the past. Even when making love, she conceded, her mind would wander off. Regardless of the situation, be it the work day, a vacation, her childrens' visits, or the lovemaking, the event in question would be over before she ever realized it had happened. In the end, it seemed, Nancy would be invariably left with little more than regrets over what she *could* have done, or the hope that "next time" things would be better. One of her primary goals, she proclaimed sadly, was to "one day start enjoying things." Between echoes of yesterday, and noises of tomorrow, it was a wonder she could hear anything at all!

Over the next few weeks, I introduced Nancy to a number of music and sound related techniques—many of which are discussed and explained throughout this book—to assist her in gaining a keener sense of moment-to-moment experiencing. Through these techniques, Nancy began to regain her ability to be in the present, and to recognize and appreciate life as it was taking place. Rather than focusing on expectations of what "may happen," or "why" things had happened in the past, she became increasingly more adept at noticing *what* was taking place in the present, and *how* events unfolded as they randomly occurred. With practice, she became better able to appreciate the present and to focus on who she was at that moment in time rather than dwelling over who she had been, or what she would probably never be. She came to realize that 48 was "really not so very old!" Details about her childrens' visits became increasingly vivid, and she returned from a week long vacation recounting clear, rich recollections of a wonderful adventure she had undertaken with her husband.

ENJOYMENT ONLY EXISTS IN THE HEAR AND NOW.
LISTEN TO PLEASURES AS YOU RECEIVE THEM,
AT THAT MOMENT.
MEMORIES ARE ECHOES OF PLEASURES
THAT ONCE WERE.

Although some of the "psycho-music" approaches used in Nancy's treatment were designed to address her specific concerns, and her personal situation, a number of them were simple, general exercises which anyone can try. One such exercise we labeled "The Sound Hunt," and the purpose was to use the time during her morning walks to take notice of as many sounds as she could detect. As she heard these passing sounds, she was to simply take notice and listen to them, at that moment, and then move on. Since Nancy's walks took her around the neighborhood, where she regularly saw children playing, or going about their daily business, another suggestion was for her to actively take note of how children are invariably immersed in the moment. As she would begin to ponder over how much better it would have been if she had gained these insights into her issues earlier in life, my suggestion was simply for her to remind herself that, whenever she arrived at certain realizations, that would be "the right time." Finally, since old habits are hard to break, it was suggested that, once in a while, she allow herself to drift off, *on purpose*. In general, she was encouraged to follow and trust her own rhythms and to transcend future obstacles and past concerns by acknowledging the value of common things, listening intently, and being consciously present in the things she did.

Quite often we speak, or think, in a past ("I wish I had done that!") or future ("I'll get to that later!") mode. Throughout this book you will have seen the phrase "here and now" used interchangeably with "heAr and now" with accentuation on the "A." The purpose of this is to consistently alert and remind the reader to use any detectable sound cues (music, passing traffic, the breeze, singing birds, air conditioning, a purring cat, someone's voice, one's own breathing) to remain anchored in the present. The phrase "heAr and now" is also meant to remind readers to listen to their own inner (as well as outer) dialogues and work toward becoming more grounded in the present.

Each moment in time is the only moment there is.
This moment is not measured linearly.

The sound emerging from this moment is the only sound.
It is free of the past or the future.[3]

An excellent way to become more adept at recognizing and enjoying each present moment is by developing our ability to become grounded. "The technique of grounding, used to anchor a person in a flashback to the here and now, is accomplished by the very act of playing a musical instrument. . . . The instrument/music acts as transitional object, bridging internal and external worlds as well as past and present. Although circumstances of the past may not be changed, a new way of relating is discovered. . . . Musical improvisation gives the individual the power to respond. . . . Improvisation goes beyond the telling of the details, combining the story, the emotions and an active response."[4] If you are a musician, whether novice, amateur, or professional, an excellent way to become grounded in the heAr and now is through improvisation with your instrument(s).

Through improvisation, "We can hear the person coming into being as he or she creates a relationship in time."[5]

The benefits that can be gained from this technique, of course, are not limited to musicians. Although many of the exercises that appear throughout this book provide effective ways to experience the benefits of grounding, or to enhance one's present moment awareness, some of the more specific ways through which grounding can be accessed—whether you are a musician or not—are presented in Exercise 9, Giving Up Control: Letting Go; Exercise 20, Listening and Communication Enhancement; Exercise 21, Enhancing Listening Sensitivity; and Exercise 35, Finding Your Mantric Sound.

Music can bring us to the awareness of the eternal Now because it can be experienced only in the present.[6]

3. Joanne Crandall, *Self-Transformation through Music* (Wheaton, IL: The Theosophical Publishing House, 1986), p. 18.
4. Stephanie Volkman, "Music Therapy and the Treatment of Trauma-Induced Dissociative Disorders," *The Arts in Psychotherapy*, 1993, 20, 3, pp. 243–252 (p. 250).
5. David Aldridge, "Physiological Change, Communication, and the Playing of Improvised Music: Some Proposals for Research," *The Arts in Psychotherapy*, 1991, 18, 1, pp. 59–64.
6. Crandall, *Self-Transformation through Music*, p. 17.

Finally, think of the phrase "heAr and now" in itself as offering a simple "hook" to remind yourself to listen, so that they may hear.

> The statement of music is made moment by moment, what it expresses comes to life as it moves in time.[7]

There is a reason this is happening now.

Sound Idea

Nothing is coincidence.

---

7. P. Nordoff and C. Robbins, *Therapy in Music for Handicapped Children* (London: Gollancz, 1971), p. 7.

25

Letting Go

A smile sounds like a beautiful melody.

" Just let go!" It sounds so simple. The fact is, of course, it isn't. For just a moment, form a fist. Squeeze it tight, and hold it. Hold it for ten seconds, and then, for ten seconds longer. As you count each passing second, feel the tension, stress, and discomfort mount and accumulate in your fingers and your hand. Tune in to the awareness of how good your hand and fingers will feel in just a few seconds, once you let go and allow your clutching grip to return to the state of peace and natural relaxation it knew just a few seconds ago. After a total of twenty seconds have elapsed, give yourself the message to actively "let go!" and bask in the pleasure of your simple reward. The strain relieved, the tightness and tension flutter away like butterflies suddenly released from inside of a paper bag.

Having experienced this simple event, this letting go of a mere twenty seconds of *voluntary* tension, just imagine how good it would feel to let go of issues, thoughts, feelings, concerns, fears, worries, anxieties, tensions and distress which you have held onto for hours, days, weeks, months, years!

The concept of "letting go" is one among many which resonate throughout this book. In effect, it is one of the primary notions underlying most of the topics covered in this book. But how *do* we let go?

> When the delight is over, they still will not let go of it: they surround its memory with ritual worship, they fall on their knees to talk about it, play music and sing, fast and discipline themselves in honor of the eight delights. When the delights become a religion, how can you control them?[1]

Although referred to freely—and quite extensively— throughout much of the "New Age" and "alternative" literature that has found popularity over the past few years, the notion of "letting go" is still misunderstood or seemingly misinterpreted by many people. In that sense, letting go is almost a "mystically magical concept."

Letting go is about unattachment—about our capability to remain involved in an issue or an object without remaining attached to it. A case in point would be an artist who paints for a living. Throughout a career, this artist will very likely create any number of works which required, or inspired, significant amounts of involvement. To earn a living, however, the artist must usually be able to remain ultimately unconnected to these creations and "let them go" to the highest bidder.

> If you want to accord with the Tao,
> just do your job, then let go.[2]

A similar situation is often encountered by those of us in the helping professions (social workers, therapists, psychologists, members of the clergy, medical personnel). Although listening, and "being there" with our clients or patients is essential in the "heAr and now," once the interaction is over it is time to emotionally "let go." Paramedics, for instance, are often faced with shocking, frightful, and sometimes tragically horrifying events with which they must become rapidly, and intensively involved. Once the patient is signed off at the hospital, however, the professional needs to let go and discard any attachment to the injured person's condition, regardless of its gravity. The notion of "heAr now, let go later" is also shared among those in other professions—the beauticians, bartenders, cab drivers, masseurs and masseuses—who listen as part of their (unwritten) job descriptions.

1. Thomas Merton, *The Way of Chuang Tzu* (New York: New Directions, 1965), p. 71.
2. Lao-Tzu, *Tao Te Ching*, Stephen Mitchell, trans. (New York: HarperCollins, 1988), chapter 24, lines 13, 14.

The skill of "letting go" is particularly important for psychotherapists, clinicians, and others in similar professions who hear one heartbreaking story after the next. Without this skill, one can quickly encounter professional burn-out. While involvement with the individual in the present is essential for clinical work, the ability to let go—or release any attachment, personal attraction, or affection for a patient—is as imperative as empathically "staying with" that individual during a session. It is not about alienation or indifference, but about separation through emotional detachment. It is a sensitive objectivity or distancing from any bond or association which is, as everything else in life, time limited.

Sound Idea

As often as possible surround yourself
with music and take a melodic vacation
to an exotic paradise inside your mind.

The simplicity of "letting go" is exemplified by its omnipresence in our everyday activities. The following examples of "letting go" are often taken for granted:

- Sneezing;
- Crying;
- Laughing;
- Falling asleep;
- Screaming in support of a team;
- Singing from the heart (or, in the shower);
- Yawning;
- Sighing;
- Stretching;
- Smiling;
- Reaching an orgasm.

And so, letting go is about release. As a concept, letting go does not consist of actively "doing" anything in particular, but of allowing, yielding, or surrendering. "Being," rather than "trying to be."[3] As a process, however, "letting go" can involve actively working toward changing unwanted, unhealthy, or even dysfunctional thought patterns, behavioral habits, or emotional trappings that interfere with our quality of life. In a way, letting go is about doing by way of *not* doing!

A common problem we encounter as psychologists involves some of our patients' inability to reach orgasm during sexual intercourse. Sylvia, a 26-year-old recently married woman, presented with such a situation. Prior to the onset of the condition, Sylvia had come to me with unrelated issues including premarital counseling. Her family physician, concluding that her difficulties appeared to be psychological, referred her to our office for consultation. After our initial meeting, I suggested that Sylvia consider a highly reputable specialty clinic which happened to be located fairly close to their home. However, due to the intimacy of her issue, and the fact that we had already established a trusting relationship, she indicated she felt more comfortable addressing this concern with me first.

Following an evaluation and discussion about her presenting concerns, it became apparent—as acknowledged by Sylvia—that her inorgasmic condition seemed to be due to her inability to release, or let go. Ironically, as is often the case with the inability to let go, Sylvia felt she was merely "trying too hard." Rather than "enjoying the experience and flowing with the moment," she would begin to anticipate[4] and visualize the (anti)climactic event even before foreplay.

Drawing from a large number of studies that suggested using music may be helpful in this situation, I recommended that we attempt a psychomusicological approach to try and trigger her orgasmic potential. For example, studies using music have found that it effectively serves as a "pacemaker," helping two interacting persons "synchronize their frequencies."[5] Other studies strongly support the notion that music is a highly effective relaxation-inducing agent which helps to decrease tension and reduce anxiety.[6] Still, other findings have indicated that music functions as

3. See Being versus Trying to Be, page 261.
4. See Expectations, page 293.
5. R. Haas, S. Distenfeld and K. Axen, "Effects of Perceived Musical Rhythm on Respiratory Pattern," *Journal of Applied Physiology*, 1986, 26, pp. 1185–1191.
6. See F. Borgeat, "Psychophysicological Effects of Two Different Relaxation Procedures: Progressive Relaxation and Subliminal Relaxation," *Psychiatric Journal of the University of Ottawa*, 1983, 8, pp. 181–185; and J. P. Scartelli, "The Effect of EMG Biofeedback and Sedative Music, EMG Biofeedback Only, and Sedative Music Only on Frontalis Muscle Relaxation Ability," *Journal of Music Therapy*, 1984, 21, pp. 67–78.

an excellent catalyst to block out extraneous obtrusive stimuli, such as noises, helping us to concentrate "on the moment" while focusing on the immediacy of the situation.[7] Further, music has been found to effectively increase environmental stimulation by providing a pleasant atmosphere as well as functioning as a powerful, albeit non-threatening, stimulus.[8] Finally, and perhaps more directly relevant to this particular situation, music has also been found to be instrumental in helping to release tension.[9] Music, it seemed, could hold a key to Sylvia's circumstances. Sylvia fondly recalled how effective Ravel's "Bolero" seemed to be in the movie "10," which starred Bo Derek and Dudley Moore.

I suggested that Sylvia and her partner adapt music as a potential "aphrodisiac" during their next lovemaking session. Over the next few weeks, Sylvia and her husband experimented to a number of different musical backdrops. Although at first the music did not seem to have its ultimately desired effect Sylvia indicated that it was helping her to relax; that it was very helpful in cutting down her internal, anxiety provoking "psychological noises"[10]; and that it was certainly helping her to focus on the heAr and now of their sexual intimacies much more effectively. In addition she felt that the musical tapestries added a romantic flair as well as diversity to their sexual repertoire.[11]

After a few tries at achieving an orgasm, Sylvia returned to my office indicating that, "for whatever reason," one night she found herself yielding to the rhythms of the music. During their lovemaking the seductive effects of "Mahogany Nights" by Al Gromer Khan (one which I had recommended as a personal favorite) had "allowed" her to finally surrender to the moment and release herself to the pleasures of a wonderful orgasm. Although she continued to prefer having music as a regular part of their sexual regimen, she quickly became increasingly more adept at finding her point of abandon, regardless of the musical background. By letting go, she

---

7. See. V. N. Stratton and A. H. Zalanowski, "The Effect of Background Music on Verbal Interaction in Groups," *Journal of Music Therapy*, 1984a, 21, pp. 16–21; and J. E. Borling, "The Effects of Sedative Music on Alpha Rhythms and Focused Attention in High-Creative and Low-Creative Subjects," *Journal of Music Therapy*, 1981,18, pp. 101–108.

8. See D. E. Wolfe, "The Effect of Interrupted and Continuous Music on Bodily Movement and Task Performance of Third Grade Students," *Journal of Music Therapy*, 1982, 9, pp. 74–85; and R. Brim, "The Effect of Personality Variables, Dogmatism and Repression-Sensitization Upon Response to Music," *Journal of Music Therapy*, 1978, 15, pp. 74–87.

9. W. Gantz, H. M. Gartenberg, M. L. Pearson and S. O. Schiller, "Gratifications and Expectations Associated with Pop Music Among Adolescents," *Popular Music and Society*, 1978, 6, pp. 81–89.

10. See Psychological Noise, page 281.

11. For more on the latter, refer to Romantic Intimacy, page 183.

was finally able to begin trusting her own inner pulse, while bonding har-
moniously with her partner's personal rhythms.

Letting go, like anything and everything else, takes practice. The
more we practice, the better we become at it. Further, like anything and
everything else, it's best to start small, and build up from there. With this
in mind, what follows is an exercise to assist us in becoming more comfortable with the basic *process* of letting go.

> Concentrating on what you are doing at the moment is simply
> a matter of letting go of what you are not doing at the
> moment.[12]

EXERCISE 30:
Letting Go

1. Build yourself a hierarchy of things which you would like to "let go of,"
or release. Begin the list with something very simple. Something which
you know you will have little, or no trouble letting go of. Gradually, as you
become more adept at the process of letting go, begin to slowly add
increasingly difficult issues to your list. Some examples may include:

- Inhaling, holding the breath for a second or two, then letting it out.
- Holding a helium filled balloon by its string, and releasing
  it.
- Yielding the right of way to a motorist.
- Not holding on to comments made by a rude office recep-
  tionist over the phone.
- Restraining from raising your voice during an escalating
  argument.
- Refraining from resorting to abusive language or cursing
  during a heated argument.
- Experiencing a disappointment, but not staying disappointed.

12. J. J. Gibbs, *Dancing With Your Books: The Zen Way of Studying* (New York: Plume, 1990), p. 18.

- Expecting a particular result, but detaching from it once it does not come to pass.
- Telling someone you love them.
- Rooting for a favorite team which happens to lose a game, and later not obsessing over the loss.
- Having a depressing thought, or experience, then leaving the sadness behind.
- Becoming anxious in a stressful situation, then discharging the anxiety in a positive, healthy manner.
- Losing a possession, then putting it into perspective.
- Being afraid of a certain obstacle, going through the fear, then discharging it.
- Telling someone you like them.
- Grieving over the loss of a loved one, eventually releasing the pain.
- Feeling, or thinking you need to hold on. Then letting go.

Since nothing lasts forever, it is also good practice to let go of things of which we are fond, for example;

- Rooting for a favorite team which happens to win a game, then celebrating, but keeping your sense of excitement in proper perspective.
- Noticing and acknowledging that you look particularly good on a given day, then not letting it go to your head.
- Accepting a compliment, then refraining from spending the rest of the day fishing for additional, validating ones.
- Experiencing a personal or professional breakthrough, feeling the sense of accomplishment, pride or relief, then moving on.
- Having a particularly pleasant experience, then using it as a source of refreshing energy without turning it into an ascending fantasy.

In other words, try to remain objective and detached, viewing and experiencing the event from a "third person" perspective. Allow the experience, but stay away from becoming part of it, or allowing it to become a part of you.

2. Letting go also involves adapting a whole new state of mind, a brand new system of interpretive thoughts, reactive emotions and corresponding behaviors. With practice, and conscious development of awareness and will-power, we can begin to recognize the negative, self-defeating, and otherwise unhealthy patterns of thinking which we need to rid from our daily repertoire. Quite often, these may involve:

- Unrealistic expectations ("I will consistently outsell my co-workers every month"). *Let go, then replace with a more adaptive statement, such as*: "Each month I'll do the best I can, sometimes I'll be the top salesperson, other months I won't. Either way I'll be content with having done my best."

- Internalization of other's thoughts and feelings with regard to how things "should" be ("Men should never show their emotions"). *Let go, then replace with a more adaptive statement, such as*: "I have the right to feel my feelings and to express them."

- Self-defeating statements ("I am never going to find a job"); or overgeneralizing ("If I don't get this job it will prove that I am a failure"). *Let go, then replace with a more adaptive statement, such as*: "If I am not selected for this job I'll use the process as a learning experience and apply what I've learned during my next interview."

- Perfectionism ("If I make a mistake I don't deserve to be here"). *Let go, then replace with a more adaptive statement, such as*: "Everyone makes mistakes, I have as much right to be here and learn from my mistakes as anyone else."

- Unconditional acceptance of destructive or self-defeating rules and habits ("There's no sense in me asking someone out on a date, I'm just no good at that!"). *Let go, then replace with a more adaptive statement such as*: "I'm going to ask this person out; if I'm rejected I will probably feel badly. Then I will let those feelings go. If I *get* the date I will probably feel happy. Then I will go on with the rest of my day."

In other words, regardless of the situation, let go of any attachments to the end result. Accept that it's impossible to control another person's responses.[13]

---

13. See Control, page 87.

WHEN LETTING GO,
WATCH THE DRAMA OF YOUR LIFE
AS IT UNFOLDS AROUND YOU.
DETACH FROM THE FEELING, AND
FLOW WITH THE EXPERIENCE.
DANCE TO THE TUNE AS IT PLAYS.
WHEN IT'S OVER, MOVE ON.

3. Having recognized your need to let go of the various self-deprecating, destructive, and paralyzing self-statements, beliefs, and philosophies to which you adhere, you first need to visualize yourself *actively* taking control of your present reality and *creating* the desired changes.

> [A] musical composition such as an improvisation is an acceptable form in which we can expose some of our wilder and more out-of-control feelings.[14]

EXERCISE 31:
Selecting Your Soundtracks

In this exercise you get to function as actor, producer, director, and choreographer as you create your own mental soundtrack, opera, or music video.

Whenever a music background is consciously selected or created to convey a desired emotional response to a particular event, it is carefully chosen to elicit very specific thoughts and feelings. Once that particular music has been associated with that specific event, such as a scene in a movie, the original feelings aroused when watching that scene are often reactivated by hearing the music in any other context.[15]

Select a piece of music which relates, as closely as possible, to the energy you feel you may need to create a mental "music video" of a letting go experience. For instance, if asking your office partner to "stop smoking

---

14. Leslie Bunt, *Music Therapy: An Art Beyond Words* (London: Routledge, 1994), page 34.
15. See Contextual Cuing, page 287.

in your office" arouses feelings of anxiety, you may wish to select music for your visualization which elicits a feeling of relaxation and helps to reduce your anxiety. Conversely, if what you need to "let go" of feelings you are harboring toward your roommate is a jolt of energy, practice the visualization conveying your concern to a background of upbeat, stimulating, or even defiant music. (See Letting Go Musical Menu.)[16]

Just as a director will choose different musical backgrounds to fit a mood, or elicit diverse emotions in a play or movie, you can choose whatever musical scores you feel will provide the activating aural backdrop to your letting go process.

For instance, afflicted with self-statements such as, "There's no sense in me asking someone out on a date, I'm just no good at that!," you may choose a visualization which portrays you as a confident, smooth, self-assured individual. A person for whom "asking someone out on a date" is no more threatening, scary, or complicated than asking a store clerk if they have a particular sweater in your size, the expected reply will ultimately be "yes or no." In effect, the response you get in either situation (asking for a date, or asking for a sweater in your size) does not say anything in particular about you as a person. You are taking a risk without anticipation or expectation and, whatever the response, you can live with the rejection, be it the date, or the sweater. In either case, if the answer is "no," let it go, and go elsewhere.

Accordingly, you need a music background for your "music video." As such, you need to select the proper aural background for your visualization. If the "letting go" of your fear of rejection involves anxiety, select a soothing, relaxing musical piece. If you need to feel "pumped up," for the event, select an invigorating, arousing number. If what you need is to set the mood of confidence or romance, select a musical background which will elicit, and later help to "cue" that sense of confidence, daring, passion, adventure, or courtship for your encounter.

Later, whenever the moment arrives, or the need arises, you may consciously "cue-in" to the acoustic memory[17] of that same musical selection to help trigger your newly acquired "letting go" abilities as necessary.

When your work is done and fame has been achieved, retire into the background; for this is the Way of Heaven.[18]

16. See also Stimulating Musical Menu, page 20, Soothing Musical Menu, page 55, Music for Dealing with Anger, page 73, and suggested Big Band selections, page 160.

17. See Acoustic Memory, page 291.

18. Lionel Giles, *The Sayings of Lao Tzu* (London: John Murray, 1905), p. 24.

♩

Musical Menu 20
Music for Letting Go
(CDs, TAPES, ALBUMS)

Popular and "Alternative" Music Suggestions

B-52's: *Cosmic Thing*
Belly: *King,* or *Star*
Bonny Raitt: *The Bonnie Raitt Collection,* or *Road Tested*
Tracy Bonham: *The Burdens of Being Upright*
The Big Chill: *Original Motion Picture Soundtrack*
The Black Crowes: *Shake Your Money Maker*
The Darling Buds: *Erotica*
Counting Crows: *August & Everything After,* or, *Recovering the Satellites*
Sheryl Crow: *Sheryl Crow*
The Grateful Dead: *What a Long, Strange Trip It's Been*
Elastica: *Elastica*
Garbage: *Garbage*
Kula Shaker: *K*
Cyndi Lauper: *She's So Unusual,* or *Greatest Hits*
John Lennon: *Plastic Ono Band* (up-beat selections)
Dave Mathews Band: *Under the Table & Dreaming,* or, *Crash*
Morphine: *Cure For Pain*
Alanis Morissette: *Jagged Little Pill*
Joan Osbourne: *Relish*
Rusted Root: *When I Woke*
Sly & The Family Stone: *Greatest Hits*
Sugarcubes: *Life's Too Good*
Cheap Trick: *Live at Budokan*
Neil Young (with Pearl Jam): *Mirrorball,* or *Ragged Glory*

26

Being Versus Trying to Be

*Composing music, we are in the process of having been, being and
becoming all at once.*

Water is harmony. The rain kisses the streams. The streams flow
into rivers. Rivers follow their path to the lakes and the oceans,
their dance becomes the rain. By simply being, water becomes itself. Be
like water. When hot, become steam. When cold, become ice. When dancing, be the rhythm. By simply being, become yourself.

To be, or to try to be—that is our struggle! From the moment when
we are born, we begin to learn, and as we learn, we somehow come to believe
that very few things come to be without struggling. We struggle to crawl,
to stand, to say our first word, to climb out of our cribs and reach up into
the cookie jar. From the very beginning, we are rewarded for "trying," but
rarely—if ever—for simply "being." Reinforced for abandoning nature's
flow, we struggle through life unconsciously—though actively—trying to
forget and replace the pure essence of being. As taught by the great master,
Lao Tzu, we become so entranced by a society that blunts our awareness to
our individuality that we begin to believe that we are the masks we wear.

Being one with the Tao of music, helps us to transcend the fleeting
notion of "being," taking us to a place within ourselves where we may simply "be." "Being" versus "trying to be" is one of the most common struggles

we each face in our daily lives. Even before awakening each day we are already "trying" to wake up on time. We then "try" to get to work, school, the gym, or any other destination on time. "Being" on time, incidentally, is very, very important. Our society and culture dictate it. Phrases such as, "Be a man," or "Try to act like a lady," tend to color, or distort, our personalities. We find ourselves somewhere in the middle of "being" who we are, and "trying" to conform to someone else's expectations of what, or who, we are supposed to be. As a result, we easily confront others with phrases such as, "*Why* are you that way?" or respond with comments such as, "I'm *trying* to be different!"

AN ARTIST, CREATING,
AN ATHLETE, COMPETING,
AN AUDIENCE, LISTENING,
ALL LOSE TRACK OF TIME.
REGARDLESS OF THEIR PATH
ALL ARE ONE WITH THE TAO.

On our way to work we are at times sent off with a, "Have a nice day!" to which we may reply, "I'll try!" Similarly, a lot of us send our children off to school with, "Try to be careful!" Throughout our daily grinds, we "try" to maintain a well balanced diet, "try" to exercise on a regular basis, and "try" to get along with others and make good impressions. We "try" not to fall asleep during meetings and, while "trying" to function to the best of our ability, we "try" to be productive. As students we "try" to pay attention in class and obtain good grades. At the gym we "try" to get through our routines or defeat our opponent at racquetball. Working at home often becomes "trying" to find motivation to be productive so that we may take care of our respective domestic responsibilities. At the end of the day we "try" to get home on time as we "try" to observe the rules of the road, such as driving somewhere near the speed limit and "trying" to drive as safely as possible. On our way home we "try" to be mindful of errands that need to get done so we don't have to venture out again. Back home we "try" to spend some time with our families and keep up with day-to-day issues, events and responsibilities. During the week we remind each other, and ourselves, to "try" and have some fun—or be productive—over the weekend. Come the weekend, we "try" to enjoy ourselves or to get something done. For a lot of people, exhausted after a day of "trying," the day ends with "trying" to fall asleep. It's a trying world.

But how much time do we spend simply "being?"

Most of us tend to fall into the trap of defining, or describing, ourselves by one or more labels. "I *am* a student . . . a housewife/husband . . . an architect . . . a nurse . . . a mother/father." Inadvertently, we often get caught up in the struggle of "trying" to fulfill our expectations of what our corresponding roles "*should* be."[1]

Have you ever considered the distinction between simply "being" who you are, and "trying" to live up to a certain image or role? "Trying" often tends to involve the traps of fulfilling internal and external expectations of what, or who, we "should" be and "why" we should be (i.e., think, feel, act) a certain way. To a lot of people at the office, for example, I "am" a psychologist, or a doctor. Subjectively, when things are running smoothly throughout the day I sometimes become aware that I am "being" a doctor, comfortably "flowing" with a particular role in an effortless manner. At other times, however, my mind may drift or I may find myself somewhat struggling—or "trying"— to assist one of my patients. During those times I become aware that I am "trying" to be a psychologist, or a doctor. In our professional capacities, as in any other life roles, "being" feels natural and relaxed. As I stated above, it "flows." There is an openness which seems to embrace everything. When a songwriter enters a state of no-mind, the "zone," the song writes itself. Whenever a performer is "being," rather than "trying to be," one can't tell the singer from the song.

While "being," we seem to "float" through our days. We hover over barriers and soar over obstacles. We flow within our own stream, emerging. Solutions seem to surge from our still and peaceful minds. It's a feeling akin to sailing across calm seas, gliding at wind speed propelled by soft, gentle breezes. While in the "being" mode we do what we do, when and where we do it, in just the way we do it. Without need for reason, we simply *are*. "Being" we are at once vulnerable and strong. "Being" confused, sad or angry is somehow okay. Like yin and yang, we are intuitively aware of the duality of these feelings or states of mind which are mirror images of being clear-minded, happy, or relaxed. "Being" can only occur in the heAr and now. "Being," in my mind, is the closest us mortals can come to flying.

To drop the need to understand the world and simply to be in the world, in life, in music—this may be the new direction of humanity.[2]

1. See Shoulds and Musts, page 311.
2. Joanne Crandall, *Self-Transformation through Music* (Wheaton, IL: Theosophical Publishing House, 1986), p. 34.

"Trying," on the other hand, sometimes borders on grappling or strug-gling. Issues, or life itself, somehow become a sort of contest. We "get by" by climbing over obstacles and stumbling around barriers, "coping." We find ourselves "acting" as ourselves, or someone else, *because* of some rea-son. "Trying to be" we succumb to expected, prescribed and preconceived roles, habits, mannerisms, images, and facades. Problem solving, project-ing, analyzing, interpreting, and "trying" to guess what will come next, we feel stifled or even overwhelmed. We "try" to avert past mistakes and avoid future problems, missing out on the potential possibilities within and without us in the heAr and now. Confused, sad, or angry we "try" to figure out "why?" We ponder whether we should be feeling a certain way. We fall short of our expectations. Trying, in some ways, feels like we're at times fighting against ourselves and the world, swimming upstream. As a result, when our movements match our inner rhythms it feels like a dance. When our movements are made to conform to external rhythms, it becomes a struggle.

> The Balinese speak of "the other mind" as a state of being that can be reached through dancing and music. . . . There is free-dom from the restrictions of actual time and complete absorp-tion in the "Timeless Now of the Divine Spirit," the loss of self in being.[3]

In interpersonal relations we sometimes fall in the trap of being versus try-ing to be "real" (genuine, authentic). When we are "being," we do not have to be concerned about whether we are, or are not, being authentic, genuine or real. If the concern appears, we are "trying." If we are authentic, we're "being."

> Being in unity with each situation,
> we respond in total harmony.[4]

IF YOU'RE GOING TO BE ANYTHING,
BE LISTENING.

---

3. John Blacking, *How Musical is Man?* (Seattle: University of Washington Press., 2nd ed., 1976), p. 51–52.
4. Tarthang Tulku, *Openness Mind* (Berkeley: Dharma Publishing, 1978), p. 124.

Additional Reading

For additional reading regarding the notion of "Being Versus Trying to Be," you may refer to the following books:

Herbert Benson. *Beyond the Relaxation Response.* New York: Times Books, 1984.

James F. T. Bugental. *The Search for Existential Identity.* San Francisco: Jossey-Bass, 1979.

Thich Nhat Hanh. *Peace is Every Step: The Path of Mindfulness in Everday Life.* New York: Bantam, 1991.

Susan Jeffers. *Feel the Fear and Do It Anyway.* San Diego, CA: Harcourt Brace, 1987.

Harold Kushner. *When All You Ever Wanted Isn't Enough.* New York: Summit Books, 1986.

Daniel J. Levinson. *Seasons of a Man's Life.* New York: Ballantine, 1978.

Matthew McKay and Patrick Fanning. *Self-Esteem.* Oakland, CA: New Harbinger, 1987.

Stephen Mitchell. *Tao Te Ching.* New York: Harper Perennial, 1991.

Mildred Newman and Bernard Berkowitz. *How to Take Charge of Your Life.* Orlando: Harcourt Brace, 1977.

Martin Seligman. *Learned Optimism: The Skill to Conquer Life's Obstacles, Large and Small.* New York: Pocket Books, 1990.

Keith Thompson (ed.). *To Be a Man: In Search of the Deep Masculine.* Los Angeles: Jeremy P. Tarcher, 1991.

Roger N. Walsh and Frances Vaughan. *Beyond Ego: Transpersonal Dimensions in Psychology.* New York: St. Martin's Press, 1980.

Jon Kabat-Zinn. *Wherever You Go There You Are.* New York: Hyperion, 1994.

27

With a clear mind,
you can think forever.

Once heard, music is but an expression of Tao,
echoes are reflections of Tao.

Clearing the Mind

*Instead of gathering knowledge, you should clear your mind. If your
mind is clear, true knowledge is already yours.*[1]

Cathy was having problems clearing her mind of what she described
as almost constant mind chatter, or, what I like to refer to as "psychological noise."[2] This "internal static" seemed to be so "loud" in her own
mind that she sometimes found it difficult to listen to others while having a regular conversation. Needless to say, attempts at sitting still
throughout her staff meetings, or focusing during her biweekly night
classes, felt overwhelming.

As a matter of fact, Cathy's description of her almost ceaseless intrusive chatter seemed to fit almost perfectly my own definition of "psychological noise." In effect, her description was as follows. The instant she
began to awaken each morning, intrusive, bothersome thoughts began to
invade her mind. This "invasion" of her mental privacy, which severely
interrupted her normal reasoning processes, endured throughout the day
and persisted until she finally fell asleep each night. Her thoughts ranged
from worrying about things outside her control, such as what could go

---

1. Shunryu Suzuki, *Zen Mind, Beginner's Mind* (New York: Weatherhill, 1983), p. 84.
2. See Psychological Noise, page 281.

wrong during the day (getting a flat tire, or being caught in heavy traffic which would make her late for work), to things for which she would feel humiliated (forgetting something important, such as picking her two children up after school, or getting them to their activities on time). Although she did not obsess over any thought in particular, a barrage of endless and unrelated issues seemed to parade through her mind as "an endless train."

Due to the fact that she was raising two children on her own, attending night school, and holding down a full time job Cathy did not have the time, nor the money, to come to therapy on a regular basis. She was also staunchly opposed to medication, but was in search of "something which could help still her mind and get her through this period" in her life. I suggested that she try to quiet her mind with music.

Cathy preferred '70s rhythm and blues music. My "prescription" was for her to either purchase, or choose from her collection, a number of selections which she liked to listen to or sing along with. Since Cathy spent a lot of time commuting, utilization of her travel time seemed to be ideal. Whenever Cathy's mind seemed to be going at full speed, the suggestion was for her to indulge herself with energetic, pounding music with strong rhythms and fast, penetrating tempos. She liked to listen to her music loud. My suggestion, therefore, was for her to try and match the external volume of her music to the volume of her own, internal clanging, to get the music's vibration to match her own, and in effect receive a "musical massage." The purpose was to achieve a sense of "rhythmic synchronicity"[3] with her external environment.

Whenever the psychological noise began to quell, my suggestion was that she tone the music down as well, continuously matching her musical selections to adapt to the level of her own, fluctuating internal condition. The suggestion worked like a charm. Cathy found herself "flushing" her "psychological noises" very effectively during her once dreaded cross-town journeys, arriving at each destination clear-minded and refreshed. As she practiced this technique more often, she found that her need to access the loud and pounding tunes began to decrease, and she began to acclimate to the softer, more soothing selections. In other words, the music was helping her modify her emotional and mental states through entrainment.[4] Having this opportunity to quiet her internal chattering throughout the day proved immensely helpful in her ability to concentrate on her daily responsibilities much more effectively. Before long, Cathy found herself able to listen during meetings and night classes, able to integrate and

3. See Rhythmic Synchronicity, page 275.
4. See Entrainment, page 317.

retain the material, as well as able to contribute her own creative ideas much better than she had in years.

If we look beneath the clamor and clutter of our lives, we recognize our inner rhythms, which are part of the overarching rhythms of nature.[5]

EXERCISE 32:
Clearing the Mind

Listening to external music silences our inner noises.

1. For this exercise you will be assembling an entrainment music sequence. Find a few musical selections which *match* your *present* disturbing mood (frustration, confusion). See Musical Menus 12–14 (pages 160–161), Musical Menu 6, Music for Dealing with Anger (page 73), Musical Menu 20, Music for Letting Go (page 259), and Musical Menu 1, Anti-Depressed Mood Entrainment Sequence (page 16).

2. Find a few other selections which fall somewhere between your *present* internal state and the state you *want to achieve* (calm, cheerful). (Refer to page 55 for soothing music suggestions, and choose selections that fall *somewhere between* Number 1 above, and Number 3, below).

3. Complete your musical sequence with a few musical pieces that match your desired state (relaxation, positivity) as closely as possible. This should be music which you feel would "sound" as close as possible to the way you *want to feel* by the end of this exercise. (Choose selections that closely reflect your *desired* mood state. Also, see Soothing Musical Rhythmic Synchronicity Menu, page 55.)

4. Sit or lie comfortably, with eyes closed. Initiate deep breathing.[6] As the music begins to play, allow your mind to focus on, and flow with, the feel of the music.

---

5. Diane Dreher, *The Tao of Inner Peace* (New York: HarperCollins, 1991), p. xiv.
6. See Breathing, page 333.

5. Without trying[7], simply allow your body to respond and adapt to the changing musical pulses. Rather than using your body to dance to the music, allow the music to dance through your mind, like gelatin—or water—responding to pulsating vibrations.

6. With each passing moment, be present[8] with the music. Remain actively aware of your emotions as these blend and flow with the feel of the music. Hear your thoughts as they bond with and are transformed by the musical ideas underlying the musical compositions.

7. Listen to how the beat underlying the music shakes loose your cluttering thoughts and feelings. As this occurs, listen to how the melodies merge with these thoughts and emotions, causing them to flow and mobilize throughout your being, dislodged and moving fluidly and effortlessly. In time, lie back and "watch" as the rhythm of the instruments brushes and sweeps them, "escorting" them out of your body and mind, and off into oblivion. Listen, and surrender to your changing mood states as they are transformed by the gentle, yet powerfully persuasive energies elicited by the music.

8. As the musical sequence enters the selections reflecting your desired state, feel yourself literally *becoming* that state. Actively allow the music to penetrate and fill your body, heart, and mind, and to transform your vibrational state from cluttered to clear.

9. Once the musical sequence is complete, and has gone full circle, allow your "acoustic memory"[9] to continue echoing through you, resonating the clearing, flowing and positive energies you just imbibed.

10. Continue to breathe in harmony, enjoying the silence resonating within your clear mind.

> *How can sweet, harmonious melody exist in the midst of*
> *modern din—the clamor of traffic, social commotion, emotional*
> *confusion, noise pollution? Our inner music is inaudible.*
> *To hear it, we need to let go, until we arrive at the silence.*

7. See Being versus Trying to Be, page 261.
8. See HeAr and Now, page 243.
9. See Acoustic Memory, page 291.

An empty sort of mind is valuable for finding pearls and tails and things because it can see what's in front of it. An Overstuffed mind is unable to. While the Clear mind listens to a bird singing, the Stuffed-Full-of-Knowledge-and-Cleverness mind wonders what kind of bird is singing.[10]

Sound Idea

Once in a while, exercise your right
not to listen.

---

10. Benjamin Hoff, *The Tao of Pooh* (New York: Penguin Books, 1983), p. 146.

Additional Reading

For further reading on how music may help to clear the mind you may refer to the following articles:

S. H. Burleson, D. B. Center and H. Reeves, "The Effect of Background Music on Task Performance in Psychotic Children," *Journal of Music Therapy*, 1989, 26, pp. 198–205.

K. Gfeller, "Musical Components and Styles Preferred by Young Adults for Aerobic Fitness Activities," *Journal of Music Therapy*, 1988, 25, pp. 28–43.

J. P. Scartelli, "The Effect of EMG Biofeedback and Sedative Music, EMG Biofeedback Only, and Sedative Music Only on Frontalis Muscle Relaxation Ability," *Journal of Music Therapy*, 1984, 21, pp. 67–78.

C. A. Smith and L. W. Morris, "Differential Effects of Stimulative and Sedative Music on Anxiety, Concentration and Performance," *Psychological Reports*, 1977, 41, pp. 1047–1053.

V. N. Stratton and A. H. Zalanowski, "The Relationship Between Music, Degree of Liking and Self-Reported Relaxation," *Journal of Music Therapy*, 1984b, 21, pp. 184–192.

R. H. Wolf and T. L. Weiner, "Effects of Four Noise Conditions on Arithmetic Performance," *Perceptual and Motor Skills*, 1972, 35, pp. 929–930.

CONCEPTS AND TERMS

All the music that there is, each note that is written, every melody that has been conceived, and those which have yet to be, have always existed. We simply need to find them.

Rhythmic Synchronicity

*Strike a membrane with a stick, the ear fills with noise—
unmelodious, inharmonic sound. Strike it a second time,
a third, you've got rhythm.*[1]

According to Carl Seashore, in *Psychology of Music*, there are eleven basic ways by which rhythm affects our perception. In effect, rhythm does the following:

- Favors perception by grouping;
- Adjusts the strain of attention;
- Gives us a feeling of balance;
- Gives us a feeling of freedom, luxury, and expanse;
- Gives us a feeling of power;
- Stimulates and lulls (contradictory as this may seem);
- Is instinctive;
- Finds resonance in the whole organism;
- Arouses sustained and enriching association;
- Reaches out in extraordinary detail and complexity with progressive mastery; and

---

1. Mickey Hart, *Drumming at the Edge of Magic* (San Francisco: HarperSanFrancisco, 1990), p 12.

- Results in play, which is the free self-expression for the pleasure of expression.[2]

Throughout our lives we encounter countless instances of "finding our rhythm" as well as "being in sync." For example, during a recent trip to New York City, I took advantage of the city's multidimensional and diverse environments and seized every opportunity to venture off in random explorations. Being from a small town with a decidedly slower pace than Manhattan's, each time I set foot outside of my hotel, I felt as if I were entering an interstate highway during rush hour. The city's rhythms, I quickly realized, were quite different from my own. The New Yorkers' pace was quick, sharp, staccato. Regardless of their physical characteristics, sex, age, race, or direction, the host multitudes appeared somehow swifter and seemingly more aggressive in their tempo. I was out of sync. While they were "being" in New York, I was "trying to be" there. As I stepped aside to observe this reality, I realized that while people were moving more rapidly than I was accustomed, their movements were smooth, congruent, and somehow seemingly coordinated in spite of their enormous legions. Not unlike a clock, a well-oiled machine, or a well-disciplined, exhaustively rehearsed marching band, these multitudes who appeared unaware of each other, or their surroundings, were "in sync."

But was their walking tempo truly the issue? Making a mental note of their rate of velocity, I set my internal odometer and once again attempted to blend with the troupes. Nope. Within moments I found myself walking too fast and slowed down. Almost instantly, someone quickly side-stepped around me. I apologized. Too late, she was gone. As I turned to apologize, I felt the equivalent of slamming one's brakes in the middle of heavy traffic and braced for a collision with the incoming throngs. Somehow, without breaking stride, much as birds do when they migrate in "v" patterns south for the winter, the herds smoothly glided around me. I was fascinated. Marching to the tune of honking taxis, distant sirens, exotic accents, and complementary internal clocks, they had rhythmic synchronicity.[3]

Toward the end of my five-day visit, I was beginning to flow. I had let go of trying to fit in, and by simply being there, I had begun to devel-

2. See Carl E. Seashore, *Psychology of Music* (New York: Dover Publications, 1967), pp. 140–145.

3. For an in-depth discussion on the notion of rhythmic synchronicity see: John M. Ortiz, "The Facilitating Effects of Soothing Background Music on An Initial Counseling Session," Pennsylvania State University, Doctoral dissertation, 1991d, pp. 227–249. For related readings on the above the following books are also recommended: George Leonard, *The Silent Pulse* (New York: E. P. Dutton, 1978); Joachim-Ernst Berendt, *Nadha Brahma: The World is Sound* (Rochester, VT: Destiny Books, 1987); and Carl E. Seashore, *Psychology of Music* (New York: Dover Publications, 1967).

op a sort of complementary harmony. A few weeks later, during a vacation in London, I had a similar experience.

> Sometimes we need to modify our rhythms to harmonize with people and situations around us. One way to do this is with music.[4]

Rhythmic synchronicity, it's good to be home. One of the best examples of rhythmic synchronicity can be found in the poetic sweeps exhibited by well balanced crew teams. Through sheer determination and a commitment to perfecting their sport, these well honed teams transform endless hours of training and practice into an elegant showcase of rhythmic harmony. Other fine examples of this mutual synchronization can be seen in refined marching bands, musical combos, championship sports teams, Olympic skating couples, choirs, and military drill teams.

Other instances of this amazing phenomenon include ideal dancing (or lovemaking) partners. Among such partners, each advance or swaying movement seems to flow effortlessly with one's own. Even sudden, abrupt changes are somehow anticipated, satisfyingly endorsing and confirming one's own movements. Poetry in motion. Yet another example is found among interpersonal conversations, when two people in "rhythmic sync" literally finish each other's sentences. Sharing a "common pulse" they tend to agree on basically everything. In effect, they find themselves "being," rather than "trying" to be,[5] as if they were speaking in free-verse.

Rhythmic synchronicity also pertains to those unique feelings we tend to experience when we share time with a special friend, a friend whom we trust and with whom we feel completely at ease. Somehow, there is a melodious and empathic resonance that vibrates between the two individuals. Even when in disagreement, or in the midst of argument, the relationship feels non-threatening, safe, precious and rare. Not restricted to people, a lot of us find similar affinities with our pets as well as other animals.

Closely related to the notion of "rhythmic synchronicity"[6] is that of entrainment, a phenomenon which involves harmonious relationships and the similarity of frequency between two or more rhythms. "Entrainment" has been described by J. R. Evans as "the modification of one rhythmic phenomenon by the flow of another." The implication is that "persons

---

4. Diane Dreher, *The Tao of Inner Peace* (New York: HarperCollins, 1991), p. 104.
5. See Being versus Trying to Be, page 261.
6. See Rhythmic Synchronicity, page 275.

with similar rhythms or rhythm hierarchies find it easier to resonate with or entrain to each other,"[7] so that entrainment between persons may be enhanced through empathy, or increased liking between two individuals.[8]

In a similar vein, the notion of complementarity is described by T. J. Tracey and P. B. Ray as a "means of conceptualizing the communicational harmony and conflict in a relationship." According to Tracey and Ray, relationships characterized by high degrees of complementarity "tend to be productive because each participant more frequently follows the influence attempts of the other." They add that "little conflict exists over what is done by whom, and these relationships are characterized as comfortable," and, further, that these complementary relationships "tend to persist over time because the needs of each person are being satisfied."[9]

Some examples of a *lack* of rhythmic synchronicity include couples who simply "cannot get along," sport teams which "fall apart," musical groups which sound unappealing, and out-of-town tourists hopelessly lost in strange environments.

A more specific example of rhythmic *dis*-synchronicity is typically found among people who are recent arrivals from foreign cultures. First, as in my New York City example, these individuals indeed become "strangers in a strange land." Mechanically, their body rhythms are "out of sync" with those around them. Second, particularly in small towns, exotic physical characteristics (skin color, phenotype, mode of dress) tend to set them apart from the "norm," making them easy targets for those who feel "uncomfortable" among people who are "different" from themselves. Third, distinctive accents and foreign languages will quickly set different peoples apart from one another. Even if the two share a common language (English) different linguistic styles and patterns (volume, accent, modulation, pitch, relative clarity, pace) often result in making some people feel uneasy and even threatened, effectively disrupting attempts at communication and socialization. Fourth, cultural styles of body language (proximity, posture orientation, grooming, degree and speed of intimacy, gestures) play significant roles in one's ability to effectively acclimate and assimilate into new cultures. As a result, these people often become disheartened or discouraged in foreign environments and enter a cycle which can result in

7. J. R. Evans, "Dysrhythmia and Disorders of Learning and Behavior," in J. R. Evans and M. Clynes (eds.) *Rhythm in Psychological, Linguistic and Musical Processes* (Springfield, IL: Charles C. Thomas, 1986), pp. 249–274 (p. 251).

8. For more on Entrainment, see page 317.

9. T. J. Tracey and P. B. Ray, "Stages of Successful Time-Limited Counseling: An Interactional Examination," *Journal of Counseling Psychology*, 1984, 31, pp. 13–27 (p. 14).

decreased self-esteem, depression, anger, anxiety, incompetence, loneliness, frustration, or social isolation and alienation.

As is true among our own peoples, all cultures and societies have their own type of general rhythmic styles. Similarly, we each have our own music. One very effective way I have found to assist individuals from other cultures with their assimilation into our society is by encouraging exposure to our music. In effect, my most popular and common prescription for my cross-cultural patients calls for them to literally saturate themselves with what they typically and affectionally refer to as "American music."

Since each person's *idea* of what "American music" may be varies enormously, I simply suggest, and encourage, them to "listen to American music" and they take it from there. Since that general term is completely relative to each individual (foreign or domestic) it is best left to each person to choose where their "American music" preferences lead. If they *truly* have no idea of what I am talking about (which is rare since "American music" in its many forms is popular throughout the world) I suggest that they purchase a radio and simply experiment with various stations, settling on ones they like. The bottom line is that, in this country, there are basically as many musical forms as there are people. Regardless of what type, or types, of music one feels an affinity toward, we will ultimately meet other individuals from particular segments of the population who share similar attractions. Conversely, just as there are many people with whom we all share many similarities, there are as many who appear to live in completely different realities from our own. In other words, regardless of what music (or anything else for that matter) one identifies with, it is never going to be representative of all people.

In effect, the best we can do is open ourselves up to the rhythms and melodies that make us feel "in sync" with ourselves and allow those same sounds to help us to bridge our differences and teach us how to communicate with one another. Other methods that I have found to be effective in helping to establish a sense of rhythmic synchronicity across cultures include active socialization and interpersonal interactions, enrolling in interesting courses at a local school or college, and—the one which seems to be the most popular—watching television and movies.

Without effective communication skills, or sense of rhythmic synchronicity, people can encounter a number of situations which may have both direct and indirect crippling effects affecting their ability to function as healthy and productive individuals. In this sense, a lack of "rhythmic synchronicity" may affect one's opportunity for academic advancement (the inability to relate to others in academic situations), professional career promotions (the inability to incorporate unwritten and unspoken company rules and regulations), or acculturating to a new setting (the inability to adapt to interpersonal challenges presented by societal expectations when these are incongruent with our own).

VIBRATIONS ARE ENERGIES IN DANCE.

LISTEN FOR THE TAO WITHIN THE SOUNDS OF SILENCE.
ATTENDED TO, IT CANNOT BE HEARD. EACH NOTE CONTAINS
ITS OWN SYMPHONY . . . EACH BEAT, ITS OWN PATTERN . . .
EACH BREATH, ITS OWN MELODY . . . EACH THOUGHT, ITS
OWN HARMONY. AMIDST THE NOISE, EMBRACE THE SILENCE.

Psychological Noise
and Masking

Music has no value or morals. Music does not think. When music
replaces our thoughts we are in trance and are open to suggestion.
There is no longer a question of thinking. We are in motion.[1]

Throughout this book you will encounter the term "psychological
noise." In general, this is a term I have introduced to define all of
those intrusive, unwanted thoughts and mental images that get in our way
while we are trying to relax, concentrate, or go on with our moment-to-
moment experiencing without those internal (and at times, infernal) inter-
ferences. "The clamoring of what the Zen masters call our monkey mind
turns our attention away from the all-important moment."[2]

Other terms which help to convey the meaning of "psychological
noise" may include:

- Internal voices;
- Mind clutter;
- Mental static, turmoil or interference;
- Feeling disconcerted, confounded, puzzled, confused,
  blurred, befuddled;

1. John Beaulieu, *Music and Sound in the Healing Arts* (New York: Station Hill Press, 1987), p. 76.
2. J. J. Gibbs, *Dancing with Your Books: The Zen Way of Studying* (New York: Plume, 1990), p. 20.

- Mind in a haze or a daze, in disarray, in a fog;
- Mind is racing.

"Psychological noises" are those intrusive, pesky thoughts which keep "attacking" our attempts at having a peaceful, clear, and orderly mind. We tend to become most aware of them when *trying* to meditate or to fall asleep. They are unsettling and upsetting. They tangle rational thinking and blur our reasoning processes. They are those worrisome and demanding thoughts which haunt us with "whys?" and "shoulds."[3] At times they become so overwhelming that I have heard people describe them as feeling "trapped in a house of mirrors with no way out!" Others have described it as feeling as if their heads are "about to explode!" At their worst "psychological noises" feel like chaos, or mental pandemonium.

Psychological noise clutters and confuses our minds. Its presence jumbles normal moment-to-moment events, and forces us to claw and fight our way through mazes of unnecessary mental distractions and emotional agitations. It clogs and muddles our sensitivity, fogs our intuition, congests our creativity and turns rational thinking into disorder. Psychological noise comes in many guises and is usually laced with:

- *Self-defeating words* such as: should, ought, must ("I *should* have gotten an A," "I *must* get a raise," "I *ought* to be smarter than that!").

- *Emotionally upsetting phrases* such as: "but what if . . . ," "I will never be able to . . . ," "I just can't . . . ," "don't they see that . . ."

- *Unrealistic expectations*: "I never miss a day of work, so why should any of my employees?" "I can't be late today, there better not be any traffic or I'm going to be truly upset!"

- *Over-emoting* (allowing our emotions to cloud our intellect): "I feel so *lonely*, I must be a really *pathetic* person!", "I feel *so tired* today, I'm just *not a very healthy* person!"

- *Catastrophizing*: "If I don't win this race I will *always* be thought of as a *loser*," "During my talk I'll probably forget my lines and *everyone will laugh* at me!" "I have a spot on my arm, if I have it checked out they'll find out it's cancer and I will die a long, agonizing death just like my uncle!"

3. See Whys, page 303, and Shoulds, page 311.

- *Magnification*: "If I do *anything* wrong during this interview they will *never* offer me the job and *no one* will ever hire me!"

- *Arbitrary inference* (inferring the worst from scanty information): "I can't remember that phone number, that means I'm losing my memory, which can only mean that I'm developing Alzheimer's!" "I can't shake this cold, and I'm feeling run down, these are all basic symptoms of AIDS!"

- *Focusing on the negative*: "What's the point of following this team, they're *losers*!" "Going to music concerts is *dangerous*!" "This weather is really *unfair*!"

- *Personalizing*: "I just know it had to be *my* fault," "Every time *I* come over something bad happens!" "If *I* watch the game they'll lose!"

- *Exaggerations*: "This will *never* end!" "This job is *unbearable*!" "There's no way I'm traveling by plane, they are *always* crashing!"

- "*Whys*!?" The word "why," in particular, seems to be a very popular instigator of psychological noise. "*Why* does this always happens to me?" "*Why* do you act that way?" "*Why* are people like that?" "*Why* can't you see things my way?" Actually, at times simply the word "why" itself seems to be a psychological noise all on its own!

As you can see, psychological noise creates chaos out of silence. Therefore, by using music to fill those hollow silences with musical melodies, and positive harmonies, or replacing the chaos with rhythmic structure and musical cadences, we can lessen and appease our psychological noise. Throughout this book, a number of "music adjunct" exercises are discussing various ways to help us to counteract, diminish, and eliminate psychological noise.

Sometimes, to get rid of the noise, try singing, playing an instrument, or reciting poetry to a musical background. Through music we can externally manifest our internal states. As indicated by Anthony Storr, music can provide "a temporary retreat which promotes a reordering process within the mind, and thus aids our adaptation to the external world rather than providing an escape from it."[4] Using music to help counteract, minimize, or even eliminate psychological noise is particularly effective.

Although music is highly effective in countering, or silencing psychological noise, there are a number of other sounds which are at least as effective. At times, depending on individual taste and the situation at hand, these sounds, known as "white noise" or "masking," (also called sound shields, or sound screens) often have a very satisfying and practical effect screening or blocking out internal or external noises.[5]

Although there are commercially available machines that are specifically designed to produce these masking sounds (sound screens), similar effects can be gained from a common house fan, air conditioner, or any other appliance which produces a continuous hum, soothing murmur, or otherwise low and sustained sound. The same effect can also be gained through natural sounds, such as those which emanate from perpetually careening waterfalls, flowing ocean waves, gurgling streams, and persevering winds. In addition, a lot of the "white noise" machines on the market provide various masking sound options, including digital imitations of the above, and other, natural sounds. Although a bit too exotic for some people, there are some who find comfort in the drone produced by the Indian instrument, the tambura, which generates a hypnotic sound and can have an effect similar to that of a "white noise."

What the "white noise" appears to do is compete, and often win out, against the relentless barrage of psychological noise which invades our minds. For a lot of us, these psychological noises may begin as a simple thought or concern. These mostly harmless thoughts may then begin to escalate as we obsess over the initial concern, extending it further and deeper, adding increasing numbers of catastrophic possibilities and potential (usually negative) scenarios. While this is going on, other related or unrelated thoughts begin to join in, accumulating to the point where they become jumbled and confounding. The thoughts, by now a "psychological noise," appear to take control or priority over other, more immediate or practical concerns, until we feel helpless in our attempts to quell them or make them stop. Recently, I had a patient describe the above feeling, adding he wished he could "open his head up for a few seconds and shake the voices out!" He described the feeling as similar to having water inside one's ear, "You just want to tilt your head and pound on the other side until it comes out!"

The *external* "white noise," then, seems to function as competition to the *internal* psychological noises, each vying for equal time. Since the (white noise) sound competing against the psychological noises is contin-

---

4. Anthony Storr, *Music and the Mind* (New York: Free Press, 1992), p. 105.
5. See Carl E. Seashore, *Psychology of Music* (New York: Dover Publications, 1967), p. 62.

uous and unyielding, the mind eventually gives up, and can eventually relax. By helping to quiet the internal voices, the external white noise enables the yielding mind to fall asleep, to more effectively meditate, or to think about the issues at hand more clearly.

Music " . . . exerts a masking effect on auditory perception."[6]

Additional Reading

For further readings on how sound and music may affect psychological noise you may refer to the following articles:

S. H. Burleson, D. B. Center and H. Reeves, "The Effect of Background Music on Task Performance in Psychotic Children," *Journal of Music Therapy*, 1989, 26, pp. 198–205.

J. Colbert, "The Effect of Musical Stimulation on Recall in High and Low Anxiety College Students" (Doctoral dissertation, New York University, 1960). *Dissertation Abstracts*, 21, 3172.

K. Gfeller, "Musical Components and Styles Preferred by Young Adults for Aerobic Fitness Activities," *Journal of Music Therapy*, 1988, 25, pp. 28–43.

L. K. Miller and M. Schyb, "Facilitation and Interference by Background Music," *Journal of Music Therapy*, 1989, 26, pp. 42–54.

J. P. Scartelli, "The Effect of EMG Biofeedback and Sedative Music, EMG Biofeedback Only, and Sedative Music Only on Frontalis Muscle Relaxation Ability," *Journal of Music Therapy*, 1984, 21, pp. 67–78.

C. A. Smith and L. W. Morris, "Differential Effects of Stimulative and Sedative Music on Anxiety, Concentration and Performance," *Psychological Reports*, 1977, 41, pp. 1047–1053.

R. H. Wolf and T. L. Weiner, "Effects of Four Noise Conditions on Arithmetic Performance," *Perceptual and Motor Skills*, 1972, 35, pp. 929–930.

---

6. Dafina Dalbokova and Pencho Kolev, "Cognitive and Affective Relations in Perception of Auditory Stimuli in the Presence of Music," *Psychomusicology*, 11, 1992, pp. 141–151. (p. 141).

LEARNING EVENTS CAN BE ALMOST ENTIRELY
IDIOSYNCRATIC. LOVERS RECALL SPECIAL
OCCASIONS THROUGH "THEIR MUSIC."[1]

Contextual Cuing

{M}usic acquires its emotional value by association.[2]

A s listeners, we attach very private imagery and meanings to music as a result of the music's association with our personal experiences.

> "Some writers become obsessed with cheap and tawdry country and western songs, others with one special prelude or tone poem. I think the music they choose creates a mental frame around the essence of the book. Every time the music plays, it recreates the emotional terrain the writer knows the book to live in. Acting as a mnemonic of sorts, it guides a fetishistic listener to the identical state of alert calm . . . [3]

For a lot of us, at some point or other throughout our lives, music serves to open entirely new or alternate realities or subcultures. It introduces fresh ways of thinking or feeling about, and listening to, ourselves and the

---

1. Mark Meerum Terwogt and Flora van Grinsven, "Musical Expression of Moodstates," *Psychology of Music*, 1991, 19, 99–109 (p. 100).
2. Terwogt and van Grinsven, "Musical Expression of Moodstates," p. 109.
3. Diane Ackerman, *A Natural History of the Senses* (New York: Random House, 1990), p. 297.

world around us. "Music has often encoded entire movements of human life which were virtually non-existent until the musical referent made its appearance. The Beatles' early singles began the creation of an entire sub-culture by encoding it in music. A few years later, the album *Sgt. Pepper* did the same again."[4]

Although these effects most often touch or inspire us at a personal level, timely tunes will sometimes coincide with unfolding social or political events striking a universal chord. "A stirring, patriotic song during wartime can encode, unify and intensify the thoughts of an entire nation."[5]

Music recreates a mental and emotional representation of the essence of the moment when it was first heard. Once a particular moment or experience has been cued contextually to music, each time the music is heard, it recreates the emotional terrain where the person's experience resonates. Later, when the music is heard, it acts as a rhythmic mnemonic, or contextual cue, returning us to revisit that moment, or feeling, now frozen in audible time.

When a musical piece is composed, it reflects that song-writer's sense of life *at that moment*. This feeling, transposed into music as translation of the emotion felt by the composer at that very moment, lives on—at some level— in the composition. Through the music, we are able to not merely hear, but in relative terms somewhat feel—filtered through our own emotional interpretations—the original emotions felt by the musical author.

A couple I recently met were discussing their vacation in the Bahamas two winters ago. While in the islands, they related that "everywhere they went, reggae music would be playing!" Although they had both been aware of this type of music prior to their trip, they had never assigned any "extramusical associations" to it. In other words, they had not associated reggae music with anything other than the lively, rhythmic music, itself. The music held no personal, or special meaning. Since their trip, however, they state that every time they hear reggae music it takes them "right back to the islands!" Regardless of where they are, or what they are doing at the moment, when reggae music plays they can "taste the tropical drinks;" "feel the warm, ocean breezes, smell the Caribbean spices," and even "see the bright, omnipresent colors" they associate with that particular vacation. The music, in effect, acts as an auditory cue that triggers those memories which are, at some level, reexperienced through all five senses.

---

4. David Tame, *The Secret Power of Music* (Rochester, VT: Destiny Books, 1984), p. 149.
5. Tame, *The Secret Power of Music*, p. 149.

Because of music's powerful ability to sift into our unconscious, we often tend to establish extramusical connections with events that occur in tandem with a particular musical background. Whenever these emotional connections are made, associating the music with the event, the music becomes a cue which, when heard, emotionally returns us to that context. Another way to explain this phenomenon is through "classical conditioning."

A common example of extramusical association in affective response to music is classical conditioning, or association by contiguity. In certain instances, musical stimuli evoke emotional response not because of the music's structural properties, but because the music has, in the past, accompanied stimuli with emotional effects.[6]

Throughout this book, these "extramusical associations," or "associations by contiguity," are referred to as "contextually cued" associations, or "contextual cuing." The purpose of using this latter phrase is to illustrate the ability of music, or any other specific sounds, to emotionally or mentally "return us" to a particular place or time, or trigger a specific feeling or memory that we may consciously, or unconsciously, associate with a distinctive sound. These powerful cuing properties are featured as a primary tool to assist the reader in reaping some of the invaluable effects that can be gained by using music, or sounds, as a complement to a number of other psychological techniques.

Sound Idea

Next time you feel the impulse to talk, use that urge as a cue to listen.

Songs and poems would become vital mnemonic and cohesive tools for the construction of a new society, and musical skill would, indeed be a skill for survival.[7]

6. Robert F. Unkefer, *Music Therapy in the Treatment of Adults with Mental Disorders* (New York: Schirmer Books, 1990), p. 78.

7. John Sloboda, *The Musical Mind* (Oxford: Oxford University Press, 1985), p. 268.

Additional Reading

For further readings on how sound and music may affect contextual cuing, you may refer to the following articles:

Cora L. Diaz de Chumaceiro, "What Song Comes to Mind: Induced Song Recall: Transference/Countertransference in Dyadic Music Associations in Treatment and Supervision," *The Arts in Psychotherapy*, 1992, 19, 5, pp. 325–332 (p. 331).

Hamid Hekmat and James Hertel, "Pain Attenuating Effects of Preferred Versus Non-preferred Music Interventions," *Psychology of Music*, 1993, 21, 2, pp. 163–173 (p. 164).

Carl E. Seashore, *Psychology of Music* (New York: Dover Publications, 1967), p. 144.

Steven M. Smith, "Background Music and Context-Dependent Memory," *American Journal of Psychology*, 1985, 98, 4, pp. 591–603 (p. 596).

Anthony Storr, *Music and the Mind* (New York: The Free Press, 1992), p. 21.

[M]USIC CAN HELP US TO REVIEW EARLIER STAGES
IN OUR LIFE AND RE-LIVE THE FULL IMPACT OF
THOSE EMOTIONAL MOMENTS.[1]

Acoustic Memory

*{W}e look back and connect various pieces of music with
significant life events.*[2]

For the purposes of this book, the term "acoustic memory" is defined or
meant as a catch phrase to encompass all of the sounds, musical or otherwise, stored in our memories. Every sound—musical or otherwise—that
tends to "cue" or alert us to some noteworthy event, issue or concern from
our past, sounds which spark or trigger old memories, and those which
remind or inspire us to take action, are stored in our "acoustic memory."

Our acoustic memory is a reservoir of every auditory experience,
thought, feeling or event that has been contextually cued[3] into our collective unconscious. Thunder, rain, wind, laughter, voices which recall certain faces, tunes that return to us to various places, all reverberate in our
acoustic memories. We can access our acoustic memories by using music
and other sounds. In this manner, we cue ourselves back to the flow and
harmony experienced when we first associated a particular tune or sound
with a specific event in our lives. These are connections of music-to-event
which, for some personal reason, became stored in our acoustic memory.

---

1. Leslie Bunt, *Music Therapy: An Art Beyond Words* (London: Routledge, 1994), p. 159.
2. Bunt, *Music Therapy*, p. 158.
3. See Contextual Cuing, page 287.

For example, if we limit ourselves to playing the same type of music whenever we practice relaxation, that music will eventually become affiliated with our relaxation regimen. Before long, having assimilated those familiar sounds into our acoustic memory, their mere presence will convey or awaken feelings of calm, or relaxation.

> Music drawn from memory has many of the same effects as real music coming from the external world.[4]

As a result, simply playing the music as background will often trigger a similar sense of ease and repose developed and integrated during our relaxation sessions. Likewise, hearing music which we have affiliated with love-making, exercise, or any other activity, will tend to cue these sound-event connections, triggering our (past) recollections or whetting (future) desires to engage in those activities in the present.

> Songs can be seen as major repositories of knowledge that can be passed on from one generation to the next. We in the West may be far removed from the Aborigines' deep knowledge of "songlines" and use of music as a "map reference" and "memory bank" . . . [5]

Although a number of sections throughout this book make reference to our "acoustic memory," the reader is particularly referred to the sections on Contextual Cuing (page 287), and Memory Recall (page 105), to obtain a broader perspective on how these areas are all closely interrelated.

---

4. Anthony Storr, *Music and the Mind* (New York: The Free Press, 1992), p. 124.
5. Bunt, *Music Therapy*, p. 72.

Expectations

Formless, music shapes itself. Harmonizing with the spirit of all things, music finds balance. Being free, without restrain or expectation, music approaches the Tao.

We all grow up and go through life "expecting" things. On our birthdays and during holidays most of us *expect* gifts. Children, in particular, are often conditioned to anticipate certain amounts of money to be spent on them for special occasions. As a consequence, it is remarkable how many people, after major holidays, make appointments to discuss how hurt and rejected they feel for not getting what they expected.

Nonetheless, we all schedule our days around expectations. Assuming that things will get done, expecting packages to arrive on time, supposing that others will see things as we do, waiting for that "special" phone call that never seems to arrive. We expect that the alarm clock will awaken us in time, that when we flick the proper switch, electricity will flow and our breakfasts will be cooked. Each morning we climb into our cars, turn the ignition, and expect that they will start. If we leave home at a certain time, and drive at a certain speed, we expect to arrive at work on time. When we stop at stop signs, or traffic lights, we expect that the cars behind us will stop as well. If things go "as expected," we arrive at the office, safe and sound, and on time. But what happens when one of those events fails to take place? When they occur, as expected, we typically do not feel exhilarated, thrilled, or even experience a mild sense of happiness that things went "as expected." Instead, we take these events for granted. We *expect* them. However, if any of those expectations fall short they can throw us into a mild (or worse) state of panic.

FOR EVERY SOUND,
THERE ARE A MILLION EXPECTATIONS.
FOR EVERY EXPECTATION,
THERE ARE A MILLION SOUNDS.

The purpose of this section is to assist those among us who tend to burden ourselves with unnecessary, unproductive, and even harmful habits of expectation or anticipation. As in the section on asking "why?," there is a significant, although very narrow difference, between healthy, or rational expectations ("Gravity will continue to work in the same manner today as it did yesterday") and unhealthy, or disruptive ones ("My favorite team defeated their rivals last year so I'm *positive* they will win again this season"). Concern occurs when our emotional lives become either disrupted due to unrealized expectations, or dependent on them ("I expected my team to win, they did not, now nothing is going to go my way!").[1]

BEWARE OF THE FILTERS THROUGH WHICH YOU HEAR.
SOMETIMES THE SOUND IS AN ECHO
OF YOUR INNER FEARS.

Most of us tend to be creatures of habit. We shun change, and drive home from work the same way every day. Entering a familiar room, we typically return to the same seat, *our* seat, and expect others to return to *their* seat, the one where they sat last time. And they usually do! At the grocer, we buy the same brand of milk, cheese, and bread, week after week, feel most comfortable in familiar restaurants, sitting in our favorite booths. We maintain a certain type of wardrobe, a "uniform" through which we cannot only be readily identified, but stereotyped. "Jim, gray pants, white

---

1. See Whys, page 303.

shirt, black tie, conservative." "Bob, long hair, wore that green shirt once, wears those wild ties, he's different." Variations from the "norm" just seem to take too much energy to figure out, it's much easier to categorize, to prejudge. It takes less of an effort to simply put people into well-defined capsules, neat little boxes, bubbles.

On a larger scale, a lot of people tend to drive the same model car their parents drove. Even if they went away to college, many eventually find their way back home after graduation, buy a house—either one similar to their parents', or similar to the one their parents wanted—and settle down near (or in) an old familiar neighborhood. They were expected to. They vote for the same political party as their parents did, share similar world views and philosophies, follow the same athletic teams, and worship the same religion. "Everyone," including themselves, assumed they would. If they don't, it often creates a fair amount of conflict, confusion, and resentment. "They've broken rank, abandoned us, they're traitors, they have gone to the other side, *our* side will now be weaker because they did not do *as expected,* and so we must now shun them from the tribe. If other members from the tribe care to join them, we will alienate them as well." They did not do as expected.

> Consider the words, "Baa, baa, black sheep." Try to imagine that you have never seen them before, and that you therefore have a completely open mind as to what is likely to come next. The task is impossible. As a consequence, whatever comes next occurs not in a vacuum, but is inevitably evaluated in terms of what has gone before.[2]

Imagine living life one step at a time without assumptions, preconceptions, or expectations. Rather than spending days, or even weeks, hoping that "special package" arrives "today," you would instead wake up each day, go on with your daily activities, and eventually, one day, the package would simply be there!

A simple good morning. A pleasant hello. A gentle "Isn't it a great day?" accompanied by a warm, friendly smile. A creative twist wrapping up the plot at the conclusion of a good, suspenseful book. An unlisted, extra "bonus" song at the end of a CD. The 13th cookie in the dozen. A refund in the mail from something long forgotten. How much sweeter things are when they just appear, unexpectedly!

2. John Booth Davies, *The Psychology of Music* (Stanford: Stanford University Press, 1978), p. 74.

FILLED WITH EXPECTATIONS
WE ARE EMPTY.
VOID OF EXPECTATIONS, WE ARE FULL.

Here are other scenarios. You're watching your favorite team and *assume* it is going to win. It *must*, after all it is *your* team! Instead, imagine turning the game on, watching the game as it develops, enjoying each and every play as it occurs in the here and now, letting go of any anticipated outcome.

On a regular morning—not your birthday, a holiday, or an anniversary—you walk into your living room and notice someone in your household has thoughtfully taken the trouble, time, and money to present you with a gift! You open it and inside a box you find exactly that, a gift! A totally unexpected token of appreciation. Think of how good it feels when you receive something unexpectedly. A phone call, a letter, a card, a visit from an old friend, a hug or kiss from your child that comes from out of nowhere. How differently those things feel when they occur unexpectedly. Suddenly, something is there, something happens, and there lies the sense of wonderment.

> If you are too strongly attached to future expectations and you are constantly comparing some desirable state that you think should have arrived to what is, you often will be disappointed and confused by the gap between your expectation and reality.[3]

You're in an unknown department store. Someone approaches you and asks if you need help. Not because that person works there, but simply because you appear befuddled, as if you *need* help. Your car breaks down—unexpectedly—in the middle of rush hour traffic. You feel confused, disoriented. As cars zoom past you, blaring their horns, offering head shakes and unkind gestures, someone pulls over. Not a policeman, or a new car salesman, but simply a kind person who's ready to take the time to give you a hand. Unexpectedly.

Limited by anticipation, restricted by the past, the listener
attends to the future while neglecting the now. Confined

---

3. J. J. Gibbs, *Dancing with Your Books: The Zen Way of Studying* (New York: Plume, 1990), p. 41.

by a trained ear, the technician listens for the structure and
misses the melody. Bound by the predictable, the perfectionist
examines the precision and misses the expression.
Distress arises from expectations, fulfillment
comes from openness to the now.

Living in anticipation of what "should," or "will likely" happen takes the joy out of life's surprises. It robs the wonders from each developing moment. Whether our assumptions are self-imposed ("The work took me longer than I assumed . . "), rooted in circumstances outside of our control ("Traffic was heavier than I expected." "The merchandise was more expensive than I had counted on . . . ") , or projected on others ("My partner did not follow up like I had anticipated . . . ") these unrealistic expectations often set us up for let downs which can result in feelings of anxiety, frustration, alienation, depression, or even low self-esteem.

Often, those types of expectations have two possible outcomes. First, if what we assume will take place, does, no big deal, another predictable outcome, we break even. If what we assumed would take place does *not*, however, we become disappointed, dejected, at times even feeling somehow responsible for the foiled outcome. When these situations occur, a dysfunctional response may be: "I knew this would happen, things *never* work out the way I *expect* them to!" Or, "I can't count on *anyone* for *anything*, *nothing ever* gets done unless I do *everything* myself!"

Instead, by letting go of unrealistic assumptions, and tuning into moment to moment experiencing, we can minimize, or in many cases even eliminate, the stress and other negative consequences which result from placing unfounded, and even unfair, assumptions on ourselves, others, and our environment.

Going through life expecting that something specific will happen can often set us up for a downfall. On the other hand, expectation or anticipation of unfolding events is often necessary, just as in the section on asking "why?", it is important to become aware of times when we may be setting ourselves up by harboring unrealistic or irrational expectations that may somehow backfire or affect us negatively.

What people expect to hear seems to have an influence on what they do hear.[4]

---

4. C. R. Anderson and T. W. Tunks, "The Influence of Expectency on Harmonic Perception," *Psychomusicology*, 1992, 11, pp. 3–14 (p.11).

Through the years I have known people who use one of two personal approaches to try to defeat, or override, expectations. Let's take a look at them.

Technique Number 1 is to expect that "nothing is going to go right." With this expectation, the reasoning seems to be that "if anything goes right at all, then I'm ahead!" One problem with operating from this mode is that it often makes people function from a negative perspective. For a lot of people, it even takes a sort of superstitious edge. For instance, I have spoken with people who feel that if they live with the motto, "nothing good ever happens to me!" then, whenever something *good* occurs, they feel like they are "ahead." Some even take this type of reasoning further and choose to negate good outcomes for fear that if they begin to *expect* good things, these good things will stop happening. They instead opt to tell themselves that, "Although it worked out this time, I bet it doesn't happen again!" This way they feel "safe."

Technique Number 2 is to expect that "everything is going to go just the way I planned!" Here, the reasoning seems to be that "if you expect good things to happen, then they will!" The problem with *this* mode of reasoning for some people is that whenever something "bad" happens they tend to feel devastated, as if their "method" has failed them. Single events like these can make people question their entire belief systems.

So what can we do?

1. *Keep it in the heAr and now.* We can attempt to remain mentally and emotionally open to life's events as they occur. Most expectations are based on past or future events, rather than the heAr and now. We tend to draw from past history and hope, or anticipate, that similar events will unfold in the same manner in the future. We also tend to look into the future and try to prophesize, predict, or forecast based on our expectations. And, of course, there is nothing wrong with that. It becomes a problem, however, when we base our lives on these expectations.

> Goals and expectations are not what we are doing in the moment. They are not the reality of the here and now. They are at best abstractions of what will happen if everything goes according to plan.[5]

2. *Put your expectations in perspective.* How realistic are your expectations? Are you setting yourself up for a fall? Is expecting this certain event to take

5. Gibbs, *Dancing with Your Books*, p. 41.

place necessary, or would it be emotionally safer to consider, and prepare for, the available options, or to simply "wait and see what happens?"

> All misery is created by the activity of the mind. Can you let go of words and ideas, attitudes and expectations?[6]

3. *Try to not depend on expectations.* It's fine to expect that something may take place, and then emotionally let it go if it does not. However, *depending* on a particular course of events occurring can be a risky and vulnerable position to take.

> Go in with an empty mind. Go in without expectations.[7]

4. *Never project your expectations on others.* Expecting that other people will behave, think, or feel as you do can often be quite precarious and sometimes even dangerous. This is particularly true when people discuss "touchy" personal issues involving religion, politics, and philosophy. If you decide to take a strong, honest stand on an issue, be aware that a lot of people will be taking opposing, or contrasting sides.

> Expectations block your development and limit your horizons.[8]

5. *Be aware of the difference between aspirations and expectations.* "One sure clue as to whether we're being motivated by aspiration or expectation is that aspiration is always satisfying; it may not be pleasant, but it is always satisfying. Expectation, on the other hand, is always unsatisfying, because it comes from our little minds, our egos."[9]

> A pitfall of participating exclusively in familiar forms of music is that expectation creeps in: we are not totally engaged in sound as it is happening but instead eagerly await what we know will follow.[10]

6. Brian Walker, *Hua Hu Ching: The Teachings of Lao Tzu* (Livingston, MT: Clark City Press, 1993), p. 36.
7. Gibbs, *Dancing with Your Books*, p. 86.
8. Chungliang Al Huang and Jerry Lynch, *Thinking Body, Dancing Mind* (New York: Bantam, 1992), p. 132.
9. Charlotte Joko Beck, *Every Day Zen* (San Francisco: HarperSanFrancisco, 1989), p. 133.
10. Joanne Crandall, *Self-Transformation Through Music* (Wheaton, IL: Theosophical Publishing House, 1986), p 17–18.

EXERCISE 33:

Unexpecting

As you practice this exercise, allow yourself to "non-focus," or to simply "let go" of any expectations, assumptions, or preconceived ideas regarding what feelings or thoughts the music may or may not elicit in you.

1. Select the first piece of music you encounter. You may even try choosing a piece with your eyes closed.

2. Sit or lie comfortably, with eyes closed. As the music begins to play, allow your mind to drift, following the sound waves wherever they may take you.

3. Allow your body to simply feel the musical rhythms, feeling each pulse as it happens . . . in the moment.

4. With each passing moment, be present with the music. Be receptive— but not analytical—to any thoughts you may have, images you may encounter, emotions you may feel.

5. Allow your inner self to flow with the music as it unfolds and surrounds you, without expectation on how you "should" be feeling, or what you "hope to achieve" from this exercise.

6. Assume nothing. Expect only the unexpected. Anticipate only the fact that, by letting go of self-imposed constraints, and flowing with the here and now, the possibilities are endless.

The Tao of music has no beginning, and no end. It is one continuous, uninterrupted melody. It is only our limited expectations which create the boundaries, restricting our awareness of the totality of its sound. Today, encounter each situation, each moment, each event with no expectation other than that *something* will occur. Listen with a still, empty, non-judgmental and unbiased mind. This receptive, inner silence will provide a deeper awareness to the message within the sound, and the sound beneath the message. Through harmony, we connect with all living things. Through complementarity, we flow along the path. Anticipation leads to expectation. Concentrating on the outcome impedes the process. With no-mind, there is no anticipation—being mindful, there is no expectation. Concentration embodies thinking, thinking obstructs harmony. Outcomes imply doing, doing obstructs complementarity. Through mindfulness we become one with the Tao. Having no expectations, you will have no limitations.

> [L]ike a samurai warrior, expect nothing and become ready for anything.[11]

---

11. Huang and Lynch, *Thinking Body, Dancing Mind*, p. 132.

Whys

*Music is never about why. It is about who, what, when,
where, and how.*

Most of us often become preoccupied with wanting to know "why?" As children, we sometimes act as barometers intended to measure just how much our parents actually know ("Why is the sky blue?" "Why is it dark at night?"). Regardless of our actual knowledge—or the practicality of our answers—the "whys" just keep coming. "Why can't I stay up later? Why do I have to eat this? Why do I have to be quiet?"

As teenagers, our quest to know "why" does not diminish, it just takes a different form. "Why can't I borrow the car? Why do I have to be in by 11:00? My older brother gets to have sleepovers, why can't I?"

As adults, rhetorical "whys" maintain their prevalence: "Why is this person riding my rear bumper? Why is there never enough time? Why can't this family just get along?"

After a while, asking "why," whether from ourselves, others, or the world around us, seems to become a habit. The pondering, in effect, is rhetorical. We are often not actually searching for an answer but rather "buying time," or being too lazy to search for the underlying reasons ourselves. We want *the* answer and we want it *now*!

A lot of responses to "why" are often either subjective opinions, defensive retorts, wild speculations, or made-up fantasies. In an attempt to keep our reputations intact as "dispensers of wisdom," we sometimes fall into the trap of offering any number of misguided metaphysical-type answers or explanations to life's most confounding questions ("The earth is round because of the way it spins!"). The fact that most people do not really *expect* coherent answers to "why" is constantly validated by typical, day-to-day common replies. How else can one explain how an answer such as, "Because that's just the way people are!" would suffice as a plausible and reasonable explanation to anything?

It is not hard to see the stumbling blocks presented by Zen for a culture like ours that begins everything with a question and is constantly asking, "Why?"[1]

The bottom line is that, more often than not, most people—including ourselves—do not *know* "why." That is not to say that we should *never* ask "why?" A visit to a physician to diagnose an ear infection, for example, is in dire need of a "why?" "Why does my ear hurt?" requires a correct diagnosis from your physician who, after suggesting "because you have an ear infection!" may prescribe ear drops and an antibiotic.

WITHOUT UNDERSTANDING MUSIC THEORY,
WE CAN APPRECIATE MUSIC AS PLEASURE OR ART.
WITHOUT KNOWING, WE DANCE.
WITHOUT UNDERSTANDING, WE SING.
WITHOUT LEARNING, WE KNOW.

Another perfectly reasonable plea worthy of a "why" may evolve after detecting a worrisome noise coming out of our car's engine. Taking the car in for assessment we may ask the mechanic "why" the car may be making that noise? But, do we actually *need* to know "why" the noise is there? Would it not make more sense to describe the noise: *what* it sounds like, *where* it is coming from, *when* it occurs, and *how* often? And later, ask *when*

1. Edward T. Hall, *The Dance of Life: The Other Dimension of Time* (New York: Doubleday, 1983), p. 93.

will the car be ready and *how much* is it going to cost to have it repaired? In such situations, a long, detailed, and technical explanation (for most people) as to "why" the noise is there is typically a waste of time. Further, a lot of the time mechanics (as do any other professionals for that matter) may not really know "why" themselves.

Most often, professionals merely diagnose the situation, find the "what" that needs to be fixed or replaced, and offer suggestions on taking care of the "how, when and where." The "why," on the other hand, may range in *speculation* anywhere from "*Could be* that the company used a cheap alloy on this model" to "This is what happens when you drive too fast, too slow, too often, not enough, etc." In other words, the bottom line is, "Fix my car, I need to get to work!"

> [Q]uestions beginning with the word "why" are likely to arouse the same defensive emotional reactions parents aroused when they "ask" a child, "Why did you do that?" "Why do you feel that?" These are rhetorical questions which communicate disapproval. The patient rarely gets past hearing the disapproval and reacting defensively to it, with no gain in information about himself.[2]

A similar situation may involve a young man, or woman, who is continually refused a date by someone he or she finds attractive. "Why won't you go out with me?" may sound like a reasonable and rational request for information. However, what often occurs after a supplication such as this is that, regardless of the reply ("I'm busy that night," "I'm visiting a sick friend," "That's the night I usually wash my hair," etc.), a lot of the time we are left wondering if that, indeed, is the "true" reason for our being rejected. In other words, most of the time it is impossible to know if the "because" we receive is indeed the "absolute truth." I have dealt with many patients who, after begging for such answers in these types of situations, and receiving straightforward, perfectly reasonable responses ("I'm very flattered but, as I mentioned before, I'm married!") continue to obsess over what the "real reason" may be for the rejection.

---

2. Ralph Crowley, "Sullivan's Concept of Participant—Observations" (a symposium), *Contemporary Psychoanalysis,* Vol. 13, p. 356.

Raising Awareness to Unnecessary "Whys"

During an ordinary day, take mental notes of just how many times you burden yourself, or others in casual conversation, with rhetorical "whys."

"Why do I always catch this (traffic) light?"
"Why do people drive so slow/fast?"
"Why is someone parked in my spot?"
"Why is this person so intent in getting in front of me in line?
"Why is this machine out of diet soda?"
"Why do secretaries always put me on hold?"

Asking "why?" quite often draws us away from the issue at hand. It creates circles, loops or (worse) downward spirals of inescapable rhetoric. Responses to "why" also tend to change constantly, depending on one's mood, immediate situation, and available data. As we enter the endless maze of "because" probabilities we encounter a cosmic universe of potential replies that can whorl our minds off into infinity. Just as we think we've "got" the answer, another "yeah, but . . . ," or, "but if . . . ," comes along to pull us further and deeper into the black hole of not knowing.

Sound Idea

Be okay with not knowing! Let go.
It's okay to *not know.* A lot of times,
"I don't know . . . that's a good
question!" is a perfectly good, sane,
and acceptable answer.

The following story is illustrative of how being obsessed with "knowing why" can become a focal, and sometimes destructive, point in our lives.

When we can give up the convention of knowing for simply
experiencing, therapy progresses.[3]

A while back, Ted, a 47-year-old male, began therapy shortly after his wife of twenty-two years—Iris—had left him. Ted's primary presenting concern

3. Greg Johanson and Ron Kurtz, *Grace Unfolding* (New York: Bell Tower, 1991), p. 59.

was his desire to know "why?" Why, after all of their years of closeness, and growing old together had his wife decided to leave him? A couple of years before their breakup, Iris sat down with Ted and explained to him that she was "unhappy with their marriage." The couple went to marriage therapy for a while to no avail. Due to a number of developing events over the years, Iris felt that they had grown apart and were no longer compatible. There was no other person in the picture, and her desire was to go out on her own and "try to start a new life." Even after months of therapy, during which Iris had openly come clean with Ted, consistently voicing the above feelings, and reasons for a divorce, Ted wanted to know why.

Over the course of the first few months after their breakup, Ted spent a lot of his time desperately looking for the answer, the real reason why his wife had left him. During this time, he had managed to come up with a number of (what to him appeared to be) plausible reasons, each of which inevitably superseded the earlier, more irrational or unjustified reasons. Rather than accepting that he and Iris had grown apart and focusing on getting on with his life, Ted continued to be obsessed with *why*. Eventually, after several months, Ted began to finally let go of his destructive and futile quest for *the answer*. He accepted that they had simply grown apart, and that he had, in fact, not done anything in particular that had created the split.

In the meantime, however, Ted wasted an enormous amount of time, money, and energy in pursuit of something so simple that it had become too complicated for him to understand, or allow himself to accept. Once he was able to let go of why, Ted was finally able to listen to his internal voices and come to terms with *what* happened (Iris left him), when (two years ago), how (after years of trying to work it out, and debating options, she announced her plans to move out), and where (from their former home into her new apartment in an adjoining town) he was able to count his losses and move on. "Why?" had become a psychological noise[4] in his mind, blocking his ability to hear the obvious and preventing him from getting his life back in harmony.

MUSIC ENABLES THE OBSERVING SELF
TO REACH NEW LEVELS OF AWARENESS
WHILE PROVIDING THE GUIDING STRUCTURE FOR
INNER, PERSONAL EXPLORATION.

---

4. See Psychological Noise, page 281.

Quite often, the answers to our "whys" lie wide awake in our minds. We just don't want to hear them. Those requests for "why," then, are, in fact, supplications for validation from an external source. In other words, we simply want to hear what we want to hear, when, where, and how we want to hear it. Further, if validation is received (the respondent actually tells us exactly what we want to hear, as in the example above) we often end up refuting this validation—the "because"—and begin to either doubt our own interpretation of the situation (Maybe what I thought was *the reason* is *not really* why!"), or to question how it was that this individual was able to figure out "exactly what we wanted to hear" ("Well, I guess she's just going to keep playing this game and avoiding the real issue!") thereby invalidating their validation!

> Composing, performing, or listening to music with our full attention upon the sound is to discover the life beyond description or meaning, the life that simply *is*.[5]

In my work, I have met many people who torture themselves in this manner throughout their lives. They wake up, go through the day, and go to sleep wondering "why?" Often, they even dream solutions or possible replies to their infinite inquiries. During our sessions they implore: "But I need to know *why*!", seemingly believing that I, or someone I may refer them to, will indeed have *the absolute answer*.

> [Y]ou might say that there is more to Knowing than just being correct.[6]

For the purpose of the exercises suggested throughout this book I recommend keeping "whys" to a minimum. In effect, whenever you feel the urge to ask "why?" about to surface, I suggest you try approaching those situations with the help of figure 1, which I have shared with many of my patients throughout the years

Figure 1 is meant to provide a visual image, a cognitive map, for approaching future situations. In other words, next time you encounter a situation which begs interpretation, rather than obsessing over "why", consider the "what (or who), where, when, and how" of the event. For example, when you encounter a red traffic light, instead of asking yourself

5. Joanne Crandall, *Self-Transformation Through Music*, (Wheaton, IL: Theosopical Publishing House, 1986), p. 34.
6. Benjamin Hoff, *The Tao of Pooh* (New York: Penguin Books, 1983), p. 29.

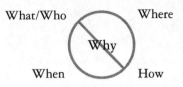

Figure 1. Handling your "whys."

"Why?" and becoming upset, simply *acknowledge* the red light ("What do you know, a red light!") and ask:

- "What do I need to do?" Stop.
- "When?" Now.
- "Where?" Here.
- "For how long?" Until the signal light changes to green.

Simple, practical, cut and dry. With practice, this approach will save a lot of unnecessary wear and tear on your nerves and your mind. In time, you will become more adept at applying the above formula to a lot of day-to-day situations where wondering why is encumbering and unnecessary. Save your mental energy for more important situations, and while you sit at the light, use that opportunity to listen to the music playing on your car CD player, tape deck, or radio, and do some deep breathing!

> When someone holds up a flower and shows it to you, he wants you to see it. If you keep thinking, you miss the flower. The person who was not thinking, who was just himself, was able to encounter the flower in depth, and he smiled.[7]

---

7. Thich Nhat Hanh, *Peace is Every Step* (New York: Bantam, 1991), p.43.

Shoulds and Musts

If-ing
If I could only start again . . .
If I could go back in time . . .
If I were just a few years younger . . .
Create tomorrow's past today.

66 I should know more about computers!" How often do you punish yourself with self-statements such as what you "should" be doing, "must" accomplish, "ought" to have, and "got to" get done sometime between the end of the day and the time right before you die? According to Dr. Albert Ellis, the founder of Rational Emotive Therapy (RET):

> [A[t the heart of psychological disturbance lies the tendency of humans to make devout, absolutistic evaluations of the perceived events in their lives. As has been shown, these evaluations are couched in the form of dogmatic "musts," "shoulds," "have to's," "got to's," and "oughts."[1]

Discussing RET and Ellis's theories, Dr. Gerald Corey indicates that:

> In Ellis's view, it is absolutistic and *must*urbatory thinking that is the foundation of human problems. The basic irra-

1. Albert Ellis and Windy Dryden, *The Practice of Rational Emotive Therapy* (New York: Springer Publishing, 1987), p. 14.

tional beliefs of individuals can be summarized by three major *musts:*

1. "I *must* perform well and be approved of by significant others. If I don't, then it is *awful*, I *cannot stand* it, and I am a *rotten person.*"

2. "You *must* treat me fairly. When you don't, it is *horrible*, and I *cannot bear* it."

3. "Conditions *must* be the way I want them to be. It is *terrible* when they are not, and I *cannot stand* living in such an *awful* world."[2]

There are several approaches we can use to combat, neutralize or minimize irrational and disruptive self-statements.

1. *We can try to raise our awareness.* We can keep track of the times we use words such as "should," "must," "ought," "got to," and "have to" in our daily self-statements. For example, when we come up with a negative self-statement, such as "No one likes me, what's the sense of trying!?" we have the choice to replace it with something more adaptive, positive, and reasonable. One such statement may be: "It's true that some people don't like me, but there are others who do. Either way, I'm not going to allow others' opinions of me to control my life."

2. *We can replace our negative self-talk with positive self-talk.* For example, replace comments, such as "I am a failure," with more rational statements such as "I fail sometimes, at some things, but I succeed at other things."

3. *We can listen to ourselves.* Sounds simple doesn't it? Try to remain aware of the internal messages you give yourself; it's very difficult, but, with practice, it gets easier. Also, we can listen to how we frame statements when we speak to others. If you find yourself tending to stress the negative ("That's never going to happen!"), try to replace those thoughts and statements with more positive remarks ("Anything can happen!" or "Stranger things have happened!").

4. *We can set realistic goals for ourselves.* Rather than pressuring ourselves with thoughts such as; "I should (or, I must) finish this job in one day," we

---

2. Gerald Corey, *Theory and Practice of Counseling and Psychotherapy* (Pacific Grove, CA: Brooks/Cole Publishing, 1982), p. 173.

can choose to replace such thoughts with more beneficial self-statements ("I will do my best to finish this today, if I don't, it won't be the end of the world").

5. *We can practice letting things go.* Recognize events over which you have no control and let them go. For example, consider a self-statement, such as, "I ought to be taller, why am I so short?" If you are an adult and have finished growing it's time to start to focus on other things. *Let it go!*

6. *We can dispute our irrational beliefs.* When we notice an irrational thought creeping in, we can zero in on it and debate it, replacing it with more rational, productive thoughts. For instance, "It *always* rains when I wash my car." Does it really? Or "I *always* pick the slowest line at the grocery store!" Do you actually? When you find yourself making such self-statements, dispute them! "Always" is a very powerful word, put it in perspective.

Sound Idea

Hushing the "shoulds," with
every opportunity, replace
"I should . . ." with "I shhhh. . ."

In order to gain a deeper, more detailed understanding of issues involving "shoulding" and "musting" habits, I strongly suggest Albert Ellis' literature on Rational Emotive Therapy[3] For our purposes, however, the above brief perspectives on these notions, along with references to them found throughout the book, "should" suffice.

> [I]t is a fundamental truth of Zen that straining is the enemy
> of rhythm."[4]

---

3. Ellis and Dryden, *The Practice of Rational Emotive Therapy*, 1987.
4. Edward T. Hall, *The Dance of Life* (New York: Anchor Press/Doubleday, 1983), p. 67.

Additional Reading

For further reading on the uses of music as adjunct to RET, you may also refer to the following articles:

D. R. Bryant, "A Cognitive Approach to Therapy through Music," *Journal of Music Therapy*, 1987, 24, pp. 27–34.

M. Maultsby, "Combining Music Therapy and Rational Behavior Therapy," *Journal of Music Therapy*, 1977, 14, pp. 89–97.

TECHNIQUES

The vitality that generates our search for the lost chord,
is the sound of the chord itself.

Entrainment

*In walking to our own comfortable tempo with musical support,
for example, we are learning to synchronize a movement with a
sound. At such moments the response produced occurs in synchrony
with the appearance of the stimulus: this is often described as
"rhythmic entrainment."*[1]

In 1665, Christian Huygens, a Dutch scientist, observed that mounting two pendulum clocks side by side would result in their acquiring a complementary rhythm. In essence, they would both establish a mutual beat, or synchronicity, superior to that which could be achieved by mechanical means. In other words, the two clocks would eventually be flowing concurrently, or "in sync." Later, scientists called this phenomenon "mutual phase-locking of two oscillators," or "entrainment." The reason for this universal phenomenon, according to George Leonard is that "nature seeks the most efficient energy state, and it takes less energy to pulse in cooperation than in opposition."[2]

Essentially, living organisms are oscillators. Any number of individuals who are involved in a harmonious activity, such as singing, rowing, or marching, are experiencing entrainment. The two (or more) individuals suddenly find themselves joined in a comfortable, mutual relationship with

1. Leslie Bunt, *Music Therapy: An Art Beyond Words* (London: Routledge, 1994), p. 62.
2. George Leonard, *The Silent Pulse* (New York: E. P. Dutton, 1978), pp. 13–14.

one another. They are "in tune," "in harmony," or "in sync." In other words, the closer we allow ourselves to link with someone else's rhythm, the better we will be able to understand, and relate to that individual. Through entrainment, the more one person joins in with another's rhythm, the closer those two individuals will become. Entrainment, then, involves a pacing, gaining rapport, or melding between two or more systems (individuals). Another example of entrainment would be when a public speaker, or performance artist, reaches that point of junction with an audience when they are all flowing, or even at times breathing together, as one unit. Entrainment is the basis of efficient flow and communication.

At normal activity, the human heart beats approximately between seventy and eighty times per minute. Whenever we are exposed to music with a tempo which exceeds this regular heartbeat, that music will—depending on other circumstances—have a stimulating, anxiety raising, or irritating effect on us. A slower external tempo, conversely, will have a soothing, slowing down, or calming effect.

> [E]ntrainment music has been found to be superior to other types of music in eliciting psychophysiological changes with chronic pain/disease patients . . .[3]

Musically, entrainment involves a merging with, or synchronizing to, the pulse of the music. From a musical perspective—for example—a state of relaxation is typically achieved or enhanced through exposure to "largo," or "adagio" movements. These slow, calming movements are typically found in music by composers from the Baroque era (music from the period between 1600–1750) such as Bach, Telemann, Corelli, Vivaldi, Handel, Scarlatti, Pachelbel, Purcell, Couperin, and many others from that period in history. (For a more detailed discussion, the reader is referred to *Superlearning*, by Ostrander and Schroeder.)

> It is possible that live entrainment music can not only elicit a maximized immune response, but also increase patient compliance with home imagery practice.[4]

The principle of entrainment is closely related to the "iso" (isomorphic) principle which suggests that one's mood should be matched to the mood of the music and then gradually moved into a desired direction.

---

3. Mark S. Rider and Cathy Weldin, "Imagery, Improvisation, and Immunity," *The Arts in Psychotherapy*, 1990, 17, 3, pp. 211–216 (p. 215).
4. Rider & Weldin, "Imagery, Improvisation, and Immunity," p. 215.

Entrainment is the ability to observe and enter into the rhythms of another. . . . The *iso* principle is one of the most natural and intuitive techniques for moving into a new rhythm. With the iso principle, a change in tempo and mood is accomplished by entraining to the present mood and slowly altering the pace in the desired direction. . . . Rather than a quick change to a fast or dynamic mood, the use of the iso principle moves the mood gradually, almost unnoticeably into a different state.[5]

Here is an example. You have just spent a stressed-filled day at the office, or have had an anxiety arousing conflict with a supervisor or spouse. At this point, the last thing you feel like doing is listening to a piece of "soothing, relaxing" music. What you actually *want* and *need* to do is to somehow *reach an internal state* of calm or relaxation. One way you can get to that point is by using music in accordance with entrainment, or the "iso" principle. In effect, music can be strategically used to effect, and modify, any particular mood, or moods.

In effect, entrainment is a process of *joining with the feeling* portrayed by the music, or *bonding* with the essence of the performance. It's a feeling of mutuality, or shared commonality, which we can vicariously enjoy along with a song and its performer. By simply listening to the "feel," and/or song lyrics, one somehow "knows" that the performer "has been there before," or has "felt what we are feeling right now." Somehow, it's reassuring to know that there is someone else out there who not only understands our feelings, or our struggle, but who can also express them, creatively through their music.

[E]ntrainment music designed to calm an anxious person would initially evoke tense, chaotic feelings and transition into calming music.[6]

Adapting Entrainment to Our Personal Needs

The essence of using the principle of "iso," along with entrainment, is as follows. First, you need to match (entrain) your internal state, your feel-

5. Chris Brewer, "Orchestrating Learning Skills," *Open Ear*, 1996, 1, pp. 14-18 (pp. 14, 15).
6. Rider and Weldin, "Imagery, Improvisation, and Immunity," p. 212.

ings (anxiety, depression, anger), to that of your *immediate* external environment. In other words, if you are feeling anxious, you would preferably select music to match or reflect your *present* mood—that of stress or anxiety—as closely as possible. Obviously, in order to reflect the "feel," or sensations associated with stress or anxiety, the music should contain similar mood elements such as intensity, tension, force, and—depending on your level of anxiety—maybe even a sense of infuriation. Also, although not *necessarily* loud, the type of music typically preferred for this particular mood state is usually up-tempo and hard-driven. The objective is to match the *feel* of the music with the feeling of your *present* emotional state.

Secondly, as you become entrained, you will be feeling more comfortable with the music reflecting your present internal state (the tension in the music will "feel" as tense as you do). As you begin to feel "as one" with the music, the next step is to *gradually* modify the tempo of the music in the direction of the internal state you *want to achieve* (calm, relaxed). An anxious or stressed individual would want to play a sequence of songs which will gradually *descend* in terms of the amount of anxiety reflected by the musical selections. In effect, the feel of these selections should start off matching your present, anxious state, and move "downward," culminating in the feeling of relaxation or calmness you are seeking.

In addition, the music *you* choose needs to include selections which echo, reflect, or resonate those particular feelings which *you*, not someone else, are experiencing. In other words, you may have a next door neighbor, friend, or partner who thinks that you "should" feel that a particular type of music, or selection, is "relaxing." Likewise, a magazine article or book chapter written by an expert may suggest that a particular recording elicits a mode of tranquillity. These suggestions (just like the ones suggested throughout this book) however, are meant as just that, suggestions, and are—at best—derived from selections which have been described as soothing by a certain percentage of individuals surveyed by that author or researcher.

Although those suggested selections may in fact work wonderfully for someone else, this helps very little in your situation unless that is the feeling which the music evokes in you. In this case, you are the expert and, as such, you are the ultimate authority in deciding what sounds, and feels, "anxious," "moderately anxious," "moderately relaxing," and "calming" to you, right here, right now. The best way to utilize music to achieve entrainment, and modify your internal state from an undesirable mood (anxiety) to a more desirable and healthy one (relaxation), is to create your own entrainment tape from personally chosen musical selections. So, although well-intended and thoroughly researched musical suggestions are included throughout this book for your convenience, or to serve as a guide along with the exercises, whenever possible, I strongly recommend that you choose your own music based on personal preferences.

> [A]ccording to John Phillips of the group, the Mamas and the Papas, "by carefully controlling the sequence of rhythms" any rock group can create audience hysteria consciously and deliberately. "We know how to do it," he said, "Anybody knows how to do it."[7]

Making Your Own Entrainment Tape[8]

Although entrainment tapes can be made to alter a number of different types of moods (see *Modifying Other Moods* at the end of this section), as portrayed in various exercises, the following general example will use "anxiety" for illustrative purposes.

1. Take an audio tape recorder and a tape of 30 to 45 minutes (per side) in duration. (Although an entrainment sequence does not have to be taped, it is often much more time efficient, in the long run, to record your music sequence(s) onto a tape which you will be able to use more than once). If your purpose is to modify (i.e., entrain) a mood state that you struggle with and wish to modify on a fairly regular basis, then the time you spend on preparing your entrainment tape(s) will be time well spent.

2. Choose a few (two or three) musical selections which match your present mood (anxiety) and record them at the beginning of the tape.

3. Following those initial (anxiety-like) selections, select and record a number of other musical selections (three or four) which fall somewhere between your present internal state (anxious) and the state you want to achieve (calm). In this case, the selections should sequentially diminish in intensity, tension, force, etc., when compared to the first few which you selected to match your initial, anxious mood.

---

7. David Tame, *The Secret Power of Music* (Rochester, VT: Destiny, 1984), pp. 153–154.

8. Before using copyrighted material to compile an audio entrainment sequence, or reproducing such prerecorded material for any purpose, be sure to first obtain written permission from the publisher.

4. Gradually, you will want to complete your taped musical sequence with a few (three or four) musical pieces which match your desired state (relaxation) as closely as possible. These selections should have elements which reflect the mood you want to achieve—that opposite of tension or anxiety—such as ease, tranquillity, peace, contentment or relaxation.

As a metaphor, think of using an entrainment tape to gradually alter your mood as analogous to gently "nudging" someone awake in the morning. This approach, you will agree, is preferable to awakening to the jolting shock of a car alarm, a barking dog, or a splash of ice-cold water on your face.

Unlike most of the other techniques which are presented throughout this book, these entrainment selections can be either instrumental, or lyrical, or a combination of both. As a matter of fact, an added benefit of making your personalized entrainment tape based on songs with lyrical content is that you can match the songs' messages, or themes, to your own present (or ongoing) struggles, feelings, or issues. As an example, if you are feeling particularly fed up with your present job, you may want to begin the tape with a song, such as "Don't Give Up" by Peter Gabriel, move into other tunes, such as "Learning To Fly," by Tom Petty and the Heartbreakers, and end the sequence with a piece like "Take This Job and Shove It!" by Johnny Paycheck.[9]

On the other hand, entrainment tapes, although fun to make, can be time consuming and tedious. Unless you find yourself encountering a particular mood state on a regular basis (being irritated by traffic, or a difficult coworker), a more eclectic tape moving you from anxiety to relaxation in general may be more useful and time efficient. However, if you have the time, and a fairly extensive musical library, another option is to make yourself a number of entrainment tapes, each designed to alter any number of recurring moods and have these at your disposal for immediate access. As you will find, quite often the process of selecting the songs and making the tapes themselves is not only fun, but extremely therapeutic! In many cases, the act of creating your own personal tapes—which involves both thinking about the music, listening to the selections, and being physically, mentally, and emotionally exposed to the changing vibrations as you search, select, and record them—often helps to alter your mood, modifying it in the direction *you* desire.

9. Specific musical selections, or artists, listed throughout this book are meant only as examples to help illustrate the exercises being discussed. They are in no way meant to be suggestive of which songs, or artists, any particular individual "should" use, nor to promote the songs or artists indicated.

To Summarize:

- Select a 90-minute blank audio-tape to record your entrainment sequence.

- Find a few musical selections (10–15 minutes total) which match your *present* mood (anxiety).

- Find a number of other selections (10–15 minutes total) which fall somewhere between your present internal state and the state you *want to achieve* (calm).

- Culminate your musical-entrainment sequence with musical pieces (10–15 minutes total) which match your goal, or desired mood-state (relaxation), as closely as possible.

Your entrainment tape, or tapes, are now ready to be played as often as you need them.

Modifying Other Moods

As mentioned above, entrainment (iso) can be used to modify a number of your present, existing moods in ANY direction. For instance, one can use entrainment to help lift a mood of sadness or mild depression, and transform it into one of joy, comfort, or contentment. In the same manner, you would start with a selection reflecting your present depressed mood ("Comfortably Numb," by Pink Floyd, or "I'm So Lonesome I Could Cry," by Elvis or B. J. Thomas), systematically move your mood upward ("I Am, I Said," by Neil Diamond), and culminate with selections exemplifying the mood you want to achieve ("All You Need is Love" by the Beatles). Again, the choice—like the responsibility—is yours. For an example on putting together a musical entrainment sequence, see the Sample Anti-Depressed Mood Entrainment Sequence, page 16.

One final advantage to the availability of a personal entrainment tape library is that these can be played in the background, affecting our changing moods in desirable directions while we carry on with our regular daily activities. Remember, entrainment is primarily a passive process of subjecting ourselves to the vibrations and feelings emoted through the music. We can use our entrainment tapes as background music to help activate our own emotional and mental transformation while washing dishes, doing the laundry, preparing dinner, working on our car, or relaxing in the tub.

ONLY BY FOLLOWING OUR INNER RHYTHMS
CAN WE FIND THE PEACE TO HARMONIZE AND BE IN ACCORDANCE
WITH THE RHYTHM OF THOSE AROUND US.
HAVING ATTAINED INNER HARMONY, CONFORMING TO OTHERS
FOLLOWS ACCORDINGLY.

Additional Reading

For further readings related to rhythm and entrainment the following research article, books and book chapter are suggested:

Chris B. Brewer, *Rhythms of Learning: Creative Tools for Developing Life Skills* (Tucson: Sepher Press, 1996).

J. R. Evans, "Dysrhythmia and Disorders of Learning and Behavior," in J. R. Evans and M. Clynes (eds.), *Rhythm in Psychological, Linguistic and Musical Processes* (Springfield, IL: Charles C. Thomas, 1986), pp. 249–274.

George Leonard, *The Silent Pulse* (New York: E. P. Dutton, 1978).

Sheila Ostrander and Lynn Schroeder, *Superlearning* (New York: Dell, 1979).

M. S. Rider, "Treating Chronic Disease and Pain with Music-Mediated Imagery," *The Arts in Psychotherapy,* 1987, 14, pp. 113–120.

Affirmations

*Affirmations are very important tools for awakening to the Tao
and living with its forces.[2]*

The following three basic rules can be used to create affirmations:

1. *Personalize your affirmations.* Always use *positive* words, thoughts, and feelings with which *you* feel comfortable. You may choose common, everyday words such as "good, calm, happy, energized, excited," or others which you may not use in daily language, but which may help trigger definite feelings of positivity for yourself, such as "lively, animated, vigorous, vivacious."

Play with different words until you find one that *sounds* right for *you*. One that fits *your* personal vibrations. Allow your mental tone to be assertive and confident.

In forming your affirmations, always avoid using negative terms such as; "annoyed, angry, sad, unlucky, or hopeless." For example, it is best that you *not* construct phrases with double negative terms such as; "I will *not* be *angry*," or "I *won't* be *sad*" anymore," but rather; "I am calm," or "I am happy."

1. Chungliang Al Huang and Jerry Lynch, *Thinking Body, Dancing Mind* (New York: Bantam Books, 1992), p. 25.
2. Huang and Lynch, *Thinking Body, Dancing Mind*, p. 23.

2. *Always use the first person* (I, me, mine). Construct your affirmations to reflect the heAr and now, or the future, and thus *become active in creating your own reality.* For instance; "I can handle this," "I can listen without expectations," "I create my own harmony."[3]

3. *Keep it simple.* Always create short and simple affirmations (affirmative phrases) which you can remember easily, and which have a personal ring to you and your situation. Think of it as writing a catchy song hook, such as "I Feel Fine" (The Beatles), "I Can Hear Music" (The Beach Boys), or "I Hear a Symphony" (The Supremes). See the end of this section for a list of song title affirmation ideas which spans sixty years!

> With affirmations, you can change patterns of negative thought that, like tape recordings in your head, continue to play old, counterproductive tunes.[4]

Whether you are singing your affirmations, speaking them aloud or repeating them within your mind, as you do, feel them echoing and resonating deep within you, like a mantra.[5] Eventually, with enough practice and determination, you will be able to replace your old self-defeating statements and negative criticisms with positive reflections and constructive observations about yourself and the world around you.

Remember, learning a new mode of listening to your self-statements will be similar to learning to play an instrument that you have never attempted to play before. At first, it will quite likely feel frustrating, awkward, and, at times, maybe even hopeless. However, with determination and will power, you will eventually find your inner rhythm. Eventually, you will develop the ability to hear the melodies within the noise, and the harmony within the discord.

> The principles of Music and Living aren't all that different, we think.[6]

Sound Idea

One day, in the near future, take a
health day.

---

3. See HeAr and Now, page 243, and Expectations, page 293.
4. Huang and Lynch, *Thinking Body, Dancing Mind*, p. 23.
5. See Mantric Sounds, page 339.
6. Benjamin Hoff, *The Tao of Pooh* (New York: Penguin Books, 1983), p. 59.

♪

MUSICAL MENU 21

Sixty-Five Years of Song-Title Affirmations

1931: "I Got Rhythm"
1934: "Anything Goes"
1934: "No, No, a Thousand Times No!"
1936: "I'm Shooting High"
1936: "Let's Face the Music and Dance"
1938: "Thanks For the Memories"
1939: "I Get Along Without You Very Well"
1940: "I'm Nobody's Baby"
1940: "It's a Wonderful World"
1940: "Practice Makes Perfect"
1942: "This is Worth Fighting For"
1944: "I'll Get By"
1945: "Accentuate the Positive"
1945: "I'm Beginning to See the Light"
1945: "My Dreams Are Getting Better All the Time"
1945: "No Can Do"
1948: "Now Is the Hour"
1949: "I Can Dream, Can't I?"
1953: "Pretend"
1954: "Little Things Mean a Lot"
1956: "Memories Are Made of This"
1958: "Get a Job"
1959: "High Hopes"
1959: "I've Had It"
1959: "It Don't Matter to Me"
1960: "It's Now or Never"
1961: "Make Someone Happy"
1963: "Our Day Will Come"
1965: "I Feel Fine"
1965: "On a Clear Day You Can See Forever"
1966: "The Last Word in Lonesome is Me"
1967: "Release Me"
1968: "All You Need is Love"

1968: "I've Gotta Be Me"
1969: "Come Together"
1969: "My Way"
1970: "Ain't No Mountain High Enough"
1970: "Everything is Beautiful"
1970: "Let It Be"
1971: "I Am . . . I Said"
1971: "I Won't Mention It Again"
1972: "I Am Woman"
1972: "I Can See Clearly Now"
1972: "Imagine"
1972: "It's Going to Take Some Time"
1972: "We Can Make It Together"
1974: "Keep On Singing"
1975: "Love Will Keep Us Together"
1976: "Sorry Seems to Be the Hardest Word"
1977: "My Heart Belongs to Me"
1980: "Yes, I'm Ready"
1981: "I Don't Need You"
1982: "Let's Hang On"
1983: "I Won't Hold You Back"
1984: "Against All Odds"
1985: "Just As I Am"
1986: "No One is to Blame"
1986: "This Is the Time"
1988: "Roll With It"
1989: "Get On Your Feet"
1989: "Listen to Your Heart"
1991: "Help Yourself"
1994: "Breathe Again"
1995: "If I Wanted To"
1995: "I Believe"
1996: "Exhale"
1996: "Free as a Bird"

Thought Stopping

Sometimes silence is the sweetest sound.

"Thought stopping" is a popular behavioral technique used to interrupt, minimize, or eliminate "psychological noise," or those sometimes obsessive, repetitive, and unwanted fears and anxieties that intrude while we are trying to concentrate on necessary issues. These thoughts are often negative, self-destructive, self-defeating, anxiety-provoking or irrational self-statements, or annoying internal mental messages. Since research has demonstrated that these repetitive negative and anxious thoughts often lead to negative, anxious feelings, thought stopping techniques can function as a beneficial and practical ally in reducing stress and negativity.

Although there are a number of "thought stopping" techniques used by professional clinicians, and discussed in various self-help books, the following, extracted from *The Relaxation and Stress Reduction Workbook,* is particularly well detailed:

> Thought stopping involves concentrating on the unwanted thoughts and, after a short time, suddenly stopping and emptying your mind. The command "stop" or a loud noise is general-

ly used to interrupt the unpleasant thoughts. There are three explanations for the success of thought stopping: 1. The command "stop" serves as a punishment, and behavior which is consistently punished is likely to be inhibited. 2. The command "stop" acts as a distractor, and the imperative self-instruction is incompatible with obsessive phobic thoughts. 3. Thought stopping is an assertive response and can be followed by thought substitutions of reassuring or self-accepting statements.[1]

The exercises found throughout this book offer a number of variations on the above thought-stopping technique. These can be used as tools to effectively reduce unnecessary psychological noise, minimize stress, and counteract negative thinking patterns.

Sound Idea

Begin with stopping one thought
at a time.

Following are some techniques more specifically designed to assist with thought stopping.

Technique 1: The Neon Sign

1. Close your eyes and take a deep, cleansing breath.

2. Focus your concentration on the exact thought which you wish to stop. Identify it consciously and clearly.

3. Using your "mind's eye," "look up" into your forehead and visualize a word, such as "Stop!" "Enough!" "Clear!" "Quiet!" or any other which may help you block, counteract, or eliminate the intruding negative thought(s) or message(s). To help with this image, you may try visualizing, or picturing the image of a glowing neon sign as if it were actually flashing in the inside of your forehead. If you have difficulty with the imaging, try the following:

1. M. Davis, E. R. Eshelman and M. McKay, *The Relaxation & Stress Reduction Workbook* (Oakland, CA: New Harbinger Publications, 1988), p. 91.

Imprinting a word image:

- Take a bright marker, preferably fluorescent, and on a white sheet of paper draw the desired word in clear, block letters (BREATHE, QUIET!).

- Place the paper with the written word directly in front of you.

- While taking a few deep breaths, continue to stare at the word, allowing it to become imprinted in your mind.

- In your mind's eye, begin transferring the word image from the paper into your forehead as you allow your eyes to close, allowing the mind to retain the image for longer periods of time.

- Once you feel that you can actually maintain the image within your mind's eye you can now lie back and continue with the exercise.

- If the image fades completely, you may either continue the exercise while focusing on the memory of the image, or simply take a moment and stare at the written word again, allowing your mind to reincorporate the word image and then return to the exercise.

Technique 2: Shaking Off the Thought

If the above technique does not seem to be working for you, you may try a more assertive approach. For example, try clapping your hands together, splashing cool water on your face, or clearing your throat. While you do one of the above, imagine the troublesome thought actually "shaking loose" and being dislodged from your consciousness. If it does not work at first, try it several times until the negative thought is successfully cleared from your mind.

Technique 3: Thought Editing

Another very effective technique you can use is mentally tuning in to any song to which you know the words. As you feel the negative thought(s) beginning to intrude, actively "turn-on" the song inside your mind and sing along, either out loud or in your head. While the song "plays" within your mind, try and listen to how its lyrics quickly and effectively begin to "flush out" and replace the unwanted thoughts from your mind.

Displacing the undesirable thoughts with *positive* song images ("Good Day Sunshine," The Beatles; "Good Vibrations," The Beach Boys; "I Will Survive," Gloria Gaynor) is even more powerful and has the extra advantage of replacing the negative thoughts with uplifting, positive associations. (See pages 327–328 for affirmative musical suggestions spanning over six decades!)

Having interrupted and dislodged the negative thought(s) replace these with more positive, adaptive, and actively purposeful self-statements such as, "I *can* do it! I *will* do just *fine*! I *can* handle this!" or any other thought or phrase you feel is appropriate and relevant to the present situation.

Technique 4. A Tune for a Thought

As you go on with your daily tasks, surround yourself (home stereo, portable player, car deck) with music which reflects the mood you wish to incorporate. In other words, if you wish to slow down rapid, negative thoughts, you may wish to play some *soothing music* (see Soothing Music, page 55); whereas if you wish to get out of a depressive "funk," you may wish to try some *stimulating music* (see Stimulating Music, page 20). Other music ideas may be gathered from Music for Letting Go (page 257), Music for Dealing with Anger (page 73), or Music for Altered States (page 241), or Centering Music (page 228).

IN LIFE'S SEQUENCE OF SONGS
WE SIMPLY NEED TO STAY IN TUNE.

Breathing

Breathe, you are alive![2]

Breathing. It is the first thing we do when we enter this world, and the last thing we do before we leave it. Although most of us do not own biofeedback equipment, have our own personal guru, or have ready access to breathtaking mountains or panoramic meadows, we do have the *magic* of our breathing. Although we often take this basic function for granted, breathing is the most effective, readily available method we have for stress reduction.

> In our busy society, it is a great fortune to breathe consciously from time to time. We can practice conscious breathing not only while sitting in a meditation room, but also while working at the office or at home, while driving our car, or sitting on a bus, wherever we are, at any time throughout the day.[3]

1. Jon Kabat-Zinn, *Wherever You Go There You Are: Mindfulness Meditation in Everyday Life* (New York: Hyperion, 1994), p. 18.
2. Thich Nhat Hanh, *Peace is Every Step* (New York: Bantam Books, 1991), p. 9.
3. Hanh, *Peace is Every Step*, pp. 9-10.

Breathing, of course, can be done from any position. However, following is the *suggested* pose recommended for practicing your breathing during this exercise: lie down on a (soft but firm) comfortable surface, with knees bent—or legs bent at the knees and supported by a chair—and feet about ten inches apart, so that the lower back is comfortably flattened. This exercise may be done either with your eyes closed, or where you can fixate your vision by selecting a particular spot, directly ahead.

EXERCISE 34:

Discovering Your Magical Breath

1. *Becoming aware of your breathing.* We cannot change something without first becoming aware of it, and then acknowledging it. Initially, simply focus on your breathing. For right now, without trying to change or adapt your breathing, simply notice and become aware of it.

Are you breathing through your nose or your mouth? Listen to the rhythm of your breathing. Are your breaths short, rapid and shallow? Or are they deep, steady and slow?

During this stage many people feel as if they have just "discovered" their breathing for the first time in their lives!

2. *Diaphragmatic breathing.* Having *become aware* of your breathing, you are now ready to move on.

As you breathe, place your hands on your lower abdomen, resting your thumbs on your belly button, and feel the abdomen rise . . . and fall. If you feel your chest rising higher than your abdomen, you will want to direct the breath deeper into the abdomen. Concentrate on inhaling, and exhaling, through your nostrils.

To enhance your sense of centering, try *lightly* pressing your tongue against the roof of your mouth, breathe deeply and slowly through your nostrils and exhale through your *slightly* parted lips.

3. *Visualizing the breath's journey.* To help you direct the breath into your abdomen, try this visualization.

• Imagine your breathing apparatus—your mouth, throat, chest and abdomen—to be a large balloon.

• As you inhale, focus on directing the breath to the bottom of the balloon—the abdomen. Once your abdomen feels comfortably filled with air, bring your inhalation upward, filling the rib cage, chest, lungs, and up into your shoulders.

• Hold the breath for just a couple of seconds. At this point, allow the breath to be exhaled from your body slowly and comfortably. Feel your breath as it rises, moving upward from deep within your belly and passing through your rib cage, chest, lungs, throat, and finally, slowly exhaled through your nostrils. As if releasing the air from a balloon, visualize the air from down within the abdomen surging upward, releasing the tension from your body and mind.

4. *Practice.* With practice (10–15 minutes, twice a day) we can quickly learn to "activate" this mind-body cleansing, deep breathing routine with little effort. Once acquired, this skill can be "triggered" whenever needed to release tension, frustration, anger, or any other emotion that needs to be discharged from the body. Deep breathing can also be used as a preventative technique to avoid stress from accumulating, or even to reduce or eliminate pain.

The goal here is to direct our *in*halation from our nose and mouth, through the throat, past our chests as the air fills our lungs, and into our abdomens, then *ex*haling in the reverse order. Softly, slowly, and comfortably. When thoughts begin to intrude, we need to gently remind ourselves that we will "think about that later," and return our concentration to the *breathing.* We may also try visualizing the word "breathe" (or any other word which feels comfortable, or natural, and seems to do the trick) as if it were written across the inside of our foreheads. This can become a very effective technique which helps us concentrate on what we're trying to do, as well as helping to block-out, flush, or purge any number of unwanted thoughts.[4]

5. *Breathing naturally.* Do not forget that breathing is a *natural* phenomenon. If you find yourself "trying" to breathe "the right way," or the way it "should be done," just take a few minutes from the time you have set aside for practice and *allow your body to breathe*, naturally and comfortably. Do not exaggerate or force your attempts, but simply pay attention to your body's signals. If you begin to feel lightheaded, or dizzy, you are probably "try-

---

4. See Thought Stopping, page 329, Affirmations, page 325, Mantric Sounds, page 339, and Psychological Noise, page 281.

ing too hard." If that occurs, just let go of the breathing as an exercise for the time being and try again later.[5]

If you feel as if all you are getting accomplished on your first few tries is simply lying there and breathing, you will have already begun to move in the right direction. Remember, this is *not a contest* to see how quickly you can learn to do this right, or how long you can stretch the breathing as the breaths glide and swirl throughout your body. It is an opportunity for your mind and body to revitalize and rejuvenate itself. If your breathing feels natural, and leaves you feeling relaxed and recharged, there lies the magic.

6. Once you begin to feel comfortable with letting go of the "right" way of doing it, try the abdominal, diaphragmatic, or "belly" breathing again. Remember, your body *already knows* how to do this, so give your rational mind a few minutes off, and allow it to happen. Now . . . breathe!

> We don't need to wait until we have asthma to enjoy our breathing.[6]

For music that provides calming backgrounds and helps stabilize the breath, or for doing breathing exercises, suggested selections are:

- Nawang Khechog: *Sounds of Inner Peace*
- Nawang Khechog: *Sounds of Peace*
- Tony Scott: *Music for Zen Meditation*
- R. Carlos Nakai: *Canyon Trilogy*
- Jon Bernoff and Marcus Allen: *Breathe* or *Petals*

In addition, look at other suggestions listed in Meditation Music, page 230, Soothing Music, page 55, Chanting Music, page 347, and Music for Altered States, page 241.

> Controlling the rhythm, volume, and frequency of breathing is inherent in all qigong, and one of the ways to do this is through the repetition of sounds coupled with listening and feeling in the body the resultant vibration. This is not mere hypnotic chanting or prayer. It is stimulation through har-

---

5. See Being versus Trying to Be, page 261, and Shoulds, page 311.
6. Hanh, *Peace is Every Step*, p. 77.

monics, the controlling of breath, and the soothing of the mind through listening to the sound.[7]

Treat yourself to a "musical breathing" break. Choose a particularly soothing, contemplative musical piece. Find a quiet, and comfortable place. If possible, use headphones to help isolate yourself from any external distractions or undesired sounds. As your chosen, peaceful selection plays, allow your breath to travel in, through, and out of your body and mind with the aid of the music. Breathe in the music . . . breathe out the music. Breathe it in . . . breathe it out. Allow the rhythm to guide the music . . . Allow the melodies to calm your thoughts . . . Breathe them in . . . breathe them out . . .

Sound Idea

Breathe . . . mindfully!

---

7. Deng Ming-Dao, *Scholar Warrior: An Introduction to the Tao in Everyday Life*, (San Fancisco: HarperSanFrancisco, 1990), p. 47. Readers may also want to investigate qigong, a form of art related to tai chi, which is discussed in detail in this book.

Mantric Sounds

*Music often bypasses the higher, thinking centers of the brain and
appeals directly to the deeper levels—like a mantra used in
meditation or an image conjured in the mind.*[2]

A baby cooing, a cat purring, or anyone moaning with pleasure is
emitting a mantra. In general, mantras fulfill similar purposes as
chanting and toning.[3] The basic premise is releasing unwanted, negative
energies, while recycling our more positive, healthy vibrations.

Rather than encouraging you to consider joining an exotic sect or
organization that would be quite willing to sell you a "personal" mantra,
in this section I will present a way by which you may select music of your
choice to use as your own personal "musical mantric sound."

The basic functions of your "musical mantric sound" will be to assist
you in clearing your mind, focusing, and increasing feelings of well being
and positivity. Why or how you select your mantra does not matter.
Rather, all that is important is what it does for you when and where you
need it.

Mantras consist of vibrations.[4]

1. Joachim-Ernst Berendt, *Nada Brahma: The World is Sound* (Rochester, VT: Destiny Books, 1987), p. 26.
2. William Poole, *The Heart of Healing* (Atlanta: Turner Publishing, 1993), p. 135.
3. See Chanting, page 345, and Toning, page 349.
4. Berendt, *Nada Brahma*, p. 27.

EXERCISE 35:

Finding Your Mantric Sound

1. Choose a song, preferably instrumental, which you find particularly soothing, quieting, and/or pleasant. (See Soothing Musical Menu, page 55).

2. As the music plays, close your eyes and allow your breath to merge and flow with the rhythm.

3. Once you begin to feel "in sync" (comfortable, flowing) with the music, allow your rational, analytical mind to let go and allow your inner ear to focus on any one particular sound or instrument within the song that seems to connect with you at the moment (your "mantric instrument" or "mantric sound").

> Lama Govinda speaks of the "mantra as primordial sound and as archetypal word symbol." Mantric formulas are "pre-lin-guistic." They are "primordial sounds which express feelings but not concepts, emotions rather than ideas."[5]

One very effective "mantric sound" is the drone played by the Indian instrument, the tambura, which is usually played as accompaniment to sitar and tabla music. Hypnotic percussion beats used as the "backbone" of rhythm sessions often also provide excellent "mantric sounds." The reason does not matter. Enter the experience without any expectation of which sound or instrument "may" or "probably will" strike a chord in you. Just trust that *when* it touches you, you will know it. Regardless of the instrument or sound you tune in to (drum, keyboard, strings, bass, horn, violin) simply allow yourself to "be" with that sound in the "heAr and now."[6]

4. As your "inner ear" connects with this sound, allow yourself to begin to mimic, or intone this sound in any manner that flows naturally and effort-lessly from your inner self. As the song plays continue to "follow" the pat-terns played by your particular "mantric instrument" or sound. To the best

5. Berendt, *Nada Brahma*, p. 40.
6. See Expectations, page 293, Being Versus Trying to Be, page 261, and HeAr and Now, page 243.

of your ability continue to concentrate on, and emit your corresponding sound, "in sync" with your mantric instrument.

5. You may find yourself following the bass line, keyboard melody, horn blasts, violin sweeps, a tambura's drone, a tabla's rhythm or any other sound. Regardless of the sound or instrument you "hook in to," try and maintain your focus and concentration on that one sound or instrument throughout the song. If the instrument or sound you selected happens to be one which "comes and goes" throughout the musical piece try and keep pace with the tempo, or pace of the music, and concentrate on "listening for" the sound or instrument as it appears and disappears throughout the composition. (See Meditation Musical Menu, page 230, for suggestions.)

6. At first, you will notice that thoughts and emotions will continue to surface and "attack" you as you attempt to follow these exercises. That's perfectly normal and to be expected. As this occurs, just acknowledge that the thoughts are there, but detach yourself from them to the best of your ability, and continue, as often as necessary, to return your concentration to your "mantric instrument or sound." With practice, these "thought invasions" or "psychological noises"[7] will eventually begin to diminish, and *at times* even completely dissipate for long periods of time. So, in summary, when your mind wanders off (and it will!) simply acknowledge the diversion and return to the music, climbing back "on board" via your "mantric sound."

7. You may try this technique with different compositions and styles of music, opening your "inner ear" up to different mantric sounds or instruments with each occasion. Also, you may choose to return to the same tune as above, repeating the previous procedure. Even if your inner ear hooks into the same exact sound or instrument as during your initial listening experience, you will be surprised at how many different sounds you may hear, and how many different feelings are evoked by the music during each subsequent musical exploration.

> In his book *Mantras: Sacred Words of Power* John Blofeld tells of an old monk who was asked where his cheerful serenity came from. His answer was that it was the sound of the mantras that enabled him to experience his inner harmony with the *tao,* the primal path and sense of existence.[8]

7. See Psychological Noise, page 281.

Just remember, no one ever learned to play an instrument flawlessly without practice, dedication, commitment, and the desire to improve. The same type of effort, willpower, and personal sacrifice that it takes to perfect any sort of worthwhile endeavor will likewise pay off in these situations.

♪

MUSICAL MENU 22:

Mantric Music

(CDS, TAPES, ALBUMS)

These selections can inspire or assist you in guiding your mantras, or mantric sounds:

> Patrick Bernhardt: *Atlantic Angels*.
> Patrick Bernhardt: *Solaris Universalis*.
> Singh Kaur and Kim Robertson: *Crimson Collection, Vols. 1 & 2*.
> Henry Marshall: *Mantras 1*, and *Mantras 2*.

See also suggestions included in the Meditation Musical Menu, page 230, and Chanting Musical Menu, page 347.

> Mantras emerge from the mantric sound, in Sanskrit *bija,* or "seed." Mantras are germinating seeds that sprout oneness. They are "tools of becoming one."9

8. Berendt, *Nada Brahma,* p. 41.
9. Berendt, *Nada Brahma,* p. 27.

Music Sources

A number of additional Meditation, Chanting and Mantra audio selections can be obtained through:

The Hanuman Foundation
524 San Anselmo Ave., Suite 203
San Anselmo, CA 94960

Sounds True
735 Walnut Street
Boulder, CO 80302

Insight Recordings
P.O. Box 700
San Jacinto, CA 92383

Pacific Spirit
Whole Life Products
1334 Pacific Avenue
Forest Grove, OR 97116

ISHK Book Service
P.O. Box 176
Los Altos, CA 94022

Omega Institute for Holistic
Studies
260 Lake Drive
Rhinebeck, NY 12572-3212

Chanting

*Chants help us to reach our darkest resources. Inspiring movement,
touching our emptiness, guiding our path through the mysteries,
without ever disturbing the darkness that surrounds them.*

Chanting can be an excellent technique to assist us in bringing our
attention to the heAr and now. It is quite effective for inducing
thought stopping, clearing the mind, and neutralizing "psychological
noise."[2]

Similar to toning and mantras, chanting can be used to help attain
inner harmony, release stored up energies, and gain spontaneity in the
heAr and now. Through chanting we can help to produce positive vibrational fields around ourselves, enabling us to dispel fears, block out negative vibrations, reduce anxiety, lift depression, enhance healing, generate
positive energies, and help to clear our minds.[3]

As you chant, listen to the feelings and thoughts which are automatically released, and be in tune to any messages which may be spontaneously liberated in the process.

1. Brian Walker, *Hua Hu Ching: The Teachings of Lao Tzu* (Livingston, MT: Clark City Press, 1993),
p. 58.
2. See HeAr and Now, page 243, Thought Stopping, page 329, Clearing the Mind, page 267, and
Psychological Noise, page 281.
3. See Toning, page 349, and Mantric Sounds, page 339.

Following are some basic, simple chanting suggestions. See Chanting Musical Menu, page 347, for selections suggested for guiding, or inspiring chants.

EXERCISE 36:

Discovering Your Personal Chant

1. Take a deep breath, filling your abdomen. As you release the breath surging through your throat, shoulders, upper chest, chest, and finally your abdomen, allow the sound "OM" (pronounced AUM) to be released from the depths of your innermost being.

2. Imagine yourself emitting your inner energies by using this sound as a vehicle. As you begin to reach the end of your breath, carry the humming sound of the "M" (" . . . Mmmmm . . . ") to the conclusion of the exhalation. As you release these sounds, allow the breath to "escort" them from deep inside of you. Listen to them as they flow effortlessly and liberally.

3. For deeper centering, or concentration, in your mind's eye you may actively try and visualize the letter "M" as it slowly fades and "disappears" off into the "distance," merging and blending with the murmur of all the sounds that surround you.

4. As you practice your chanting, you may choose to experiment with various basic simple sounds which sound particularly pleasing or cleansing to you. These may routinely change, or be modified according to your personal preference and specific need at any particular moment. Some of the sounds may include; "Om," "Ah," or "Hum," (or these three may be combined as "Om-Ah-Hum"), or, in a variation such as, "Ah-A-E-O-OO."

5. Finally, you may choose to further personalize your chant by "letting go" or releasing your anxieties, depression, or any other feelings of discomfort to the accompanying sound of a particular word (or phrase) which may have special relevance for you at the moment, or one which may hold a deep meaning in your life. Some of these may include *short* phrases ("I am") or words such as "heal, calm, peace, flow" or any other words or sounds which may prove effective in helping you to attain the feeling *you* need at the moment.

If you say *OM* in the correct way, leading the sound from the head through the chest down into the belly, then the entire body will start to vibrate. The *M* in particular, spoken forcefully, can make the body vibrate for a long time. In fact, the body will continue to vibrate when the mantra (beginning again with *O*) is "threaded" into the head once more and led down again. At that point, not only chest, stomach, and belly will be vibrating, but also the head and (if you have practiced enough) even your arms and legs. Related to this technique of saying and singing *OM* is the multivoice singing technique of Tibetan monks.[4]

Your chant . . . spiraling through hollow canyons, as breeze through prairies, as wind through trees, as a murmuring creek, as a roaring river.

♪

MUSICAL MENU 23
Chanting Music
(CDs, TAPES, ALBUMS)

Suggested selections for guiding, or inspiring chants:

The Benedictine Monks of Santo Domingo de Silos: *Chant* Vols. 1 & 2)
Dik Darnell: *Following the Circle*
Dik Darnell: *Voice of the Four Winds*
Robert Gass and On Wings of Song: *Shri Ram*
Jonathan Goldman: *Gateways Men's Drumming and Chanting*
Randall Gray: *One Hand Clapping*
The Gyuto Monks: *Freedom Chants From the Roof of the World*
David Hykes and the Harmonic Choir: *Harmonic Meetings*
Kriyananda: *Mantra*
Bill Miller and Robert Mirabel with Smokey Town: *Native Suite: Chants, Dances.*
Ravi Shankar: *Chants of India*

4. Joachim-Ernst Berendt, *Nada Brahma: The World is Sound* (Rochester, VT: Destiny Books, 1987), pp. 131-132.

Jon Shore: *Tibetan Memories*
Valley of the Sun Artists: *The Eternal Om*
Alan Watts: *Om: The Sound of Hinduism*

See also Meditation Musical Menu, page 230, for additional musical suggestions.

Music Sources

A number of additional Meditation, Chanting and Mantra audio selections can be obtained through:

The Hanuman Foundation
Suite 203, 524 San Anselmo Ave.
San Anselmo, CA 94960

Pacific Spirit
Whole Life Products
1334 Pacific Avenue
Forest Grove, OR 97116

Insight Recordings
P.O. Box 700
San Jacinto, CA 92383

Omega Institute for Holistic
    Studies
260 Lake Drive
Rhinebeck, NY 12572-3212

ISHK Book Service
P.O. Box 176
Los Altos, CA 94022

Sounds True
735 Walnut Street
Boulder, CO 80302

Living Arts
P.O. Box 2939
Venice, CA 90291-2939

Toning

{Toning is} a matter of freeing the body and letting the sounds
emerge naturally and spontaneously.[1]

Toning is basically a process of spontaneously "letting go" of basic,
natural sounds to attain a sense of centering, balance, or harmony.
Some natural examples of toning are:

- Yawning when tired;
- Moaning when in pain (or when experiencing ecstatic
  pleasures);
- Sobbing or crying when sad, laughing or whistling when
  happy;
- Taking deep breaths when relieved;
- Moaning, groaning, and sighing during sex;
- Screaming when excited.

In each case, the release of these internal tensions results in a healthy harmonizing of our bodies, minds, and emotions.

1. John Beaulieu, *Music and Sound in the Healing Arts* (New York: Station Hill Press, 1987), p. 115.

We can use music as an adjunct to help us to induce the benefits of toning in any, or all, of the following ways.

EXERCISE 37:

Toning through Natural Release

1. Play any selection that reflects your present emotional state. (For musical suggestions refer to the section which best reflects your emotional or mental state at the moment. For example, if feeling "down," refer to Depressed Mood, page 3, if feeling "frustrated" refer to Anger, page 61, or perhaps Stress, page 51.)

2. As the music plays, allow yourself to make any sound that the music seems to arouse, provoke or elicit from you. For example, if you are sad, playing a melancholy song may help stir up your underlying emotions of sadness, allowing you to release your feelings through sighing, whining, sniffling, moaning, sobbing, or crying. If you are feeling particularly joyful and excited, but feel a bit apprehensive about releasing these emotions liberally, you may want to try loosening these inhibitions or reservations with musical assistance. A good upbeat, stimulating song will "give you permission" to release those inner feelings through humming, voicing the instruments, or "la-la-ing" your way through the melody lines. (See Stimulating Musical Menu, page 20.)

3. Whatever emotions you may be feeling at the moment, however, the only "rule" is to allow your internal sounds to be expressed, or released, naturally, effortlessly, and spontaneously. The music is mainly used to *facilitate* the emancipation of what is already on the brink of expression. In other words, at the tip of your tongue. (Refer to page 249 for some musical suggestions, as well as a general overview on the process of Letting Go.)

4. Once you begin to feel comfortable with the subtle expression of your disengaged sounds, you may want to move up toward liberal *exaggeration* of these sounds. Some visualizations which may be helpful in these situations include pretending you are a cartoon character, young child, or animal; mimicking a particularly amusing or "exotic" person in your past or present life; or pretending you are actually one of the instruments, or characters, in the music which you are listening to (opera is particularly good for this!).

EXERCISE 38:

Toning While Making Love

In a different setting, you may choose to use a particularly inspiring musical piece to unbind toning during romantic intimacy. Music in this situation serves a number of purposes. First, by helping to set, and maintain, a sensuously seductive ambiance it acts as an "acoustic aphrodisiac." Second, music helps to eliminate extraneous sounds and contain internal sounds (those you and your partner make) while creating a more personal and private environment. Third, it helps to stimulate the discharge of pent up emotions, verbally, emotionally, and physiologically. Finally, psychologically, the fact that the music is already "filling up" the room with sounds helps to reduce inhibitions related to "letting go," or releasing your own melodic passions.

EXERCISE 39:

Toning During a Stroll

Take a walk around your city, town, or local countryside. As you walk around, tune in (or "tone in") to the sounds which surround you. As you become comfortable with your acoustic surroundings allow yourself to harmonize with the various sounds you encounter through toning (or "tuning in"). Whistle with the birds, hum with the electric wires, rattle with the train, whoosh with the airplanes, roar with the lawn mowers, breathe with the trees.

> When you hum (and the simple humming that many people do they do not know is a kind of inner granting) even if you don't sing, the breath is going deep from where it came.[2]

Since most of the time we have absolutely no control over the endless sounds that surround us, we can choose to use these techniques to help us

2. Joan Allekote and Marsha Maslan, "Sri Karunamayee: An In-Depth Interview," *Open Ear*, 1996, 1, p. 8.

react more positively to many of the otherwise "harmful" sounds and noises in our environment. In effect, each sound we encounter will—with the help of our heAr and now awareness—function as a cue to help us create yet another opportunity for harmonizing, balancing and developing a healthful attitude toward our environment.

Intone a sound audibly, then less and less audibly as feeling deepens into *this silent harmony.*[3]

3. Paul Reps, *Zen Flesh, Zen Bones* (New York: Anchor Books, 1989), p. 164.

SPECIAL TOPICS

Don't wait, play music for your children, now.

WHAT A SAD, BORING UNIVERSE, IF ALL MUSIC
WERE THE SAME.

Choosing One's Music

Choosing your own music is like finding your own way,
you have to do it yourself.

History consistently supports the fact that, throughout time, music has been "an indispensable factor in healing the sick. The medicine man was doctor, lawyer, priest, philosopher, botanist, and musician. The right song had to be used with the right medicine. Each member had his own songs, some of which he composed and others he had to buy, as no one was allowed to sing another's song."[1]

More recently, the scientific community has corroborated what our forefathers suspected all along. In using music as an adjunct to ameliorating pain, for example, findings have indicated that "choice of preferred music may assist the client in pain coping above and beyond listening to music that is pre-chosen for them and possibly non-preferred. The control of musical selection may have profound effects on the ability of participants to cope with pain because of an increased sense of control and self-efficacy."[2]

1. Marion Bauer and Ethel Peyser, *Music Through the Ages* (New York: G. P. Putnam's Sons, 1932), p. 9.
2. Hamid Hekmat and James Hertel, "Attenuating Effects of Preferred Versus Non-Preferred Music Interventions," *Psychology of Music*, 1993, 21, 2, pp. 163–173 (p. 170).

Among the many pleasures in our diverse universe, our freedom to make personal choices based on individual taste would rank very highly for most of us. Regardless of the similarities we may share with close friends or family members, each of us has a personal leaning toward particular things that tend to help define us as unique individuals. A distinctive perfume or cologne, jeans which "fit like a glove," well-cooked versus raw, vodka rather than rum, brick instead of log homes, stocks over mutual funds. The universe of differences is, literally, endless. Although a particular person may be okay with the color brown, all things considered, that individual may have a definite preference for gray, blue, or any other color. An so it is with music. In general, not one musical tune sounds—or feels—the same to any two people. Music is experienced as "good" or "bad" according to how closely it relates to one's particular reality at any specific time and place.

Attempts to analyze where our musical preferences originated, or how they developed, is often complicated. For instance, "fetuses spend many months listening to various rumblings in the mother's gut, the whooshing of blood through veins and arteries, and the rhythmic thump of the mother's heart—which may account in part for the healing agency of rhythm and music for many people later in life. The fetus hears voices as well—particularly and most consistently its mother's voice. Research has shown that a newborn infant already recognizes its mother's voice and prefers it to less familiar voices. Similarly, babies show a preference for a melody they heard while in the womb over other melodies."[3]

> Specific musical training most probably does influence aesthetic appreciation, but it has little to do with the emotional value of the music.[4]

An individual's musical preference, like anything else, is therefore highly subjective, personal and relative. What may feel soothing to one may well feel disturbing, or even irritating to others. In the course of my workshops, I have found that Indian music, in particular, is one musical form which tends to evoke very contradictory effects among audiences. While a few people in the audience seem to find these tunes not only relaxing but pleasantly trance inducing, or hypnotic, others describe the same compositions as annoying, disquieting, or even offensive. The above illustrates a perfect example of the importance of considering individual preferences when choosing a musical background!

3. William Poole, *The Heart of Healing* (Atlanta: Turner Publishing, 1993), p. 141.
4. Mark Meerum Terwogt and Flora van Grinsven, "Musical Expression of Moodstates," *Psychology of Music*, 1991, 19, pp. 99–109 (p. 109).

If a piece of music moves a variety of listeners, it is probably not because of its outward form but because of what the form means to each listener in terms of human experience. The same piece of music may move different people in the same sort of way, but for different reasons.[5]

The way we are affected by music depends on a number of variables. According to research, they fall into three major categories: musical, situational, and subject. In other words, one's preference for particular types of music depends on the music itself, the situation one is in at the moment (the heAr and now), and a number of personality characteristics. Five specific personal characteristics which have been found to affect musical preference, or taste, include: mood, personality, musical training, gender, and age.[6]

Extroverts, for example, have been found to have a leaning toward highly arousing music such as jazz, while others seem to prefer hard rock. Some persons who tend to remain open to new experiences, on the other hand, have been found to lean toward new age, classical, jazz, reggae, folk-ethnic and soul music.[7] Still another study found that conservatives tend to prefer familiar music, whereas liberals are typically more receptive to unfamiliar tunes.[8]

Likewise, some of the particular musical elements that affect a listener include rhythm, volume, the composition's complexity, variation in pitch, repetition within the tune itself, and the type of music. Situational factors, which include repeated hearings, expectation effects, teaching methods, community attitudes, peer influences, socioeconomic relationships, educational level and musical training have all been found to influence our individual tastes for different types of music.[9]

It is rather striking that the durations of our heartbeats and of our spontaneous and preferred tempi do seem to fall within a similar range.[10]

5. John Blacking, *How Musical is Man?* (Seattle: University of Washington Press,1990), p. 52.
6. See B. L. Wheeler, "The Relationship between Musical and Activity Elements of Music Therapy Sessions and Client Responses: An Exploratory Study," *Music Therapy*, 1985, 5, pp. 52–60.
7. Stephen Dollinger, "Personality and Music Preference: Extraversion and Excitement Seeking or Openness to Experience?" *Psychology of Music*, 1993, 21, 1, pp. 73–77.
8. M. R. Glasgow, A. M. Cartier and G. D. Wilson, "Conservation, Sensation Seeking, and Music Preferences," *Personality and Individual Differences*, 1985, 6, pp. 395–396.
9. J. David Boyle, Glen L. Hosterman and Darhyl S. Ramsey, "Factors Influencing Pop Music Preferences of Young People," *Journal of Research in Music Education*, 1981, pp. 47–55.
10. Leslie Bunt, *Music Therapy: An Art Beyond Words* (New York: Routledge, 1994), p. 57.

Other factors that may influence one's leaning toward a particular type of music may include familiarity with the music, culture, and one's ability to discriminate fine distinctions within music in general, and specific tunes or compositions in particular. Successful composers of popular music through the ages, for example, from Mozart, through Gershwin, to Lennon and McCartney seem to be able to tap into universal rhythms and melodies, somehow echoing our culture's collective unconscious. When released, these songs and compositions seem to sound, and feel, somehow comfortably familiar, while simultaneously eliciting a sense of fresh excitement. Expressed as music, these commonly shared feelings seem to fill timely emotional voids during our developmental transitions. Other studies have indicated that certain variables, such as socioeconomic status, political affiliation, and level of intelligence affect an individual's musical preferences.

Regardless of how our musical leanings became ingrained, however, there are some sound characteristics which mutually move us in certain general emotional, physical or psychological directions. For example, over time, professional and lay people alike have realized that certain sound patterns motivate us, while others tend to evoke peace or relaxation. "Psychiatrist Roberto Assagioli prescribed different music for his patients: marches to quicken the energies of depressed people, waltzes to calm the overly anxious. . . . To slow down and relax, I listen to Bach, Vivaldi, or new age meditation music."[11] Although there are certain universals within music which tend to be shared by many people, there is no substitute for choosing one's own musical backgrounds in accordance with personal preferences.

Just as all forms of music cannot be expected to appeal to each and every individual, all individuals cannot be expected to be attracted to any one particular form of music.

Throughout this book, readers will find that specific music selections are suggested for various exercises. As follows from the discussion above, however, readers should keep in mind that, although these general suggestions may satisfy the needs of many individuals, they are by no means intended to fulfill everyone's needs. On the other hand, the suggested selections may well serve as a starting point for many people. Whenever possible, however, readers are strongly encouraged to delve into their musical unconscious and allow the music from within to surface, guiding the adventurous search for rhythmic synchronicity.[12]

11. Diane Dreher, *The Tao of Inner Peace* (New York: HarperCollins, 1991), p. 104.
12. See Rhythmic Synchronicity, page 275.

Additional Reading

For further reading on preferred music you may refer to the following articles:

W. B. Davis and M. H. Thaut, "The Influence of Preferred Relaxing Music on Measures of State Anxiety, Relaxation, and Physiological Responses," *Journal of Music Therapy*, 1989, 26, pp. 168–187.

N. A. Hadsell, "Multivariate Analyses of Musicians' and Nonmusicians' Ratings of Pre-Categorized Stimulative and Sedative Music," *Journal of Music Therapy*, 1989, 26, pp. 106–114.

V. N. Stratton and A. H. Zalanowski, "The Effect of Background Music on Verbal Interaction in Groups," *Journal of Music Therapy*, 1984a, 21, pp. 16–21.

V. N. Stratton and A. H. Zalanowski, "The Relationship between Music, Degree of Liking and Self-Reported Relaxation," *Journal of Music Therapy*, 1984b, 21, pp. 184–192.

D. B. Taylor, "Subject Responses to Precategorized Stimulative and Sedative Music," *Journal of Music Therapy*, 1973, 10, pp. 86–94.

Anna Unyk, Sandra Trehub, Laurel Trainor and Glen Schellenberg, "Lullabies and Simplicity: A Cross-Cultural Perspective," *Psychology of Music*, 1992, 20, 1, pp. 15–28 (p. 25).

J. Wapnick, "A Review of Research on Attitude and Preference," *Bulletin of the Council for Research in Music Education*, 1976, 48, pp. 1–20.

WHATEVER WE CHOOSE,
THAT BECOMES OUR REALITY.

The Spiral Sojourn

*{A}ll life is part of a great rhythmic process of creation and
destruction, of death and rebirth, and Shiva's dance symbolizes this
eternal lifedeath rhythm which goes on in endless cycles.*[1]

Among the many ways we may reach our "special place," ascending
or descending to it (the direction is *our* choice!) by way of the Spiral
Sojourn is a technique which is particularly effective. The Spiral Sojourn is
simply a progressive relaxation exercise designed to help us integrate deep
breathing, relaxation, and visualization skills for a number of purposes.

Music is multi-dimensional and multi-directional. How we
use music can be beautifully represented in this image of the
spiral, a shape so fundamental to life.[2]

The Music

True to the nature of this book, each Spiral Sojourn trip, or visualization
should be accompanied by a musical background. Carefully selected, the

1. Fritjof Capra, *The Tao of Physics* (Boston: Shambhala, 1985), p. 242. Note: Shiva is described as the
Hindu dancing god, the "King of Dancers."
2. Leslie Bunt, *Music Therapy: An Art Beyond Words* (London: Routledge, 1994), p. 159.

music should be quite effective in helping you achieve a quicker and deeper state of relaxation, more vivid visualizations, and smoother transitions into altered states of consciousness. As it helps you to attune to your own inner vibrational state, the music may also function to block out unwanted extraneous sounds, help you to tune in to your own inner voices, and help to set your own pace by way of its tempo and rhythmic structures.[3]

> Music is a sort of dream architecture which passes in filmy clouds and disappears into nothingness.[4]

Introduction to Your Special Place, by Way of the Spiral Sojourn

The following is a simple, passive exercise by which you may, at anytime, experience the harmony of the Tao of music. There are five basic components underlying each exercise. These include:

- Deep breathing;
- Being in the heAr and now;
- Letting go (mentally, physically, and emotionally);
- Joining with the music;
- Holding no expectations.

EXERCISE 40:
The Spiral Sojourn

1. The magic you once knew as a child still echoes in your mind. It is still there, you just need to reclaim it. Let go, follow the music and it will take you back to that place where dreams reside.

---

3. See Musical Menus on pages 55, 228, and 241.
4. Percy Scholes, from *The Listener's Guide to Music* (1919), in *A Dictionary of Musical Quotations,* Ian Crofton and Donald Fraser, eds. (New York: Schirmer Books, 1985), p. 49.

2. Select a piece of music you wish to explore. Instrumental music is best. This may be any style or genre, any type or form, simple or exotic, fast or slow, long or short. It's your choice, the Tao of music abides in every sound.

3. Wear loose, comfortable clothes and socks. Nothing restrictive, tight, or anything which will make you too warm, or expose you to the cold.

4. Select a warm, quiet and comfortable place where you may sit, or lie down without being disturbed. Unplug the phone. Place a "do not disturb" sign on your door. Let anyone else around know that you wish to not be disturbed for the amount of time you wish to explore the Tao of music. Make sure that the volume on your record (cassette, disc) player is adjusted to your liking.

5. Lie down, make yourself comfortable and turn on your musical selection. Immediately, begin your slow . . . deep . . . breathing . . . and begin to consciously let go of your tensions, concerns, and any conscious thoughts that may be interfering.

6. During this time you have no place to go but here. Physically or mentally. You have selected this time for yourself. This is not a time to balance your checkbook . . . nor to wash the dishes . . . nor read the newspaper . . . nor to work on the garden . . . nor make phone calls. Those other things you did earlier, or you will do later. This is your time to relax. To enjoy. To travel within the Tao.

7. As the music begins to unfold, allow your mind to savor the sounds. Allow the melody to empty your mind. Feel the rhythm caress a subtle smile on the inside of your face. Watch how the smile surfaces on the outside of your face.

8. Whenever thoughts attempt to intrude—and they WILL—allow yourself to "let go. . . . " Do not TRY to let go, but simply "give yourself permission" to let go. After all, this is YOUR time. HeAr and now.

9. Return to the flow of the music. At first, this may be rather difficult. It's like learning any new skill, like learning to play a musical instrument. With practice, you become better, and better. With patience, it becomes easier, and easier. With time, you begin to flow. You become sensitized to the mode of what you are doing and you eventually "become one." You assimilate, or rhythmically synchronize, with the event of the moment. It becomes okay.

10. Allow the music to bathe your mind, your self, your spirit. Without expectations, allow the melody to take you where it leads. Let go of all control. Allow any and all images the music conjures up to surface, and greet them with a smile.

11. When thoughts again invade, return to the music. The pattern of the bass . . . the sweeping strings . . . the swaying violins . . . the beat of the drum . . . the glow of the brass . . . the thrill of the guitar . . . the breathing of the flute. . . .

12. If thoughts become too much, and you need to return to the Tao of music, try and focus on the phrase, "I am listening." As you do, repeat it again and again in your mind. You may choose to actually verbalize it very softly, very subtly and lightly, barely allowing the words, blending into one, to empty from your mouth in a whisper. Feel the "m" murmur and resonate in your mind like an echo. Watch it fade and disappear as it blends with the notes within the melody. Ride the "Mmmmmm" back to the heAr and now.

13. As you breathe, breathe in the music. Visualize the melody entering your body with each inhalation. "See" the music entering your body like a white, clear, healthy light. Watch it flow throughout your mind, clearing it of every negative thought, every concern, every tension. With each exhalation, see those thoughts, concerns and tensions being purged out of your body in the form of a dark and muddy haze. Breathe the music into each and every corner of your being. Continue to watch as the spiraling melodies purify your body. Feel and listen to how the music enters your body, emptying and cleansing it of anything unhealthy, negative, or undesired.

14. Feel the vibrations of the music energizing you. Feel how the music, resonating through your self, harmonizes your being with your environment. Listen to your internal energy harmonizing with your external surroundings. Visualize your aura glowing, blending and dancing with the Tao of music.

15. Feel the rhythm of your being synchronizing with the rhythm of the music. Lose your self in the pulsing midst of the rhythmic synchronicity.

16. Stay with the music. Let it take you where it goes. Up, down, sidewinding left and right, spiraling into infinity. Any way you go, is the

right way. Any path it takes will take you there. Wherever you go, there you will be, for that moment. Let go.

17. As the music concludes, allow it to bring you back.

18. Before you allow yourself to return completely, know that you can return to that path whenever you wish. Know that the music you choose will take you there. That the magic is in the process, in the letting go of your mind. Know that the Tao of music vibrates inside you, always. That the echo of your experience resonates within you. That as long as you are aware of being here, at this moment, you will hear the music of the Tao.

> This cycle or spiral is found repeatedly in diagrams, glyphs and mandalas worldwide, reflecting a property or expression of human consciousness harmonizing and relating to the greater consciousness or the universe.[5]

Summary

Once you have become more acquainted with the above processes you will no longer need the reminders, procedures, and suggestions described above. With practice, you will eventually develop your own approach and find the path through listening, and then hear your own way through the path.

To assist you in your transition, below is a summarized, slightly advanced version of the journey.

- The magic you once knew as a child still echoes in your mind. It is still there, you just need to reclaim it.
- Lie down, make yourself comfortable and turn on your musical selection. Breathe. . . .
- During this time you have no place to go but here. This is *your* time.
- Allow your mind to savor the music. Allow the melody to empty your mind. Listen to your inner smile.
- Let go. You are here, now.
- Dance with the flow of the music.
- Listen to your musical images.

5. R. J. Stewart, *Music and the Elemental Psyche* (Rochester, VT: Destiny Books, 1987), p. 111.

- Focus on the mantra (affirmation) "I am listening" as you follow the musical path of the Tao.

- Breathe in the music. Let the melody embrace you. Feel the harmony.

- Feel the musical energies blending with your aura. Resonate with the yin and yang.

- Lose your self in the pulsing midst of the rhythmic synchronicity.

- Trust your instincts, your inner primordial sounds.

- As the music ends, allow it to bring you back.

- Before you allow yourself to return completely, know that you can return to that path whenever you wish. Know that the music you choose will take you there, that the magic is in the process, in the letting go of your mind. Know that the Tao of music vibrates inside you, always, that the echo of your experience resonates within you. As long as you are aware of being here, at this moment, you will hear the music of the Tao.

Throughout this book, as the exercises suggest that you "initiate your Spiral Sojourn," consult your "inner guide," or go to your "special place," you need only refer back to this section and review these basic directions to comply with that portion of each exercise.

> The spiral is an excellent symbol for the path of individuation, because it combines the sense of movement along an inner axis with the image of circumambulating a center. If one imagines a line along one side of a spiral form, and pictures the ego as moving along it, we have a sense of the way in which one continually comes back to the same problems but at a different level with each turn of the spiral. To paraphrase T. S. Eliot, in *Four Quartets*, it is like finding that our end was in our beginning, but we come to know it for the first time.[6]

6. James A. Hall, *The Jungian Experience: Analysis and Individuation* (Toronto: Inner City Books, 1986), p. 49.

Your Special Place

Music is fourth dimension.[2]

Your special place is a term given to an imaginary place of retreat, a sanctuary deep within yourself where you may feel totally and absolutely safe, comfortable, at peace, secure, positive and in control of your environment. Although imaginary, your special place is an actual or virtual place, either indoors or out, which is indeed quite real to *you*.

> The level of imagination is giving ourselves permission to have images with the sounds. For example, when we go to a concert we do not simply "hear violins;" we close our eyes and let the music take us to magical places.[3]

When we were children, our special place was that realm in our minds where imaginary friends dwelled; where stuffed animals spoke, emoted, laughed, and at times provided us with support and even advice. It was a

---

1. Leslie Bunt, *Music Therapy: An Art Beyond Words* (London: Routledge, 1994), p. 36.
2. Joan Allekote and Marsha Maslan, "Sri Karunamayee: An In-Depth Interview," *Open Ear*, 1996, 1, p. 8.
3. John Beaulieu, *Music and Sound in the Healing Arts* (New York: Station Hill Press, 1987), p. 14.

uniquely magical, and sometimes mysterious place where we were the ultimate, omnipotent, and omniscient authority. Although as both children and adults some of us may be lucky enough to have an actual, tangible special site (a room, basement, barn, workshed, spot in the woods) where we can hide out, get away, or go in times of need, the special place referred to here is one which dwells *inside* us. An exclusive place which *we* can access, and to which only *we* hold the "enchanted key."

> I share Plato's conviction that musical training is a potent instrument "because rhythm and harmony find their way into the inward places of the soul."[4]

As it vibrates within the recesses of our imagination, our special place can, in actuality, be any number of places, such as an imaginary forest, beach, castle, mansion, meadow, lakeside cabin, a ship out on the ocean, tower, etc. Limited only by our own inner creativity, this special place can be something out of our past such as a childhood room, treehouse, elementary school library, or something completely unorthodox, such as a cloud, magic carpet, or recluse mountain top. In effect, our special place does not have to be explainable by rational thought. Its physical or emotional characteristics are exempt from any sort of deductible, analyzable, or rational components. It just *is*.

Our special place is a private and personal space where we can relax and feel safe and comfortable "letting down our guard." There, we can meditate, contemplate, freely expose our deepest emotions, explore our innermost intuitions, or have private dialogues with other aspects of our personality which are usually embodied or manifested as our "inner guide."[5] There, we make all the rules, control all consequences, and allow only the presence of people with whom we choose to share our time and space. If anything or anyone becomes uncomfortable, negative, or annoying, we have complete jurisdiction over their existence. Their actuality is dependent on our moment to moment discretion.

Since your special place is there to provide you with immediate sanctuary, its characteristics can be altered and modified to fit your special, personal needs with each passing moment. Whenever you ascend, or descend, into your special place, allow yourself the luxury of completely detaching from any and all expectations (expecting events to unfold in pre-

---

4. Anthony Storr, *Music and the Mind* (New York: The Free Press, 1992), p. 126.
5. See Inner Guide, page 371.

scribed patterns, particular people to appear, or things to be a certain way) and limitations (you can have a swimming pool in a cloud, you can fly, levitate, or summon a magic flying carpet at anytime). Wherever you enter, there you'll be.

> When we take part in music, or listen to an absorbing performance, we are temporarily protected from the input of other external stimuli. We enter a special, secluded world in which order prevails and from which the incongruous is excluded.[6]

---

6. Storr, *Music and the Mind*, p. 105.

WE CARRY WITH US THE WONDERS WE SEEK
WITHOUT US.[1]

Inner Guide

What music expresses is the inner *spirit.*[2]

Some of us, the lucky ones, grow up with the advantage of an older, "wiser" person who serves as a "guiding light" or role model, showing us the ropes, sharing practical advice, and making our life's path a little smoother. If we are fortunate, this individual turns out to be trustworthy, kind, caring, and reliable. If we are *very* fortunate, this individual will also have a sense of humor, be highly creative, and instill in us a sense of inner awareness and healthy ambition. While this "outer guide" may be a parent, relative, or sibling, he or she may also be a neighbor, close family friend, teacher, sports coach, or any other person with whom we feel a certain affinity. If a positive relationship develops, it will be based on a mutual sense of respect, fondness and—most importantly—a natural, comfortable fit between the two auric fields (the electromagnetic energies which radiate in the form of our auras).

These "outer guides," are kindred spirits, soul mates. An "inner guide," on the other hand, is an *internal* version of the above helpful, sup-

1. Sir Thomas Browne, in Jon Winokur, *Zen To Go* (New York: Plume, 1990), p. 119.
2. Anthony Storr, *Music and the Mind* (New York: The Free Press, 1992), p. 140.

portive entity. The notion of the Jungian archetype, the *Self*, helps to describe some dimensions of this image of an "inner guide."

> The word Self does not refer to the individual self, but the whole of the personality—ego, consciousness, personal and collective unconscious. Its numinous power is centering.
>
> The Self appears in dream, myths, and fairy tales as the king, the hero, the prophet, the savior. It appears as the magic circle, the square, and the cross; it is the total union of opposites. The Self is a united duality as Tao and yang and yin. It appears as the mandala.[3]

For the purposes of this book, an "inner guide" can be described in a number of ways. The "inner guide" can be thought of as a reflection of our innermost, wiser "self," our vibrational double. Accessed through visualizations, it (he/she) can appear in the form of any person, character, image, or presence whom we encounter in our journeys to our special place.[4] It/she/he is a sort of "ethereal entity" in whose presence we feel a sense of trust, confidence, comfort, peace, and safety. For those of us who developed with the advantage of a positive "outer guide," our "inner guide" will usually include some of the characteristics of this external figure, or it may reflect a composite of our various "outer guides."

Our "inner guide" can also be a legendary, mythical, imaginary, or internal manifestation of an actual person—or even animal—from our past, or even our future! In that sense, our "inner guide" may even be one of our "future selves!" Further, it can be a virtual incarnation of an older and wiser you, reaching back in time to lend advice to your present, younger incarnation. On the other hand, the "inner guide" may surface in the form of an *earlier*, younger you, reawakening inner child material, or dormant memories and experiences whose time has finally arrived.[5] While these younger incarnations of ourselves may bring with them the advantage of objective innocence and the fresh energy of unjaded youth, our future versions benefit from experience, patience and priceless maturity. This is manifested through an essence which we perceive as "wiser," and to whom we feel a strong affinity. It is both the epitome and extension of our inner self and may communicate through sounds, feelings, images, scents,

---

3. Harry A. Wilmer, *Practical Jung* (Wilmette, IL: Chiron Publications, 1987), pp. 80, 81.

4. See Special Place, page 367.

5. For excellent reading in this area, I highly recommend Jane Roberts' wonderful book, *The Education of Oversoul Seven*, recently released as part of *The Oversoul Seven Trilogy* (San Rafael, CA: Amber, Allen, 1995).

signals, symbols, visualizations, colors, or in any other manner that may resonate within the mutuality of our universal unconscious.

> Eyes closed, see your inner being in detail. Thus *see* your true nature.[6]

Manifested as a "being," or "presence" with whom we share a special sense of rhythmic synchronicity,[7] our "inner guide" is a definitive compilation of all that we are, all we have been, and all we are yet to be. In short, when we encounter our "inner guide," we are confronting the essence of our naked self. In discourse, we are hearing our own echoes. As we observe, the reflections we see are our own. Whenever we follow, we are leading the way.

EXERCISE 41:
Accessing Your Inner Guide

1. Select a favorite piece of soothing music (see page 55 for a Soothing Musical Menu, or page 230 for a Meditational Musical Menu), initiate a Spiral Sojourn[8] and descend/ascend into your Special Place.

2. Having reached your safe, quiet space, allow yourself to bask in the calming, harmonious vibrations as these surround, soothe, and energize you. As you become more comfortable, and feel ready to greet your inner guide, allow yourself to "look out" into your (internal) distance and imagine that you see a figure approaching.

3. If the figure who approaches you as your proposed inner guide makes you feel in any way anxious, unsafe, or uncomfortable, you have complete control to reject it. If this occurs, stop, return to your breathing[9] and continue your internal search through a different "path" until you encounter a positive presence with whom you feel completely at ease.

6. Paul Reps, *Zen Flesh, Zen Bones: A Collection of Zen and Pre-Zen Writings* (New York: Anchor Books, 1989), p. 163.
7. See Rhythmic Synchronicity, page 375.
8. See Spiral Sojourn, page 361.
9. See Breathing, page 333.

4. As an amiable, benevolent figure enters your vibrational field, imagine your two selves greeting. As you listen, imagine yourself bonding and feeling safe, secure, and completely comfortable in the company of this peaceful and trustworthy figure.

5. Visualize your selves engaging in some form of discourse which may be through verbal, telepathic, or any other form of communication. Through your intuition, hear yourself becoming increasingly aware of the superior level of this figure's wisdom, its good intentions, and its commitment to your best welfare.

6. As time passes, and you develop, grow, and change, be aware that your inner guide may very well also experience changes which will resonate with, or echo, your own. Likewise, if you encounter more than one inner guide throughout your spiral sojourns, realize that they are all extensions or abbreviations of your inner self, each with its own specialty, or purpose.

7. As you conclude each meeting, or discussion with your inner guide, consciously activate your acoustic memory,[10] making a mental note to mentally and emotionally store the experience acquired through this encounter with your inner guide. As you return to full consciousness in the real world, you will be returning to your daily activities with the full benefit of your inner encounter.

8. Finally, regardless of the suggestions, explanations, or advice you receive from any of your inner guides, don't forget that, ultimately, *you* are *always* in control of, and responsible for, all your thoughts, actions, and behaviors.

Listen to music that bridges the three spheres of your being.[11]

. . . AND SO, FOR NOW,
I'D LIKE TO END THIS ON A GOOD NOTE.

---

10. See Acoustic Memory, page 291.
11. Brian Walker, *Hua Hu Ching: The Teachings of Lao Tzu* (Livingston, MT: Clark City Press, 1992), p. 52.

Bibliography

Ackerman, Diane. (1990). *A Natural History of the Senses*. New York: Random House.

Aldridge, David. (1996). *Music Therapy Research and Practice in Medicine: From Out of the Silence*. London: Jessica Kingsley Publishers, Ltd.

————. (1991). "Physiological Change, Communication, and the Playing of Improvised Music: Some Proposals for Research." *The Arts in Psychotherapy*, 18, 1, pp. 59–64.

Aldridge, David and Gudrun. (1992). "Two Epistemologies: Music Therapy and Medicine in the Treatment of Dementia." *The Arts in Psychotherapy*, 19, 4, pp. 243–256.

Allekote, Joan and Maslan, Marsha. (1996). "Sri Karunamayee: An In-Depth Interview." *Open Ear*, 1, pp. 6–11.

Anderson, C. R. and Tunks, T. W. (1992). "The Influence of Expectency on Harmonic Perception." *Psychomusicology*, 11, pp. 3–14.

Ansdell, Gary. (1995). *Music for Life: Aspects of Creative Music Therapy with Adult Clients*. London: Jessica Kingsley Publishers, Ltd.

Assagioli, Roberto. (1982). *Psychosynthesis*. New York: Penguin.

Austin, Diane Snow and Dvorkin, Janice M. (1993). "Resistance in Individual Music Therapy." *The Arts in Psychotherapy*, 20, 5, pp. 423–430.

Azar, Beth. (1996). "New Studies of Music Support Old Theories about People's Musical Preferences." *The APA Monitor*, American Psychological Association, April, 26, 4, p. 22.

Bailey, L. M. (1986). Music Therapy in Pain Management." *Journal of Pain and Symptom Management*, 1, pp. 25–28.

Bandura, Albert. (1977). *Social Learning Theory*. Englewood Cliffs, NJ: Prentice–Hall.

Bauer, Gregory P. (1990). *Wit and Wisdom in Dynamic Psychotherapy*. Northfield, NJ: Jason Aronson.

Bauer, Marion and Peyser, Ethel. (1932). *Music Through the Ages*. New York, NY: G.P. Putnam's Sons.

Beaulieu, John. (1987). *Music and Sound in the Healing Arts*. Barrytown, NY: Station Hill Press.

Beck, Charlotte Joko. (1989). *Every Day Zen: Love and Work*. San Francisco: HarperSanFrancisco.

Berendt, Joachim-Ernst. (1987). *Nada Brahma: The World is Sound*. Rochester, VT: Destiny Books, Helmut Bredigkeit, trans.

Bever, T. G. (1988). "A Cognitive Theory of Emotion and Aesthetics in Music." *Psychomusicology*, 7, pp. 165–175.

Blacking, John. (1990). *How Musical is Man?* Seattle: University of Washington Press.

Bonny, H. L. (1986). "Music and Healing. *Music Therapy*, 6A, pp. 3–12.

Borgeat, F. (1983). "Psychophysicological Effects of Two Different Relaxation Procedures: Progressive Relaxation and Subliminal Relaxation." *Psychiatric Journal of the University of Ottawa*, 8, pp. 181–185.

Borling, J. E. (1981). "The Effects of Sedative Music on Alpha Rhythms and Focused Attention in High-Creative and Low-Creative Subjects." *Journal of Music Therapy*, 18, pp. 101–108.

Bowman, R. P. (1987). "Approaches for Counseling Children through Music." *Elementary School Guidance and Counseling*, 19, pp. 284–291.

Boyle, J. David, Hosterman, Glen L. and Ramsey, Darhyl S. (1981). "Factors Influencing Pop Music Preferences of Young People." *Journal of Research in Music Education*, 29,1, pp. 47–55.

Brewer, Chris. (1996). "Orchestrating Learning Skills." *Open Ear*, 1.

———. (1996). *Rhythms of Learning: Creative Tools for Developing Life Skills*. Tucson: Sepher Press.

Brim, R. (1978). "The Effect of Personality Variables, Dogmatism and Repression-Sensitization Upon Response to Music," *Journal of Music Therapy*, 15, pp. 74–87.

Bryant, D. R. (1987). "A Cognitive Approach to Therapy through Music." *Journal of Music Therapy*, 24, pp. 27–34.

Brydon, K. A. and Nugent, W. R. (1979). "Musical Metaphor as a Means of Therapeutic Communication." *Journal of Music Therapy*, 16, pp. 149–153.

Bunt, Leslie. (1994). *Music Therapy: An Art Beyond Words*. London: Routledge.

Bunt, L., Wren, V. and Pike, D. (1987). "Music Therapy in a General Hospital's Psychiatric Unit—An Evaluation of a Pilot Eight Week Programme." *Journal of British Music Therapy*, 1, pp. 22–28.

Burleson, S. H., Center, D. B. and Reeves, H. (1989). "The Effect of Background Music on Task Performance in Psychotic Children," *Journal of Music Therapy*, 26, pp. 198–205.

Campbell, Don. (1991). *Music Physician: For Times to Come*. Wheaton, IL: Theosophical Publishing House.

————. (1989). *The Roar of Silence: Healing Powers of Breath, Tone and Music*. Wheaton, IL: Theosophical Publishing House.

Capra, Fritjof. (1985). *The Tao of Physics*. Boston: Shambhala.

Colbert, J. (1960). "The Effect of Musical Stimulation on Recall in High and Low Anxiety College Students." Unpublished doctoral dissertation, New York University. Dissertation Abstracts, 21, 3172.

Cooper, J. C. (1991). *Taoism: The Way of the Mystic*. London: Mandala.

Corey, Gerald. (1982). *Theory and Practice of Counseling and Psychotherapy*. Pacific Grove, CA: Brooks/Cole Publishing.

Crandall, Joanne. (1986). *Self-Transformation Through Music*. Wheaton, IL: Theosophical Publishing House.

Crofton, Ian and Fraser, Donald. (1985). *A Dictionary of Musical Quotations*. New York: Schirmer Books.

Crowley, Ralph. (1977) "Sullivan's Concept of Participant–Observation (a symposium)." *Contemporry Psychoanalysis*, Vol. 13, pp. 347–386.

Curtis, S. L. (1986). "The Effect of Music on Pain Relief & Relaxation of the Terminally Ill." *Journal of Music Therapy*, 23, pp. 10–24.

Dalbokova, Dafina and Kolev, Pencho. (1992). "Cognitive and Affective Relations in Perception of Auditory Stimuli in the Presence of Music." *Psychomusicology*, 11, pp. 141–151.

Dass, Ram and Gorman, Paul. (1985). *How Can I Help?* New York: Alfred A. Knopf.

Davies, John Booth. (1978). *The Psychology of Music*. Stanford: Stanford University Press.

Davis, M., Eshelman, E. R. and McKay, M. (1988). *The Relaxation and Stress Reduction Workbook*. Oakland: New Harbinger Publications.

Davis, W. B. and Thaut, M. H. (1989). "The Influence of Preferred Relaxing Music on Measures of State Anxiety, Relaxation, and Physiological Responses." *Journal of Music Therapy*, 26, pp. 168–187.

de Chumaceiro, Cora L. Diaz. (1992). "What Song Comes to Mind: Induced Song Recall: Transference/Countertransference in Dyadic Music Associations in Treatment and Supervision." *The Arts in Psychotherapy*, 19, 5, pp. 325–332.

Decuir, Anthony. (1991). "Trends in Music and Family Therapy." *The Arts in Psychotherapy*, 18, pp. 195–199.

Devlin, H. J. and Sawatzky, D. D. (1987). "The Effects of Background Music in a Simulated Initial Counselling Session with Female Subjects." *Canadian Journal of Counselling*, 21, pp. 125–132.

Diserens, C. M. (1923). "Reactions to Musical Stimuli." *The Psychological Bulletin*, 20, pp. 173–199.

Dollinger, Stephen. (1993). "Personality and Music Preference: Extraversion and Excitement-Seeking or Openness to Experience?" *Psychology of Music*, 21, 1, pp. 73–77.

Dowling, W. J. and Harwood, D. L. (1986). *Music Cognition*. New York: Academic Press.

Dreher, Diane. (1991). *The Tao of Inner Peace*. New York: HarperCollins.

Edwards, Jane. (1995). "You Are Singing Beautifully: Music Therapy and Debridement Bath." *The Arts in Psychotherapy*, 22, 1, pp. 53–56.

Ellis, Albert and Dryden, Windy. (1987). *The Practice of Rational Emotive Therapy*. New York: Springer Publishing.

Evans, J. R., (1986). "Dysrhythmia and Disorders of Learning and Behavior." In J. R. Evans and M. Clynes (eds.), *Rhythm in Psychological, Linguistic and Musical Processes*. Springfield, IL: Charles C. Thomas, pp. 249–274.

Fromm, Erich, Suzuki, D. T. and De Martino, Richard. (1970). *Zen Buddhism and Psychoanalysis*. New York: Harper Colophon Books.

Gantz, W., Gartenberg, H. M., Pearson, M. L. and Schiller, S. O. (1978). "Gratifications and Expectations Associated with Pop Music Among Adolescents." *Popular Music and Society*, 6, pp. 81–89.

Gfeller, Kate. (1988). "Musical Components and Styles Preferred by Young Adults for Aerobic Fitness Activities." *Journal of Music Therapy*, 25, pp. 28–43.

Gibbons, Alicia Clair. (1977). "Popular Music Preferences of Elderly People." *Journal of Music Therapy*, 24, pp.180–189.

Gibbs, J. J. (1990). *Dancing With Your Books: The Zen Way of Studying*. New York: Plume.

Glasgow, M. R., Cartier, A. M. and Wilson, G. D. (1985). "Conservation, Sensation-Seeking, and Music Preferences." *Personality and Individual Differences*, 6, pp. 395–396.

Glasser, William. (1984). *Control Theory: A New Explanation of How We Control Our Lives*. New York: HarperCollins.

Glassford, P. V. (1972). "Staff Experimental Relaxation Group." *Australian Occupational Therapy Journal*, L9, pp. 51–54.

Goldman, J. S. (1988). "Toward a New Consciousness of the Sonic Healing Arts: The Therapeutic Use of Sound and Music for Personal and Planetary Health and Transformation." *Music Therapy*, 7, pp. 28–33.

Greenberg, R. P. and Fisher, S. (1971). "Some Differential Effects of Music on Projective and Structured Psychological Tests." *Psychological Reports*, 28, pp. 817–818.

Grigg, Ray. (1989). *The Tao of Being*. Atlanta: Humanics New Age.

Groeneweg, G., Stan, E. A., Celser, A., MacBeth, L., Vrbancic, M. I. (1988). "The Effect of Background Music on the Vocational Behavior of Mentally Handicapped Adults." *Journal of Music Therapy*, 25, pp.118–134.

Haas, R., Distenfeld, S. and Axen, K. (1986). "Effects of Perceived Musical Rhythm on Respiratory Pattern." *Journal of Applied Physiology,* 26, pp. 1185–1191.

Hadsell, N. A. (1989). "Multivariate Analyses of Musicians' and Nonmusicians' Ratings of Pre-Categorized Stimulative and Sedative Music." *Journal of Music Therapy*, 26, pp. 106–114.

Hall, Edward T. (1983). *The Dance of Life*. New York: Anchor Press/ Doubleday.

Hall, James A. (1986). *The Jungian Experience: Analysis and Individuation*. Toronto: Inner City Books.

Halpern, Steven and Savary, Louis. (1985). *Sound Health: The Music and Sounds That Make Us Whole*. New York: HarperCollins.

Hamel, Peter Michael. (1986). *Through Music to the Self*. Shaftesbury, England: Element Books.

Hanh, Thich Nhat. (1991). *Peace is Every Step*. New York: Bantam Books.

Hanser, S., Larson, S. and O'Connell, A. (1983). "The Effect of Music on Relaxation of Expectant Mothers During Labor." *Journal of Music Therapy*, 20, pp. 50–58.

Harper, B. L. (1985). "Say It, Review It, Enhance It with a Song." *Elementary School Guidance and Counseling*, pp. 218–221.

Harris, Robert. (1991). *What to Listen for in Mozart*. New York: Simon and Schuster.

Hart, Mickey (1990). *Drumming at the Edge of Magic*. San Francisco: HarperSanFrancisco.

Hekmat, Hamid and Hertel, James. (1993). "Pain Attenuating Effects of Preferred Versus Non-Preferred Music Interventions." *Psychology of Music*, 21, 2, pp. 163–173.

Hoff, Benjamin. (1983). *The Tao of Pooh*. New York: Penguin Books.

Holbrook, Morris and Anand, Punam (1990). "Effects of Tempo and Situational Arousal on the Listener's Perceptual and Affective Responses to Music." *Psychology of Music*, 18, 2, pp. 150–162.

Hope, H., (1971). "Music has charms." *Nursing Mirror*, 132, pp. 40–41.

Huang, Chungliang Al and Jerry Lynch. (1992). *Thinking Body, Dancing Mind*. New York: Bantam Books.

Hunter, H. (1974). "An Investigation of Psychological and Physiological Changes Apparently Elicited by Musical Stimuli." *Psychology of Music*, 2, pp. 53–68.

Hyde, I. M. (1924). "Effects of Music Upon Electrocardiograms and Blood Pressure." *Journal of Experimental Psychology*, 7, 213–224.

Jellison, J. A. (1975). "The Effect of Music on Autonomic Stress Responses and Verbal Reports," in C. K. Madsen, R. D. Greer and C. H. Madsen, Jr. (eds.), *Research in Music Behavior: Modifying Music Behavior in the Classroom*. New York: Teachers College Press, pp. 235–271.

Johanson, Greg and Kurtz, Ron. (1991). *Grace Unfolding*. New York: Bell Tower.

Jung, Carl G. (1974). *Dreams*. Princeton: Princeton University Press, R. F. C. Hull trans.

———. (1964). *Man and His Symbols*. New York: Doubleday.

———. (1965). *Memories, Dreams, Reflections*. Aniela Jaffe, ed. New York: Vintage Books.

Kabat-Zinn, Jon. (1994). *Wherever You Go There You Are: Mindfulness Meditation in Everyday Life*. New York: Hyperion.

Kenny, Carolyn Bereznak. (1995). *Listening, Playing, Creating: Essays on the Power of Sound*. Albany: State University of New York Press.

Leonard, George. (1978). *The Silent Pulse*. New York: E. P. Dutton.

Levinson, Jerrold. (1990). *Music, Art, and Metaphysics*. Ithaca: Cornell University Press.

Linoff, M. G. and West, C. M. (1983). "Relaxation Training Systematically Combined with Music: Treatment of Tension Headaches in a Geriatric Patient." *International Journal of Behavioral Geriatrics*, 1, pp. 11–16.

Logan, T. B. and Roberts, A. R. (1984). "The Effects of Different Types of Relaxation Music on Tension Level." *Journal of Music Therapy*, 21, pp. 177–185.

Martin, M. (1990). "On the Induction of Mood." *Clinical Psychology Review*, 10, pp. 669–697.

Maultsby, M. (1977). "Combining Music Therapy and Rational Behavior Therapy." *Journal of Music Therapy*, 14, pp. 89–97.

McDermott, K. (1988). "Music Soothes." *The Magazine of Case Western Reserve University*, 1, p. 40.

McGuire, William and Hull, R. F .C. (1977). *C. G. Jung Speaking: Interviews and Encounters*. Princeton: Princeton University Press.

Merritt, Stephanie (1990). *Mind, Music and Imagery*. New York: Penguin Books.

Merton, Thomas. (1965). *The Way of Chuang Tzu*. New York: New Directions.

Meyer, L. B. (1966). *Emotion and Meaning in Music*. Chicago: University of Chicago Press.

Miller, L. K. and Schyb, M. (1989). "Facilitation and Interference by Background Music." *Journal of Music Therapy*, 26, pp. 42–54.

Ming-Dao, Deng. (1990). *Scholar Warrior: An Introduction to the Tao in Everyday Life*. San Fancisco: HarperSanFrancisco.

Morrongiello, Barbara. (1992). "Effects of Training on Children's Perception of Music: A Review." *Psychology of Music*, 20, 1, pp. 29–41.

Nielzèn, S. and Cesarec, Z. (1981). "On the Perception of Emotional Meaning in Music." *Psychology of Music*, 9, pp. 17–31.

Nordoff, P. and C. Robbins. (1971). *Therapy in Music for Handicapped Children*. London: Gollancz.

Ortiz, J. M. (1991). *The Facilitating Effects of Soothing Background Music on an Initial Counseling Session*. Unpublished Doctoral Dissertation, Pennsylvania State University, call# Thesis,1991d, Ortiz,JM.

———. (1990). "Music as Sound Campus Ecology." *The Campus Ecologist*, 8, 4, pp. 1–4.

Ostrander, Sheila and Schroeder, Lynn (1979). *Superlearning*. New York: Dell.

Peretti, P. D. and Swenson, K. (1974). "Effects of Music on Anxiety as Determined by Physiological Skin Responses." *Journal of Research in Music Education*, 22, pp. 278–283.

Peretti, P. O. (1975). "Changes in Galvanic Skin Response as Affected by Musical Selection, Sex, and Academic Discipline." *Journal of Psychology*, 89, pp. 183–187.

Pignatiello, M. R., Camp, C. J. and Rasar, L. (1986). "Musical Mood Induction: An Alternative to the Velten Technique." *Journal of Abnormal Psychology*, 95, pp. 295–297.

Pirsig, Robert M. (1974). *Zen and the Art of Motorcycle Maintenance*. New York: Morrow.

Plato. (1977). *Timaeus and Critias*. Desmond Lee, trans. London: Penguin.

Poole, William. (1993). *The Heart of Healing*. Atlanta: Turner Publishing.

Pope, Alexander. "The Dunciad," in John Bartlett: *Familiar Quotations*. Boston: Little, Brown & Co.

Priestley, M. (1987). "Music and the Shadow." *Music Therapy*, 6, pp. 20–27.

———. (1976). "Music, Freud and the Port of Entry." *Nursing Times*, pp. 1940–1941.

Rawson, Hugh and Miner, Margaret. (1986). *The New International Dictionary of Quotations*. New York: E. P. Dutton.

Reps, Paul. (1989). *Zen Flesh, Zen Bones: A Collection of Zen and Pre-Zen Writings*. New York: Anchor Books.

Reynolds, S. B. (1984). "Biofeedback, Relaxation Training, and Music: Homeostasis for Coping with Stress." *Biofeedback and Self-Regulation*, 9, pp. 169–179.

Rider, M. S. (1987). "Treating Chronic Disease and Pain with Music-Mediated Imagery." *The Arts in Psychotherapy*, 14, pp. 113–120.

Rider, M. S. and Weldin, Cathy. (1990). "Imagery, Improvisation, and Immunity." *The Arts in Psychotherapy*, 17, 3, pp. 211–216.

Rider, M. S., Floyd, J. and Kirpatrick, J. (1985). "The Effects of Music, Imagery, and Relaxation on Adrenal Corticosteroids and the Re-entrainment of Circadian Rhythms." *Journal of Music Therapy*, 22, pp. 46–58.

Roberts, Jane. (1995). *The Oversoul Seven Trilogy*. San Rafael, CA: Amber-Allen Publishing.

Roberts, T. B. and Roberts, A. R. (1984). "The Effects of Different Types of Relaxation Music on Tension Level," *Journal of Music Therapy*, 21, pp. 177–185.

Roger, John and McWilliams, Peter. (1991). *Do It! Let's Get Off Our Buts*. Los Angeles: Prelude Press.

Rohner, S. J. and Miller, R. (1980). "Degrees of Familiar and Affective Music and Their Effects on State Anxiety." *Journal of Music Therapy*, 17, pp. 2–15.

Scarantino, Barbara Anne. (1987). *Music Power: Creative Living Through the Joys of Music*. New York: Dodd, Mead & Company.

Scartelli, J. P. (1984). "The Effect of EMG Biofeedback and Sedative Music, EMG Biofeedback Only, and Sedative Music Only on Frontalis Muscle Relaxation Ability." *Journal of Music Therapy*, 21, pp. 67–78.

Scartelli, J. P. and Borling, J. E. (1986). "The Effects of Sequenced Versus Simultaneous EMG Biofeedback and Sedative Music on Frontalis Relaxation Training." *Journal of Music Therapy*, 23, pp. 157–165.

Schuster, B. L. (1985). "The Effect of Music Listening on Blood Pressure Fluctuations in Adult Hemodialysis Patients." *Journal of Music Therapy*, 22, pp. 146–153.

Scott, Cyril. (1981). *Music: Its Secret Influence Throughout the Ages*. York Beach, ME: Samuel Weiser; Reprint: Sun, 1995.

Sears, W. W. (1968). "Processes in Music Therapy." In E. T. Gaston (ed.), *Music in Therapy*. New York: Macmillan, pp. 116–136.

Seashore, Carl E. (1967). *Psychology of Music*. New York: Dover Publications, Inc.

Shehan, P. K. (1983). "Student Preferences for Ethnic Music Styles." *Contributions to Music Education*, 9, 21–28.

Sloboda, John. (1985). *The Musical Mind*. Oxford: Oxford University Press.

Smeijsters, Henk, Wijzenbeek, Gaby and van Nieuwenhuijzen Niek. (1995). "The Effect of Musical Excerpts on the Evocation of Values for Depressed Patients." *Journal of Music Therapy*, 32, 3, pp. 167–188.

Smith, C. A. and Morris, L. W.. (1977). "Differential Effects of Stimulative and Sedative Music on Anxiety, Concentration and Performance." *Psychological Reports*, 41, pp. 1047–1053.

Smith, David S. (1994). "An Age-Based Comparison of Humor in Selected Musical Compositions." *Journal of Music Therapy*, 31, 3, pp. 206–219.

———. (1989). "Preferences for Differentiated Frequency Loudness Levels in Older Adult Music Listening." *Journal of Music Therapy*, 36, 1, pp. 18–29.

Smith, Steven M. (1985). "Background Music and Context-Dependent Memory." *American Journal of Psychology*, 98, 4, pp. 591– 603.

Stainback, S. B., Stainback, W. C. and Hallahan, D. P. (1973). "Effects of Background Music on Learning. *Exceptional Children*, 40, pp. 109–110.

Steele, A. L. and Jorgenson, H. A. (1971). "Music Therapy: An Effective Solution to Problems in Related Disciplines." *Journal of Music Therapy*, 8, pp. 131–145.

Stewart, R. J. (1987). *Music and the Elemental Psyche*. Rochester, VT: Destiny Books.

———. (1990). *Music, Power & Harmony: A Workbook of Music and Inner Forces*. New York: Sterling.

Storr, Anthony. (1992). *Music and the Mind*. New York: The Free Press.

Stoudenmire, J. A. (1975). "A Comparison of Muscle Relaxation Training and Music in the Reduction of State and Trait Anxiety. *Journal of Clinical Psychology*, 31, pp. 490–492.

Stratton, V. N. and Zalanowski, A. H. (1989). "The Effects of Music and Paintings on Mood." *Journal of Music Therapy*, 26, pp. 30–41.

———. (1984a). "The Effect of Background Music on Verbal Interaction in Groups." *Journal of Music Therapy*, 21, pp. 16–21.

———. (1984b). "The Relationship Between Music, Degree of Liking and Self-Reported Relaxation." *Journal of Music Therapy*, 21, pp. 184–192.

———. Summer, L. (1981). "Guided Imagery and Music with the Elderly." *Music Therapy*, 1, pp. 39–42.

Suzuki, Shunryu. (1983). *Zen Mind, Beginner's Mind*. New York: Weatherhill.

Swanwick, K. (1975). "Can There Be Objectivity in Listening to Music?" *Psychology of Music*, 3, pp. 17–23.

Tame, David. (1984). *The Secret Power of Music*. Rochester, VT: Destiny Books.

Taylor, D. B. (1973). "Subject Responses to Precategorized Stimulative and Sedative Music." *Journal of Music Therapy*, 10, pp. 86–94.

Terwogt, Mark Meerum, and van Grinsven, Flora. (1991). "Musical Expression of Moodstates." *Psychology of Music*,19, pp. 99–109.

Thaut, M. H. (1989). "The Influence of Music Therapy Interventions on Self-Rated Changes in Relaxation, Affect, and Thought in Psychiatric Prisoner-Patients." *Journal of Music Therapy*, 23, pp. 155–166.

Tracey, T. J. and Ray, P. B. (1984). "Stages of Successful Time-Limited Counseling: An Interactional Examination." *Journal of Counseling Psychology*, 31, pp. 13-27.

Tulku, Tarthang. (1978). *Openness Mind*. Berkeley: Dharma Publishing.

Unkefer, Robert F. (1990). *"Music Therapy in the Treatment of Adults with Mental Disorders*. New York: Schirmer Books.

Unyk, Anna, Trehub, Sandra, Trainor, Laurel and Schellenberg, Glen (1992). "Lullabies and Simplicity: A Cross-Cultural Perspective." *Psychology of Music*, 20, 1, pp. 15–28.

Volkman, Stephanie. (1993). "Music Therapy and the Treatment of Trauma-Induced Dissociative Disorders." *The Arts in Psychotherapy*, 20, 3, pp. 243–252.

Wadeson, H. (1982). "Art Therapy." In S. Abt and I. Stewart (eds), *The Newer Therapies*. New York: Van Nostrand.

Walker, Brian. *Hua Hu Ching: The Teachings of Lao Tzu*. Livingston, MT: Clark City Press, 1993.

Wapnick, J. (1976). "A Review of Research on Attitude and Preference." *Bulletin of the Council for Research in Music Education*, 48, pp. 1–20.

Webster, C. (1973). "Relaxation, Music and Cardiology: The Physiological and Psychological Consequences of their Interrelation." *Australian Occupational Therapy Journal*, 20, pp. 9–20.

Wheeler, B. L. (1985). "The Relationship Between Musical and Activity Elements of Music Therapy Sessions and Client Responses: An Exploratory Study." *Music Therapy*, 5, pp. 52–60.

Whitehead, A. N. (1969). *Symbolism: Its meaning and effect*. New York: Capricorn Books.

Wilmer, Harry A. (1987). *Practical Jung*. Wilmette, IL: Chiron Publications.

Winokur, Jon. (1990). *Zen To Go*. New York: Dover Publications, Inc.

Wolf, R. H. and Weiner, T. L. (1972). "Effects of Four Noise Conditions on Arithmetic Performance." *Perceptual and Motor Skills*, 35, pp. 929–930.

Wolfe, D. E. (1982). "The Effect of Interrupted and Continuous Music on Bodily Movement and Task Performance of Third Grade Students." *Journal of Music Therapy*, 9, pp. 74–85.

Index

abuse, 64
Ackerman, Diane, 190, 224, 287
affirmations, 325
aging, 141
Aldridge, David, 128, 145, 247
Aldridge, Gudrun, 145
Allekote, Joan, 11, 13, 32, 44, 351, 367
aloneness, 174
altered states, music for, 241
alternative music, 25, 74
Anand, Punam, xix
Anderson, C. R. 297
anger, 61
    dealing with, 65, 73
    ten ways to arouse, 64
anxiety, 64
appetite, loss of, 6
arguments, 64
Assagioli, Roberto, 157
Austin, Diane Snow, 130
awareness, raising our, 312
Axen, K. 252
Bandura, A. 88
Baroque music, 55, 202
Bauer, Marion, 355
Beaulieu, John, 3, 183, 218, 219, 225,
    281, 349, 367

Beck, Charlotte Joko, xxi, 42, 67, 125,
    299
being in sync, 276
being versus trying to be, 252, 261
beliefs, disputing irrational, 313
Berendt, Joachim-Ernst, 276, 339, 342,
    347
Big Band, 197
Blacking, John, 264, 357
Blofeld, John, 341
body language, 215
Bonny, Helen L. 94, 165
Borgeat, F., 97, 252
Borling, J. E., 95, 253
Boyle, J. David, 357
breathing, 66, 333
Brewer, Chris, 319
Brim, R., 253
Browne, Sir Thomas, 371
Brydon, K. A., 165
Bunt, Leslie, 107, 180, 206, 226, 257,
    291, 292, 317, 357, 361, 367
Burns, Robert, 186
calm, inner, 223
Capra, Fritjof, 361
Cartier, A. M., 357
case histories

Angelique, 51
Cathy, 267
Charlotte, 235
Daphne, 155
Donna, 3
Frank, 61
Iris, 306
Jamal and Jaime, 37
Jean, 120
Lelia, 77
Nancy, 244
Sally, 133
Sylvia, 253
catastrophizing, 282
centering, 233
    music, 228
Cesarec, Z., 165, 207
challenges, 129
change, 125
    engendering growth, 128
chanting, 345
    music, 347
classical music, 17, 19, 21, 48, 73
    romantic, 196
Clynes, M., 278
Cole, Nat King, 196
Coltrane, John, 198
communication, improving, 165, 177
companionship, 173
concentrating, 167
control, 87
Cooper, J. C., xvi, 69
Corey, Gerald, Dr., 311, 312
Crandall, Joanne, 8, 56, 119, 126, 128,
    130, 178, 179, 247, 264, 299, 308
creativity, 233
criticism, 7
Crofton, Ian, 77, 80, 105
Crowley, Ralph, 305
cuing, 107
    contextual, 287
Curtis, S. L., 95
Dalbokova, Dafina, 285
Dass, Ram, 87, 95, 213, 219
Davies, John Booth, 295
Davis, M., 330
Davis, W. B., 94
Decuir, Anthony, 119, 166

de Martino, Richard, xvi
depressed mood, bonding and moving
    away from, 19
depression, 5, 119
Devlin, H. J., 202, 207
discipline, 53
Diserens, C. M., 94
Distenfeld, S., 252
Dollinger, Stephen, 357
Dreher, Diane, xiii, xxi, 5, 6, 37, 43, 44,
    65, 68, 87, 125, 130, 135, 237,
    269, 277, 358
Dryden, Windy, 11, 311, 313
Dvorkin, Janice M., 130
ear, educating the, 213
eating, compulsive, 6
Edwards, Jane, 31
Ellis, Albert, 11, 311, 313
entrainment, 317
    adapting, 319
    making a tape, 321
entrainment sequence
    anti-depressed mood, 16
    Big Band, 160
    limited budget, 161
    '60's pop, 160
Eshelman, E. R., 330
Evans, J. R., 277, 278
exaggerations, 283
exercise, 53
    accessing your inner guide, 373
    beating procrastination, 138
    centering through music, 229
    clearing the mind, 269
    creating new memories, 130
    discovering your magical breathing,
        334
    discovering your personal chant, 346
    dispelling anger, 71
    diverting another person's anger, 69
    enhancing creativity, 238
    enhancing listening sensitivity, 180
    finding your center, 227
    finding your personal mantric sound,
        340
    giving up control, 90
    improving learning skills, 207
    letting go, 254

letting go of chronic anger, 67
lifting a depressed mood, 8
listening, 216
listening and communication enhancement, 169
magic nightclub, 192
moving out of the blues, 13
musical memories, 108
pain elimination/reduction, 32
reasons, to, 153
reducing stress, 97
rejuvenation through music, 142
selecting your soundtracks, 257
self-enhancing, changing noise to harmony, 42
sound convergence, 224
sound sleeping, 82
spiral sojourn, 362
time management through music, 115
toning through natural release, 350
toning and walking, 351
toning while making love, 351
training through entrainment, 157
unexpecting, 300
using music to memorize word lists, 203
using music to slow your pace, 117
using music to speed your pace, 116
using music to trigger emotional responses, 121
expectations, 293
    techniques for defeating or overriding, 298
    unrealistic, 282
extramusical associations, 289
fatigue, 6
feedback, 215
Fraser, Donald, 77, 80, 105
Fromm, Erich, xvi
frustration, 64
G., Kenny, 199
Gantz, W., 253
Gartenberg, H. M., 253
Gfeller, Kate, 152, 153
Gibbs, J. J., 202, 254, 281, 296, 298, 299
Giles, Lionel, 258
Glasgow, M. R., 357
Glasser, William, 91

goals, realistic, 312
Gordon, Dexter, 197
Gorman, Paul, 87, 95, 213, 219
greatest hit music, 26
grief and loss, 119
Grigg, Ray, xvi
growth, 125, 129
guide, inner, 371
Haas, R., 252
habits, 53, 294
Hall, Edward T., xiv, xvi, xviii, xxi, 8, 56, 111, 114, 116, 117, 125, 177, 191, 304, 313, 366
Hamel, Peter Michael, 29
Hanh, Thich Nhat, 30, 54, 71, 123, 159, 309, 333, 336
Hanser, S., 94
Harris, Robert, 217, 243
Hart, Mickey, 275
HeAr and Now, 243
Hekmat, Hamid, xix, 30, 355
Hertel, James, xix, 30, 355
Hoff, Benjamin, 6, 48, 126, 233, 271, 308, 326
Holbrook, Morris, xix
Hosterman, Glen L., 357
Huang, Chungliang Al, 45, 299, 301, 325, 326
Hunter, H., 202, 207
Huygens, Christian, 317
Hyde, I. M., 94
hypersensitivity, 64
hypersomnia, 6
impatience, 65
injustice, 65
insomnia, 6
inspirational music, 48
irritations, external, 64
Johanson, Greg, 52, 90, 154, 229, 306
Jung, C. G., xxii
Kabat-Zinn, Jon, 333
Khechog, Nawang, 224
Kolev, Pencho, 285
Kurtz, Ron, 52, 90, 154, 229, 306
Lao-Tzu, 250, 261
Larson, S., 94
Lee, Desmond, 72
Leonard, George, 276, 317

letting go, 54, 249, 254, 259, 313
   music for, 259
Linoff, M. G., 94
listen, 215, 216
   how to, 213
listening, subliminal, 218
Logan, T. B., 208
loneliness, 173, 174
lovemaking, 184
low tolerance, 64
Lynch, Jerry, 45, 299, 301, 325, 326
magic nightclub, 186, 192
mantric music, 342
masking, 281
Maslan, Marsha, 11, 13, 32, 44, 351, 367
McKay, M., 330
McWilliams, John-Roger, 133
McWilliams, Peter, 133
meditation music, 230
memory, 105
   acoustic, 219, 291
menus, musical, 15
Merritt, Stephanie, 151, 155
Merton, Thomas, xvi, 250
Miller, L. K., 95
mind
   clearing, 267
   motivating, 201
Miner, Margaret, 106
Ming-Dao, Deng, 337
moods
   depressed, 3
   modifying, 323
Morgan, Frank, 198
Morrongiello, Barbara, 168
musex, making, 184
music, 7, 12, 31, 201, 288, 361
   aphrodisiac powers of, 183
   Baroque, 202
   choosing one's, 355
   helping, 154
   and physical exercise, 151
   relaxation, 96
   selecting, 157
   sources, 210, 231, 343, 348
music-box tune suggestions, 210
musts, 311
Narcolepsy, 81

needs, personal, 319
negative, focusing on, 283
new age music, 20, 49, 56
Nielzèn, S., 165, 207
noise
   psychological, 64, 281
   white, 82, 284
Nordoff, P., 248
Nugent, W. R., 165
O'Connell, A., 94
Ortiz, John M., xix, 168, 207, 276
Ostrander, Sheila, 202, 207
over-emoting, 282
pain, 29
   elimination/reduction, 32
patterns, competitive, 53
Pearson, M. L., 253
perfectionism, 135
personalizing, 283
Peyser, Ethel, 355
Pirsig, Robert, 244
place, your special, 362, 367
Poole, William, 31, 339, 356
pop-rock music, 16
Pope, Alexander, 77
popular music, 19, 22, 58, 73, 74
procrastination, 133
project, never, 299
Quebec, Ike, 198
Ramsey, Darhyl S., 357
Rawson, Hugh, 106
Ray, P. B., 278
relationship issues, 177
relaxation, 93
release, 251
Reps, Paul, 352, 373
Reynolds, S. B., 94
Rider, Mark S., 318, 319
Robbins, C., 248
Roberts, A. R., 208
Roberts, Jane, 372
romantic magic nightclub music, 194
Sawatzky, D. D., 202, 207
Scarantino, Barbara Anne, 152, 188, 189,
   237, 238
Scartelli, J. P., 94, 95, 252
scenarios, 296
Schiller, O., 253

Scholes, Percy, 362
Schroeder, Lynn, 202, 207
Schuster, B. L., 95
Schyb, M., 95
Scott, Cyril, 183, 184
Seashore, Carl E., xviii, xx, 42, 45, 87,
    129, 201, 205, 275, 276, 284
self-esteem, 37
    low, 37
self-statements, positive, 53
self-talk, replacing negative, 312
shoulds, 311
silence, 223, 225
Sleep Terror Disorder, 81
sleeplessness, 77
Sloboda, John, 289
Smeijsters, Henk, 7
song-title affirmations, sixty-five years of,
    327
soothing music, 55
sound
    mantric, 339
    suggestions, 213
    synchronizing, 218
spatial reasoning, 201
speculation, 305
spiral sojourn, 361, 362
Stanton, Elizabeth Cady, 179
Stewart, R. J., 12, 88, 187, 365
stimulating music, 20
Storr, Anthony, xviii, 6, 9, 10, 16, 57, 97,
    116, 117, 151, 174, 208, 236, 284,
    292, 368, 369, 371
Stratton, V. N., 166, 253
stress, 51
Suzuki, D. T., xvi
Suzuki, Shunryu, 127, 267
synchronicity, rhythmic, 275
Tame, David, 184, 203, 288, 321
Tennyson, Alfred Lord, 85
Terwogt, Mark Meerum, 287, 356

Thaut, M. H., 94
thought stopping, 66, 329
    neon sign technique, 330
    shaking off the thought technique, 331
    thought editing technique, 331
    a tune for thought technique, 332
time
    management, 111
    traveling in, 219
toning, 349
top songs
    of the '30's, 145
    of the '40's, 146
    of the '50's, 146
    of the '60's, 147
    of the '70's, 148
Tracey, T. J., 278
trying, 264
Tulku, Tarthang, 264
Tunks, T. W., 297
unattachment, 250
Unkefer, Robert F., 289
unlistening, 216
van Grinsven, Flora, 287, 356
van Nieuwenhuijzen, Niek, 7
Volkman, Stephanie, 108, 247
Walker, Brian, 299, 345, 374
Wapnick, J., 208
Webster, Ben, 197
Webster, C., 94
Weldin, Cathy, 318, 319
West, C. M., 94
Wheeler, B. L., 94, 357
whys, 303
    unnecessary, raising awareness to, 306
Wijzenbeek, Gaby, 7
Wilmer, Harry A., 372
Wilson, G. D., 357
Wolfe, D. E., 253
words, self-defeating, 282
Zalanowski, A. H., 166, 253

John M. Ortiz, Ph.D. is a composer and multi-instrumentalist—he has written hundreds of songs and plays nine instruments. He loves music! He is also a licensed psychologist and certified clinical hypnotist who has a strong transpersonal and mind, body, spirit orientation. He received his Ph.D. in Counseling Psychology from the Pennsylvania State University, a Masters degree in Counseling Psychology from Nova University in Florida, a B.S. in Psychology from Virginia Commonwealth University, and has also studied Okinawan Karate, Southern Shaolin Kung-Fu, Yang style Tai Chi, fencing, and is an avid swimmer. He earned a dissertation scholars award for his doctoral thesis which proposed, and later substantiated, the benefits of using music as an adjunct to counseling. Author of a number of psycho-musicology related articles, he is presently on the editorial board of the American Counseling Association's *Journal of Counseling and Development*, is listed in the National Register of Health Service Providers in Psychology, and works with music with his clients every day. He participates in workshops, and travels internationally to teach people how they can use music to improve their lives. He lives in Pennsylvania with his wife, Roz.

For a list of available audio resources designed to complement some of the exercises found throughout *The Tao of Music: Sound Psychology*, please send a SASE to:

Dr. John M. Ortiz, Director
The Institute of Applied Psychomusicology
P.O. Box 145
Camp Hill, PA 17001

Dr. Ortiz may also be contacted in care of the publisher.

Samuel Weiser, Inc.
P.O. Box 612
York Beach, ME 03910-0612